Demography and Population Problems

Demography and Population Problems

Sachin Verma

RANDOM PUBLICATIONS
NEW DELHI (INDIA)

Demography and Population Problems

ISBN 978-93-5111-412-3

© Reserved

All Rights Reserved. No Part of this book may be reproduced in any manner without written permission.

Published in 2014 in India by

RANDOM PUBLICATIONS

4376-A/4B, Gali Murari Lal, Ansari Road
New Delhi-110 002
Phone : +91-11-43580356, +91-11-23289044
e-mail: randomexports@gmail.com, sales@randompublications.com, info@randompublications.com

Reprinted 2023

Type Setting by : Keystoneprintads, Delhi-110051
Digitally Printed at: Replika Press Pvt. Ltd.

Preface

It is impossible to generalize about problems of population on the continental or international levels. The wide divergence in population density and growth, and in the level of resources available within a country, precludes a common attitude toward demographic increase. In addition adequate demographic data is not available. Reliable demographic data and analysis are required as a basis for planning in all developing countries.

Most population studies focus on the subjects of mortality, migration, and resultant growth, which is then related to production and consumption. The environment, both the physical and cultural setting, influences elements of population growth, yet there have been few studies in which the effect of the environment on population is considered. Such consideration should be part of any study, plan, or policy on population. In addition to growth, environmental factors are often responsible for the distribution and density of population. These factors cause some areas to remain unsettled while others are overpopulated. In the overpopulated areas, environmental degradation results when the capacity of the land to support the human and animal population is exceeded.

The natural productivity of marginal lands in the tropics and subtropics often exceeds the yields presently obtained from using these lands for cultivation or animal husbandry. An adequate survey of arable lands and the natural productivity of the various biomes for the entire developing world are required. A program should be instituted to encourage the settlement of those fertile areas now unoccupied or sparsely occupied for social, historical, or traditional reasons.

Developing countries need to explore and evaluate their natural resources. They should also be encouraged to diversify their economic resources and supplement them with some measure of industrialization. Malnutrition, inadequate health and sanitary facilities, and illiteracy, as well as certain social factors, are the real causes of poverty and backwardness. The developing countries should be helped to increase the life expectancy of their population and the productivity of their manpower. Modern technology is needed to increase the skills of the population. These measures go hand in hand with increasing the capability of the land to sustain a better-fed, better-equipped, and more productive population.

We hope that the discussion made in this book will help the readers to understand and learnt about the different aspects of "Demography and Population Problems" in a most comprehensive way.

I thank all members of my team who have helped in the preparation of the book. My special thanks go to "Random Publications" who have published the book.

– ***Sachin Verma***

Contents

1

Population in Mughal India—A Backdrop

ESTIMATES OF POPULATION OF MUGHAL INDIA

It was, however, hard to rest content with an admission that a definitive demographic history of India from c. 1601 to 1872 is impossible. No phase of economic history can be studied without allowing for demographic factor. For pre-modern societies, population growth is often considered as a major index of economic growth. It is, therefore, legitimate to attempt estimating the Indian population on the basis of quantitative data of diverse kind that are available to us.

On the Basis of the Extent of Cultivated Area

Moreland made the first attempt to estimate the population with the help of the data of the A'in-i Akbari. He tried to determine the population of Northern India on the basis of the figures given in the A'in. This work gives figures for arazi (measured area) which he took to represent the gross cropped area. Comparing the arazi with the gross cultivation at the beginning of this century and assuming a constant correspondence between the extent of cultivation and the size of the population right through the intervening period, he concluded that from "Multan to Monghyr" there were 30 to 40 million people at the end of the 16th century.

Applying Civilian: Soldier Ratio

For the Deccan and South India, Moreland took as the basis of his calculations the military strength of the Vijaynagar Empire and Deccan Sultanates. Taking a rather arbitrary ratio of 1:30 between the soldiers and civilian population, he estimated the population of the reign at 30 millions. Allowing for other territories lying within the pre-1947 limits of India but not covered by his two basic assumptions, he put the population of Akbar's Empire in 1600 at 60 millions, and of India as a whole at 100 millions.

These estimates received wide acceptance. Nevertheless, Moreland's basic assumptions (and therefore his figures) are questionable. For estimating the population of Northern India he makes the assumptions that (a) measurement was made of the cultivated land only; and (b) it was carried out by the Mughal administration to completion in all localities for which any figures are offered. It has been shown on the basis of textual as well as statistical evidence that the arazi of the A'in was area measured for revenue purposes which included, besides the cultivated area current, fallows and some cultivable and uncultivable waste.

Moreover, measurement by no means was completed everywhere. Thus, Moreland's estimate of the population of Northern India loses much of its credibility. It is weaker still for Deccan and South India. The army: civilian ratio is not only arbitrary but undependable; the comparison with the pre-World War I France and Germany seems, in particular to be quite inept, since the military: civilian ratios maintainable in modern states and economies are so variable. Any of these can by no stretch of the imagination be used to set limits for the range of military: civilian ratios in pre-modern regimes in the tropical zones. This is apart from the fact that Moreland's count of the number of troops in the Deccan kingdoms was based on very general statements by European travellers.

However, Moreland has given inadequate weight to the areas outside the two regions. To make an appropriate allowance for these regions, Kingsley Davis raised Moreland's estimate for the whole of India to 125 millions in his book Population of India and Pakistan. This modification, reasonable insofar as it goes, does not, of course, remove the more substantial objections to Moreland's method indicated above. In spite of the various objections to the estimates of Moreland, it still remains legitimate to use the extent of cultivation to make an estimate of population. The arazi figures of the A'in can provide the means of working out the extent of cultivation in 1601.

Making allowance for cultivable and uncultivable waste included in the arazi and establishing the extent of measurement in various parts of the Mughal Empire, Shireen Moosvi in her book Economy of the Mughal Empire has concluded that the area under cultivation in Mughal Empire in 1601 was about 55 per cent of the cultivated area in the corresponding region in 1909-10. This estimate receives further reinforcement from the extent of cultivation worked out by Ifran Habib from a detailed analysis and comparison of the number and size of villages in various regions of the Empire in the 17th century and in 1881. Irfan Habib suggests that the area under plough in the 17th century was more than one-half but less than two-thirds of the ploughed area in 1900.

On the basis of the above mentioned analysis, Shireen Moosvi makes the following three assumptions:

- The total cultivation in 1601 was 50 to 55 per cent of what it was during the first decade of the present century.
- The urban population was 15 per cent of the total and, thus, the rural population was 85 per cent of the total population.

- The average agricultural holding in 1601 was 107 per cent larger than in 1901.
- She gives the estimate of the population of India in the 17th century as between 140 and 150 millions.

Using Total and Per Capita Land Revenue

Another significant attempt to estimate population, by using different kinds of data was made by Ashok V. Desai. This required rather complex assumptions. Desai compared the purchasing power of the lowest urban wages on the basis first of prices and wages given in the A'in and, then, of all-India average prices and wages of the early 1960s. The yields and crop rates given by Abul Fazl provide him with a means of measuring the total food consumption in Akbar's time which was 1/5th of what it was in the 1960s (cultivation was then concentrated in the areas with highest yields). He found that the productivity per unit of the area should have been 25 to 30 per cent higher in 1595 than in 1961. This in turn enables him to estimate the productivity per worker in agriculture at a level twice as high in 1595 as in 1961.

Basing himself on the statistics of consumption in the 1960s, Desai extrapolated the level of consumption in 1595 and found that the consumption level was somewhere between 1.4 and 1.8 times the modern level. He then proceeds to breakdown the average consumption at the end of the 16th century for each major agricultural item. With these figures at hand and taking into account other relevant modern data, Desai worked out the area under the various crops per capita which he then multiplied by the revenue rates, to estimate per capita land revenue.

Dividing the total jama (which Desai treats as the total land revenue) by this estimated per capita revenue, the population of the Empire works out at about 65 millions which confirms Moreland's estimate. Desai's assumptions and method have been criticised by Alan Heston and Shireen Moosvi. Heston's main objection is that the yields for 1595 have been overestimated. While Shireen Moosvi makes some more serious objections, namely, he used modern all-India statistics to compare with 16th century data. Since the prices and wages in the A'in are those of the imperial camp and, therefore, apply to Agra (and possibly to Lahore), it is surely inappropriate to compare these with modern all-India average.

In the same way, the A'in's standard crop rates applied either to the immediate vicinity of Sher Shah's capital, Delhi, or at the most to the region where the later dastur-ul amals (schedules of revenue rates) were in force, i.e., mainly Uttar Pradesh, Haryana and Punjab. These are thus not comparable to all-India yields. Moreover, Desai divided the total jama of the Empire by the hypothetical land-tax per capita without making any distinction between the zabt provinces (for which the various cash-revenue rates had been framed) and the other regions where the tax incidence might have been at a different level altogether. Another assumption of his which requires correction is that the jama was equal to the total land revenue whereas, given the purpose for which it was fixed, it could have only been an estimate of the net income from tax-realization by the jagirdars to whom the revenue were assigned. Moreover, the pattern of consumption in Akbar's India was not comparable to that of 1960s because the Mughal Empire was mainly confined to wheat-eating region, and oil seeds consumption could not possibly be as high in 1595 as in the 1960s.

Shireen Moosvi makes use of the basic method suggested by Desai but modifies his assumption for 1870s to meet the objections raised. She uses the data available for 1860-70 for purposes of comparison and extrapolations; first, working out the population for five provinces of Akbar's India that were under zabt and then assuming that the population ratio of these provinces to that of the Empire, and of the latter to the whole of India, have remained constant since 1601, estimates the population of Akbar's Empire at 100 millions and that of India (pre 1947 boundaries) at 145 millions.

AVERAGE RATE OF POPULATION GROWTH

Taking the population of India to be around 145 millions in 1601 and 225 millions in 1871—this being the total counted by the first census of 1872 (as modified by Davis to allow fuller territorial coverage), the compound annual rate of growth of the country's population for the period 1601 to 1872 comes to 0.21% per annum. Adopting this rate and given the two population figures for 1601 and 1872, one gets for 1801 a population of some 210 millions. This offers a welcome corroboration of our estimates: the most acceptable estimates for 1801 based on quite different arguments and calculations range from 198 millions to 207 millions. The rate of population growth during the last three decades of the 19th century (1872-1901) was 0.37 per cent per annum—a rate higher than the one we have deduced for the long period of 1601-1801, but not in itself a very high rate of growth.

Comparison with Contemporary Europe

The accompanying Table gives population growth rates (compound) calculated from estimates of European countries drawn from a well-known text book of European economic history 1600-1700

- Spain and Portugal 0.12
- Italy 0.00
- France 0.08
- British Isles 0.31
- Germany 0.00
- Switzerland 0.18
- Russia 0.12
- Total 0.10

These estimates show that compared to the European demographic experience, the Mughal Empire was by no means exceptionally sluggish in raising its population. The rate of 0.21 per cent on the contrary suggests an economy in which there was some room for 'national savings' and net increase in food production, although the growth, on balance, was slow. The slowness must have come from natural calamities like famines as well as man-made factors (of which the heavy revenue demand could have been one).

If one had data for estimating populations of some intermediate points, such as the year 1650 and 1700, one could perhaps have worked out the rate of population growth for shorter periods and obtain a closer view of the efficiency of Mughal economy within those periods. Such estimates would have been helpful, too, in indicating whether the rate of population growth in the 18th century (period of the dissolution of the Mughal Empire) signified any different movement in the economy than the one for the 17th century (the classic period of that Empire).

Implications of the Rate of Growth

An overall annual rate of growth of 0.2 per cent for the period 1601-1801 suggests some interesting inferences about the Mughal Indian economy. If population growth is regarded as an index of the efficiency of a pre-capitalist economy, the Mughal economy could not be deemed to have been absolutely static or stagnant for the population tended to grow between 36 and 44% in two hundred years.

COMPOSITION OF THE POPULATION: RURAL AND URBAN

There is again no direct data about the proportion of urban population. Ifran Habib has made an attempt to estimate urban population on the basis of the pattern of consumption of agricultural produce. The Mughal ruling class tended to lay claim on one half of the total agricultural produce, but all of it was not taken away from the rural sector. Assuming that about a quarter of the total agricultural produce was reaching towns, and, making allowance for the higher ratio of raw material in the agricultural produce consumed in the towns, he assumes the urban population to be over 15 per cent of the total population.

Estimated Population in Various Towns

Nizamuddin Ahmad in his Tabaqat-i Akbari (c. 1593) records that in Akbar's Empire there were 120 big towns and 3,200 townships. Taking the total population of Akbar's Empire to be nearly 100 millions and the urban population as 15 per cent of it, the average size of these 3,200 towns works out at about 5000 each. However, in the Mughal Empire there were quite a few big towns. The European travellers provide estimated population of some major cities as follows:

Town	Year	Estimate
Agra	1609	500,000
Delhi	1659-66	500,000
Lahore	1581	400,000
Thatta	1631-35	225,000
Ahemdabad	1663	100,000-200,000
Surat	1663	200,000
Patna	1631	200,000
Dacca	1630	200,000
Masulipatam	1672	200,000

2

Process of Growing Up: Functions and Problems

MALE REPRODUCTIVE SYSTEM AND FUNCTIONING

PHYSIOLOGICAL CHANGES AT THE ONSET OF ADOLESCENCE

As you all might know, adolescence is a very important period in a person's life because it prepares a child for his life as grown up. This is the time when he is no longer a child, but not yet an adult; when he begins to find a number of changes taking place in himself, Delarge compares adolescence with "the building of a house as the house: is being built the dreadful noise of a hammering and the ugly scaffolding reaching up into the sky can be rather depressing and irritating; but when the house is finished it is nice to look at and pleasant to live in". Most of you would have experienced the turmoil of this age. But, remember that just as noisy hammering is a necessary part of the building of a house, the unhappy moments of adolescence are necessary part of growing up. The term adolescence comes from the Latin word adolescere, meaning 'to grow' or 'to grow to maturity'. It includes mental, emotional, and social maturity as well as physical maturity. This point of view has been expressed by Piaget when he said:

- "Psychologically, adolescence is the age when the individual becomes integrated into the society of adults, the age when the child no longer feels that he is below the level of his elders, but equal, at least in rights..... This integration into adult society has many effective aspects more or less linked with puberty.... It also includes very profound intellectual changes. The intellectual transformations typical of the adolescent's thinking enable him to achieve his integration into the social relationships of adults, which is infact, the most general characteristic of this period of development".

In other words, you can say that all the developmental tasks of adolescence are focused on overcoming childish attitudes and behaviour patterns and preparing for adulthood. The developmental tasks of adolescence require a major change in the child's habitual attitudes and patterns of behaviour. Fundamentally, the need for mastering the developmental tasks in the relatively short time that adolescents have reason for much of the stress that plagues many adolescents.

You may, perhaps, be aware of how difficult it is for adolescents to accept their physiques if, from earliest childhood, they have a glamourized concept of what they wanted to look like when they are grown up. It takes time to revise this concept and to learn ways to improve their appearance so that it will conform more to their earlier ideals. Also, because of antagonism towards people of the opposite sex that often develops during late childhood or puberty, learning new relationships with members of the opposite sex, actually, is quite difficult.

Most of the adolescents experience emotional instability from time to time, which is a logical consequence of the necessity of making adjustments to new patterns of behaviour and to new social expectations. While adolescent emotions are often intense, uncontrolled, and seemingly irrational, there is generally an improvement in emotional behaviour with each passing year.

Erikson, in his book "Eight Ages of Man" argued that all human beings pass through eight stages of development which are determined by our genes. He was of the view that each of these stages of development must be resolved successfully before the individual can move to the next higher stage of development. On the psychological level, argues Erikson, even though adolescents can think abstractly and do realize that their views are not the only valid views in the world, they continue to assume that everyone is as obsessed with their behaviour as they are. It is this assumption that accounts for their ego-centrism—their self centeredness.

Social Adjustments

One of the most difficult developmental tasks of adolescence relates to social adjustments. Because adolescents spend most of their time outside home with members of their peer groups, it is understandable that peers would have a greater influence on adolescents' attitudes, speech, interest, appearance and behaviour than the family has. Most adolescents, for example, discover that if they wear the same type of clothes as popular group members wear, their chances of acceptance are enhanced. Of all the changes that take place in social attitudes and behaviour, the most pronounced is the area of heterosexual relationships.

In a short period of time, adolescents make the radical shift from disliking members of the opposite sex to preferring their companionship to that of members of their own sex. As a result of broader opportunities of social participation, social insight improves among older adolescents. They develop new values concerning the selection of friends and also concerning social acceptance. They also develop a strong 'interest themselves', partly because they realize that their social acceptance is markedly influenced by their general appearance, and partly because, they know the social group judges them in terms of their material possessions. Their interests, as you might be aware, tend to range from their appearance, achievements, their independences, education, and religion and so on.

Physical Changes

During adolescence, besides the changes on the psychological and social level, physical changes are among the most striking and amazing. Here we will discuss the physical changes in the body of a male adolescent. The event marking the beginning of manhood (usually between the ages of 13 and 15 years) is the secretion of gonad tropic hormones by the pituitary gland, which is situated at the base of the brain.

They cause the testicles to mature and in turn to secrete their own hormones (androgens), the most important of which is testosterone. Testosterone is responsible for the many physical changes taking place during adolescence. First of all, the teenager starts growing up fast. The shape of his body and the muscles now begin to grow firmer. The voice begins to "break": it becomes deeper in sound but until it has found its proper adult pitch, it sounds rather rough. Hair starts growing near genital organs and round the anus, under the armpits and on the lower part of the abdomen (the so called pubic region, hence, the name "puberty" is also given to this stage).

Hair also starts growing on the face, first on the upper lips, and then on the cheeks, chin and anterior neck. Later on (in some men), hair also grows on the chest and abdomen. It may happen to some boys that one or both of the breasts get slightly enlarged. This situation is normal and temporary. A boy need not worry that the body is becoming feminized. The enlargement will disappear automatically in a few months or years.

It is the testicles and the penis that make the real difference during adolescence. The male sex glands and the testicles do not begin to work in the normal way until sometime between the ages of twelve to fifteen. But, when the testicles begin to release the male hormones through the blood-stream to the rest of the body, the adolescent boy begins to appear much more masculine. At the same time the penis becomes longer and thicker and the testicles held in the scrotum becomes larger and firmer.

Soon the testicles will be to produce their first sperms or life cell: this means that the boy is capable of becoming a father. For a better understanding, we will now discuss the various organs of the male reproductive system along with their functions. The males reproductive system is not cyclical and thus, not as hormonally or endocrinologically complex as that of the female, which we shall study in detail in the next unit.

SCROTUM AND TESTICLES

The major sexual endocrine glands are the two testes or testicles, which are contained and protected in a sac-like structure called the scrotum. The word 'testes' is derived from the word 'testify' meaning to 'witness. It is based on the ancient custom of taking oath by solemnly placing the hands on the genitals. Scrotum is a sac of skin, divided into two parts, which holds the testes, epididymides, and a portion of the vas deferens.

When the skin is stretched a large number of small glands are visible, which resemble pimples. These are entirely normal. The scrotum protects the testes from any injury. Each testis is enclosed in a tough fibrous shealt and suspended from a spermatic cord in a separate compartment of the scrotal sac. Each of these characteristics has important practical consequences. When the organ attempts to swell, for example, during an infection, the unyielding cover will not give way but will choke its delicate structures. This condition, which occurs when an adult male develops mumps involving the testes, may result in sterility. Prepubescent boys are in no danger as their sperm producing structures are not yet functional and thus not subject to damage.

Temperature Difference

It is important for you to note that spermatogenesis, the production of sperm, is highly sensitive to temperature differences. It is hampered by the warm environment inside the body and the testes proceed optimally within the scrotal sac where temperatures are somewhat lower. In fact, the scrotum keeps the testes upto 5 degrees cooler than normal body temperature in order to allow for production of sperm. The scrotum is situated as a projection outside the body since within the body the temperature would be higher. Muscle fibres are attached to the inner surface of the skin, which contract during sexual excitement or when it is cold. The scrotum then becomes rounded small and wrinkled. When it is warm, the scrotum hangs lower and is pear shaped in appearance. This adjustability helps to maintain a steady temperature. This facilitates the proper production of sperms.

Structure of the Testes

The testes, two oval-shaped bodies suspended in the scrotum, are the most important glands of the entire reproductive system. Upto the age of fourteen, the testes are approximately only 10 percent of their mature size. Then, there is rapid growth for a year or two, after which the growth slows down, the testes are fully developed by the age of twenty-one. The testicles contain two groups of structures which perform different functions. One is a series of cells: interstitial cells (meaning: situated between) which secrete the male sex hormones. The other group of structures is the seminiferous tubules which are a very large number of fine hairs like tubules in which the sperm are formed. This network of tiny tubules in the testes constantly produces sperm, beginning at puberty, but no sperm is produced until then. Testes descend from the abdomen of male baby normally shortly before or just after birth. The testes also produce the male sex hormones testosterone. Estrogen is also produced in minute amounts by the testes, as well as by the liver.

Developments of Testes

At the foetal stage of a male, testes develop in abdominal cavity of the foetus. Then they gradually descend to the edge of the pelvis. Usually, by the eighth month of intrauterine life, they descend into the scrotum. However, in few cases they make this descent during the post-natal period or in infancy. Sometimes, we may come across child with one testicle only, or even without testicles, because they do not descend into the scrotum and are retained within the abdomen. This situation is called cryptorchism (hidden testicles). It is obligatory that the testes descend prior to puberty because undescended testes are sterile.

They get irreversibly damaged by the higher temperatures present in the body. It may happen, sometimes that one or both testes become enlarged with or without pain. In this case, it is necessary to consult a doctor. The scrotum may at times, becomes apparently enlarged by liquid collection around the testes (hydrocele). At other times some veins above the testicles become enlarged and may ache (veriocele). You would be aware of the fact that with the advancement of medical sciences, it is now possible to correct any developmental complications medically or surgically. Parents should take care to detect such complications in children. It can be easily done while bathing a child or dressing him.

Problems with Undescended Testes

Some of the problems related to undescended testes include development of 'rupture' or inguinal hernia and cancer. This can happen to any child. Therefore, it is advisable that those parents take necessary care to observe such abnormalities. In some cases, one of the testes may descend while the other may not. In such cases also medical help should be sought. There is no harm in removing one of the testes surgically if it does not descend. You should keep in mind that such a surgical removal would not affect the reproductive system. It is very necessary for parents to be aware of the pros and cons of such developments. They may need counselling before the surgery is done on her child. When the child notices that one of his testes is missing, it can embarrass him. It is the duty of his parents to explain to him the reasons, how he lost one of his testes. Parents should also instill in him confidence, so that he does not worry about the missing organ. Parents should take utmost care to keep these facts confidential between themselves and their child.

Testosterone

When the testes mature they begin to produce the male hormones. This highly complex chemical compound is called the testosterone. Men are not the only ones who make testosterone; women make some too. But men make about 10 times more testosterone than women. Testosterone does more than just allow men to make sperm. It is carried to various parts of the reproductive system where it directs each part in its physical growth. As you have read earlier in this unit, it triggers the growth of facial hair, causes men's voice to deepen, their muscles to develop and the genital organs themselves to grow in size. Later in life, testosterone also plays a role in balding. At maturity, the left testes generally will hang lower than the right one and the scrotum becomes darkened and wrinkled.

THE SPERM

Inside each testicle there are hundreds of fine tubules, closely packed. With the help of microscope, we can see the inside of these tubes which is lined with millions of cells. You already know that the testicles produce hormones which the blood carries to all the cells of the body. Another function of the testes is to produce spermatozoa or the sperm cells. The sperms are among the smallest cells in the human body, so small that we need a microscope to see them. It is possible to differentiate between the two groups of sperms, according to their sizes and shapes. One group is formed by small, round headed sperms carrying the Y chromosomes (androsperms), and the other groups of larger, oval-shaped sperms carrying the X chromosomes (gymnosperms). Sperm production takes place in the somniferous or sperm bearing tubules. These tubules are very long and measure hundreds of feet, which permit the production of millions of sperm, or what we call 'the tiny life cells' during a male's fertile lifetime. When you see them under a microscope, you will find that sperms are shaped like seeds and have a long tail. The movements of the tail make the sperm move in a straight direction when they are ejaculated (suddenly emitted) from the penis.

Male Reproductive System

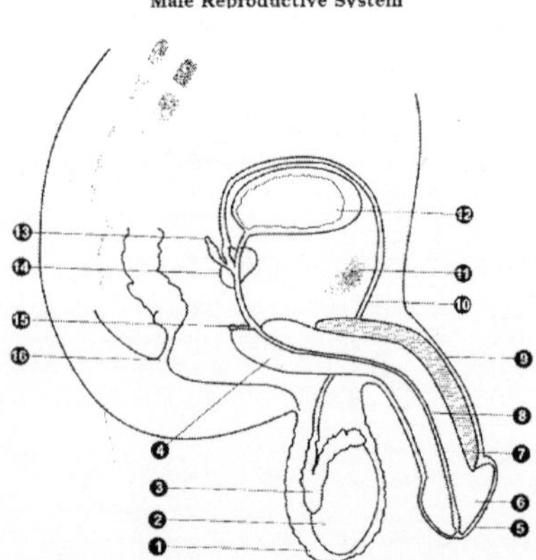

Fig. 1. Scrotum, 2. Testicle, 3. Epididymis, 4. Corpus Spongiosum, 5. Foreskin, 6. Glans, 7. Corpus Cavernosum, 8. Urethra, 9. Shaft of Penis, 10. Vas Deferens, 11. Public Bone, 12. Urinary Bladder, 13. Seminal Vesicle, 14. Prostate Gland, 15. Cowper's Gland, 16. Anus

Epididymides

Sperms are produced in the testes, and mature in the epididymides, each of which is a tube tightly coiled over the top and behind each testes, in the shape of a helmet. On straightening, each tube may measure about twenty feet. This provides a vast capacity for the storage of semen. Mature sperms move from the epididymides to the vas deferens. The vas deferens are two long, narrow tubes that carry the sperms from each epididymis to the seminal vesicles. There are two seminal vesicles located beneath the bladder. The seminal vesicles produce seminal fluid, in which the sperms move and are nourished. Seminal fluid combined with secretions from the prostrate and cowper's glands is called semen.

Vas Deferens

The shorter and straighter continuation of the epididymis, known as the vas deferens, is one of the components of the spermatic cord from which the testicles get suspended. During its upward course within the scrotum, vas deferens can be felt as a firm cord, before it disappears in to the abdominal cavity. You should be aware of the fact that since this structure is easily located, and surgically accessible, it is most convenient target for sterilizing men. This operation, known as vasectomy, simply involves the cutting or tying of the vas deferens (on both sides) through two small incisions performed under local anesthesia. Vasectomy results in permanent sterility (a man becomes sterile, because the sperms will not be able to reach the urethra); but this does not have any impact on the sexual desire, performance or male characteristics. There is not even any noticeable effect upon the quantity of ejaculate because of the volume sperm contribution to semen is very little.

Re-establishing fertility in a man who has undergone vasectomy is very rare although it is not an impossible task. But, when a person wants to opt for vasectomy, it is important for him to seek necessary counselling and guidance. A person should make sure that he has all the necessary information on vasectomy, before opting for it. In fact some religious teaching do not permit vasectomy. Therefore, one should examine all such matters from the concerned religious or spiritual guides.

Ejaculations

The tip of the vas deferens joins the duct of the seminal vesicle to form the ejaculatory duct. Mature sperms move from the epididymides into the vas deferens. During sexual excitement, the vas deferens and the other internal reproductive organs tighten and relax in a pulse-like rhythm. The contractions push the sperms through the vas deferens into urethra. In the urethra, fluids from the prostate gland, seminal vesicles, and cowper's gland mix to form semen. The semen is pushed through the urethra by pulse-like contractions, and at the peak of sexual excitement, the semen exits through the opening of the urethra in the glands of the penis. This process is known as ejaculation. The seminal vesicle situated behind the urinary bladder produces a gelatinous, yellowish secretion which mixes with the sperm, thickens the semen and gives it greater volume. The seminal vesicles produce also the sugar fructose which is essential for giving the sperms the capacity of fertilizing the egg.

Erection

Distension of the seminal vesicles when full of secretions stimulates the phenomenon of erection (stiffness of the penis). Also a full distended urinary bladder can press on the seminal vesicle and give rise to erection. This explains the frequent occurrence of erection in the morning because the urinary bladder is usually full of urine collected during the night.

Prostate Gland

The prostate gland is located below the bladder. It produces a thin alkaline fluid that helps the sperm to become mobile and active and able to make their journey into the female reproductive system. It gives the semen its characteristic odour and viscosity. The prostatic secretion accounts for much of the volume of semen and neutralizes the acid in a man's urethra and a women's vagina. In older men, sometimes the prostate enlarges, causing difficulty in urination. Cancer of prostate is also a common feature in many older men.

Cowper's Glands

There are two cowper's glands attached to the urethra as it descends from the prostate gland. The cowper's glands secrete the fluid that makes the seminal fluid sticky. The secretion from this gland is the fluid that forms on the end of the penis, when a man initially becomes sexually aroused. It was in the seventeenth century, when William Cowper first described the function of this gland. Therefore, it has been named after him. You should not confuse the fluid produced by cowper's glands with semen. However, the important fact is that this fluid also may contain some quantity of sperms, which can also, at times result in pregnancy, even if an intercourse has not ended in ejaculation.

THE PENIS

The penis is a soft, cylindrical organ that hangs under the abdomen at the junction of the thighs. It is formed of two parts: the body or shaft, and a smooth part shaped like a helmet called glands. The body of the penis is formed by three parallel cylinder of spongy tissue: two are in an upper position (each one is called 'corpuscavernosum' or hollow body) that are responsible for the stiffness of the erected penis and a softer one is below them ('corpus spongiosum' or spongy body) expanding on the top of the penis to form the glands. The urethra runs through the middle of the spongy body. Urethra in the male is a tube that originates from the bladder, and passes through the spongy body, to the opening in the glands of the penis. It carries urine from the bladder, and semen from the vas deferens. The urethra in male remains closed to urine during erection of the penis on ejaculation.

Erection

The three cylindrical bodies of the penis are made of soft tissue, which contain numerous blood vessels. These are known as erectile tissue. During sexual excitement, when blood flows through the blood vessels, they swell and exert pressure inside the penis, in effect it is erected upward in appearance, length and stiffness. This is called erection. The penis can become erected very early in male's life. However, ejaculation cannot take place until puberty, when sperm production begins.

Functions of Penis

The penis begins to grow in size only after it receives the male hormones from the testicles when the boy is 11 or 12, and attains adult size when he is about 20. The penis is an organ which serves two purposes. One of its functions is to pass urine. The other function is related to reproduction. This male sex organ is specially designed by nature, when firm and erect, to fit into the vagina of the female as the channel for passing semen from the man's reproductive organ into the woman's reproductive organ during sexual intercourse.

Foreskin

The penis has no bone. As you have read earlier, it ends in a nut-shaped enlargement called glands, which is soft. In uncircumcised men, the foreskin covers the glans. The glans is highly sensitive. It is equivalent to the clitoris in a woman, as a source of sexual pleasure. The foreskin, also known as the prepuce, is a retraceable tube of skin that covers and protects the glans of the penis. It is connected to the rim of the glans on its undersurface by a thin bridge of tissue called the frenulum, and this, if it is short, can tear and bleed during intercourse.

Around the crown of the glands, in certain men, many small white spots can be seen. These are frequently found and are quite normal. The glans, the frenulum, and the crown are the most sensitive parts of the penis because they consist of a great number of nerves. During erection, this skin usually stretches out leaving the glans uncovered, otherwise, if it is too tight on the top (a condition known as phimosis), it prevents the free movements of the penis during sexual intercourse and does not allow a proper cleaning of the glans.

It may also be possible that in some new born babies the foreskin is stuck to the glans. In infancy, it may be difficult to pull it back. In such cases, it is always advisable for the parents to consult a doctor when taking a child for immunization.

Circumcision

The surgical removal of the foreskin known as circumcision leaves the glans permanently exposed. In some societies, cultures and religions, it is custom to have all boys circumcised. You might be aware, for instance that among the Jews and Muslims, circumcision of boys has a religious significance. This makes urinating easier. In the light of information available regarding HIV/AIDS, it is often advised to circumcise boys as one of the ways of preventing the spread of HIV. This is because during intercourse, the foreskin can hold back female secretions. If there are breaks or sores, on the penis or glans, the HIV (or any other infection) can enter the body of the man, if his partner is HIV positive (or infected).

Cleanliness

It is healthy for males to wash their genital organs daily. Uncircumcised men should pull back the foreskin and wash the organs, in particular the inner parts. If the glans and inner part of the foreskin are not washed often, a thick and yellowish substance collects underneath (called the smegma) and may cause irritation and burning sensation. Regular cleaning will prevent organs from itching, irritation and developing sores.

Size of Penis

No other organ in the entire body varies so greatly in size from individual to individual. The size of the penis has caused many a boy much misgiving. A boy ought to know that the size of the penis has nothing to do with the degree of 'manliness' in him. This is a highly fallacious notion that has lead to the development of inferiority complex in many uninformed and misinformed adolescents. They feel that they probably are less competent and potent to be sexually competent than other grown up men. A normal sized penis is usually three or four inches long.

It enlarges to about six inches in length when erect, and about one to three centimeters in diameter. Perfectly normal and adequate penises can be considerably smaller in size. However, in some exceptional cases, penises larger than 13 inches have been reported. The size and shape of the penis has very little to do with the competence of the man in giving or receiving sexual satisfaction. It is also a fact that smaller penises tend to get proportionately larger than penises that are larger in size to start with.

Wet Dreams

During adolescence, the male starts getting a new experience, called 'night emissions'. Night emissions are a periodic discharge of semen (stored up sperm and fluid) generally occurring during sleep. Now and then, while he is asleep, the semen comes out spontaneously from an adolescent's penis. This phenomenon may occur from one or two to several times a month. The release of semen is often accompanied, in sleep, by a dream which is erotic in nature. Hence, this phenomenon is also referred to as 'wet dreams'. Often adolescents may be dismayed that they have such dreams. They may be out of keeping with their accepted standards. It is not wise to take the imagery of dreams at its face value. The dream merely symbolizes the expression of the periodic physical and psychological tension. The emissions should be considered a consequence of the abundant daily presence of semen in the genitals, as a compensation in case of prolonged abstinence from sexual activity.

All of us should remember that these night emissions or 'wet dreams' are natures' normal safety valve for accumulated semen. This phase is a natural part of boy's development. He should be informed in advance about this fact and assured that there is no reason to be alarmed about when it does happen. It is just the sign that he is growing up in a healthy and normal manner. He can also be advised to channelize his energies into vigorous work and play, and various hobbies and interest.

FEMALE REPRODUCTIVE SYSTEM AND FUNCTIONING

CHANGES AT THE ONSET OF ADOLESCENCE

Adolescence is often described as a phase of life that begins in biology and ends in society. The change is evident in the physical as well as psychological and social development. You have already read in the earlier unit that a sure sign of reaching adolescence is the onset of rapid physical changes in the body. These changes are experienced not simply as increase in size, but also as addition of physical characteristics and sensations. We have already said that when rapid changes in body size and proportions take place, physical changes in the reproductive system also occur leading to sexual maturity. By now you know that the internal and external body parts that are necessary for reproduction are collectively referred to as the Reproductive System.

Although many of the reproductive organs are present in children from the very beginning, these are very small in size and inactive until the time of puberty. Sexual maturation consists of two types of changes in the reproductive system, the primary and the secondary. Those that relate to the primary sex organs such as the penis and testes in males, and the vagina and the ovaries in females are called primary sex characteristics; whereas associated changes visible on the body are referred to as secondary sex characteristics. These include breast development in females, facial hair or beard in males, and growth of under-arm and pubic hair in both sexes.

Among girls, the first sign of puberty is usually the appearance of a small rise around the nipple called the breast bud. Breast development begins before adolescence, sometimes between nine and eleven years. Prior to the bud-stage during pre adolescence, the papillae (or nipples) have already become elevated. In the bud stage, the dark area around the nipple, called the areola, enlarges and the papillae become raised. The remaining stages in breast development that occur up to the end of adolescence are: the enlargement continues and the papillae and areola form a secondary mound; the areola recedes and there is shaping of the breast; and finally the papillae project out.

The appearance of pubic hair takes place soon after the breast bud stage in most girls, although in some girls it may appear first. Growth of the uterus and the vagina occurs along with breast development. Growth in the other parts of the female genital organs, i.e. labia and the clitoris also take place. The ovaries become enlarged and the cells that eventually mature into ova (egg) begin to ripen. The most dramatic and perhaps the most important to the girl is the event of the first menstrual period. The first menstruation is called menarche. It consists of a flow of sticky blood in small amounts from the vagina.

Menarche is one of the later signs of puberty in girls and occurs about 18 months after the growth spurt reaches its peak. Among Indian girls menarche is reached sometimes between 11 and 15 years, the average being 13 years. The early menstrual periods might be slightly irregular i.e they may not occur at the same time interval every month. It is normal to have early or delayed menstrual period for about two years. While menarche does signify that the female reproduction system, including the ovaries, the uterus and the fallopian tubes have reached maturity, these are not yet ready for the full reproductive function, i.e. to bear a child. The remaining secondary sex characteristics in girls appear after the menarche. Growth of pubic hair and breast development are completed while axillary hair appears. These changes may take a fair amount of time. Some may complete the process in one-and-a half to two years while others may take up to five years. However, any duration within this range is normal.

As you are perhaps familiar, every child is born with the genes received from the parents that are responsible for her or his resemblance to them and their ancestors. Following the same rule, the girl's age of menarche is likely to be similar to the mother's menarcheal age, provided there have not been any major changes in the girl's health status. Further, it has been found that in different parts of the world, girls attain menarche at different ages, especially when they belong to different racial groups. Indian girls from different backgrounds are found to have a slightly lower age at menarche (12.5 years), compared to those of European and American origin (12.8 years).

Nutrition is an important factor in health. If the nutrients required by the body at a particular stage are not present in the diet, it can affect many aspects of health, including advancing the age of menarche in girls. The energy requirements of a girl approaching womanhood are much greater than those during childhood. You should know that the average Indian middle-class girl has been found to consume inadequate amount of nutrients. For this reason, the age of menarche among rural and urban poor girls, is later than that of urban affluent girls, presumably with better nutritional status. We will now study in detail the female reproductive system. We will also learn about menstruation, pregnancy and other significant aspects related to them. The female reproductive system consists of the external genital (vulva) and an internal group of organs.

THE EXTERNAL ORGANS

The external genitalia of the female are known as vulva, which means "covering' or the pudendum, meaning "a thing of shame". The vulva is the area between the thighs behind a hairy part which is in front (mons pubis). The mons pubis (also called Mount of Venus, the Greek Goddess of love) consists of a pad of fatty tissue covering the pubic bone. The mons pubis is covered with pubic hair which appears at the time of puberty. The pubic hair is stiff, coarse and curly. The thickness and curliness of the hair depends not only on the hormones but also on racial and genetic factors. The area covered with pubic hair in a female looks like a inverted triangle, the upper line being straight. In some girls the hair might extend upto the navel and creep around and inside of the thighs. In some, the pubic hair may be very thin and sparse. Both types are perfectly normal. The vulva include the clitoris, labia majora, labia minora and the urethra.

The Clitoris

The clitoris is small cylindrical organ resembling the penis but with a hook shape. It is about the size of a pea that is located in the soft folds of the labia that meet just above the opening of the urethra. The clitoris contains many nerve endings and is therefore, highly sensitive. The clitoris swells during sexual excitement and becomes source of sexual pleasure when stimulated. The woman's clitoris and the glans of a man's penis are equivalent external sex organs. The clitoris has hardly any reproductive function. Its main purpose is attainment of sexual pleasure. However, clitoris is usually stimulated by midwives during childbirth in order to enable the expansion of the vagina for the smooth passage of the baby. Thus it has great importance for most of the women in India who are assisted by midwives for childbirth in their homes. Like penis it consists of spongy, erectile tissue. Even though the clitoris swells during sexual excitement, it does not become erect, because its overhanging prepuce, the upper layer of the labia minora, holds it down. The clitoris is an area more sensitive than any other part of the body, even more than the vagina itself.

In some societies, the practice of female circumcision or what is called 'clitoridectomy' is still prevalent. You should know that it is a mutilating procedure whereby the clitoris is amputated. We cannot provide any justification for such a crude practice. In other words, in some male dominated societies women are still viewed as mere objects of pleasure, consequently men fail to see them as equal partners in their lives. With the removal of the clitoris, the woman loses her sexual pleasures. It is believed that clitoridectomy will prevent women from becoming promiscuous and would remain loyal to their husbands. We need to educate people against such painful and wrong ideas which are nothing but misconceptions.

Female Reproductive System : External View

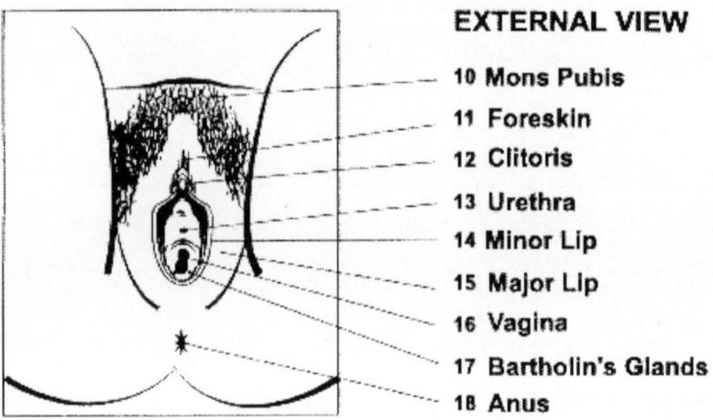

The Labia Majora

The most visible part of the female genitalia is the slight protuberance known as the mons pubis or mons veneris (Mount of Venus), which gets covered with the pubic hair following puberty. The major lips or labia majora that curve downward between the thighs vary in prominence. The labia-majora or out-lips, are two folds of skin located at the outermost on either side of the vagina. They protect the clitoris, and the urethra and vaginal openings.

The Labia Minora and Urethra

The inner edges and surrounding areas are hairless. Along the inner edges of the labia majora are two-folds of tissue called the inner or minor lips or the labia minora. The colour varies from light pink to brownish black and the texture from fairly smooth to wrinkled. At the upper end, the labia minora join to form a fold of skin called the prepuce (or foreskin) that encloses the clitoris. The labia minora and the clitoris have a rich blood supply, and an extensive network of sensory fibres and elastic tissue. The structures lying in between the labia minora from above downwards are: the clitoris, the urethra and the vaginal opening. The urethra, as you might be knowing is not a part of the female reproductive system. Its sole function is to pass urine from the bladder. You have already read in the previous unit that the urethra in male is a passage for both urine and semen.

The Skene's and Bartholin's Gland

The Skene's and Bartholin's glands are located in the labia minora. The Skene's glands are one each side of the opening to the urethra. The Bartholin's glands are on each side of the opening to the vagina, at the lower one third of the labia majora. The Bartholin's glands consist of two small round bodies, which are the counterpart of the Cowper's glands in the male. Each gland opens by means of a duct at the side of the hymen. It secretes sticky mucus during sexual stimulation, which lubricates the entrance to the vagina and its surrounding parts in preparation for coitus. These glands secrete freely only under sexual excitement. Occasionally, one of these glands can fill with mucus and form a painless swelling known as a Bartholin's cyst. At times the gland may become infected and form a painful abscess.

THE INTERNAL ORGANS

Situated deep within the female body are the organs for sexual development as well as for the reproduction of life. To protect these organs against possible accident or injury, they are housed in a strong, basin-like bone structure called the pelvis. The hip bones are the outer boundaries of the pelvis, while the backbone at the rear and strong muscles at front provide complete protection. The internal organs broadly consist of the vagina, uterus, fallopian tubes and ovaries. blood supply, and an extensive network of sensory fibres and elastic tissue. The structures lying in between the labia minora from above downwards are: the clitoris, the urethra and the vaginal opening. The urethra, as you might be knowing is not a part of the female reproductive system. Its sole function is to pass urine from the bladder. You have already read in the previous unit that the urethra in male is a passage for both urine and semen.

The Skene's and Bartholin's Gland

The Skene's and Bartholin's glands are located in the labia minora. The Skene's glands are one each side of the opening to the urethra. The Bartholin's glands are on each side of the opening to the vagina, at the lower one third of the labia majora. The Bartholin's glands consist of two small round bodies, which are the counterpart of the Cowper's glands in the male. Each gland opens by means of a duct at the side of the hymen. It secretes sticky mucus during sexual stimulation, which lubricates the entrance to the vagina and its surrounding parts in preparation for coitus. These glands secrete freely only under sexual excitement. Occasionally, one of these glands can fill with mucus and form a painless swelling known as a Bartholin's cyst. At times the gland may become infected and form a painful abscess.

THE INTERNAL ORGANS

Situated deep within the female body are the organs for sexual development as well as for the reproduction of life. To protect these organs against possible accident or injury, they are housed in a strong, basin-like bone structure called the pelvis. The hip bones are the outer boundaries of the pelvis, while the backbone at the rear and strong muscles at front provide complete protection. The internal organs broadly consist of the vagina, uterus, fallopian tubes and ovaries.

The Female Reproductive System

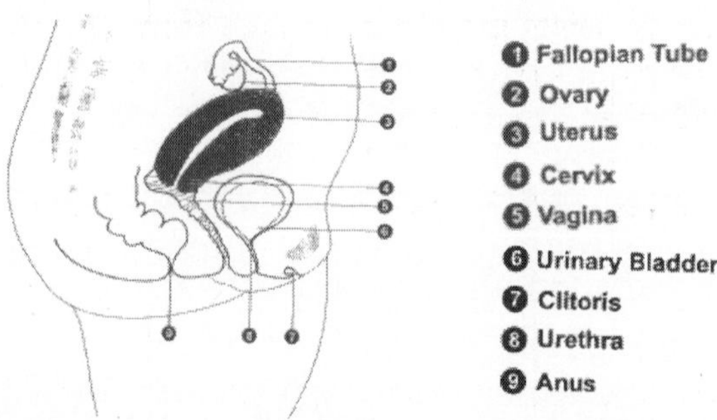

Although this is a very rare phenomenon, surgical help should be sought to avoid further complication. The early symptoms are the swelling of vagina and the uterus as a result of the accumulated menstrual fluid, which has no outlet. In a few cases, some women may have a thicker or tougher hymen than the average or normal hymen. This is likely to cause much discomfort and pain during the first intercourse. Such cases, however, are very rare and might need surgical help. The surgical correction does not require one to have bed-rest or medication. It is only a simple procedure lasting a couple of minutes. As we said earlier, the opening in the middle of the hymen will permit the passage of a sanitary tampon. In most cases, this passage cannot accommodate an erect penis without tearing it. Since some hymens can withstand intercourse, while other get torn accidentally in nonsexual activities like certain kinds of exercise, bicycle or horseback riding or while squatting on the ground, the presence or absence of an intact hymen does not constitute a reliable criterion of whether or not a girl has had an intercourse. Very often, the girl is not even aware that anything has occurred when her hymen breaks during a fall or while taking part in activities like sports.

In many cultures, people believe that a girl without a hymen is no longer a 'virgin'— that a boy perhaps has put his penis in her vagina. But that may not always be true. Virginity has nothing to do with whether or not the hymen is present. There is no way for anyone to tell whether the hymen was broken in intercourse or in an accident.

The Vagina

The vagina is a muscular tube or passage way that connects the neck of the uterus and the external opening at the vulva. It is about four to five inches long. The inner wall of the vagina is lined by a membrane which has large folds giving it a wrinkled appearance. The inner wall of the vagina is moist due to certain secretions which are acidic and serve a protective purpose against germs causing diseases. At the time of sexual excitement this fluid is slightly increased, serving the purpose of lubrication, that makes it easy for the penis to enter the vagina.

Vaginal Discharge

This moisture consists mainly of mucus from the cervix and a watery fluid which comes from the vagina walls; it is scanty and is not sufficient to mark the underclothes. When woman experiences persistent increase in quality of vaginal secretion, we call it leucorrhoea which can occur in a number of diseases. It is often offensive in smell and has a different colour from the normal liquid, usually staining the underclothes. At times a foreign body may be the cause, at other times, taking contraceptive pills for a long time, antibiotics, or a fungus called monillia is commonly responsible. The vaginal discharge in these cases is thick, curdy white, causing inflammation of the vagina and vulva. Other causes of discharge include a common infection of the vagina with a germ called Trichomonas. This germ is transmitted between the partners during sexual intercourse and it may cause itching and swelling of the vulva, inflammation of the vagina and pain during intercourse. This infection is easily curable and both the woman and the man should be treated.

Misinformation

The front and rear walls of the vagina are normally in contact. This permits distension and has the effect of allowing the passage to adapt to a penis of any shape and size. It is never too narrow for intercourse. There is misinformation about the length and width of vagina both among men and women. Some men observe that some vaginas 'feel tight' and others 'feel lax'. Similarly, some women support the observation that the 'fit' during intercourse varies from one person to another. The vagina is sensitive only in its out 3-4 cms. The inner walls have only a few nerve endings sensitive to touch, and this makes the vagina relatively insensitive so that even local operations can be carried on without pain.

Uses of Vagina

Thus as you may have observed, the vagina has essentially three uses:

i) It provides a way for the baby to leave the uterus. Hence, the vagina is also called the 'birth canal'.
ii) It receives the man's penis during sexual intercourse. That is how the sperm get inside the uterus.
iii) It provides a path for menstrual fluid to leave the body. However, you must know that urine does not pass through the vagina.

The Uterus

The uterus, which is commonly known as the womb, is the child-bearing organ. It is a pear-shaped muscular organ that lies between the urinary bladder in front and the rectum behind. It is about 8 cms in length and 5 cms in breadth at the upper end and 1 inch at the lower end. The upper part of the uterus is connected to the tubes and called the body of the uterus. The portion of the body above the tubal attachment is called the fundus, while the lower portion is known as the cervix and it projects into the vagina. The interior of the uterus is a narrow, triangle shaped cavity. This cavity is lined with a special membrane called the endometrium, and is surrounded by thick muscular walls. This narrow cavity undergoes extensive changes in pregnancy and during the menstrual cycle. The endometrium thickens under the stimulus of the two sex hormones in preparation of pregnancy. During pregnancy the embryo and the foetus develop in the uterus which sits down deep in the lower abdomen.

The muscles of the uterus contract during labour to deliver the foetus from the uterus. The uterus is the strongest muscle in the woman's body. You should note that it is so strong, that it is able to push the baby out at childbirth. Inside the muscular walls of the uterus is a very rich lining. This lining feeds the growing foetus during pregnancy. However, if fertilization does not take place by the joining of the ovum and the sperm, that is if the woman does not become pregnant, then the thickened lining of the womb to produce discharge of blood. This blood and lining pass down through the vagina to the outside of the body, at the vulva. This process is known as menstruation or monthly period about which you will read in further detail later in this unit.

The Greek word for uterus is 'hystera'. The surgical removal of the uterus is medically termed as hysterectomy. Originally, the psychologically common word 'hysteria' was associated with the uterus. The wandering of the uterus in search for a child was termed as 'hysteria' by the Greek physicians. The uterus remains very small until the age of puberty. It is about the size of one's fist. It starts growing along with other reproductive organs and reaches maturity when the girl is about 18-20 years old. When the woman is not pregnant, as you have already read, the inside walls of the uterus touch each other. When she is pregnant, they spread apart to make room for the foetus. The pregnant uterus can become as large as a mediumsized Watermelon. As mentioned earlier, a man's body constantly produces sperm while a woman's body produces only one ovum at a time in a month. But, when the woman is pregnant, the ovaries stop producing ova. This means that a mother-to-be stops having periods during the nine months it takes her baby to be properly formed within her, until it is born.

The Ovaries

The ovaries are two female sex glands, the counterpart of the testes in the male. These glands are small and almond-shaped located on each side of the uterus and are attached by ligament. Each of them is about 3-5 cms long, 2-5 cms wide and one cm thick. The ovaries are the most important organs of the entire female reproductive apparatus, and correspond in function of the male testicles. You should know that it has the dual function of production of germ cells and sex hormones. The ovaries are smaller than the testes and remain within the abdominal cavity of the foetus.

The ovaries produce ova which are the female reproductive cells. In the male, sperm production starts at the age of puberty and continues till old age, where in the female, even at birth, the ovaries contain a fixed number of eggs or ova (200,000 to 400,000). As girl grows, some of these eggs die, so that the number of eggs the ovaries contain are about 10,000 immature ova. Each egg is enclosed in a separate sac called the primordial follicle. During the fertile period of a woman (average from 13- 14 to 45-50 years of age) for every ovum that completely matures, untold number of immature ova are lost the attempt and become mere microscopic specs of scar tissue embedded in the substance of the ovary. During the fertile period, less than 500 of these eggs ripen and are released into the fallopian tubes. The egg is laden with nourishment to sustain a growing pre embryo in its first few days. The egg is the largest human cell.

You should note that mostly, the cells of the human body measure only 1/10 of the egg which in turn has a diameter of 1/5 mm. It is about the size of a dot of a newsprint. The shape of the egg is spherical, like a ball, and inside it there is its nucleus which contains the female chromosome. The egg is released from one ovary during ovulation beginning at puberty. The ovaries also produce female sex hormones—estrogen and progesterone as well as small amounts of testosterone.

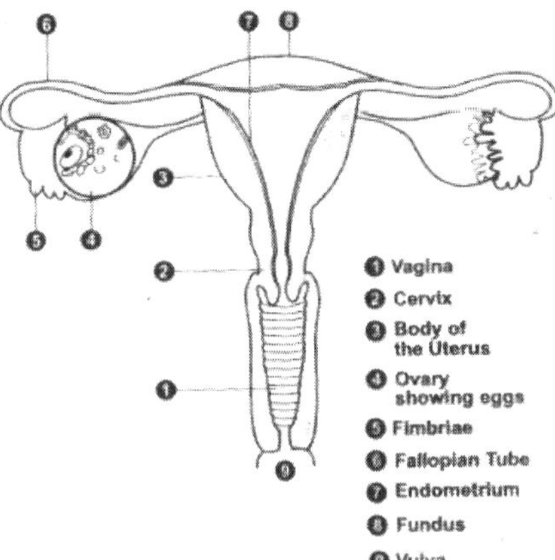

The development of the primordial follicle (the sac which encloses an egg) into a mature follicle (also called the Graafian follicle) is under the control of the pituitary gland located at the base of the brain, which secretes the follicle stimulating hormone. The ripening follicle secretes estrogen, in increasing amounts, which reaches its maximum just before ovulation. At this moment, the chosen mature follicle bulges on the surface of the ovary like a small blister.

When pituitary releases a second hormone, called the Luteinising Hormone, it causes the follicle to break and release the ovum. The event is called ovulation. The released ovum is drawn into the fallopian tube by the finger like ends of the tube itself. This released ovum has a life span of 12-24 hours, and this is the most fertile period of woman's cycle. The mature of follicle, after the release of the egg, becomes a small yellow body (called the corpus luteum), which secretes two hormones: estrogen and progesterone. The presence of these two hormones in the blood signals the pituitary to stop its activity. At the end of the cycle, as corpus luteum fades, the level of estrogen progesterone drops and the pituitary again begins to stimulate the ovaries and the whole process is repeated in a new cycle.

Between 45 and 50 years of age, the ovaries gradually stop responding to the stimulation of the pituitary gland, with the result that the eggs and the hormones of the ovary are not produced. Ovulation occurs with decreasing frequency, the cycles become more and more irregular and after some time menstruations stop completely. The period when the reproductive processes are coming to a halt is called premenopause. Once menstruation has completely stopped for a full year, the woman is said to have reached menopause.

The Fallopian Tubes

Gabriello Fallopio was an anatomist of the sixteenth century who thought that the two tubes found on each side of the uterus are 'ventilators' of the uterus. The Fallopian tubes are named after him. The fallopian tubes are a pair of muscular hollow channels, about 8-10 cms long, which extend from the top of each side of the uterus to the ovaries. The ovarian ends of these tubes are entirely free as they do not touch the ovaries. The outer edge of each of the tubes, as discussed earlier, cap the ovaries with finger like ends or fringes. These are known as the fimbriae. The function of the fimbriae is to sweep a mature egg from the ovary into the tube.

Each tube is lined with a membrane which possesses tiny hair like structures called cilia. These cilia move in such a way so as to push the egg towards the uterus, when contractions take place in the tubes. The egg can live in the fallopian tube for about 24 hours. However, the life of a sperm in the woman's body is about four days. After that the sperm dies. Whenever fertilization of the egg takes place it occurs at the junction of the middle of one third of the tube. Once the egg and sperm unite in the process of fertilization, it is known as zygote. Sometimes, the zygote gets implanted in the wall of the fallopian tube.

That means the fertilized zygote could not reach the uterus; this is called an 'ectopic pregnancy', or out of place pregnancy. It is very dangerous for the pregnant woman. Such pregnancies cannot come to full term of nine months and break the tube. This causes the death of the foetus. Therefore, it is advisable for every pregnant woman to seek the help of a qualified physician and regularly go for check up. An ultra-sound examination can satisfactorily tell us all about the position and growth of the foetus in the womb. Therefore, if it is detected that a woman is having a tubal pregnancy, prompt medical intervention can save the woman from further complications. It is important for you to note that tubectomy or the sterilization of woman is done by cutting the fallopian tubes. This is much more complicated procedure than vasectomy, in which surgery is done on the vas deferens of the male to sterilize him.

The Breasts

The breasts are another pair of reproductive organ in the female. The breasts contain milk glands that produce milk and the milk ducts that carry the milk to the nipple so that the infant is able to have its feed. These milk glands and milk ducts are surrounded and protected by fatty tissue. The fact that a female has breasts does not mean they produce milk. The production of milk starts only after childbirth. When a woman is pregnant, her body begins to produce the pregnancy hormones. These hormones help the breast to grow and get ready to make milk. It also helps every part of the woman's body to adapt to being pregnant.

There is no specific size and shape for breasts. Some women have large breasts while others have small one. In certain cases, some women may have one larger breast and a smaller breast. The size and shape of the breasts have no effect on the ability to feed a baby. On the outside of the breast is nipple, through which the baby can suck the milk. It is surrounded by a circle of dark coloured skin. It is called the areola. Normally, pregnant women experience milk discomfort or pain when pressed upon around their breasts. This is only a positive sign of pregnancy. Nevertheless, one common disease prevalent among women is breast cancer. It is most common in women about thirty-five years of age, though, it can also affect younger women. Since one in ten women are reported to be suffering from breast cancer, it is suggested that women should regularly check their breasts for lumps. A gyneacologist can give you information about how to check the breasts. This, though, is not required before the girl has had her first period.

MENSTRUAL CYCLE AND THE ONSET OF PUBERTY

During puberty, under the influence of estrogen, the pre-pubescent girl gradually turns into a woman, the contours of her body change, her breasts enlarge, and her genital organs develop more fully. Gradually, after some erratic starts and stops, she also starts to menstruate, and there appears a monthly 'bleeding' from the vagina. This usually starts at the age of 12-13 years. However, she becomes fully fertile and sexually a mature woman several years after the onset of these changes.

Menstruation is the flow of blood, fluid and tissue out of the uterus through the vagina. It may last between three to seven days. The menstrual cycle is the time from the beginning of one period to the beginning of the next one. Usually, menstrual cycles last about 28 days. However, some may last for about 20 days or so, whereas, in some cases they may extend to 35 or 40 days. In exceptional cases, they may still last longer even for a couple of months. These variations may be caused by sickness, nervous tension, emotional upset, physical injury, traveling fatigue, change in climate or other circumstances.

When pregnancy begins, menstrual cycles and ovulation stop. Progesterone and estrogen continue to be produced by the uterine lining while the embryo grows into a foetus. The presence of progesterone also stops the ovulation process for the duration of the pregnancy. Once the woman is no longer pregnant or fully nursing, the normal pattern of the menstrual cycle is resumed. After childbirth, usually the menstrual cycle resumes only after about 100 days. However, in some women, it may resume only after six months. There is misconception that a subsequent pregnancy may not occur as long as a woman continues to breast-feed her child. This is not true. Pregnancy can occur even while one is breast-feeding child.

It is important for you to understand that menstruation is a normal part of a female's life. Therefore, it should not be regarded as a sickness. In fact, if menstruation does not take place within the teenage period of a girls' life, she should consult the family doctor for necessary guidance and advice. Many superstitions and fear were associated to it before medical science brought to us the knowledge about this phenomenon and its association with the female reproductive system. Some girls and women may have cramps on the first day or two of their periods. Some may have mood swings or depression. They may become uncomfortable before each of their period begin. They may have physical or emotional discomfort upto two weeks before menstruating. This is called premenstrual syndrome (PMS). It happens in fewer than half of all women between the ages of 14 and 50.

It is important for mother to take special care to instruct their daughters about this important phenomenon in the reproductive system of the female. Their failure often causes the girls to develop an attitude of shame and secrecy. Some mothers hesitate talking about these matters to their daughters. As a result, the children also feel puzzled and frightened by their experience at the first menstruation, especially when it occurs at a time when they are not prepared for it. However, in some societies parents eagerly await the first menstruation of their daughter in order to celebrate it. During the period of menstruation, there is no need for a women to restrain from her normal activities. On the whole, however, it is advisable to avoid strenuous activities. There are also certain myths surrounding menstruation, that it is a 'curse' and therefore, several restrictions are imposed upon women during this period (which are being strictly observed in many Indian families). With the break up of the joint family system though, there are changes taking place in this area.

The first time menstruation happens, it is called 'menarche'. Many families celebrate 'menarche' as the time when a girl becomes a woman. You may call them 'puberty rites'. Some families are more private about menarche. But, regardless of the celebration, it is an exciting and important moment in a girl's life. In many cases, menstruation is accompanied by feelings of fatigue, weakness, headache, changing moods, irritable temper, and cramps in the lower abdomen. If a girl/women suffers from serious cramps or any other cyclic disturbance, a girl/women should consult her doctor. Excessive menstrual bleeding is always a serious matter, requiring medical care, and may be dangerous because of the repeated loss of blood. In some young girls, during the initial years of menstruation, several months may elapse between periods. This is not a cause of worry. Gradually, the normal cycle is resumed.

The Females Sex Hormones

Hormones are chemicals in one's body which are secreted into the blood stream by the endocrine glands. The term 'hormone' has its origin in the early years of this century. Etymologically, hormone got its name from the Greek work for 'excite'. So far, over twenty hormones have been discovered, and many of these have some bearing on the sexual development and function. Hormones that play a central role in this regard are known as the sex hormones. Those that occur in higher concentration in the male are known as the male sex hormones (androgens), and those that are more abundantly produced in the female are the female sex hormones (estrogens and progesterone). The female sex hormones are produced in the ovaries. The ovaries start producing these female sex hormones during puberty. They play a very important role in the female reproductive life and have far reaching effects on the body of the woman.

PREGNANCY AND HEALTH CARE

Now that you are familiar with the male and female reproductive apparatus, you will be able to appreciate the wonderfully ingenious way nature has adapted both systems for the one purpose they were originally intended to bring together the male and female cells. If sexual intercourse takes place in the period of ovulation, the consequence may be the fertilization of the egg and hence, pregnancy.

Fertilization

During intercourse, about 200-300 millions of sperms are ejaculated in the vagina. The sperms move at a speed of 10-12 cms per hour, propelled by the movement, of their tails. The survival and transport of sperms are greatly helped by the alkaline and watery mucus secreted by the cervix, present before and during ovulation. When one sperm touches the egg, the former secretes a substance that facilitates the penetration of the head of the sperm through a hole formed in the wall of the ovum. At this time, the tail of the sperm drops off. At the same point of time, the outer membrane of the egg hardens, preventing the other sperms from entering. The nucleus of the sperm unites with that of the ovum to form a single nucleus. This entire process is called fertilization, and the ovum is now called a zygote (yoked together).

Growth of the Child During Pregnancy

As the zygote is pushed slowly towards the uterus, rapid changes take place. It first divides into two cells, which remain attached to each other; then into four cells and so on. After five days, it reaches the uterus and resembles a fruit with many seeds. It is called the 'morula'. By the tenth day after fertilization, the zygote measures about 2 mm in diameter. For pregnancy to continue, a continued production of nutritive substances in the mother is achieved through a hormone which is secreted by the chorionic villi after implantation.

This hormone is called the Human Chorionic Gonadotrophin (HCG), and it stimulates the corpus luteum in the ovary to increase its size and produce progesterone and estrogen. The hormones produced by the corpus luteum are important to the continuation of pregnancy only during the first twelve weeks. After that, the production of hormones is increasingly taken over by the placenta, which produces HCG, estrogen and progesterone.

The HCG is found in the urine of woman in significant quantity 14 days after the first missed period and reaches a peak between the 70th and 100th day after ovulation. Therefore, one's pregnancy test can be confirmed by testing the urine at the end of the second week after first day of the missed menstruation. From the moment of fertilization till the second week the growing cell mass is called a zygote. From the second to the eighth week it is referred to as an embryo, and from the eighth week till birth it is called foetus. The first twelve weeks of pregnancy are the most important and vulnerable, because all the vital organs, the heart and brain are being formed. Due precautions should be taken during this period to avoid X-rays, certain drugs and exposure to viruses.

Every living organism requires nourishment for its growth and needs to get rid of its waste products. For the foetus, the placenta serves these needs. The placenta is an oval organ about eight inches in diameter when fully developed, and is attached to the endometrium. It prevents the blood of the mother from entering into the circulation of the foetus, while allowing the passage of oxygen and nourishing elements, and simultaneously helping to excrete the waste products of the foetus. The foetus is connected to the placenta by the umbilical cord which contains blood attached to the navel of the baby. The placenta, in turn, is attached to the inner-lining of the cavity of the uterus, and is, therefore, in direct contact with the blood of the mother, which is the source of nutrition to the foetus.

It is advisable for the woman that for all the time during her pregnancy she should undergo regular check ups in order to make sure that the new life within her is developing in a healthy manner. Also, between 16 to 36 weeks of pregnancy, the vaccine, tetanus toxoid should be administered to her. Therefore, it is advisable to consult a qualified physician while one is pregnant.

Delivery

Two hundred and sixty six days after fertilization the foetus is completely developed. The word 'delivery' refers to the birth of the baby. However, the whole process can be described in three stages. The first stage is the uterine contractions (or labour pain, as you can call it), which are rhythmic contractions of the uterus. They are painful to the mother and occur at intervals of 10- 15 minutes, each wave of pain lasting for about 30 seconds. With these contractions, the foetus is forced downwards. The stage usually lasts about 12-18 hours for the first child and about 8 hours for subsequent babies.

The second stage begins when the cervix is fully dilated and ends with the delivery of the baby. With each uterine contraction, the head of the child is pushed downwards. Then, one shoulder appears followed by the other, and soon the rest of the body is delivered. With the change in temperature, the child is stimulated to cry. A few seconds after the umbilical cord has been cut, air flows into the child's lungs for the first time in order to oxygenate the blood. This stage lasts for about an hour in the first delivery and 10 to 30 minutes in the subsequent deliveries. In the third stage, following the birth of the child, the placenta is expelled. This stage may last from 10 to 30 minutes. After the birth of the child, the uterus shrinks in size and so does the area where the placenta is detached from the uterine wall. With this stage, the whole process of delivery is completed.

Physical and Emotional Care of the Child in the Womb

At no other time during the life span are there more serious hazards to development or of a more serious nature than during the relatively short period before birth. These may be physical or psychological. Therefore, you should note that appropriate physical and emotional care of the child in the womb is of utmost importance.

Care Regarding Physical Factors

Certain conditions have been found to influence the foetus physically in more ways than one. Maternal nutrition plays a vital role in the normal development, especially the development of the foetal brain. Excessive smoking and drinking are detrimental to normal development, specially during the periods of the embryo and foetus. Also, maternal age has often been reported as a condition that may lead to the possibility of physical hazard during prenatal period. Certain kinds of work are more likely to disturb the prenatal development than others. Chemicals and other hazards faced by women working in places like hospitals, beauty parlours and factories may be responsible for the increasing number of birth defects and miscarriages. As Burnham (1976) pointed out, "The potential damage to the foetus and the possible genetic damage which may occur when pregnant women go to work appears to be an important medical problem".

Care Regarding Psychological Factors

Like the physical factors associated with the prenatal period, the psychological factors can have persistent effects on the individual's development. During the early formative years, there are three important psychological hazards to the unborn child's well being. These are traditional beliefs about prenatal development, maternal stress during prenatal period, and unfavourable attitudes towards the unborn child on the part of people who will play significant roles in the child's life. There are also traditional beliefs about the causes of developmental irregularities which often hold the mother responsible. Acceptance of these lead to feelings of guilt on the part of the mother, resentments towards her on the part of the father (husband), and tendency for the mother to overprotect the child as a form of compensation for the harm she believes she has caused. Another important psychological factor, maternal stress, can be the result of fear, anger, grief, jealousy or envy.

Causes of maternal stress during pregnancy include not wanting a child because of marital or economic difficulties or because having a child will interfere with educational or vocational plans' feelings of inadequacy for the parental role; and fears that the child will be physically deformed or mentally deficient. Maternal stress affects the developing child both before and after birth. Before birth, severe and persistent glandular imbalance due to stress may result in irregularities in the developing child and complications of delivery or even prematurity. Maternal anxiety affects uterine contractions, with the result that the labour lasts longer than normal and the chances of complications are greater because the infant must be delivered by instruments. Prolonged and extreme maternal stress during the period of the foetus frequently causes more illness during the first three years of the child's life than is experienced by children who had a more favourable foetal environment.

There is evidence that many unfavourable attitudes towards children, begin to develop when their potential arrival becomes known to parents, siblings, relatives and neighbours. If the child is not wanted, or at least, not wanted at this time, attitudes unfavourable from then start. A father to-be-may blame his wife for being careless and make her feel guilty about not preventing the pregnancy. This will lead to marital friction and resentment toward the child when it is born. Therefore, a couple should always seek appropriate counselling, both when the foetus is developing and when child is born.

EARLY STAGES OF HUMAN GROWTH: BIOLOGICAL, SOCIAL, PSYCHOLOGICAL AND DEVELOPMENTAL ASPECTS

CONCEPTION AND HUMAN DEVELOPMENT

A husband and wife who love each other have a very special and intimate ways to knowing and loving one another deeply. They show it, among other things, by sharing their bodies and joining them. This is possible because a man's body and woman's body are made in such a way that they can join together. This process is called coitus of sexual intercourse. There are certain specific positions that the husband and wife take during the sexual intercourse. The most common position that in which the woman lies of her back with her thighs separated, while man over her in close contact with her body.

The husband's penis penetrates into the wife's vagina. During these few moments the husband's semen flows from his penis into the wife's vagina. This very intimate act between husband and wife helps them to love and understand each other: it is called 'making love'. If this act happens during the fertile days of woman's menstrual cycle, there is a very high probability that she will conceive. i.e sperm present in the semen of the male will unite with the ovum of the female. This process is called fertilization.

Prenatal development begins at conception, or fertilization, when the genetic material from a male sex cell (sperm) unites with the female sex cell (ovum) to form a single cell, called a *zygote.* The zygote receives 23 chromosomes from the mother and 23 from the father, and these 46 chromosomes replicate over and over as the zygote reproduces itself through mitosis.

Different Stages of Development After Conception

As you have been told in the earlier unit, there are three stages of development after conception or during pregnancy. Let us study each of them from the point of view of development.

The Period of Zygote (Conception to Second Week)

Approximately six days after fertilization, the cells of the zygote become sticky and attach to the wall of the uterus, where implantation begins. Now the cells begin to specialize, some forming an inner cell mass, which will become the embryo, and some forming a surrounding cell mass, which will become support structures for the embryo. The zygote is still only about 0.01 inches long. Implantation takes about a week. Finally, the zygote is totally buried in the uterine wall, and the period of the zygote ends. About two weeks have passed since fertilization, which corresponds to the first missed menstrual period. By the time a woman suspects she may be pregnant, the prenatal development is well under way.

It is very important to note that with fertilization a new human life begins in all respects. Therefore, one should not be carried away by the misinformation that the foetus is only a piece of flesh without life. Because of this feeling sometimes people feel convenient to abort the foetus and many a time of the live foetus is extracted from its mother's womb for laboratory experiments. This is the most inhuman harm one can do to an unborn and defenseless child.

The Period of Embryo (Third to Eight Weeks)

All major internal and external structure form during this period. In the third week, the inner cell mass differentiates into three germ layers from which all body structures will emerge. Initially, two layers form – the endodermal layer and the ectodermal layer. The endodermal cells will develop into internal organs and glands. The ectodermal cells form the basis for parts of the body that maintain contact with the outside world—the nervous system; the sensory parts of the eye, nose, and ear, tooth enamel, skin, and hair. This is the third cell layer that appears between the endodermal and extodermal layers. This is the mesodermal layer, which will give rise to muscle, cartilage, bone, the heart, sex organs and some glands. A primitive heart begins to form and, by the end of the third week, connects to the vessels and begins to beat to form a cardiovascular system, the first organ system to become functional.

Around the fourth week, the embryo looks something like a tube of about 0.1 inch long. You should note that this period is important, because now, the environment begins to affect the development of cells. By the end of fourth week, the embryo assumes a curved form, and the upper and lower limbs have just begun to form as tiny buds. The embryo's body changes less in the fifth week, but the head and brain develop rapidly. The upper limbs now form, and the lower limbs appear and look like small paddles. In the sixth week, the head continues to grow rapidly, and differentiation of the limbs occurs as elbows, fingers, and wrists become recognizable. It is now possible to discern the ears and eyes. The limbs develop rapidly in the seventh week, and stumps appear that will form fingers and toes.

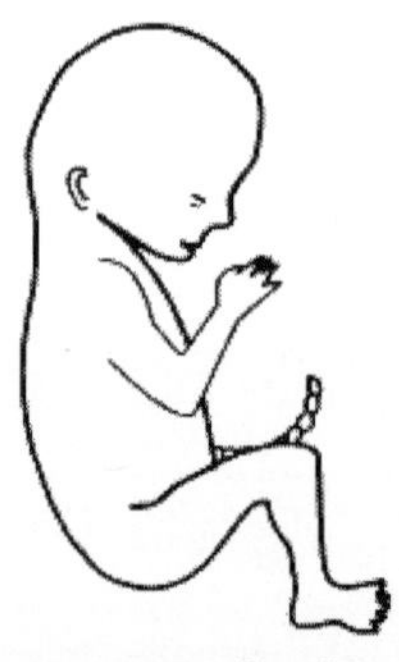

3 months foetus

By the end of the eighth week, the embryo has distinctly human features. Almost half of the embryo consists of the head. During most of this week, the eyes are open, but eyelids soon form to cover them. The eyes, ears, toes and fingers are easily distinguishable and the tail has disappeared. All internal and external organs have formed. Thus, you can see that in eight weeks a single tiny undifferentiated cell develops into a remarkable complex organism consisting of millions of cells differentiated into heart, kidneys, eyes, ears, nervous system, brain, and all the other structure that make a human being. By the end of the embryonic stage, the surrounding cells develop into three major support systems: the amniotic sac, the placenta, and the umbilical cord.

The amniotic sac is a watertight membrane filled with fluid. As the embryo grows, the amniotic sac comes to surround it, cushioning and supporting it within the uterus and providing an environment with a constant temperature. The placenta, formed from both the mother's tissue and the embryo's tissue is the organ the mother and embryo use to exchange materials. Linking the embryo to the placenta is the umbilical cord which houses the blood vessels that carry these materials. The exchange of materials take place in the placental villi. These are small blood vessels immersed in the mother's blood, but separated from it by a very thin membrane. You should note that blood does not pass between the mother and the foetus. However, oxygen and nutrients do pass from the mother's blood to the villi, and waste products of the foetus pass into the mother's blood to be carried away and excreted.

The Period of the Foetus (Ninth to Thirty Eight Week)

In this period, the principal tasks for the foetus are to further develop the already formed organ structures and to increase in size and weight. You will find it surprising that beginning its third month weighing only 0.2 ounce and measuring 2 inches in length, the average foetus is born 266 days after conception weighing about 7 to 8 pounds and measuring about 20 inches in length.

External Changes

During this period, the foetus's appearance changes drastically. The head grows first than the other parts of the body, changing its ratio from 50 percent of the body mass at 12 weeks towards 25 percent at birth. The skin which has been transparent begins to thicken during the third month. The foetus's eye move from the sides, the head to the front. Nails appear on fingers and toes by the fourth month, and pads appear at the ends of fingers that uniquely identify the individual for life. Head hair also begins to grow. A bone structure begins to support a more erect posture by six months.

Growth of Internal Organs

By three months, the brain has assumed the basic organization that marks its later subdivision – seeing, hearing, thinking, initiating activity, breathing, and so on. The 100 billion cells of the adult brain are already present in the foetus by the fifth month. Nerve cell growth and establishment of connections, begun at 19 days, continue throughout foetal development. A major mystery facing scientists is how a single zygote cell can give rise to billions of fibres that properly connect eyes, ears, touch sensors, muscles, and the parts of the brain. It is clear that environmental factors and interactions between nerve cells also play a role as (you would be aware that) no two brains are wired identically not even those of identical twins, who have exactly the same genetic material.

6 months foetus

In the third month, the kidneys begin to excrete urine into the surrounding amniotic fluid, which is freshened by the mother's body every three hours. Sexual development becomes apparent in males by the end of this month with the appearance of external sexual organs. In females the oocytes form the outer covering of the ovaries. The fallopian tubes, uterus, and vagina develop and the external labia become discernible.

Early Signs of Behaviour

Foetal activity begins in the third month when the foetus is capable of wiggling the toes, and swallowing; but the mother feels none of this. The foetus also appears to become sensitive to environmental stimulation for it moves its whole body in response to touch stimulus. By the fourth month the eyes are sensitive to light through the lids, and by the fifth month, a loud noise may activate the foetus. During this same month the foetus swims effortlessly. The foetus is now capable of kicking and turning, and may begin to display rhythms of sleep and activity.

By the seventh month, brain connections are sufficient for the foetus to exhibit a sucking reflex when the lips are touched. By seven months of age, the foetus has a slightly better chance of survival outside the mother's body.

The brain is sufficiently developed to provide at least partial regulation of breathing, swallowing, and body temperature. However, a baby born after only seven months of development will need to be provided with extra oxygen, will have to take food in very small amounts and will have to live for several weeks in an incubator for temperature control. In the eighth month, fat appears under the skin, and although the digestive system is still too immature to adequately extract nutrients from food, the foetus begins to store maternal nutrients in its body.

But even a baby born at eight months is susceptible to infection. By the eighth month, the mother's body starts contributing disease-fighting antibodies to the foetus that she has developed through her own exposure to foreign bodies. This process is not complete until nine months of foetal age and is very important, because these antibodies help to protect babies from infection until around six months of age, when they can produce their own in substantial amounts.

Importance of Conception

At the time of conception, four important conditions are determined that influence the individual's later development. The role each of these conditions plays in the individual's development explains why the time of conception is probably the most important period in the life span of the human being.

Hereditary Endowment

The first important happening at the time of conception is the determination of the newly created individual's hereditary endowment. You should note that determination of hereditary endowment affects later development in two ways. First, hereditary places limits beyond which individuals cannot go. If prenatal and postnatal conditions are favourable, and if people are strongly motivated, they can develop their inherited physical and mental traits to their maximum potential, but they can go no further. Secondly, hereditary endowment is entirely a matter of chance, there is no known way to control the number of chromosomes from the maternal or paternal side that will be passed on to the child.

Sex

Determination of sex depends on the kind of spermatozoon that unites with the ovum. As we have already discussed in the earlier unit, two kinds of mature spermatozoa are produced in equal numbers. The first contains twenty-two matched chromosomes plus one X-chromosome, the second contains twenty two matched chromosomes plus one Y-chromosome. The X and Y chromosomes are the sex determining chromosomes. The mature ovum always contains an Xchromosome. If it is fertilized by a Y bearing spermatozoon, the offspring will be girl. The sex of an individual is important to lifelong development. Studies of sex preferences for offspring have revealed that the traditional preference for a child of given sex have marked influences on parents attitudes, which in turn affect their behaviour toward the child and their relationships with the child.

It is important that we accept each child as gift of God born in his own image and likeness. Therefore, parents should gladly accept this God given gift, no matter whether the child born in a male or female, healthy or disabled. It should be noted that a girl child is born only with an X-bearing spermatozoon received from the father. Therefore women should not be blamed for giving birth a female child.

Number of Offspring

While most humans are singletons, multiple births also occur. Meredith (1975) reported that 1 out of 80 births is twins, 1 out of every 9,000 is triple, and 1 out every 570,000 is quadruplets. You are perhaps aware that when a ripe ovum is fertilized by one spermatozoon, the result will be singleton, unless the fertilized ovum (zygote) splits into two or more distinct parts during the early stages of cell cleavage. When this happens, the result will be identical twins, triplets, or other multiple births. If two or more ova are released simultaneously and are fertilized by different spermatozoa, the result will be non-identical) (or fraternal) twins, triplets, or other multiple births.

Ordinal Position

The fourth thing that happens at the time of conception is the establishment of the new child's ordinal position among siblings. While this may change within a year or after birth, the child's ordinal position remains fairly static from then on. The effect of ordinal position on the individual depends on a number of conditions, the two most important of which are the sex of the individual and how individuals feel about the roles they are expected to play. A firstborn girl, for example, who is expected to help with the housework and with the care of young siblings may resent the fact that the boys in the family have fewer domestic duties and are granted privileges and given opportunities denied to her.

A second or later born boy may resent being 'bossed' by an older female sibling or being treated as the "baby of the family" while his female siblings are given more privileges and freedom than that he is given. Some individuals enjoy the role they are expected to play as a result of their ordinal position while others do not.

INFANCY AND HUMAN DEVELOPMENT

Infancy begins with birth and ends when the infant is approximately two weeks old, by far the shortest of all developmental periods. You should note that according to medical criteria, the adjustment to life outside uterine walls is completed with the fall of the umbilical cord from the naval. According to physiological criteria it is completed when the infant has regained the weight lost after birth. Infancy is hazardous period. Physically, it is hazardous because of the difficulties of making the necessary radical adjustments to the totally new and different environment. The high infant mortality rate is evidence of this. Psychologically, infancy is the time when the attitudes of significant people toward the infant are crystallized, some of which remain relatively unchanged or are strengthened, depending on conditions at birth and on the ease or difficulty with which the infant and parents adjust.

Here it is important to mention about a vital aspect, that of immunization of the new born. Adequate care needs to be taken by parents or those responsible for taking care of the child to see that necessary vaccination and immunizations are given to the child as per schedule. Therefore parents should constantly take guidance from a qualified physician.

Conditions Influencing Adjustment to Postnatal Life

Many conditions influence the success with which infants make the necessary adjustments to postnatal life. The most important of these, as research to date indicates, are the kind of prenatal environment, the type of birth and experiences associated with it, length of the gestation period, parental attitudes and postnatal care.

Prenatal Environment

A healthy prenatal environment contributes to good adjustments in postnatal life. Inadequate prenatal care of the mother, as a result of either poverty or neglect is often responsible for the development of unfavourable conditions in the intrauterine environment which effect the developing child and lead to complications during child birth, both of which affect the kind of adjustment the infant makes. Malnutrition of the mother during pregnancy has been found to be responsible for premature births, still births, and infant mortality during the early days of life. One of the most important conditions that contribute to difficulties in postnatal adjustment is a prenatal environment characterized by prolonged and intense maternal stress. It may be noted that in some communities a mother of an unwanted female child is poorly fed and very often made to do household chores beyond her ability. This practice is inhuman and needs to be discouraged at all costs.

Kind of Birth

The second condition that influences the kind of adjustment that will be made to postnatal life is the kind of birth the infant experiences. There were five kinds of birth each with its distinctive characteristics. These are Natural or spontaneous birth, Breech birth, Transverse birth, Instrument birth and Caesarean Section.

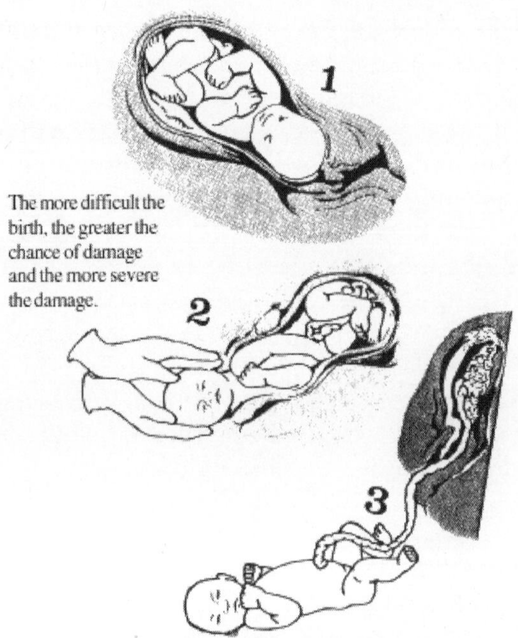

The infant who has been born spontaneously usually adjusts more quickly and more successfully to the postnatal environment that one whose birth has been difficult enough to require use of instruments or caesarean section.

Parental Attitudes

How quickly and how successfully newborn infants will adjust to postnatal life is greatly influenced by parental attitudes. When parental attitudes are unfavourable, for whatever reasons, they are reflected in the treatment of the infant that mitigates against successful adjustments to postnatal life. By contrast, parent whose attitudes are favourable treat the infant in ways that encourage good adjustment.

A relaxed mother for example, produces more milk than one who is tense and nervous, and this helps the infant to adjust to a new method of taking nourishment. Fathers who are present during delivery usually have more favourable attitude towards their children than do those who do not share the childbirth experience with their partners. In India the chances for the father to be present during delivery by the side of the mother is remote.

Physiological Functions

With the birth cry the lungs are inflated and respiration begins. The respiration rate at first ranges from forty to forty-five breathing movements per minute. By the end of the first week of life, it normally drops to approximately thirty-five per minute is more stable than it was at first. Elimination of waste begins a few hours after birth. Many voiding occur during periods of wakefulness and when the infant is quiet, usually within an hour after feeding. Defecations likewise, occur when the infant is quiet, shortly after feeding. Neonatal sleep is broken by short waking periods which occur every two or three hours, with fewer and shorter waking periods during the night than during the day.

Rhythms

The newborn baby engages in a cycle of active and quiet sleep that repeats each 50 to 60 minutes. This cycle is co-ordinated with a cycle of wakefulness that occurs once every 3 to 4 hours. Even before, the first feeding and with external distraction held a minimum, newborns still display roughly these same sleep-wake cycles. Gradually, infants adapt to the 24 - hour lightdark cycle. Sleep periods become longer at night and wake periods longer during the day, with long sleep at night emerging around 5 to 6 weeks of age.

Organized Behaviour of Newborn

Newborns are also equipped with several specific behaviour patterns that occur in response to specific stimuli such as the startle reaction to a loud sound. These highly stereotyped behaviour patterns, which occur as brief responses to specific stimulation called reflexes. The newborn also initiates activities and is capable of sustaining the over considerable period of time. Looking behaviour, sucking and crying are examples of such activities which can be referred to as congenitally organized behaviour.

Emotions of the Newborn

Emotional reactions of the newborn may be described as state of pleasantness and unpleasantness. The former is characterized by a relaxing of the body and the latter by a tensing of the body. The outstanding characteristic of the infant's emotional makeup is the complete absence of gradations of responses showing different degrees of intensity. Whatever the stimulus, the resultant emotions is intense and sudden.

Beginning of Personality

Children are born with characteristic temperamental differences that are reflected in activity rates and sensitivities. It is these differences from which the individual's personality pattern will develop. Individual differences are apparent at birth and are shown in responses to food, in crying, in motor activities, and especially, in sleep. A disturbed prenatal environment, which can result if the mother is subjected to severe or prolonged stress, may cause a modification of the newborn infant's behaviour pattern. There is also evidence that infants who are separated from their mothers after birth do not make as good as adjustment to postnatal life as infants who remain with their mothers.

BABYHOOD AND DEVELOPMENTAL ASPECTS

Babyhood occupies the first two years of life following the brief two-week period of infancy. During the babyhood months there is gradual but pronounced decrease in helplessness. Babyhood is the foundation period of life, because, at this time many behaviour patterns, many attitudes, and many patterns of emotional expression are being established. Babies grow rapidly, both physically and psychologically, there is a change not only in appearance but also in capacities. The decrease in dependency on others results from the rapid development of body control which enables babies to sit, stand and walk and to manipulate objects.

Developmental Tasks of Babyhood

The pattern of development is predictable even though different babies reach important landmarks in this pattern at slightly different ages. Therefore, it is possible to set up standards of social expectations in the form of developmental tasks. All babies, for example, are expected to learn to walk, to take solid foods, to have their organs of elimination under control, to achieve reasonable physiological stability (especially in hunger rhythm and sleep,) to learn the foundations of speech and to relate emotionally to their parents and siblings to some extent instead of being completely self-bound as they were at birth.

It is important to note that the rapid development of the nervous system, the ossification of the bones, and the strengthening of the muscles makes it possible for babies to master the developmental tasks of babyhood. Babies, who lag behind their age mates in mastering the developmental tasks appropriate of their age, may be handicapped when they reach the early childhood years and are expected to master the developmental tasks for these years. For example, a poor foundation in motor skills or in speech will make it difficult for young children to master the skills in these areas of development.

Physical Development

We should always be aware that babyhood is one of the two periods of rapid growth during the life span; the other comes at puberty. During the first six months of life, growth continues at the rapid rate characteristic of the prenatal period and then begin to slow down. In the second year, the rate of growth slows down at a very fast pace. During the first six months of life, growth continues at the rapid rate characteristic of the prenatal and then begins to slow down. In the second year, the rate of growth slows down at a very fast pace. During the first year of life the increase in weight is proportionally greater than the increase in height. During the second year, babies gain height.

At the age of four months, the baby's weight has normally doubled. At one year, babies weigh three times as much as they did at birth. Increase in weight during babyhood, comes mainly from an increase in fat tissue. At four months, the height of a baby, on an average, is between 23 and 24 inches, at one year, between 28 and 30 inches, and at two years, between 32 and 34 inches. Head growth slows down, while the trunk and limb growth increases. Thus, the baby gradually becomes less top heavy and appears more slender. Muscle fibre present at birth is in very undeveloped forms. They grow slowly during babyhood and are weak. During the second year of life, as body proportions change, babies begin to show tendencies toward characteristic body builds. The average baby has four to six of the twenty temporary teeth by the age of one and sixteen by the age of two.

The first teeth to cut through are the central incisor, and the last to appear are the molars. Non-appearance of teeth can cause concern to the parents. It is always desirable that you consult a qualified doctor in such eventuality. By the age of three months, the eye muscles are wellenough co-ordinated to enable babies to see things clearly and distinctly and the cones are also welldeveloped so that they can see colours. Hearing develops rapidly during this time. Smell and taste which are well-developed at birth continue to improve. Babies are highly responsive to all skin stimuli because of the thin texture of their skin.

Physiological Functions

Babyhood, as you might be aware, is the time to establish the fundamental physiological patterns of eating, sleeping and elimination. During the first year of babyhood, on an average night sleep increases from 8½ hours at three weeks to 10 hours at twelve weeks and then remains constant the rest of that year. During the first three months, the decline in day sleep is balanced by an increase in night sleep.

From birth until four or five months of age, all eating is the infantile form of sucking and swallowing. Chewing generally appears in the developmental pattern, a month later than biting. But both require a lot of practice before they become serviceable. After being accustomed to food in liquid form, it is difficult for babies to adjust to semisolid form. This adds to their revolt against food, even though they may like its taste. Bowel control begins, on the average, at six months and bladder control begins between the ages of fifteen and sixteen months. The habit of bowel control is established by the end of babyhood. Dryness at night cannot be achieved in the average child until several years later.

Babyhood Skills

Development of skills depends upon three important factors: an opportunity for practice, an incentive to learn, and a good model to copy with guidance to ensure that the copying will be correct. Before babyhood is over, babies acquire many skills. At first, they are unable to integrate the different parts of a skill, with the result that the skill is of little value to them. Eventually, integration takes place with practice.

Comprehension

The speaker's facial expression, tone of voice, and gestures help babies to understand what is being said to them. Pleasure, anger and fear can be comprehended as early as the third month of life. Until babies are eighteen months old, words must be reinforced with gestures, such as pointing to an object. The comprehension of the baby depends partly upon the baby's own intellectual abilities and partly on how others stimulate and encourage the baby to try to comprehend what they are saying.

Learning to Speak

Learning to speak is a long and difficult task, and because babies are not mature enough for such difficult and complicated learning during the first year of life, nature provides substitute forms of communication to be used. These substitute forms of communication are know as "pre-speech forms". Four pre-speech forms normally appear in the developmental pattern of learning to talk: crying, babbling, gesturing and the use of emotional expressions.

Tasks in Learning to Speak

Learning to speak involves three difficult tasks. Babies are learning how to pronounce words, building, and a vocabulary by associating meaning with words that can be used to communicate meanings to others, and combining words into sentences that are understandable to others. These tasks, you should note, not only involve control over the vocal mechanism but also the ability to comprehend meaning and to associate them with words which act as symbols for meanings. As you can probably understand, these tasks are far more difficult than may at first be apparent, it is understandable therefore, that only the foundation skills involves in speech will be laid.

Emotional Behaviour in Babyhood

All of us know that the emotions of babies differ markedly from those of adolescents and adults, and also from those of older children. It has often been observed that the behaviour responses accompanying baby's emotions are too great for the stimuli that give rise to them. This is especially true of anger and fear.

Common Emotional Patterns

There are certain emotional patterns that are commonly found among babies.

Anger

The common stimuli that gave rise to anger among babies are interference with attempted movements, thwarting of some wish, not letting them do what they want to do, etc. Typically, the angry response takes the form of screaming, kicking the legs, waving the arms, throwing themselves on the floor, and hold their breath.

Fear

The stimuli that are most likely to arouse fear in babies are loud noise, strange people, objects or situations, dark rooms, high place, and animals. The fear response is manifest in an attempt to withdraw from the frightening stimulus, accompanied by whimpering, crying and temporary holding of breath.

Curiosity

Anything new or unusual acts as a stimulus to curiosity, unless the newness is so pronounced that it gives rise to fear. As the fear wanes, it gives rise to curiosity. Young babies usually express curiosity by tensing the facial muscle, opening the mouth and protruding the tongue. Later, babies grasp the objects that aroused their curiosity and handle, shake, bang or suck them.

Joy

Physical well-being of the babies give rise to a feeling of joy. By the second or third month of life, babies reach to being played with, being tickled and watching or listening to others. They express their pleasure by smiling, moving their arms and legs and also by cooing, gurgling or even shouting with glee.

Affection

Anyone who plays with them caters to their needs, give rise to the babies' affection. Later, also toys and a family pet may also become objects of love for them. Babies typically, express their affection by hugging or patting, at times, even kissing the loved object or person.

Development of Socialization

You would agree that early social experience play a dominant role in determining the baby's future social relationships and patterns of behaviour towards others. Because the baby's life is centered around the home, it is here that the foundations for later social behaviour and attitudes are laid. Whether the babies grow up to become extroverted or introverted individuals depends mainly on their early social experiences. There are two reasons for the importance of these early foundations. First, the type of behaviour shown in social situations affects their personal and social adjustments. Secondly, once established, the social foundations tend to be persistent as children grow older.

Early social behaviour follows a fairly predictable pattern, though variations can and do occur as a result of health or emotional states or because of environmental conditions. During the first year of babyhood, babies are in a state of equilibrium which makes them friendly, easy to handle and pleasant to be with. Around the middle of the second year, babies tend to become fussy, unco-operative and difficult to handle. Before babyhood is over, equilibrium is restored and babies again exhibit pleasant and social behaviour.

Interest in Play

Babyhood is the stage in which babies begin to show their interest in play. You know that play at all ages is engaged in for pleasure and not for any end result. In spite of this, it makes important contributions to the babies development. It provides opportunities for many forms of learning like problem solving and creativity. Also, while playing, babies gain a lot of information about their environment, and the people and things in their environment.

Development of Understanding

All babies begin life with no meaning of the things they come in contact with in their environment. They, therefore, acquire it through maturation and learning, when they start understanding what they observe. As new meanings are acquired, babies interpret new experiences in terms of their memories of previous ones. The association of meanings with objects, people and situation results in the development of concepts. Babies show recognition of familiar people and objects and their environment through pleasurable responses, just as they regard strange people and objects with fear.

Beginning of Morality

Babies have no values and no conscience that is why their behaviour is not guided by moral standards. This means that they are neither moral nor immoral. Gradually, babies learn moral codes from their parents, as well as the necessity of conforming to these codes. Learning to behave in a morally approved manner is a long, slow process. However, the foundations are laid in babyhood. Because of their limited intelligence, babies judge the rightness or wrongness of an act in terms of the pleasure or pain it brings them rather than in terms of its good and harmful effects on others. It is important for you to note that a baby is in stage of moral development which Piaget has called morality by constraint, the first of the three stages in moral development.

This stage lasts until the age of seven or eight years and is characterized by automatic obedience to rules without reasoning or judgment.

Role of Discipline

The main purpose of discipline is to teach children what is regarded as right and wrong by the group with which they are identified. It is also important, then to make sure that they act in accordance with this knowledge. With strict discipline, involving negative reinforcement, i.e. punishing for a wrong behaviour, even young babies can be made to follow a pattern of behaviour. Before, babies are punished for wrong doing, however, they must learn what is right and what is wrong. Positive reinforcement, i.e., reward or praise for the right behaviour is equally significant for making the baby follow a disciplined pattern of behaviour. Babies are able to understand what is said in praise. Pleasant facial expressions accompanying praise motivate babies to repeat the acts that brought them such favourable responses.

Family Relationships

We are all aware that the early environment of babies is limited primarily to the home, therefore, family relationships play a dominant role in determining the future patterns of a baby's attitudes toward and behaviour in relationships with others. During the babyhood years, parent-child relationships are more important than any other family relationships. All babies need, at least during the first nine to twelve months of life, the continuous care of one person, usually the mother, or a satisfactory mother substitute. Such care not only makes them feel secure, but shows them the satisfaction they can derive from a close, personal relationship with another person.

Personality Development in Babyhood

It is very important to note that the potential for personality development is present at birth. Thomas *etal* (1970) had emphasized, 'Personality is shaped by the constant interplay of temperament and environment'. Babyhood is a critical time in the development of personality. Since the baby's environment is limited almost exclusively to the home and because the mother is the most constant companion, the kind of person she is and the kind of relationship they share will have a profound influence on the baby's personality. Genetic studies of the persistence of personality traits over a period of years have revealed that patterns established early in life remain almost unchanged as the child grows older.

LATER STAGES OF HUMAN GROWTH: BIOLOGICAL, SOCIAL, PSYCHOLOGICAL AND DEVELOPMENTAL ASPECTS

DEVELOPMENTAL ASPECTS OF CHILDHOOD

Childhood begins when the relative dependency of babyhood is over, at approximately the age of two years, and extends to the time when the child becomes sexually mature, at approximately thirteen years on an average for a girl and fourteen for a boy. After children become sexually mature, they are known as adolescents. During this long period of time – about eleven years for girls and twelve years for boys marked changes take place in the child both physically and psychologically. Because cultural pressures and expectations to learn certain things at one age are different from the pressures and expectations at another age, a child in the early part of childhood is quite different from a child in the latter part of the period.

With the dawn of childhood, behaviour problems become frequent and more troublesome. The reason is that children are developing distinctive personalities and are demanding an independence which, in most cases, they are incapable of handling successfully. In the later part of childhood, children are often not willing to do what they are told to do and are more influenced by their peers than by their parents or family members. The time when children are learning the foundations of social behaviour as a preparation for the more highly organized social life, is commonly referred to as 'pregnant age'.

This is the age when children form the habit of being achievers, under-achievers or over-achievers, which tends to persist into adulthood. In comparison to early childhood therefore, late childhood is called "gang age", the time when children's major concern is acceptance by their age-mates and membership in a gang. Although, as you have already learnt in the last unit, the foundations of some of the developmental tasks young children are expected to master before they enter school are laid in babyhood, much remains to be learned in the relatively short span of early childhood. Their ability to communicate with others and to comprehend what others say to them is still on a low level in early childhood. Similarly, they have some simple concepts of social and physical realities. Emotionally, young children must learn to give as well as to receive affection; they must learn to be outer bound instead of self-bound.

Gradually, in later childhood, the mastery of developmental tasks is no longer the sole responsibility of the parents. It now becomes the responsibility also of the child's teachers and to a lesser extent, the peer group. Although parents can help to lay the foundation of the child's learning to get along with age mates, being a member of the peer group it provides the major part of this learning experience.

Physical Development in Childhood

Growth during childhood proceeds at a slow pace as compared with the rapid rate of growth in babyhood. Early childhood is a time of relatively even growth. The major aspects of physical development include height, weight, body proportions, body build, bones and muscles, fat and teeth. The average annual increase in height is approximately three inches. Weight, on an average, increases by 3 to 4 pounds in a year. During this time, the baby look starts disappearing. Facial features remain small but the chin becomes more pronounced and the neck elongates. The body tends to become cone shaped with a flattened abdomen. The arms and legs lengthen and the hands and feet grow bigger. Differences in body build become apparent for the first time in early childhood. Some children have an endomorphic body, some have mesomorphic and some have ectomorphic body build.

The bones ossify at different rates in different parts of the body, following the laws of developmental direction. The muscles become larger, stronger and heavier. During the first four to six months of early childhood, the last four baby teeth begin to be replaced by permanent teeth. The first to come are the front central incisors. As compared to early childhood, late childhood is a period of slow and relatively uniform growth until the changes of puberty begin, approximately two years before the child becomes sexually mature, at which time growth speeds up remarkably. Body build affects both height and weight in late childhood.

Good health and good nutrition are important factors in the child's growth and development. Emotional tension likewise affects physical growth. Placid children grow faster than those who are emotionally disturbed. Sex differences in physical growth become pronounced in late childhood. Because boys begin their puberty growth spurt approximately a year later than girls they tend to be slightly shorter and lighter in weight than girls of the same age.

Skills Acquired in Childhood

Early childhood, you will agree, is the ideal age to learn skills. There are three reasons for this. First, young children enjoy repetitions and are willing to repeat an activity until they have acquired the ability to do it well. Second, young children are adventurous and, as a result, are not held back by fear of hurting themselves or of being ridiculed by peers. Third, young children learn easily and quickly because their bodies are still very pliable and because they have acquired such few skills that they do not interfere with the acquisition of new ones.

The skills of late childhood can be divided roughly into four categories:

- *Self-help Skills:* Older children should be able to eat, dress, bathe and groom themselves with almost as much speed and adeptness as an adult. But, conscious attention is necessary in early childhood.
- *Social Help Skills:* Skills in this category relate to helping others like making beds, dusting and sweeping at home or emptying wastebaskets, washing blackboards at schools, etc.
- *School Skills:* At school, the child develops skills like writing, drawing, painting, clay modeling etc.
- *Play Skills* – Older children also learn skills as throwing and catching balls, riding a bicycle, skating and swimming etc.

By the time they reach late childhood, most children are so predominantly right or left-handed that changing handedness is very difficult. Many left-handed children become ambidextrous during late childhood in that they use both hands, though there is a tendency to favour the left hand. As they learn new skills, they often discover, it is easier for them to learn by following the right handed model than by trying to adapt the right handed model to use the left hand. Consequently, some of their skills are carried out predominantly with the right hand and other with the left hand.

Emotions of Childhood

Emotions are especially intense during early childhood. This is a time of disequilibrium when children are "out of focus" in the sense that they are easily aroused to emotional outbursts and as a result, are difficult to guide. Much of the heightened emotionality characteristic of this age is psychological rather than physiological in origin. Young children experience most of the emotions normally experienced by adults. However, the stimuli that give rise to them, and the ways in which children express these emotions are markedly different. It is important for you to note that the fear-related emotional patterns—worry, anxiety and embarrassment, normally do not become important emotions until late childhood when contacts with peers and adults outside the home become more frequent and more pronounced than they were in early childhood. The prominent emotional patterns include anger, fear jealousy, curiosity, envy, joy, grief and affection. Older children acquire a strong incentive to learn to control their emotional expressions because of peer pressure and a desire for approval and acceptance. As a result, children frequently express their emotions as forcibly as they did when they were younger.

Characteristically, emotional expressions in late childhood are pleasant ones: the child giggles, or laughs uproariously, squirms, twitches, etc. Not all emotionality at this age, however, is a pleasant sort. Numerous outbursts of temper occur, and the child suffers from anxiety and feelings of frustration. Girls often dissolve into tears, whereas boys are more likely to express their annoyances or anxieties by being sullen or sulky.

Socialization

The foundation for socialization are laid as the number of contacts young children have with their peer increases with each passing year. If young children enjoy their contacts with others, even if they are only occasional, their attitudes towards future social contacts will be more favourable. Generally, during the preschool years, children find social contacts with members of their own sex more pleasurable than those with members of opposite sex.

Companions in Early Childhood

At all ages, companions may be of three different kinds – associates, playmates and friends. Associates are people who satisfy an individual's companionship needs by being in the same environment where they are watched and listened to. Playmates are people with whom individuals engage in pleasurable activities. Children prefer playmates of their own sex. Friends are not only congenial playmates, but they are also people with whom the individuals engage in pleasurable activities. Children prefer playmates of their own sex. Friends are not only congenial playmates, but they are also people with whom the individual can communicate by exchanging ideas and confidences and by asking or giving advice.

Moral Development

Moral development in early childhood is on a low level. The reason for this is that young children's intellectual development has not yet reached the point where they can learn or apply abstract principles of right and wrong. They merely learn how to act without knowing how to do so. Early childhood has been characterized by what Piaget has called "morality by constraint". In this stage of moral development, children obey rules automatically, without using reason or judgement, and they regard adults in authority as omnipotent. They also judge all acts as right or wrong in terms of their consequences, rather than in terms of the motivations behind them as early childhood comes to an end, habits of obedience should be established, provided children have had consistent discipline.

Discipline is society's way of teaching children the moral behaviour approved by the social group. In discipline, there are three other elements: rules and laws which serve as guidelines for approved behaviour, punishment for willful violation of rules and laws, and rewards for behaviour or attempts to behave in a socially approved way. During the early childhood years, major emphasis should be placed on the educational aspects of discipline and punishment given only when there is evidence that children not only know what is expected of them, but when they willfully violate these expectations. To increase young children's motivations to learn to behave in a socially approved manner, rewards serve purpose of reinforcing the motivations. Moral codes develop from generalized moral concepts.

In late childhood, moral codes are greatly influenced by the moral standards of the groups with which older children are identified. This does not mean that they abandon family moral codes in favour of the code of the 'gang'. Rather, it means that if older children must make a choice, they will go along with the gang's standards.

Sex-role Typing in Childhood

Childhood, especially early childhood is often referred to as a critical age in sex-role typing. During this stage in the developmental pattern, two important aspects of sex-role typing are expected to be mastered: learning how to play the appropriate sex role and accepting the fact that they must adopt and conform to the approved sex-role stereotypes are constellations of meanings associated with members of the male and female sex. Learning sex-role stereotypes does not guarantee sexrole typing. Young children learn to behave in accordance with the patterns outlined in the stereotypes partly by imitation but more by direct training in which they are shown how to imitate a model.

Sex-role typing, which actually, began shortly after birth, now continues with new agencies playing important roles in the typing process. Teachers and school subjects are important because of the prestige children attach to the teacher role. The different mass media likewise play important roles in sex- role typing of children. When mothers work outside the home, it affects girl's vocational aspirations and influences what girls think women should do. Unquestionable, the most important force in sex-role typing during the late childhood years comes from peer pressures. Children accept the sexrole stereotype of their gang-mates as a guide for their own behaviour and they accept the attitudes of their gang-mates towards their own and the opposite sex.

Sex-role typing influences in important ways both the behaviour and self-evaluation of children. In appearance, clothing and even in mannerisms, children try to create the impression of sex-appropriateness. Even before they have completed first grade, most children learn to aspire to what the social group regards as sexappropriate. Sex antagonism is an outgrowth of sexrole typing. When boys are encouraged to believe that they are superior to girls, it leads to a derogatory attitude towards members of the female sex, in treatment of girls as inferiors, or in tendency to make derogatory comments about girls and their achievements.

Family Relationships

We have discussed the issue of family being the most socializing influence. Not only there are more contacts with family members than with other people, but the contacts are closer, warmer and more emotionally tinged. Perhaps the most important condition influencing the kind of adjustments young children will make, both personal and social, is the type of parent-child relationship during the early childhood years. Next in significance are sibling relationships and relationships with relatives, especially grandparents.

Changes in parent-child relationships, which began during the second year of babyhood, continue throughout early childhood. As young children become more independent, parents feel that they need less care and attention than they did when they were babies. When young children do not come up to parental expectations, parents often become critical and punitive. As regards parental preference, since mothers spend more time with young children than fathers, and because they better understand troublesome behaviour, many young children prefer their mothers. As young children depend more on their parents for feelings of security and for happiness than on anyone else, poor relationships with their parents have a devastating effect.

The relationship of young children with their siblings is often frictional. Young children often feel inadequate, especially if their achievements are criticized and ridiculed by their older siblings. But not all sibling relationships are frictional. Whether the siblings are older or younger, they contribute emotional security, and teach young children how to show affection for others. Furthermore, all children learn in a family where there are siblings, to play certain role depending on their sex, their ordinal position in the family, and the age difference between them and their siblings.

Children's personal and social adjustments often depend upon two conditions. The first is the frequency of contacts with relatives. If families live in different communities, or in different states or countries, the contacts between young children and their relatives play an important role in the young child life. In the case of cousins, for example, the role will be that of a playmate, in the case of grandmother, the role is likely to be that of caretaker or surrogate mother. So long as the relationship young children have with their relatives is that of playmates, it will end to be pleasant, though there may be occasional quarrels. On the other hand, if the relative is given authority over the children, in the absence of their own parents, chances are that the relationship will be far from pleasant. The reason is that relatives rarely do things exactly as parents do. Young children accustomed to a stable pattern of living, find changes upsetting and they resent the person who makes these changes necessary.

The deterioration in family relationships which continues through early childhood, becomes increasingly detrimental to children's development as late childhood progresses. It is also responsible for much of the feelings of insecurity and the unhappiness that older children experience. There are, of course, times of peace and harmony at home. At times, older children show real affection for, and interest in, their siblings, even to the point of helping in the care of younger brother and sisters.

Personality Development in Childhood

The personality pattern begins to take form in early childhood. Because parents, siblings and other relatives constitute the social world of young children, how they feel about them and how they treat them are important factors in shaping self concepts, the core of the personality pattern. As early childhood progresses, the attitude of their peers and the way their peers treat them begin to have an effect on the children's self concepts. These early peer attitudes are important because once the foundations for the self-concept are laid, they are far less likely to change than to remain stable.

Because the environment of young children is limited to a large extent, to their homes and to family members, it is not surprising that many conditions within the family are responsible for shaping the self concept. The child training method used in the home is important in shaping the young child's developing concept of self. Strict, authoritarian discipline accompanied by frequent reprimand and had corporal punishment tend to build up resentment against all persons in authority. The aspirations parents have for their children play an important role in their developing self-concepts. When their aspirations are unrealistically high, children are doomed to failure. Regardless of how children react, failure leaves an indelible mark on their self-concepts and leads to feelings of inferiority and inadequacy. The ordinal position of children in family has an effect on their developing personalities. Each child in a family learns to play a specific role, in part by differences in the child-training methods used by parents with different children, and in part by successes and failures children have in their competition with their siblings.

DEVELOPMENTAL ASPECTS OF ADOLESCENCE

It is, therefore, an important pre-stage to adolescence, that needs specific attention. Puberty is the period in the developmental span when the child changes from an asexual being to a sexual being. During this period, the sex organs develop and an individual attains reproductive capacity. It is accompanied by changes in the physical growth and psychological aspects. The word puberty is derived from the Latin Word 'pubertas', which means age of manhood.

It refers to the physical changes that take place when the individual becomes sexually mature. Puberty, as you have been told earlier, is also a time when behaviour changes. The sex hormones secreted during this period not only affect the tissue of the body, but are also related to changes in sexual and emotional behaviour. You might be aware of some communities which recognize puberty as a time of importance in the lifespan of every individual. As a custom, they observe various rites in recognition of the fact that as their bodies changes, children are emerging from childhood into maturity. After successfully passing the tests that are an important part of the puberty rites, boys and girls are granted the rights and privileges of adulthood and are expected to assume the responsibilities that accompany that state.

It is important for you to know that scientists of today have been able to pinpoint the cause of puberty changes, and extensive studies of behaviour during this period have revealed what behavioural changes can normally be expected to occur. This knowledge acts as guidelines for parents and teachers to know what to expect of children as they progress through this period of change. Children also become aware that they are entering a new phase in their lives. Therefore, with all adjustments to new social expectations, most of them find puberty a difficult period in their lives.

The criteria most often used to determine the onset of puberty are the menarche (in girls), nocturnal emissions (in boys), and evidence derived from chemical analysis of the urine and X-rays of bone development. About five years before children become sexually mature, there is a small secretion of sex hormones in both boys and girls. The amount of hormones secreted increase with time, which eventually leads to the maturing of the structure and functioning of the sex organs. You have already read in unit 1 of this block that there is a close relationship between the pituitary gland located at the base of the brain, and the gonads, or the sex glands. Puberty in boys, as you must be well aware by now, comes later than in girls. It is usually between the ages of thirteen and sixteen that a boy's body becomes sexually mature. About 50 percent of boys mature between the ages of 14 and 15.5. Girls generally mature a year in advance of boys of their own age.

There is evidence that some children are reaching puberty earlier now than in the earlier generations. The explanations for this are better health, better prenatal and postnatal medical care, and better nutrition. Children who are slow in starting to mature—the late mature –usually mature more rapidly, once the process starts, than the average child. Fast matures have greater spurts of rapid growth, their periods of accelerated and halted growth come abruptly, and they attain adult proportions very quickly.

Puberty Growth Spurt

Children experience a period of rapid growth which indicates the onset of puberty. This is called the Puberty Growth Spurt. The growth spurt for girls begins usually between 9 to 12 years, with the peak coming, on an average, at about 13 years. From then on, the rate of growth slows down until growth gradually comes to a standstill between 17 and 18 years. For boys the growth spurt starts between 11 to 14 years, reaches the peak between 14.5 and 15.5 years, and is then followed by a gradual decline until twenty or twenty one years. During the Puberty Growth Spurt, four important physical changes occur which transform the child's body into that of an adult: changes in body size, changes in body proportions, the development of the primary sex characteristics, and the development of the secondary sex characteristics. Let us briefly examine these changes.

Changes in Body Size

Among girls, the average annual increase in the year preceding the menarche is 3 inches, though a 5 to 6 inch increase is not unusual. After the menarche, the rate of growth slows down to about 1 inch a year, coming to a standstill at around 18 years. For boys, the onset of the period of rapid growth in height comes, on an average, at 12.8 years and ends on an average, at 15.3 years, with a peak occurring at fourteen years. Weight gain comes not only from an increase in fat but also from an increase in bone and muscle tissue.

Changes in Body Proportions

Certain areas of the body, which in the early years of life were proportionally much too small, now become proportionally big because they reach their mature size sooner than other areas. This is particularly apparent in the nose, feet, and hands. It is not until the latter part of adolescence that the body attains adult proportions in all areas.

Primary Sex Characteristics

The third major physical change at puberty is the growth and development of the primary sex characteristics, the sex organs. In the case of male, the testes are only 10 percent of their mature size at the age of 14 years, then there is a rapid growth for a year or two, after which growth slows down; the testes are fully developed by the age of tewenty or twenty one. Shortly after the rapid growth is in length, followed by a gradual increase in circumference. Among the girls, all parts of the reproductive apparatus grow during puberty, though at different rates. The uterus of the average 11 or 12 year old girl, for example, weight 5.3 grams, by the age of 16, its average weight is 43 grams. The fallopian tubes, ovaries, and vagina also grow rapidly at this time. The first real indication that a girl's reproductive mechanism is becoming mature is the menarche, which we have already discussed in unit 2 of this block.

Secondary Sex Characteristics

The fourth major physical change at puberty is the development of secondary sex characteristics. As puberty progress, boys and girls become increasingly dissimilar in appearance. This change is caused by the gradual development of the secondary sex characteristics. These include growth of pubic hair and other body hair, development of the sebaceous and apocrine glands, and change in the voices of both boys and girls. Also, their skin becomes coarser, slightly sallow and the pores enlarge. The muscles increase in size and strengthen, thus giving shape to the shoulders, arms and legs. Among girls, the hips become wider and rounder, as a result of the enlargement of the pelvic bone and the development of subcutaneous fat. Shortly after the hips start to enlarge, the breasts begin to develop; the nipples enlarge and as the mammary glands develop, the breasts become larger and rounder. Among boys, slight knobs around the male mammary glands appear between the ages of twelve and fourteen. These last for several weeks and then decrease in size. While introducing unit 1, we have already discussed in brief, the various aspects of the adolescence.

Physical Changes during Adolescence

During adolescence, there is a slackening of the pace of growth and there is more marked internal than external development.

External Development

The average girl reaches her mature height between the ages of 17 and 18 and the average boy, a year or so later. Weight is now distributed over areas of the body, where there was little or no fat. Various parts of the body gradually come into proportion. For example, the trunk broadens and lengthens, and thus, the limbs no longer seem too long.

Development Concerns

Some of the concerns adolescents have about their bodies include those about 'normalcy' about 'awareness of social reactions' to different body builds, 'acne and other skin problems', the problem of 'obesity', etc. Apart from these, adolescents, both boys and girls are often concerned about their physical attractiveness. Also, for many girls, menstruation is a serious concern. This is because they suffer physical discomfort such as cramps, weight gain, headaches, backaches, swollen ankles, breast tenderness; and experience emotional changes such as mood swings, depression, restlessness and depression.

Emotionality during Adolescence

Adolescence, as you have been told earlier, has been thought of as 'period of storm and stress' a time of heightened emotional tension resulting from the physical and glandular changes that are taking place. Adolescent emotionality can be attributed mainly to the fact that boys and girls come under social pressures and face new conditions for which they received little preparation during childhood. Emotional instability is a logical consequence of the necessity of making adjustments to new patterns of behaviour and to new social expectations. While adolescent emotions are often intense, uncontrolled and seemingly irrational, there is generally an improvement in emotional behaviour with each passing year. To clear their systems of pent up emotional energy, they can do physical exercise, by play or work, by laughing or by crying.

Social Changes during Adolescence

To achieve the goal of adult patterns of socialization, the adolescent must make many new adjustments, the most important of which are adjustments to the increased influence of the peer group, changes in social behaviour, new social groupings, new values in friendship selection, new values in social acceptance and rejection, etc.

Increased Peer-Group Influence

Since adolescents spend most of their time outside the home with members of the peer group (in schools etc.), it is understandable that peers would have a greater influence on adolescent attitudes, speech, interests, appearance, and behaviour than the family has. But, as adolescence progresses, peer-group influence begins to wane. There are two reasons for this. First, most adolescents want to become individuals in their own right and to be recognized as such.

Secondly, adolescents are no longer interested in large group activities as was true during their childhood days. In adolescence, there is a tendency to narrow down friendships to smaller numbers though most adolescents want to belong to larger social group for social activities. The influence of the large social group becomes less pronounced than the influence of friends.

Changes in Social Behaviour

In social attitudes and behaviour, adolescents make the radical shift from disliking members of the opposite sex to preferring their companionship to that of members of their own sex. As a result broader opportunities for social participation, social insight and social competency improves. They are able to judge people better and also to carry on conversations, to behave appropriately, and with confidence, in social situations.

New Social Groupings

In adolescence, the social groupings of boys are larger and more loosely knit while those of girls are smaller and more sharply defined. Some common social groupings include close friends, cliques, crowds, organized groups and gangs.

New Values in Selection of Friends

Adolescents want as their friends those whose interests and values are similar to theirs, who understand them and make them feel secure, and in whom they can confide problems and discuss matters they feel they cannot share with parents or teachers. Interest in making friends of the opposite sex becomes increasingly stronger as adolescence progresses. As a result, by the end of adolescence, there is often a preference for friends of the opposite sex, though both boys and girls continue to have a few intimate friends of their own sex with whom they associate constantly.

Changes in Morality during Adolescence

When they reach adolescence, children no longer accept in an unquestioning way a moral code handed down to them by parents, teachers or even their contemporaries. They now want to build their own moral codes on the basis of concepts of right and wrong which they have changed or modified to meet their more mature level of development. There is another important change that takes place in adolescence. Since parents and teachers cannot watch adolescents as closely as they did when they were children, adolescents are expected to assume responsibility for control over their own behaviour.

Sex Interests and Sex Behaviour during Adolescence

Due to the growing interest in sex, adolescent boys and girls seek more and more information about it. Few adolescents are able to learn all they want to know about sex from their parents. Consequently, they take advantage of whatever sources of information are available to them—sex hygiene courses in school or college, discussions with their friends, books on sex, or experimentation through masturbation, petting, or intercourse. With the advent of HIV/AIDS, a need to offer sex education at the school level has become necessary. In fact in some developed countries educators have gone to the extent of suggesting 'heterosexual education' to adolescents as a result of the growing phenomena of homosexual tendencies and behaviour which they argue are not normal.

Family Relationships during Adolescence

The relationships of young adolescents with members of their families become crucial as adolescence progresses. Often, parents are reluctant in modifying their concepts of their children's abilities as they grow older; whereas adolescents think that they should be accorded the status of grown ups, now that they are capable of managing so many of their tasks of their own. Hence, the so-called 'generation gap, between adolescents and their parents. This gap is partly the result of radical changes in values and standards of behaviour that normally occur in any rapidly changing culture, and partly the result of the fact that many young people now have greater educational, social and cultural opportunities than most of their parents had when they were adolescents. Many adolescents feel that their parents do not 'understand them' and that their standards of behaviour are old fashioned. The advance in Information Technology and satellite communication network expose the adolescents to wide variety of situations which were not otherwise available earlier.

Children born to parents living away from hometown (migrant employees) miss a lot in terms of family values and traditional practices. It is therefore necessary that opportunities are provided to such children for close interaction with close family relatives as often as possible.

DEVELOPMENTAL ASPECTS OF ADULTHOOD

The term 'adult' comes from the past participle of the Latin verb 'adolescere', which means adolescence – 'adults' – which means 'grown to full size and strength' or 'matured'. Adults are, therefore, individuals who have completed their growth and are ready to assume their status in society along with other adults. During the long period of adulthood, certain physical and psychological changes occur at predictable times. Adulthood is a period of adjustments to new patterns of life and new of life and new social expectations. The adult is expected to play new roles, such as that of spouse, parent, and breadwinner, and to develop new attitudes, interests, and values in keeping with these new roles. This period is crucial because until now most boys and girls have had someone—parents, teachers, friends or others – to help them make the adjustments they are faced with. Now, as adults, they are expected to make these adjustments for themselves.

If childhood and adolescence are the periods of 'growing up', adulthood is the time for 'settling down', and assuming the responsibilities of adult life. Once individuals decide upon the pattern of life they believe will meet their needs, they develop patterns of behaviour, attitudes and values which will tend to be characteristically theirs for the remainder of their lives.

Parenthood is, probably, the most important role in the lives of most adults. The early adult years present many new problems, different in their major aspects, from the problems experienced in the earlier years of life. In the years from the beginning of adulthood, most men and women are adjusting to marriage, parenthood, and jobs. In the later adulthood years, adjustments focus more on family relationships. Alongside, many values developed during adolescence change as experience and social contact with people of different ages broaden and as values are considered from a more mature standpoint.

Social expectations from adults are clearly defined and familiar to them even before they reach maturity. They include getting started in an occupation, selecting a mate, learning to live with a marriage partner, starting a family, rearing children, managing a home, taking on civic responsibilities, and finding a congenial social group etc. How well these tasks are mastered in the early years of adulthood will influence the degree of success people will experience when they reach the peaks during middle age, and will determine how happy they will then be as well as during the closing years of their lives.

Changes in Interest in Adulthood

It is quite understandable that adolescents carry over into the adult years many of their interests. Interests change during the adult years, however.

Personal Interests

Personal interests are those related to the individual. By the time they reach adulthood, most men and women have learned to accept their physiques and to make the most of them. Although their physical appearance may not be to their liking, they have learned that little can be done to alter it, but that much can be done to improve it. As a result, the adult's major concern with appearance is in improving it. This leads to interest in beauty aids and in dieting and exercise.

Apart from appearance, young adults are interested in money because of what it can do for them now, rather than in the future. Usually, by the time they reach adulthood, young men and women have resolved the 'religious doubts' that plagued them in adolescence and have formulated a philosophy of life, based on religion, that is satisfactory to them. Along with these adults personal interest also include recreational activities which keep their spirits refreshed and renews their strength after the toil or anxiety of the day. These might include talking or sports, games, music or any other hobbies.

Social Interests

Erikson has referred to early adulthood as the time of 'isolation crisis', since it is often a lonely time for both men and women. Their friends of earlier years are often occupied with activities of their own lives. As a result, they miss the kind of social life they enjoyed during adolescence, when there was usually a congenial group to talk to or do things with. At times even young married adults are lonely and miss the companionships they enjoyed during the adolescent years.

Marital Adjustments

Marital adjustment is one of the most difficult adjustments young adults have to make. During the first year or two of marriage, the couple normally makes major adjustments to each other, to members of their families, and to their friends. While these adjustments are being made, there are often emotional tension and this is understandably a very significant period. After adjusting to each other, their families, and friends, they must adjust to parenthood. This increases the adjustment problems if it comes while the earlier adjustments are being made. More discussion on role expectations and adjustments in marital life is given in the elective cause of family education.

DEVELOPMENTAL DECLINE AND AGEING

The period during old age when physical and mental decline is slow and gradual and when compensations can be made for these decline, is known as 'senesence' – a time of growing old or ageing. Decline comes partly from physical and partly from psychological factors. The physical cause of decline is a change in the body cells, not due to a specific disease, but to the ageing process. Decline may also have psychological causes. Unfavourable attitudes towards oneself, other people, work, and life in general can lead to senility, just as changes in the brain tissue can. Individuals who have no sustaining interests after retiring from work are likely to become depressed or disorganized. How the individual copes with the strain and stresses of living will also affect the rate of decline.

Individual differences in the effects of ageing have been recognized for many centuries. People age differently because they have different hereditary endowments, different socio-economic and educational backgrounds, and different patterns of living. These differences are apparent among members of the same sex, but they are even more apparent when men and women are compared because ageing takes place at different rates for the two sexes. Often, it is expected that old people will play a decreasingly less active role in social and community affairs as well as in the business and professional worlds.

Because of unfavourable social attitudes, few rewards are associated with old age roles, no matter how successfully they are carried out. At times, feeling useless and unwanted, elderly people develop feelings of inferiority and resentment, feelings that are not conducive to good personal of social adjustments. Because of this, it is not surprising that many people develop unfavourable self-concepts. Ageing people are expected to adjust to decreasing strength and gradually failing health. This often means marked revisions in the roles they have played in the home and outside. Meeting social and civic obligations is difficult for many older people as their health fails. Sooner or later, most old people also have to adjust to the death of a spouse. It may also necessitate changes in living arrangements. As grown up children become increasingly involved in their own vocational and family affairs, the elderly can count less and less on their companionship. This means that they must establish affiliations with members of their own age group if they are to avoid loneliness.

The pattern of family life established in early adulthood starts to change with the onset of middle age. Of the many adjustments centering around family relationships that the elderly person must make, the most important ones might involve relationship with the spouse, changes in sexual behaviour, relationships with offspring, parental dependency, relationships with grandchildren etc. People who feel generally happily married find that their marriage become more satisfying to them as they grow older. With times, mutual interests are developed, the children grow up and leave home, thus drawing the partners closer together, illness or retirement on the part of the husband may make the wife feel useful again, as she did when the children were young. Satisfaction with marriage among older people is increased if their children are successful and happily married, and if they have good relationships with their grandchildren, even if their contacts with them are infrequent.

YOUTH AND THEIR CONCERNS

CONCEPT AND MEANING OF YOUTH

Youth is a time of search for meaning, for belonging and for achievement. It is a key stage of intense discovery of oneself and of one's qualities and capacities. It is point of decision-making about one's career, one's partner, and one's direction in life. Youth is phase for accepting, rejecting or reshaping one's values and beliefs, and one's stance towards status and authority. Youth has a tremendous potential that can be harnessed to bring about a creative transformation or enormous destruction.

According to the United Nations Organisation (UNO), youth is the period between 15 and 25 years which may differ from country to country e.g. 15 to 30 years, etc. However, you would agree that youth is vital transition period from childhood to adulthood, from dependence to interdependence, from being protected to being protective. It is also a time of curiosity, learning and experimenting, when special skills are acquired and mature habits are formed.

As we have already discussed in the earlier units, youth is also a stage of important physical and psychological changes as well as of the evolution of the being or the individual. Youth has always been the major concern of every society, therefore, empowering the youth for the betterment of the society is one of the most vital challenges for any country. For this purpose, it would be appropriate for us to define youth. The concept of youth can be perceived in different forms i.e.

- As an age category
- As a transitional stage between childhood and adulthood, and
- As a social construct

Youth as an Age Category

Youth as an age category is the most convenient, popular and common sense way in which youth has been defined. It is argued that this category defines youth more significantly than any other category. The experience common to all young leads them to defining themselves in certain ways as sharing the same fate.

Youth as a Transitional Stage from Childhood to Adulthood

Mitteraeur, a social scientist, identifies four significant happenings that mark the transition from childhood to adulthood. He maintains that these transitional markets have remained fairly stable over time.

They are:

- Leaving home
- Finding employment
- Setting up home
- Marriage

Mitterauer, however, points out that these transitional markets have limitations in helping us to define who youth are. The timing of these aspects of transition, their meaning, their order of occurrence differ for young men and young women, and from one region to another. For example, some transitional markets are traditionally applicable only to young men. Until recently, in many societies or cultures, recruitment into the army was for males only. Also, the very concept of youth is embedded in the practices of patriarchy — the use of the term youth usually brings a mental image of a young man. Thus, we need to, sincerely, broaden our outlook.

Youth as a Social Construct

Each and every society has its ways of seeing youth. These social constructs are not necessarily true, nor do they always show youth the way they really are. One of the best ways of understanding the social construction of youth is to study how other societies construct views of them. These views differ from society to society. A comparison of different view can help us to understand our own views. Youth can be astonishing brief period in some societies such as those where people live by hunting and gathering, because the skills required for survival are usually acquired in childhood itself. These skills are usually needed as early as possible in adult roles. In other societies, particularly late capitalist economies such as those of present-day Europe and the United States of America, the concept of youth, or at least young people, is being stretched further and further. The reason for this can be found in structural adjustment. As structural adjustment continues to create extended periods of unemployment, especially for school leavers, people tend to remain longer in the category of youth. Today, in many western countries, the category of youth even seems to include people in their early thirties.

PRIMARY FACTORS CAUSING CONCERN

Whenever we talk about youth, we discuss issues which are usually acute problems related to youth, like unemployment, alcohol and drug abuse, juvenile crimes, vandalism etc. These perceptions of the youth present them more as a challenge than an asset to any society. We ought to remember that youth are the most dynamic part of the society. To develop is their basic demand and main trait. The path for their development depends on the selection and the integration of the social goal of youth development with personal ideas and aspirations. Youth problems in the modern society and social problems with which youth are concerned are closely related to the subject of youth development. During this process of developing and evolving, the youth go through a number of changes, which affect them in various ways. They might not be prepared to accept these changes very easily and may react in different ways. Therefore, rather than perceiving youth in a negative manner we ought to pay appropriate emphasis on the factors which are a cause of concern in this regard. We can divide these factors of concern to the youth into personal factors and environmental factors.

Personal Factors

Personal factors are those which, in general, have little to do with the environmental conditions of the individual. They are in many instances related to the behavioural, biological and economic dispositions of the individual himself/herself. We are already aware that the process of growing up is a very difficult phase for all adolescents. They are not prepared to see and experience such drastic changes in their physiques. Emotional disturbance accompany these physical changes in their physiques. Emotional disturbance accompany these physical changes because of hormonal changes and they generally become irritable and uncompromising. It is in this period of development that youngsters tend to get very concerned about the normalcy of their physical characteristics. They are very conscious, all the time, of their appearance and sex-appropriateness. Based on these feelings about normalcy and sex-appropriateness, they develop 'Self-concepts' and hold to them for a long time. Just like acceptance of the changed body, the desire of acceptance of sex-roles causes the youngsters to play 'near adults', and this is one of the major developmental tasks of this age. Because of the advantages and prestige associated with the traditional male sex-role, most boys are not only willing but also eager to play it. This however, is not often true of girls.

They often enter youth with a some what blurred concept of the sex role they will be expected to play as adults, and are now confronted with the problems of accepting the traditional stereotype of the female. For some girls who have learnt to play the traditional female sex-role throughout childhood, it will not be a problem. But for others this may be a major psychological hazard to good personal and social adjustments. As adolescents attain legal maturity, they are anxious to shed the stereotype of teenagers and to create the impression that they are near adults. They often discover that dressing and acting like adult is not enough. So, some of them begin to concentrate on behaviour that is associated with the adult status – smoking, drinking, using drugs, and engaging in sex, for example. They believe this behaviour will create the image they desire.

Role of Family

Family also has an important role to play with regard to the personal factors in their development. First of all, a child's parents arc his/hcr first role models. He learns initial behaviour by merely imitating them and later, it develops into a habit. Also the values and moral that the family members inculcate in the child affect his/her life in a big way. Often in single child families, the child gets all the attention at home, and therefore, he/she is likely to become more demanding in other social settings, in terms of relationships and even material gains. Therefore, such parents should make a conscious effort to teach their child attributes like sharing, respect for others etc.

On the other hand, in families where there are two or more children, there are chances of sibling rivalry. One of the children might feel that the other gets more affection and favour from the parents, and therefore, become stubborn and rebellious in nature. It is the hands of the parents to handle these circumstances carefully and also make the children realize their mistakes and rectify them. Another very important role of family, especially parents in a child's life is their expectations from him/her. If the parents are very ambitious for their children, they might directly or indirectly pressure them to perform well, some times even to over perform, unrealistically so.

When the child is not able to meet the expectations of his/her parents, he/she might begin to lose his/her self confidence. Therefore, it is always advisable for parents to know the aptitude and capacity of their child and encourage, and not push him/her to work hard in order to achiever his/her goals.

By the time children reach adolescence, they tend to take their own decisions. Most overprotective parents stop them from doing so, thinking that they are not mature enough. But right approach would be that of 'permissiveness'; and then guiding them from time to time. This will encourage them and boost their selfconfidence. They will learn how to be independent, from their own experience.

There is another section of children who have been rendered homeless and familyless. Their families have a negative role to play by their absence in the children's life—orphans, destitutes and street children who have practically nobody to guide them live their own life from one day to the other. At times, some anti-social elements with vested interests take advantage of their situation and involve them in crime, violence etc. of which they become a part very soon. In order to prevent this, governmental and non-governmental efforts are crucial.

Environmental Factors

The most significant impact on a child's personality, after family, is the educational institution. In schools, the teacher's role is the same as that of parents at home. They help in building a child's personality by guiding them and even by reinforcing their behaviour with rewards and punishment. That is how a child learns that he/she is not supposed to do something for which he/she is rewarded for. In co-educational schools, children also learn gradually with the process of growing up what their relationships with members of the opposite sex be like.

In segregated schools, they deprived of this aspect of socialization. But, in any case, peer influence is very strong, particularly during adolescence, when children tend to identify more with peer group behaviour. Such behaviour continues till college age. This is the time when they start thinking seriously in terms of their careers. Once they have chosen their direction, they strive to achieve their respective goals. Much depends on their aptitude and interest so it is advisable that parents do not expect their children to choose a career according to their parents liking.

Once they get into employment, life changes drastically: they are no longer students. They are now expected to behave as responsible adults, and they often make conscious efforts to live up to this expectation. Another important factor regarding employment is job satisfaction. If they are satisfied with their jobs, the results show in their work.

Another important factor is that of religion. Right from childhood, we see our religion has different ritual and festivals within and outside the family. These experiences and the fact that they are born in a particular family, give them the identity of belonging to a particular religion. This religion should inculcate in them spiritual richness and rather than closing them down to narrow thinking. For example, acceptances of inter-caste, and inter-religious marriages, even if a little reluctantly, point out to the gradual lowering of the religion bound walls. Media has an important role to play as well. With the sudden influx of satellite channels, the adolescents and youth are, on the one hand, flooded with information to their advantage.

On the other hand, there is some information that can be quite misleading. Also, with the strong impact of western culture and life-style, the adolescents are driven towards it without much forethought. Also, certain forms of media such as cinema and T.V focus more on affluence and western life-styles, which are then imitated by our youth. Perhaps media should not mislead the youth by making them run after affluence rather than values and morality. Often, when in search of a life-style that the youth cannot manage to get, they get frustrated and take up improper alternatives available to them. A burning example of these can be the militants who have joint organizations like JFLF, ULFA etc.

It is a very sorry state of affairs when we lose so much of energy, in the form of youth in appropriate steps in this regard. Also it is the duty of the government to make amendments in the existing system through better policies and programmes to make youth development their prime agenda. Various establishments, whether Governmental bodies, Non-governmental organizations or community based organizations can contribute in their own way at the local and national levels. Organisations like the NCC, NSS, YMCA, YWCA, Nehru Yuvak Kendras etc. help a lot in channelizing youth power in the correct direction.

REALITIES IN A CHANGING SOCIETY

Among the indicators of the changing society visible around us are access to information technology, satellite communication etc. On the one hand, this opens up innumerable avenues for the young generation. But on the other hand, we cannot refuse to see the 'turbulence' in the changing society. As well all know too well, the youth of today is exposed to all kinds of information and knowledge which is crucial for his/ her healthy growth and development as an individual. But we should always be ready to accept that as a transitional stage to adulthood, adolescence seems a particularly vulnerable period for such exposure. This is of specific significance in a country like India where the society itself is undergoing major transition due to influences from the west, particularly in this era of liberalization. We are fast turning into a consumer society where the influence of sex, violence and materialism is only too evident. The circumstances thus created, besides being highly stressful are continuously posing a vital question: Does our young generation know how to face and adapt to these changes?

A sizeable number of educated Indian youth find themselves being along by the tide of fast growing consumer and materialistic culture. They are caught in the race for jobs and success in a world little concerned with values and morality. There is also a growing number of youth in our towns and cities who are unemployed and marginalized, and consequently at high risk of being trapped by the communalism and crime promoted by various vested interest. Many young people are also victims of sexual abuse, oppression and violence.

They struggle to cope with such situations, but they also show tremendous resistance. There is also a whole category of working youth who are occupied in menial jobs; they live on the streets or in dingy places, are exploited by others, and have little or no security. In our villages and slums, where live the vast majority of the youth of our country, the general picture is one of poverty, illiteracy and unemployment. But, there are sections of the dalits and tribals who are beginning to assert their identity. Their young people are engaged in a struggle for their self-identity; they are beginning to demand – forcefully, and at times, even violently their due share of the benefits of development.

We cannot also forget the present day scourge of the evils of alcoholism and drug-addiction afflicting many of our young people. Many young women are in the process of undoing, the victimization, discrimination and injustice to which they have been subject for a long time. They are discovering the rightful place for themselves that was hitherto denied then in the family and in society. Against this backdrop of the youth condition in India, it is somewhat heartening to find a small but significant section of youth committed at various levels to sociocultural and political change and the welfare of the community. The many social movements, organizations and processes that have emerged in recent years have been successfully tapping the generosity, dedication and professional skills of these sections of enlightened and committed youth.

These youth have been contributing in the struggle for the rights of children, of women and of the marginalized, as well as in the campaign for a clean environment, democracy and human rights. This is indeed a sign of hope and a pointer to what the young generation, if given the proper guidance and encouragement can achieve.

The grinding poverty and socio-economic inequality prevailing in India are a depressing reality for most of the younger generation. Seriously lacking in resources and opportunities, millions of youth all over the country face unemployment and oppression, and as a result their creative energies are simply underutilized or destroyed. While there is need, therefore, to provide avenues for employment to the extent possible or to assist young people in securing good jobs, they themselves should also show a creative, enterprising spirit and face up to the risks involved in taking the initiative to devise ways of self-employment.

With regard to those who are victims of sexual abuse, trafficking and exploitation, the country needs to reach out to them and work for their liberation and rehabilitation in a more active manner than has been done hitherto. Communication and fundamentalism of a militant kind are increasingly taking hold of various communities, and threatening to destroy the very fabric of the society, which is characterized by a plurality of cultures and by mutual respect and acceptance of others. We have also witnessed, in recent years, a systematic and large-scale mobilization of youth on communal planks, based mainly on an appeal to their individual and collective fears and insecurities.

An atmosphere of brutal competition and corruption leads to the narrowing down of the individual's quest for a 'better life' in materialistic teams. The result is a crisis of cultural identity as well as clash with the tradition and values. They experience identity crisis in the face of an increasingly consumer and materialistic society. They often feel confused as to where to draw the line between consumer values and human values and human values, between 'having-more' and 'beingmore'. Those who migrate to towns and cities face considerable difficulties arising out of regionalism and ethnicism. They sometimes feel lost or neglected; they may tend to form cliques according to their language or place or origin.

It is even worse when one group tends to treat another with indifference: the result is unnecessary tension, clashes and disharmony. Young people, therefore, should experience the joy of companionship and of collaboration with the peers. There are many other young people who are caught in the shackles of various other kinds of oppression. In education, at workplace, at home and at various settings in the society, women face discriminatory behaviour. Even after having ensured 'equal wages for equal work' in our directive principles of state policy, it is not really put into practice.

We ought to help bring such oppressed young people together as a group, a movement or an organization where through the very process of sharing among themselves they will already experience a great freedom form domination, and find encouragement and support in their endeavors to break their bonds and so recover their freedom and dignity as individuals. They need to take up responsible leadership and activity take part in the formation and organization of youth who are poor, voiceless and marginalized.

CHALLENGES TO THE YOUTH IN A CHANGING SOCIETY

The society today is becoming more and more competitive in all aspects. A mere academic qualification does not take anyone very far; one is asked to prove his/her calibre in getting things done, in working together with others, in increasing productivity and wealth. This competitive atmosphere is also visible in the personal life-styles of people – in the way one tries to present oneself to the public. We shall discuss some of challenges that the youth are faced with in this section.

Self-confidence

In this context, one of the first challenges before a young person is one of self-confidence. A growing up young person is trying to find his/her feet amidst the turmoil of the physical and emotional changes that he/she has to deal with. Added to this is the external pressure to perform and to prove. Very few young people get the kind of support and guidance to grow in the kind of self assurance and confidence that is needed to see them through this high pressure. The fear of not measuring up lurks deep within. Parents today add to this pressure on the young forcing them to take up various programmes of study sand exams that would ensure that the wards stand a chance in this highly competitive environment. The surge in the number of suicides among the young is part of the expression of the exasperated ones who feel they cannot reach the high expectations of their dear ones and are made to feel that they are a failure.

Family Relationships

Relationships with family members is another challenge of the young people. They are more and more pulled towards their peer groups and friends with whom they would like to spend most of their time. Suddenly, the doting father and the ever attentive mother may be considered a bit of a nuisance. The young boy and girl can do with some support and guidance in balancing their affection towards their parents and the external pull towards their peer groups.

Idealism of Youth

The young person is highly idealistic. He/she is angry at the exploitation, injustice, corruption, discrimination, poverty, hunger and other evils that threaten the harmony in society. This idealism is easily manipulated by vested interest groups that spell out their agenda in the most romantic terms. The young people are swayed by forces that would like to tap into the unselfish, impulsive energy of the young people for their own end. Communal forces, militant groups, political parties, and religious groups play havoc with the idealism of the youth, and leave them frustrated in the end.

Risk Taking

The young are willing to take risks and to experiment. They look for exhilarating experiences and accessories that are "cool". The media has understood this well. The media is out to sell glamour and happiness to the youth. "Have and be happy" seems to be the underlying message. Relationships, happiness, satisfaction, success, everything depends on what you possess and how you appear. The number of young people who do get caught up in this world of glamour and consumerism, forgetting the deeper realities of life is not small.

Rural Urban Divide

The rapid changes in technology has made the world smaller and brought people closer. The process of globalization aided by the power of technology opens up new opportunities and avenues in employment, business, travel, health care, education and a host of other conveniences thought impossible a couple of decades ago. To reap the advantages of this progress, one needs the capacity to tap into its potential. It is here that the rural youth are at a tremendous disadvantage compared to the urban youth. The urban youth are in a way highly influenced with choices of opportunities and possibilities, while the rural youth are often left with no choice other than to take what comes their way.

The kind of facilities and infrastructure development to keep pace with and take advantage of the progress of technology is denied to millions in the villages. As a result the gap between the rural youth and the urban youth is widening. Things like electricity, communication links, flow of information, financial support, training and education institutions of quality that are taken for granted in the cities are far from satisfaction in the rural areas. While some have all the advantages, others are left to struggle with very little. As a result, thousands flock to the cities in search of the "dream" life, making our cities crowded, with all its disadvantages. Some very smart ones make it big in the cities. But majority of these young men and women who flock to the cities, with little support and guidance, end up being exploited and manipulated. Our villages should become attractive enough for our young people to find a reason to stay on.

Professed Values and Lived Values

Another aspect of grave challenge to the youth is the evident dichotomy between professed values and lived values in the public sphere. Whether it is in politics at various levels, in religion, business, administration or in education, young people are bombarded with contradictory messages from those who are supposed to be leaders. The public pronouncements on honesty, transparency, communal harmony, etc. do not find actualization in deeds in day to day life. The number of public scams that are increasing day by day is a clear indication of this. What message do young minds gather when those they consider role models flout the law with impunity? What lesson does a young person get when the guilty are shielded by the same authority that is expected to render justice? The messages that our young people get from the so called "teachers" are very contradictory and the young minds are confused as to what is right and what is wrong. The message that goes out very often seems to be 'everything is fair as long as you do not get caught'. There can be no message more damaging to young minds than this.

Health Hazards

Health hazards facing the youth are much more than ever before. The threat of HIV/AIDS, the dangers of drug addiction, alcoholism, smoking and chewing pan, the increasing number of road accidents, adverse effects of environmental pollution, and the build up of stress at all levels claim more young victims each year. At the same time, the access to correct information on these health hazards and to affordable and quality health care, and counselling and guidance services is very limited to the youth. This is a cause of major concern in this present age.

Young people are eager to make their mark on the society. They need the space and the opportunity to do it. They also need guidance to make positive contribution. Adults, who are concerned for the young would ensure that the youth play their role responsibly, and walk with them to the mature adult world. Youth can do it. The society should not adopt a negative attitude towards the youth by "under estimating them".

YOUTH AND SEX RELATED ISSUES

Biologically, this is a totally new experience. Its significance is due both to the pervasiveness and to each society's expectations. It creates in the adolescents a great wonderment about themselves and a feeling of having something in common with all human beings. It influences all their relationships with each other, male or female. Boys begin to perceive sexuality essentially as a way of achieving fun and pleasure. This is partly explained by the fact that their genital organs are situated outside the body where they can be seen and touched. Girls, on the contrary do not experience this stage as a very pleasant one. Their sexual organs are within the body and therefore, they cannot be seen and touched. The beginning of the menstrual bleeding can be a frightening experience.

By now, we know that sexuality is a gift intended primarily to foster and strengthen the bond of love between a man and woman united in a life long commitment. To understand this sufficient degree of maturity is essential. In order that young people can attain this maturity, providing them with appropriate sex education at the appropriate age is very important. Mostly, issues relating to sex education and HIV/AIDS do not have immediate and easy answers. Educating young people on these topics gives an opportunity to clarify their own questions and to think of some strategies to overcome the difficulties.

Adolescents experience conflicting pressures from a variety of sources in relation to sex, which are often contradictory. There may be a desire to explore sexual identity and experiment. This may include exploring masturbation, same gender affection and a variety of other sexual activities. Along with this desire, they may also become concerned with what is okay, acceptable and permissible from the point of getting infected with sexually transmitted diseases or becoming pregnant. Many youngsters are prone to desires for short-term relationships. The messages and pressures received from the media and peer group often install in them this desire for experiment. Those who succeed in their attempt are likely to seek further opportunities.

When we are talking of sex related issue, there is a need to discuss certain aspects, or rather behaviours, which are not necessarily limited to young people, but nevertheless, young people are in the picture in a big way. Hence, in order to provide you with a better knowledge of several issues, we will discuss 'alternative sexual patterns' and 'maladaptive sexual behaviours'.

Alternative Sexual Patterns

You should note that the sexual patterns or styles in this general category are usually considered by many to be acceptable alternatives to traditional sexual patterns. Though often subject to social disapproval, there is a lack of conclusive evidence that these patterns are necessarily maladaptive, nor are persons engaging in them ordinarily subjected to legal sanctions.

Masturbation

Masturbation is defined as self-stimulation of the genitals for sexual gratification. It has been traditionally condemned on religious and moral grounds, as well as for its allegedly harmful physical effects. It is taught that masturbation is a vile habit that can be prevented with a little self-control. Many sexologists emphasize that masturbating as practiced by the average adolescent has no known harmful physiological effects and is actually a normal and healthy sexual outlet for young people. Children particularly boys who feel unhappy, lonely and unwanted may centre too much of their activity around masturbatory practices in an attempt to compensate for their frustrations.

Usually, the undesirable features of masturbation are the worry, guilt and self-devaluation that may be associated with it. Young people need to learn self control. Masturbation if carried over to marital life can have negative consequences. Sex is primarily for sharing and expressing love between a husband and wife. Excessive masturbation can lead to developing less interest in the heterosexual act in marital life which can cause strain in sexual relationship between a husband and wife. Mutual masturbation among peer (of same sex) can lead to same sex relationship which will leave its impact on one's personality. Among the Catholics (the largest denomination of Christian) masturbation is still considered a sin.

Pre-marital and Marital Patterns

Traditional sexual mores in Indian society have emphasized abstinence from sexual relations prior to marriage and fidelity in one's spouse following marriage. However, we can notice that these mores have been increasingly challenged and threatened over the years. Although there are reports that premarital sexual relations may be on the increase, there is no evidence of widespread indiscriminate sexual activity. Even among persons who, perhaps, do not consider marriage a prerequisite for sexual relations, emphasis is usually placed on some kind of loving relationship or mutual commitment before sexual involvement.

In this context, it is important for us to note a form of non-marital relationship which is gradually emerging in our society which may be called as cohabitation. In cohabitation, the person lives quite openly with a member of the opposite sex on a relatively stable basis. Such a phenomena can be noticed especially in urban India.

Prostitution

Prostitution is defined as the provision of sexual relations in return for money. Technically, there are four types of prostitution, the most common involving heterosexual relations for which the female is paid. There is also heterosexual prostitution for which the male is paid by the female; male homosexual prostitution for which a male provides sexual relations for another male and female homosexual prostitution for which a female provides sexual relations for another female. The last three types appear to be relatively are throughout the world.

Homosexuality

Homosexual behaviour is sexual behaviour directed towards a member of one's own sex. It is generally referred as 'lesbianism' for female relationships. Homosexuality has existed throughout recorded history. The ancient Greek, Roman, Persian, and Muslim civilizations all condoned a measure of homosexuality. Later in Greece and Rome, for example, homosexual prostitution existed openly. Most contemporary cultures, however, have condemned homosexuality as socially undesirable. Homosexuals may, nevertheless, be well adjusted, well educated and highly successful in their occupation.

Contrary to the popular opinion, it is not possible to divide people into two clear out groups, homosexuals and heterosexuals. You may find certain individuals whose experience and desires combine both heterosexual and homosexual components. Homosexual behaviour is considered a sin by some of the world religions, particularly the Christian.

EXPLOITATION AND OPPRESSION OF YOUTH

Over the ages, our society has been witness to various forms of oppression and exploitation directed towards certain section of the community, or at certain communities in general. Now, we are trying to break these shakles of oppression and come out to stand together. But still many groups face oppression, including working class people, women, adolescents, scheduled castes and tribes, certain religious groups, people who are differently labeled like eunuchs, lesbians and homosexuals, people surviving with HIV, drug users, single parents, unwed mothers, street children, devadasis, blood, semen and milk donors, people who have used the mental health system etc. Though all these kinds of oppressions exist for different reasons and social practices, they share certain features. Some of the shared features of oppression include exclusion from the mainstream process of decision making in the society, social and financial injustice, misinformation of facts which distorts one's perception of life and keeping one's group bound to the status quo.

People of the working class are oppressed on the basis of their position or designation nature and position of work, place of work—public versus private sector, hours of work, poor pay and perks, poor housing and opportunities for education, and limited access to lawful means of improving these needs and conditions. Women on the other hand are oppressed on the basis of their gender, discrimination in pay, limitation in opportunities for education, political participation, religious participation and job opportunities, perpetuating of unpaid care work, limitation of choice regarding pregnancy and abortion, limitations in decision making and instilling a sense of inferiority and lesser worth in comparison to men.

Young People

Also, there is a different kind of stress that youngsters have to undergo. As we have already seen the chief task and problem of adolescence is growing up to be a mature adult. The young persons feel that they are not longer children and yet, they are not grown up enough to be adults. The adolescents want to have a place among adults and yet feel inadequate in the task. They attempt to push away all parental props and take their first steps alone and unaided, and at the same time, they feel the need of their parents more than ever. Now, that they are trying to become more and more of themselves, and less and less of their parent's children, home pleasures tend to have less appeal. The world around them seems to change everyday, while their viewpoint changes even faster. The more the adolescents feel that their maturity is underrated, the more rebellious they will be and the more awkward will be their attempts to prove how grow-up they are.

This is their way of rebelling against the circumstances that cause them so much stress. At this stage, it is important to give the adolescents, adequate freedom to do their own experimenting without oppressing them. Only with freedom one can learn to be responsible. Certainly, this freedom entails risk; but the only alternative to freedom is 'overprotection'. Overprotection can render the adolescents incapable of developing their selfconfidence, sense of responsibility and social judgment. It is, therefore, essential that while providing freedom, instead of oppression, they should be guided and helped to become responsible, capable and self-dependent.

The HIV Infected

Persons living with HIV are also exploited. Often, they are not treated properly or refused treatment. They are socially ostracized; they are unwelcome in their own families. Provision for their social security, like insurance, is not available. They are being thrown out of employment. Given the present situation in India, if individuals are found to be HIV positive through a chance test they are not informed about their HIV status.

Other Groups

The drug addicts are another lot who face oppression. There are thousands of drug abusers in India who hail from every stratum of society. Millions of street-children and children of prostitutes are introduced into drug use before they reach their teenage. Unemployment and frustration have forced many youngsters from middle class families to seek the help of drugs. Affluence, bad company and lack of love and care from parents compel many people adolescents to take to drugs. Once addicted, the family, society, religious groups and the legal system look down upon them. Similar is the plight of unwed mothers, single parents and the devadasis who are despised by our tradition bound society inspite of all the advancement in knowledge and development of science and technology.

Professional blood donors, semen donors and milk donors are very much in demand. They are important as long as they can supply their precious human tissue. They also face oppression in the society by way of poverty, financial deprivation and subjection to misinformation, which distorts the perceptions of their lives. In the light of this discussion, we are led to pose questions to the society and to ourselves. Where will all this exploitation and oppression lead them? Is society not responsible if these oppressed groups take up just about any alternative, violent or illegal, to express their anger and dissatisfaction?

STRATEGIES AND SUGGESTIONS

After having discussed the problems faced by the youth, we ought to think and work out strategies and suggestions to deal with the concern of youth. Let us classify our strategies into three – Prevention, Protection, and Participation.

Prevention

A host of considerations arise in relation to the preventive strategy. The most obvious is the satisfaction of basic needs, such as food, water, shelter, health and education, which may enable people to exist without having to suffer from the pangs of insufficiency leading to social deprivations and dislocation. These needs are closely related to the fact that a majority of the nation's population still lives in rural areas, thus calling for priority allocation of resources and decentralization of power to proper rural development. Preventive education has an untapped and unlimited potential. Its long-term effects are vast. For instance, environmental education can help to prevent environmental degradation from having negative impact on children and youth. Similarly, education against drug abuse and sex education may both have positive consequences for the physical and mental welfare of children, youth and their families. For this purpose appropriate emphasis at the governmental, community and family level is required on family education in general, and on providing knowledge about HIV/AIDS, sexually transmitted diseases and drug abuse, alcoholism, smoking etc. Also, at schools and college proper facilities should be provided for counselling and guidance. Youth development should not be seen as totally independent from the other core concerns of development particularly family development. It should thus, be integrated into the planning process as one of the components calling for immediate attention.

Protection

The role of laws, policies and measures to protect children and youth holds great importance. It calls for action at national and international levels. At the national level, the existing laws and policies should be scrutinized to assess their efficiency. In this regard, much depends upon the integrity of the law makers and law-enforcers themselves. Various discriminatory laws exist against children and youth on grounds of gender, race and social origin. Female youth are not treated universally at par with male youth in many areas of law and practice. Nationality questions, access to schools, children born out of wedlock and employment potential are some widespread examples where the legal framework stumbles. These laws should be identified and reformed. Various laws particularly on social welfare and social security, exist only on paper. These should be seen as ways and means of alleviating the plight of many youngsters and their families. A lot depends upon how the state will utilize these laws to reallocate resources to guarantee social justice and equity.

Participation

Youth participation is not a new concept, but it has yet to become a reality in several areas. There are many countries, where youth groups operate constructively to promote the interests of youth and children in many fields e.g. the National Service Scheme, National Cadet Corps etc. The current challenge is to uphold the structure of participation without allowing it to be manipulated. On another front, the activities of the youth groups and other NGOs promoting child and youth development should be better integrated in the whole process of developmental entities which may be instrumental in making the development strategy effective, especially as the latter also hold a plethora of resources and powers. Just a simple glance at the children and youth on the streets and in the villages anywhere in the developing and developed world will reveal the true motivation for action.

Participation of the mentors of the youth—their parents and teachers in all such actions is very significant. Participation of youth should be highlighted in the media to send the message across to as large number of people as possible, particularly, issues which need widespread attention should be propagated.

3

Population

Explicit concern over India's rapid rise of population originated in the third decade of this century. Until 1920, India's population had been growing very slowly owing to the heavy toll from famines, epidemics, and wars. According to census reports, the population of the country within its present geographical boundaries actually declined between 1911 and 1921, from 252.1 to 251.3 million because of the high mortality inflicted by the influenza pandemic of 1918-19. It is estimated that about 5 per cent of the country's population-some 13 million persons-died in that epidemic. The population has increased steadily since 1921, largely because of epidemic, famine control and sanitation measures undertaken by the provincial governments.

For the first time, since the initiation of a systematic population census in 1881, India's population increased slightly by more than 10 per cent in a decade, with the 1931 census enumerating a population of 279.0 million. In this context, concern over such an unprecedented rapid rise in population arose from four quarters: intellectuals, social reformers, the Congress Party and the government. The intellectuals in India were mostly drawn from the upper caste elite sections of the society and many of them went to England for higher education or for training for posts in the Indian Civil services. They were, there, exposed to the Malthusian theory of population-positive and negative checks on populations growing beyond its means of subsistence. India was always cited as a basket case of poverty whose population was growing beyond its means of subsistence.

When the scholars returned to India, they set up Neo-Malthusian Leagues on patterns similar to such Leagues in England and Europe to warn the people about the dangers of population growth. The first such League to discuss and propagate on the hazards of high population growth was set up in Madras city in July 1929. The League published its first propaganda journal on the need for controlling birth rate, the 'Madras Birth Control Bulletin', in the same year. Similar Neo-Malthusian Leagues were started in subsequent years in other cities, notably in Poona and Bombay.

Madras and Bombay seem to be the two Indian cities that were first concerned about the population problem at the intellectual level which subsequently gained momentum in other cities. The interest and action from social reformers for the control of population growth originated from those activists who were primarily interested in promoting women's health and welfare especially keen on liberating women from the wheels of childbearing, preventing unwanted births, and reducing the hazards to the life and health of pregnant women who were willing to expose themselves to cruel and primitive methods of induced abortion.

They were largely influenced by the work of Margaret Sanger in the United States and Edith-Howe Martin from England. This social reform movement was initiated by Prof. R D Karve, who advocated widow-remarriage, practice of artificial methods of family planning to protect women from the hazards of unwanted pregnancies, and who started a magazine called Samaj-Swasthya in Marathi language in 1927, which was published regularly until his death in 1953. He also started the first contraceptive clinic in Girgaum, at the heart of Bombay in 1921.

This social-reform movement eventually spread to other parts of the country and was largely responsible for the establishment of Family Planning Association of India in 1949 in Bombay. At the political level, the Congress Party's attitude towards population control was tinged with scepticism mostly because of Mahatma Gandhi's strong moral opposition to the use of artificial methods of birth control. Mahatma Gandhi argued that though he was convinced that high population growth is of major social concern, the solution to reduction of fertility should not be through artificial methods of birth control, but through sexual abstinence and self discipline.

He argued that widespread use of artificial methods of family planning would ultimately lead to moral and social decay. The social reformers and intellectuals were unable to convince Mahatma Gandhi to their point of view. However, some of the princely States in India considered high population growth as a hurdle to development and social welfare. The Maharaja of Mysore commissioned, officially, two family planning clinics in 1930-one in Cheluvamba Hospital, Mysore and the other in Vani Vilas Hospital, Bangalore.

These were the first two official family planning clinics to be started in the world. The last vestiges of moralistic objections to family planning seem to have been eroded because of the Bengal famine of 1943-44, which resulted in 1.5 million deaths within a period of 12 months, and made the Government of India and the officials aware of the precariously poor conditions of people and their extreme vulnerability during conditions of famine. The report of the Bengal Famine Inquiry Committee, constituted by the Government of India which submitted its in 1945, contained a chapter on the potential dangers to the economy and life of people arising out of rapid population growth, especially a population living in abject poverty and deprived of the bare necessities of life. Mr. R A Gopalaswamy, ICS was the Member-Secretary of the Committee, who later became the Registrar General of India in 1951 and conducted the first Census of independent India.

When he became the Chief Secretary of Madras Province in 1954, he introduced a strong incentive based family planning programme. Similarly, the Bhore Committee, which was set up in 1943 to make an assessment of the health conditions in India submitted its report in 1946 and recommended a suitable health infrastructure for the country. It also stressed the need for a national programme of family planning for improving the health status of people.

The reports of these two committees, the Bhore Committee and the Bengal Famine Enquiry Committee, paved the way for the Government of India to adopt a National Programme of Family Planning in 1947. With the death of Mahatma Gandhi in 1948, the moral objections for the adoption of artificial methods of birth control seem to have waned and the official family planning programme was launched in 1952 as a part of the first five year plan. However, the Congress Party, whose values and ideals were largely shaped by the Gandhian philosophy retained, to some extent, the moralistic objections against free and unrestricted use of artificial methods of family planning.

POLICIES AND PROGRAMMES FROM 1951 TO 1976: HITTS APPROACH

This period covers the first twenty five years of the family planning programme implemented during the three five year plans, the inter-plan period, the fourth five year plan, and the first two years of the fifth five year plan 1975-76. In April 1950, the Government of India appointed a Population Policy Committee under the Chairmanship of Minister of Health and upon the Committee's recommendations, a Family Planning Cell was created in the office of the Director General of Health Services. The first five year plan document referred to a programme for Family Limitation and Population Control-terms which may be considered objectionable on humanitarian grounds now.

It sought to reduce the birth rate to the extent necessary to stabilize the population at a level consistent with the requirements of the national economy. A sum of ₹ 6.5 million was allocated by the Central Government for the family planning programme, which included a plethora of activities such as motivation, education, research and clinical services. A Demographic Training and Research Center was established in Bombay in 1956 with the assistance of United Nations for undertaking training and research on population issues. Family Planning programme was intended to be promoted through a network of family planning clinics under the assumption that there was already some intrinsic demand for family planning services and that provision of supply through clinics will induce further demand.

This clinical approach was intensified during the second plan period. The budget provision for family planning during this period increased from Rs 6.5 million to Rs 50 million. The actual expenditure incurred during the first and second five year plans was less than the budgeted amount, only Rs 1.5

and Rs 21.6 million respectively. The clinical approach of family planning promoted the methods of diaphragm, vaginal jelly, vaginal foam tablets, condoms and vasectomy in some states. During the later half of the second plan, the scheme of giving some incentive money to acceptors of vasectomy was introduced in Madras Province.

The Chief Secretary of the Madras Province, Mr. R A Gopalaswamy, postulated the concept of 'improvident maternity', which aimed at preventing all births of four and above by a strong programme of vasectomy, motivating men to undertake sterilization operations after the third child. He also estimated that if 7 vasectomies were done for 1000 population per year over a period of 10 years all improvident births could be avoided, and the birth rate could be reduced by 40 per cent. The seeds of incentive-based, target-oriented and time bound sterilization programme were thus sown in Madras province in the late fifties, which was immediately adopted in Bombay province next year, and in the next plan period in the country as a whole. The number of family planning clinics, where family planning services including sterilizations were provided, increased from 147 at the end of the first five year plan to 4,165 at the end of the second five year plan.

The slow pace of increase in contraceptive acceptance by the end of the second plan and the poor attendance in the family planning clinics indicated that the demand for family planning from the people was not as high as was expected in the plan documents. The clinic-oriented approach was hence replaced by an extension-education approach in the third five-year plan, which aimed at bringing the message and services of family planning to the people by house to house visits by the field staff employed in the Primary Health Centres and sub-centres in rural areas and government hospitals in urban areas. Shift from clinical approach to extension approach, which continues to be a pervasive methodology of family planning programme till date, was based on the following premises:

- There is a need to create a small family norm in the community by appropriate *information-education-communication* (ICE) procedures by involving opinion leaders. Six Family Planning Communication Research Centres were established in different parts of the country, to carry out field based action-research, as well as social science and demographic research for identifying and resolving field based issues in the implementation of family planning programmes.
- It is necessary to inform every eligible couple on the availability and use of contraceptive methods.
- It is necessary to provide contraceptive services to all couples in a socially and psychologically acceptable manner.

During the third plan period, family planning programme was thus made an integral part of the public health departments of all states. It was considered a part of health services in the country. The symbol of an inverted red triangle was introduced to convey the message of family planning. Various innovative measures of populariszing the programme, including carrying giant sized logos on elephant backs in various parts of the country were tried and, for the first time, a demographic goal was set. It was desired in 1962 that a crude birth rate of 25 should be achieved by 1972, a goal which is yet to be achieved in 1998.

The expenditure on Family Planning programme during the third plan period increased to Rs.248.6 million, 11 times more than the second plan. With the setting up of demographic goals for the programme and achievement of these goals being made the responsibility of the health departments, the programme became entrenched in a HITTS model i.e., Health department operated, Incentive based, Target-oriented, Time-bound and Sterilization-focussed programme.

A separate department of family planning was set up at the center and the departments of health in the states were renamed, over a period of time, as departments of health and family planning and family planning programme was fully funded from the central funds with staffing patterns and methods of functioning formulated by the central government.

In my view, 1962 saw the beginning of the HITTS approach, which lasted until 1977, leading to the 'coercive approach' during 1976-77. The period from 1966 to 69 was termed as a 'plan holiday'. However, during this period, family planning programme was integrated not only in the health system but also specifically made a part of the maternal and child health programme implemented through the Primary Health Centres (PHCs) in rural areas and Urban Family Planning Centres in towns.

The Government of India gave additional funds to state governments for recruitment of medical and para-medical staff including extension educators in the PHCs and urban health centres for working specifically for family planning. The expenditure during this three-year (1966-69) was Rs 704.6 million, almost three times the expenditure during the five years of the third plan.

Rapid expansion of the PHCs and Urban Family Planning Centres took place to pursue the HITTS model. The 1961 census showed a rising population growth rate and high fertility levels necessitating, in 1966, a postponement of the demographic goal of crude birth rate (CBR) of.25, which was again revised in 1968 aiming at CBR of 23 by 1978-79. The family planning programme got a big boost during the fourth plan period (1969-74) when the budget was increased to Rs.3150 million, though the actual expenditure was Rs.2844 million.

The infrastructure was considerably expanded and there was a strong desire on the part of the Government to resolve the population problem once and for all by organising vasectomy camps on a mass scale, so that these facilities are available for men in their own geographic proximity and the services of skilled surgeons could be optimally utilised.

In order to help women with unwanted pregnancies to have safe abortions from medically skilled personnel and not resort to primitive abortive procedures, a law liberalising induced abortion camouflaged under the term 'Medical Termination of Pregnancy Act' was passed by Parliament in 1972. The incentive amounts provided to acceptors of vasectomy and tubectomy were substantially increased, incentives were provided to motivators and to state governments by the central government for their performance in family planning, which were based essentially on the number of sterilizations done in relation to the population.

However, the 1971 census indicated that the high rates of population growth had continued unabated during the decade, with population increasing from 439.2 million in 1961 to 548.2 million in 1971 i.e., by 24.8 percent as compared to 21.5 per cent in 1951- 61. This continuing increase in population growth rate inspite of the vast network of personnel involved in the programme and sizeable expenditure from the central exchequer frustrated the policy-makers and programme administrators, which led to draconian measures during the emergency period of, 1975-76. The effective couple protection rate, which is an approximation for the contraceptive prevalence rate but based on the programme service statistics, indicates that percentage of couples protected by any modern methods of family planning was only 14.7 per cent by the end of March 1974.

The fifth plan document, which covered the period 1974-79, but implemented during 1974-78, refixed the demographic goals of achieving the birth rates as 30 by 1979 and 25 by 1984. The programme was given the highest priority by the central government during this period and the expenditure during 1974-78 rose to Rs 4,090 million, almost double per year of that in the fourth plan. Mass camps were organized with larger frequency in more states. In some classic camps such as the one conducted in Ernakulam during 1972, 65,000 vasectomies were carried out in a fortnight's time.

THE EMERGENCY PERIOD (COERCIVE APPROACH)

India went through a phase of national internal emergency under the Prime Ministership of Mrs. Indira Gandhi from June 75 to March 77, when rights of individuals were largely suppressed, freedom of the press restricted and powers of the judiciary curtailed with the government at the center assuming enormous authoritarian powers. One major impact of the emergency was felt on the population front, and was spearheaded by late Sanjay Gandhi, the second son of Mrs. Indira Gandhi. For the first time, a National Population Policy was formulated and adopted by the Parliament in April 1976, which called for a 'frontal attack on the problems of population', and which inspired the state governments to 'pass suitable legislation's to make family planning compulsory for citizens, and to stop child bearing after three children, if the 'state so desires'.

Many other measures were introduced such as stipulations to government officials in the health and revenue departments to remit given numbers of vasectomies from their areas of operation, failing which punishments were to be meted out to them. Various coercive tactics were used to control the fertility levels, mainly though increased number of vasectomies. The Commissioner for Family Planning at the center assumed enormous powers under the programme and the officials not only in the center but also in the states became powerful The incentive payments to acceptors was substantially increased and related on a sliding scale to the number of living children a couple had at the time 'Of accepting sterilization.

Innovative political and fiscal incentives were offered by the center to the state governments to implement the family planning programme. Laws, which made it compulsory for couples to stop reproduction after two or three children, were beginning to be drafted and placed before state legislatures in Maharashtra and other states for enactment. By a Constitutional Amendment, representations to parliament from each state were frozen at the 1971 census level upto the year 2001, making it politically unattractive for any state to increase its relative population size in the hope of securing greater political strength at the center. Vasectomies were conducted in railway stations, quickly arranged camp sites, and it is alleged that in the northern states of Uttar Pradesh and Bihar men were forcibly subjected to sterilization.

The strategy during this period can be termed as 'coercion'. However, news of these excesses leaked out very quickly through informal channels and there was general public agitation brewing up all over the country. The number of sterilizations done in India between April 1976 and March 1977 was 8.26 million, more than the total number done in the previous five years and more than the number done in any other country in the world until that time. The cost per sterilization was the lowest during the emergency period, at Rs 200 per sterilization compared to Rs 469 during 1973-74 and ₹ 751 during the post-emergency year 1977- 78.

However, during the period of emergency, partly due to excesses in sterilization and partly for other reasons, there was large scale political unrest and general elections were called in February 1977. The elections brought defeat to the Congress Party at the centre and in most of the states. An oft-used cliche to characterise the comprehensive family planning programme during the emergency period was that instead of bringing down the birth rate rapidly, it brought down the government. It is surprising that under an authoritarian single party rule in China, the one child family norm, which is more stringent than the measures practised in India during the emergency period, is continuing to be practised for almost two decades, without any popular unrest or international condemnation, and conversely with unabated appreciation of China's achievements in the field of population control. Even in India, the Chinese achievements in the field of population control continue to be lauded and form the basis for judging India's performance as poor.

POST-EMERGENCY PERIOD: RECOIL AND RECOVERY PHASE (1977-94)

There was a strong political reaction to the population policy of April 1976 and the coercive insistence on targets for vasectomy during the emergency period. The new government that assumed power in March 1977, changed the name of 'family planning' to 'family welfare', reduced the targets on sterilization and chose to achieve demographic change through a programme of education and motivation. A judicial commission was appointed to enquire into the wrong doings during the emergency period. A revised Population Policy adopted in 1977 was totally against compulsory sterilization and legislation of any kind and stated that 'compulsion in the area of family welfare must be ruled out for all times to come.

Our approach is educational and wholly voluntary'. The 1977 policy was welcomed as a type of liberation for the expression of individual opinions and attitudes on family size and freedom of choice of contraceptive methods to be used by couples. The backlash on the earlier programme was felt severely on the number of vasectomies done in 1977-78 which was one fifth of the number performed in the previous year, although the expenditure incurred in that year remained the same as in the previous year. However, the new government enacted into law the proposal of the earlier government of raising the minimum age at marriage (18 for girls and 21 for boys) which came into operation in October 1978.

During the provisional sixth plan period, 1978-79 and 1979-80, the programme expenditure was 2,260 million, almost equal to the amount spent in the previous two years. The period from 1977 to 1980 can be considered to be a recoil phase for the family planning programme. The change of government again in January 1980 marked a turning point in the programme and helped to restore it to some extent with emphasis continuing on its voluntary nature. During the revised sixth five year plan (1980-85), a Working Group of Population Policy was set up by the Planning Commission to formulate long-term policy goals and programme targets for family welfare programmes.

The long-term demographic goals were revised in terms of achieving Net Reproduction Rate (NRR-1) by the year 1996 for the country as a whole, on an average, and by the year 2001 in all the states. These goals are yet to be realised. It was assumed that fertility rates of a population are linked closely with the levels of development of the society, especially with female literacy and child mortality, and low fertility rates can be sustained only in the context of certain minimum levels of development and low mortality rates. These goals were translated into achieving a crude birth rate of 21, a crude death rate of 9, infant mortality rate of 60 and expectancy of life at birth of 64 years and contraceptive prevalence rate 60 per cent among eligible couples by modern methods of family planning to be achieved in all the states by the year 2000.

The health-based, time-bound, target-oriented family planning programme was revived with reduced emphasis on sterilization and greater emphasis on spacing methods and on child survival programmes. These were to be implemented through all the sub-centres and Primary Health Centres in the rural areas, without any aggressive campaigns or mass camps for sterilization as were adopted in earlier years. With greater assistance from international organisations, especially the UNICEF and the WHO, Universal Immunisation Programmes (UIP) and Expanded Programme of Immunisations (EPI) were launched in a systematic manner covering all the districts of the country in a phased manner. However, the post-emergency collapse of the family planning programme could never be revived fully in the subsequent years, especially in terms of acceptance of vasectomy by men as a good method of family planning.

With men almost refusing to come forward for vasectomy, and motivations for family size limitations continuing to rise because of the information-education campaigns and lack of easy availability of spacing methods, tubal ligation of women began to rise steadily and became a dominant method of family planning during the next five years. During the sixth plan, an allocation of Rs.10,780 million were made in the sector of family welfare while the actual expenditure was higher at Rs 14,480 million. The sixth plan increased the percapita expenditure on family planning to its highest since the implementation of the programme to ₹ 700 per sterilization equivalent. The seventh plan implemented during 1986-91 continued the low key approach to family planning adopted in the sixth plan but witnessed a slow but steady increase in number of acceptors of female sterilization in family planning.

There was greater emphasis on spacing methods in this plan and incentives were offered to younger couples not to have more than two children to accept this method. Special programmes to reduce infant and child mortality rates through Universal Immunisation Programme (UIP) started earlier were replaced by a more broader programme of Child Survival and Safe Motherhood (CSSM) implemented in collaboration with the UNICEF. However, the reduction in birth rates were smaller than anticipated in the seventh plan. By the late eighties, it came to be recognised that the mortality and fertility levels in some states are declining rapidly, more rapidly than anticipated. The crude birth rate of Kerala which was 37 in 1966, came down to 26 in 1976 and to 20.3 by 1988, below the goal of 21-the replacement level of fertility, recommended in the sixth plan document.

By 1986, the infant mortality has declined to 27 infant deaths per 1000 live births, well below the goal of 60 recommended to be reached by the year 2000. Similarly, Tamil Nadu reduced its birth rate from 33.6 in 1970-72 to 23.1 by 1989, though its infant mortality in that year was 68, much higher than that of Kerala. Clearly something striking was happening in terms of demographic transition in the southern states. This phenomenon attracted scholars from various disciplines to analyse the factors that were behind such a transition and whether these could be replicated or adapted to other areas of the country where fertility levels were declining more slowly.

A major change in the political scenario of the country was introduced by late Prime Minister Rajiv Gandhi with the passing of Constitutional Amendments 72 and 73 and enactment of Panchayati Raj and Nagar Palika Acts in 1992, setting in motion the process of democratic decentralization. These acts ushered in a three-tier system of political governance in the country, central government, state government and the panchayats in the rural areas and the nagar palikas in the urban areas upto the district level. The primary health care including family planning, primary education and provision of certain basic amenities to the people such as drinking water and roads became the responsibility of the panchayats.

Another notable feature of this act is the reservation of one third of the seats in panchayats for women members. Thus at the grass root level the women are politically empowered by this act to participate in all decision making issues pertaining to social development including family planning. This is great leap forward for the Indian democracy and empowerment of women. The process of this demographic decentralization is still going on with varying speed and intensity in different states. Generally, the states are reluctant to share their powers and resources with the elected bodies of the panchayats. In some states, even the elections to the panchayats are yet to take place.

Family planning and primary health care, legally, are now in the domain of the panchayats and nagar palikas. This democratic decentralisation has further infringed on the powers of state government to impose any strong family planning programme through its Primary Health Centres and Sub-Centres. Another notable development from the early 1990's has been organized intensification and expansion of the women's movements within the country and outside, questioning the policies and directions of the government with regard to family planning programme, in which women had to shoulder major responsibilities for fertility regulation and demographic transition.

All family planning programmes, they argue, have been ultimately targeting women through propagation of female methods of family planning, in the context of a target-oriented and incentive based system. The preponderance of female sterilizations as the dominant method of family planning in the country, it was argued, was because of the pressure brought on women by the officials in the health departments who were keen to fulfil their quotas of family planning. This was, they said, tantamount to an infringement on their fundamental rights.

Thus family planning programme landed itself in a quagmire where it could neither achieve its demographic goals of low fertility and population stabilization (through birth rate goals converted into family planning targets and pursuing these targets) nor withdraw from such a programme in the context of a continuing rise in the yearly additions to its population. In this context, in July 1993 the Government of India appointed an expert group under the chairmanship of noted agricultural scientist, Dr. M S Swaminathan for drafting a National Population Policy for consideration of the government and adoption by Parliament.

This committee, which submitted its report in 1994, recommended some basic directions of the shift in the goals of population stabilization programmes and structurally organised motivations at various levels for their effective implementation. The recommendations are yet to be accepted by the Government. Surprisingly, the goals on fertility, mortality and contraceptive use set during the eighth plan period (1992-97) on levels to be achieved by the end of the plan period have indeed been realised.

REPRODUCTIVE AND CHILD HEALTH APPROACH (RCH), 1995 ONWARDS

The Reproductive and Child Health (RCH) approach to family planning and population stabilization owes its origin to the deliberations and recommendations of the International Conference on Population and Development (ICPD), organized by the United Nations and held in Cairo in 1994. The Programme of Action formulated at the end of the conference and to which India is a signatory, postulated that population policies should be viewed as an integral part of programmes for women's development, women's rights, women's reproductive health, poverty alleviation and sustainable development. Women's concern dominated the discussions at the Cairo conference, which felt that population policies which are based on macro demographic considerations and acceptor-target-driven programmes are unnecessarily and unevenly burdening women with the task of regulating reproduction to suit macro level policies.

They argued that, henceforth, population policies should not be viewed with the sole concern of reductions in fertility rates considered desirable by planners and demographers, but by considerations of reproductive health, reproductive rights and gender equity. It was argued that developmental programmes which are not engendered are not only sustainable but also endangered. The Programme of Action adopted by the ICPD recommends a set of qualitative and quantitative development goals.

They are:

- Sustained economic growth in the context of sustainable development; education, especially for girls gender equity, equality and empowerment of women; infant, child and maternal mortality reduction; and the provision of universal access to reproductive health services, including family planning and sexual health.

The Government of India, which was a signatory to ICPD Programme of Action, promptly followed up on the recommendations by abolishing the acceptor based family planning targets since April 1995 in the country as a whole. It had already experimented with the 'target-free' approach in a few selected districts in the previous year, but the effectiveness of the approach was not properly assessed. Since 1997, officially, the Reproductive Health Approach has been adopted as the national policy of the Government of India. The official RCH programmes include the conventional maternal and child health services including immunization of children and contraceptive services to couples, treatment of reproductive tract infections (RTIS) and sexually transmitted diseases, provision of reproductive health education and services for adolescent boys and girls, screening of women near menopausal age for cervical and uterine cancer and treatment where required.

The budget required for these additional services intended to be covered under reproductive health are quite high, but almost the same amount allocated in the earlier years for the programme has been allocated. It is feared that the emphasis on contraceptive services will get diluted when budgets are not adequately increased to cover the wider goals of RCH programmes. Population concerns go beyond reproductive health, though the latter is an important contributing factor for population stabilization.

POLITICAL IMPLICATIONS OF SUSTAINED HIGH DIFFERENTIAL GROWTH OF POPULATION

The population of India as of mid-July 1998 has been estimated at 971 million. With a birth rate of 27.5 and death rate of 9 for 1996, it is growing at 1.85 per cent per year, adding 18 million per year. Among the larger states, the growth rates vary from a low of 1.15 per cent and 1.22 per cent in Tamil Nadu and Kerala to high of 2.43 per cent and 2.33 per cent in Uttar Pradesh and Rajasthan. These differentials in growth rates have been going on for the past two decades for indexed growth of the states from 1951 to 1991 with 1951 value as 100). Haryana has the highest index of 339 and Tamil Nadu the lowest at 202. The states have been growing at different rates. The political and socioeconomic implications of the persistence of such high growth rates in some of the states is mind-boggling and the apathy of the leadership to this fundamental problem is appalling. The widening demographic diversity of India's population, especially between the southern and the. northern states, are yet to be fully realized.

At the political level, with the universal adult franchise guaranteed to every citizen above 18 years of age, the states that have a higher rate of population growth will have proportionately a larger number of representatives in Parliament, and hence a better political leverage compared to the states which have a slower rate of growth of population. Indian leaders were aware of this problem and seem to have resolved it very wisely, by a

Constitutional Amendment and an Act of Parliament in 1977, by which the number of representatives to Parliament from each state was frozen at the 1971 census level, and such a freeze will be in vogue until 2000. The constitution 42nd Amendment Act 1976, section 15, has specifically been made to ensure that those states that do well in family planning programmes and control their growth rates are not penalized by reduction in their representation to Parliament. As the law stands at present, from the year 2001, the figures of 2001 census can become the basis for reallocation of number of seats to Parliament from each of the states. If this is done U.P. is expected to gain 8 seats, from 85 to 93; Rajasthan 4 seats, from 25 to 29; Madhya Pradesh 3 seats, form 40 to 43; and Haryana 1 seat, from 10 to 11.

On the other hand, the states that have been relatively successful in family planning programmes will have less representatives in Parliament than they have now. Tamil Nadu will lose 6 seats, from 39 to 33; Kerala 4 seats, from 21 to 17; Andhra Pradesh 1 seat, from 42 to 41; and Manipur one seat, from 2 to 1. By the year 2016, the states of Uttar Pradesh, Rajasthan, Madhya Pradesh and Bihar will gain by 14, 5, 4 and 2 seats respectively and the states of Tamil Nadu, Kerala, Andhra Pradesh and Karnataka will lose 8, 4, 3 and 1 seats respectively, compared to the 1991 levels.

In the current context of a still widening growth differentials among the states as revealed by the 1991 census and the recent projections by the Technical Group of the Planning Commission, there is an urgent need for the continuation of the 1977 freeze on the representation to Parliament from different states for at least another 20 years i.e. upto 2018 or until the growth differentials narrow down whereby replacement levels of fertility is realized in every large state. This is a necessary political expediency not only to encourage accelerated demographic transition in the large Hindi speaking states but also to preserve the national integrity and not penalize the states that have successfully implemented the national population policy and achieved lower levels of population growth rates as stipulated in the various developmental plans.

WIDENING INTERSTATE DISPARITIES IN HUMAN DEVELOPMENT

The Human Development Report (HDR) published by the UNDP in 1996 states that "Human Development is the end, economic growth a means". The HDRs of 1996 and earlier years have consistently define the basic objectives of development as enlarging the choices of people primarily by providing them with education, health and employment opportunities.

According to UNDP reports, human development has three essential qualitative components:

- Equality of opportunity for all people in society;
- Sustainability of such opportunities from one generation to the next; and

- Empowerment of people so that they participate in and benefit from development process.

As a first step in capturing the combined effects of the above three components, UNDP has developed and advocated a number of indices, the primary one being the Human Development Index (HDI). This index attempts to measure a country's or an area's achievements in the enhancement of human capabilities. The HDI has undergone some modifications in its computation from year to year since 1990, when it was first introduced, but it includes three indicators: life expectancy at birth to measure, the health status and longevity of people; educational attainment to represent the levels of knowledge and skills; and an appropriately adjusted real GDP per capita (in purchasing power parity-PPP-dollars) to serve as surrogate for command over resources. The HDR categorically identifies the above three parameters as essential, though not exhaustive, for choices at all levels of development. Many other opportunities remain inaccessible in their absence. The Human Development Index (HDI) was computed by the Population Foundation of India for all the large states of the country for which data are available circa 1995 and are diagramatically presented in.

It is a composite index ranging from 0 to 100, giving equal weightage to three component indices computed from the recent data on:

- The expectation of life at birth (eo) during 1991-95;
- The educational attainment of the population based on a combined measure of the projected adult literacy levels and the enrolment ratio in middle school in 1995; and
- The purchasing power-parity-price adjusted per capita net state domestic product for 1995 measured in dollar terms.

The procedures for the computation of HDI from these component values are identical to the procedures used in the UNDP report of 1996, excepting for school enrolment ratio. While the UNDP used the enrolment ratio for primary, secondary and tertiary levels, in this analysis we used the enrolment ratio only for the middle school level for which the data were considered to be the most reliable.

The HDI for India as a whole by this modification turned out to be 45 on a 0 to 100 scale, and close to the level of 44 given in the 1996 UNDP Report. India, with an HDI value of 45 ranks quite low in the comity of nations, with a rank of 135 among 174 countries studied by the UNDP. There is a good deal of variation in the HDI values across the states. Kerala with an HDI value of 63 ranks highest among the Indian states. In the international scene, its HDI score would place it at 105 in rank and above China and Egypt (with an HDI of 61). The lowest HDI values were observed in Bihar with a value of 34 and Uttar Pradesh at 36 and these values are comparable to the HDI value of Nepal (33) given in the 1996 HDR. These states will be ranked 150 and 151 at the international level. The states with HDI score of 50 and above are Haryana,

Himachal Pradesh, Kerala, Maharashtra, Punjab and Tamil Nadu. The states having scores below 40 are the large Hindi speaking states of the north: Bihar, Madhya Pradesh, Rajasthan and Uttar Pradesh.

As already mentioned, HDI is an equally weighted index of three components: index of life expectancy, index of educational attainment and index of parity adjusted per capita income. In these three components, the range of variation (in a score of 0 to 100) is from a maximum of 80 in Kerala to a minimlum of 50 in Madhya Pradesh for life expectancy; from a maximum of 93 in Kerala to 36 in Bihar in terms of educational attainment and from a maximum of 34 in Punjab to a minimum of 8 in Bihar for parity price adjusted income.

Thus the variability is higher in terms of educational attainments than in the case life expectancy or per capital income. These data reinforce the need to achieve parity among the states in terms of educational attainment i.e., adult literacy and educational enrolments as the priority item in human development, ranking higher than health and income. The correlation coefficient of HDI with the contraceptive protection rate and total fertility rate in 1995, taking the state as the unit of analysis were +0.76 and -0.75 respectively, and statistically significant implying that efforts at human development will have a significant payoff in terms of increased contraceptive use and reductions in fertility.

AN OVERVIEW OF POPULATION POLICIES AND PROGRAMMES IMPLEMENTED

A critical study of the population policies and programmes adopted in India since 1951 reveals the following major deficiencies and possible corrective measures:

- The programme placed almost a total emphasis on sterilization as the major method of family planning and the quality of services offered has been extremely poor. There is an urgent need to expand the range of choice of contraceptives and the quality of services to the couples. Though there are wide interstate differentials in these two aspects, generally the conditions are poor in most of the states and in the context of a very high level of unmet need for family planning, expressed by the women themselves in many sample surveys even in those states where fertility is very high, attention to these two aspects alone will help bring down fertility levels rather quickly. There is no need for slogans like 'one is fun' to motivate couples to adopt small family norm any more. The need of the hour is the offer of 'choice and service'.
- Though the period of emergency witnessed unnecessary imposition of coercive methods of family planning and has been strongly criticised nationally and internationally, it also witnessed introduction and enactment of some far reaching legislations, such

as the Minimum Age at Marriage Act and the freezing of the seats in Parliament and state legislatures on the basis of 1971 census until the year 2000, making it politically unattractive for the states to have a higher rate of population growth. There is a need to extend this freeze till 2028 or till all the states reach the replacement level of fertility, whichever is earlier.

- Until the sixth five year plan (1980-85), demographic goals were set in terms of crude birth rats and the target was set in terms of number of sterilization operations to be carried out on the basis of population size. These are no longer valid criteria for programme implementation. Though the target-free approach has come into vogue officially by orders from the center since April 1995, many states are continuing in their old groove of targets and sterilization, and state specific actions on this front are urgently called for. Because of the rigidity in the organizational pattern for maternal, child health and family planning programmes throughout the country and the strong insistence of the government at all levels (center, state and the district) on achieving the targets on sterilization, the delivery of maternal and child health services have suffered over the years. This has to be corrected.
- The offer of incentives to acceptors, motivators, medical and paramedical personnel involved with the sterilization programme gave a commercial touch to the whole programme and in the hands of unscrupulous administrators many 'ineligible cases' were sterilized to gain monetary benefits at the individual or state level. On many occasions, in order to get awards from the central government as the best performing state in the family planning programme, the sterilization figures were manipulated. The quality of services at the time of sterilization and follow-up care for cases with complications left much to be desired. The programme lost much of its popularity among the people though the motivational and educational programmes on small family norms have been fairly successful. All incentives to acceptors should be in the form of high quality of services and range of choice and any incentive should be, if at all, to communities through developmental programmes.
- The performance of the different states in family planning, even under a common population policy, organisational and scheme of financial assistance varied widely over the past three decades. States such as Kerala, Tamil Nadu, and Maharashtra were most successful in their family planning programmes and reduction in the fertility level than states like Uttar Pradesh, Rajasthan, Bihar and Madhya Pradesh. The factors underlying the differential performance of the states are the bureaucratic efficiency of the states; the political

commitment to the programme at the state level and the progress of the states in selected areas of socio-economic development. Development in the education of females have been found to increase the desire for small family norm and demand for family planning methods.

- The programme implicitly assumed that all married women in the reproductive ages are equal partners or contributors to the fertility of the population. No attempt was made to identify relatively more fecund couples and target the programme to them. Birth-based approach to family planning is likely to be more effective.
- Many authors have noted in their critical study of the population policy in India that the processes of decentralization of political power and decision-making through the Panchayati Raj system (wherein locally elected leaders at the level of a village or a group of villages are to be given authority to raise taxes, plan and implement local development programmes with assistance from higher levels) will eventually contribute to better quality of services. including health and family planning services. The experiences in this regard are yet to be gained.
- Demographically, the impact of the programme on fertility has been towards reduction in the fertility rates among women above the age of 30, because of the emphasis on sterilization as the major method of family planning. The programme was nibbling, as it were, on the tail end of the fertility curve. The natural fertility or fertility of women in the absence of contraception has been increasing during the past three decades among women below the age of 30 because of the forces of modernisation. We have thus a peculiar situation wherein the fertility rate of married women in the age group 20 to 29 has been increasing for the past three decades in a number of states, though significant declines in fertility have been observed only among women above the age of 30. The combination of these two factors have contributed to very slow decline in Total Fertility Rates (TFR) in some states, even in the context of a rise in contraceptive use. With increasing emphasis on spacing method and quality of care, we can hope to witness a more accelerated decline in fertility in the coming years.
- The recent paradigm shift of the family planning programme as a part of the enlarged Reproductive Health and Child Services package is a welcome step in the right direction. This will enable the programme to care of women's health, especially their reproductive health, meet their unmet needs for family planning in terms of spacing of children and limitation of family size, treatment of reproductive tract infections and sexually transmitted diseases and

improve the quality of maternal and child health services. However, implementation of a larger package of services requires additional funds and commitment from the government. India barely spends eight percent of its GDP on essential health and education services, and the expenditure on family welfare is merely one percent of its GDP. India spends far less on its educational and health programmes than many other developing countries. Unless statements of intent on reproductive health are backed by higher financial commitments from the government to the social sectors, the great expectations can hardly be translated into tangible achievements.

4

HIV/AIDS and Vulnerable Population Problems

HIV/AIDS AND WOMEN

IMPORTANCE

There are certain groups, which are vulnerable to HIV/ AIDS. Women are one such group. AIDS was first detected in the USA, in 1981 among male homosexuals. Initially there were more men being infected with AIDS virus than women, in the ratio of 10:1, but now the number of women infected with HIV is increasing. In 2003, 50% of all HIV infection were among women. By and large, HIV disease among women in the developing world has been acquired heterosexually (i.e. from man to woman).

This is due to the following facts:

- HIV infection is transmitted more effectively during sexual contact from men to women;
- Lack of education and illiteracy among women;
- Cultural beliefs regarding the role of women in the family and society; and
- Lack of economic power among women.

All the above factors influence the relative vulnerability of women and their access to means of prevention and support in the face of AIDS. Women who are infected with HIV infection can also transmit the HIV infection to others. For health care workers dealing with HIV positive women, it is important to understand the psycho-social and cultural issues as they have important implications for women and related issues such as child-bearing and breast-feeding.

STATISTICS

The UNAIDS and WHO periodically publish statistics pertaining to the spread of HIV/AIDS. According to the latest information, in the world, there are close to 38 million people living with HIV/AIDS by the beginning of 2005.

Of these 17 million [15.8-18.8 million] are women. There is nearly three-fold increase in HIV disease among women from 1985 to 1995. The median age of women with AIDS is 35 years, but in India it is much younger. The greatest rate of rise has been in Africa and in the Afro-American women in the USA. In these countries the rates are almost equal to that of men. In the year 1998, 2.1 million women were newly infected with HIV disease. 9,00,000 women died from AIDS in 1998. 4.7 million women have died from AIDS since the beginning of the epidemic. Women now present 43 percent of all over 15 years living with HIV and AIDS. There are no indications that is equalizing trend will reverse.

Table
Regional HIV/AIDS Statistics, features for women, 2003 and 2005

Religion		Number of women (15-49) living with HIV/AIDS	Age of HIV Positive adults who are women
Sub-Saharan Africa	2005	13.5 million [12.5-15.1million]	57
	2003	13.5 million [12.1-14.61 million]	57
North America	2005	220 000 [83 000-660 000]	47
& Middle East	2003	230 000 [78 000-700 000]	50
South & South	2005	1.9 million [1.1-2.8 million]	26
east Asia	2003	1.6 million [950 000-190 000]	25
East Asia &	2005	160 000 [82 000-260 000]	18
Pacific	2003	120 000 [59 000-190 000]	17
Oceania	2005	39 000 [20 000-62 000]	55
	2003	27 000 [14 000-43 000]	44
Latin America	2005	580 00 [420 00-770 000]	32
	2003	510 00 [370 00-680 000]	32
Caribbean	2005	140 000 [88 000-250 000]	50
	2003	140 000 [87 000-250 000]	50
Eastern Europe	2005	440 000 [300 000-620 000]	28
& Central Asia	2003	310 000 [210 000-430 000]	26
Western and	2005	190 000 [140 000-240 000]	27
Central Europe	2003	180 000 [150 000-220 000]	27
North America	2005	300 000 [150 000-440 000]	25
	2003	270 000 [130 000-400 000]	25
Total	2005	17.5 million [16.2-19.3 million]	46
	2003	16.5 million [15.2-18.2 million]	47

In India, the exact number of women who are infected with HIV is not known but is estimated to be around 1 million. The male to female ratio is approximately 4:1 in India (i.e. 21.06 per cent of all HIV infected cases are in women).

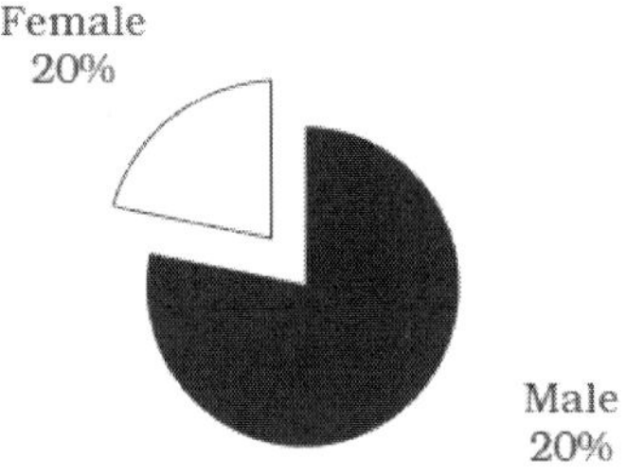

Fig. Sex-wise Distribution of AIDS Cases

SOCIO-CULTURAL FACTORS

The link between powerlessness and the risk of exposure to HIV provides the key to understanding the source of women's vulnerability to HIV infections. The social, economic and cultural subordination of women creates a context in which the women succumb silently to scourge. Following are some of the factors that make an Indian woman not only more prone to HIV infection but also less likely to seek medical attention.

Early Sexual Intercourse

Culturally, initiation to sexual intercourse begins several years earlier for females than for males. Many women are still in their mid-teens when they marry. Often women get married to much older men, who are sexually more experienced. Therefore chances for women to get HIV infected from a husband who might be indulging in sexual activities outside marriage are higher.

Source of Infection

In the developing countries nearly all HIV infection reported among women has been acquired heterosexually. Majority of the Indian women have been infected not through their own behaviour but through that of their husband. An Indian woman's greatest risk/ promiscuous of HIV infection is from her husband.

Lack of Choice

In marriage, women lack control over their lives or over that of their husband's life outside the marriage. Extramarital relationships, intravenous drug abuse, and bisexual behaviour on the part of the husband are possible routes for entry of the virus into the marital union. For these women, sexual intercourse is not a question of choice, but rather a question of survival. The wife has hardly any say in matters such as when to have sexual intercourse, or how to protect herself from HIV infection. She also does not enjoy the freedom to choose whether to become a mother or to protect the life of an unborn child from forced abortion.

Poor Access to Health, Education and Care

Women are looked upon as child bearers and child rearers. In the sociological division of labour, they have greater responsibilities towards the children and home. There is limited access to information, education and mobility. Also, more often than not, there is shortage of financial resources to pay for the use of health care facilities.

Blame

It is an unfortunate reality that when the first case of HIV/AIpS is identified within a family, the blame is most often placed upon the woman, even if the evidence contradicts this. There is fear that her family because of her perceived past behaviour will abandon her. She is forced to keep quiet and she is not in a position to argue her case.

Isolation and Stigma

HIV positive women feel extremely lonely and isolated. Fear of social stigma compels them to keep their seropositive status a secret. They are afraid of being abandoned by family, friends and the community.

Delay in Diagnosis

Indian women are often unaware of their HIV positive status or they may be the last one in their family to know their diagnosis, due to the power hierarchy in the family structure. Some women discover that they are HIV positive by accident, usually after the husband or the child is found to be symptomatic with an HIV related disease. The women will then be dealing with two crises, that of illness of her husband or child, or both, as well as her own illness.

Emotional Response

Suddenly, upon discovering the HIV positive status of spouse the woman has to deal emotionally with her husband's unfaithfulness. She may feel anger towards her husband, grief at the loss of health and status, and guilt relating to how she may have been the cause of illness in her own family, particularly for her children. She may also be filled with anxiety and worry. Undoubtedly, the situation is stressful and one in which there is lot of uncertainly about the future.

Dependency

In India, most women are dependent on their husbands or his family for food, clothing, shelter and money. It is the male partner who usually controls the financial matters at home. As a result of this, abstinence, faithfulness on man's part and using condoms for protection, which has now become the mainstay of prevention of HIV infection which is totally under the man's control.

Burden and Bereavement

From the time of her birth, the Indian female child is considered a burden, initially for her parents, and later on for her husband's family. The main aim of her biological family is to quickly marry her off. She is usually given minimum education and care before marriage. After marriage, in case of the husband's death his property and savings (if any), remain with the husband's family and in many cases, the wife goes back to her own family where she continues to be a financial and emotional burden. Many such women are also forced into prostitution for a living. In fact, most women living on prostitution have a poor background: like desertion by husband, rape, migration to cities in search of job, forced flesh trade through kidnapping or sale etc.

Pregnancy

Women are considered to be the potential bearer of sons. Many Indians believe that sons are the ones who will grow up and earn and look after the old parents while daughters are a burden who will have been given away in the marriage. Even if a woman is HIV positive, she may be under pressure to produce a son, at risk to her own life, as well as that of her unborn child.

HIV/AIDS IN WOMEN

Reasons for Transmission

The reasons for transmission of HIV disease to women are:

Sexual Promiscuity

Worldwide the cause of transmission of HIV to women is the prevalence of heterosexual promiscuity. Research indicates that the male to female transmission of HIV-1 is relatively more efficient than female to male transmission.

Sexually Transmitted Diseases

Sexually transmitted diseases, particularly those associated with genital ulcers, lead to an increased risk of HIV infection. Non-ulcerative STDs (Gonorrhea, Chlamydia, Trichomonias, and Bacterial Vaginosis) also have been associated with increased risk of HIV transmission.

Drug Abuse

In western countries at the beginning of the AIDS epidemic, drug use was one of the major factors in women acquiring HIV. Drug use in women is associated with sharing of unsterilized needles for injecting drugs and high-risk sex behaviours with multiple partners.

Communication with Spouse

The inability of the woman to compel her male sexual partner about using barrier contraception such as condoms etc., places her at risk of acquiring HIV infection and other sexually transmitted diseases. While research is still on, some studies are there on the role of oral contraception or Intra-uterine contraceptive/or IUCD devices (such as loops, copper-T etc.) in increasing the risk of HIV infection. Oral contraception may thin the vaginal epithelium, making it easier for HIV transmission and IUCD may injure the mucosa and help to transmit the virus easily.

Viral Factors

Viral load and viral characteristics play role in the risk of sexual transmission of HIV. Higher the viral load in the semen and vaginal secretions, greater the risk of transmission. Also certain sub-types of HIV virus may be associated with certain types of transmission, but again this has not been conclusively proved.

Signs and Symptoms

There are no differences in the manifestation of HIV infection among men or women. As in the male, the female also, once she has become infected with the AIDS virus, may not have any signs or symptoms at all. In a significant percentage of people, at the time of seroconversation (when the antibodies are formed) there may be flu like illness with fever, body pains, rash, headache etc. This may last for few days to weeks and then disappear. The HIV infected person may then not have any more signs and symptoms. She may continue to do her routine work of cooking and caring for children with a sexual relationship with her husband. Her blood test may be done only when her husband or her child become sick. Later on, as her CD4 count begins to fall, she becomes prone to other infections called opportunistic infections.

Opportunistic Infections

Fungal infection of the throat and oesophagus (the hollow tube that connects the mouth to the stomach) is a common opportunistic infection in women. Recurrent bacterial pneumonia and lung infections are common in women. Other infections commonly seen in HIV infected women include recurrent muco-cutaneous infections, herpes simplex infections, muco-cutaneous candidiasis, Toxoplasmosis, Tuberculosis and Cryptococcol infections.

Gynaecological Infections

Infections of the reproductive tract are referred to as gynaecological infections. Gynaecological diseases in HIV infected and non-HIV infected women are the same. Certain diseases are more common in the HIV infected women. Extensive herpes simplex ulceration may be seen in HIV infected women and it may be resistant to standard treatment. Vaginal infections such as Candidiasis, Trichoniasis, and bacterial vaginosis may be more common. Apart from the usual causes of genital ulcers like syphilis and chancaroid HIV infection can also cause genital ulcers. Pelvic inflammatory diseases are common and more aggressive in HIV infected women. Immuno-suppression has been associated with consequences of Human papillomma virus (HPV) infection includingcervical cancers. HIV associated cancers and pre-cancerous conditions in women.

It is noted that HIV positive women have higher risk of acquiring cancer of the cervix. Due to the loss of cellmediated immunity in HIV infected women, they tend to develop HPV or. Human Papillomma Virus infections, which are associated with pre-cancerous lesions. The common occurrence of HPV infection, often of multiple types, the rapid progression of Cervical Intraepithelial Neoplasia and the high rate of re-occurrence in spite of therapy and the multiple lesions, makes this an important area of concern in HIV prevention.

Treatment

In HIV disease, one has to consider two regimes of treatment:

- Specific treatment for HIV infection
- Treatment for opportunistic diseases.

Drugs that are given for specific HIV disease are called anti-retroviral drugs and several drugs are available. These drugs may be given in double or triple drug combination. These drugs are very-expensive and beyond the reach of the common man. For opportunistic diseases, there is a specific treatment depending on the disease, such as Tuberculosis, Candidiasis, Toxoplasmosis, Cryptococcus and Cytomegalovirus infections, etc.

HIV/AIDS progression and overall survival of infectfd women in comparison to men In the late eighties reports suggested a less favourable outcome for HIV infected women in comparison to men, but more recent studies have not confirmed this finding. Majority of research data suggests no difference between women and men in HIV disease progression or survival.

HIV/AIDS AND PREGNANCY

HIV/AIDS has now spread from the high-risk behaviour group to the general population. This is corroborated by the fact that a significant percentage of pregnant women who are tested for HIV in the antenatal clinics are positive and this percentage is now increasing. There are several issues to be considered in the case of HIV positive mother and pregnancy and these issues are briefly enumerated below. HIV infection does not erase women's desire and hopes for sexual bonding, intimacy and child bearing. In India, a pregnant woman is considered to be the potential bearer of a son. Her social status improves after the birth of a son. This culturally prevalent attitude should be kept in mind when counselling the HIV positive women of childbearing age.

The pregnant HIV positive mother's chance of producing an HIV positive child is 25-30 per cent. This transmission from mother to child can occur during pregnancy itself, or at the time of childbirth or during breast-feeding. The stage of HIV infection in the pregnant mother is also important. If it is in early stages of HIV infection, pregnancy has little (if any) effect on HIV infection. However in later stages of infection, especially if the mother has AIDS, the pregnancy can be more complicated. It is very important to help HIV positive women and their husbands assess the risks of giving birth to an infected child. They should consider the possibility of having an infected child, or if the child is uninfected, who will care for the child in the event of their own illness or death.

Counselling should help the women develop a plan of how she will care for her child, how her family and community will help her, and how she expects to support and care for her child if she becomes sick and dies. Whenever decisions about avoiding or terminating a pregnancy or about preparing for a possibly infected infant need to be made, they should involve both the parents. Such couples should also discuss the matter with their religious leaders or spiritual guides. The mother and her family will require psychological support during the pregnancy. She should be advised upon having regular medical check ups, use of medications and consider delivery in a hospital.

Effect of HIV on Pregnancy

Data from developing countries show that HIV infection among pregnant women is associated with increased rates of pre-term delivery, low birth weight and still birth. This has not been seen in developed countries.

Risk Factors Associated with Transmission

The risk factors associated with HIV transmission from mother to child may be sub-divided as follows:

- Virologic factors
- Maternal factors
- Placental factors
- Foetal factors
- Birth canal factors
- Obstetric factors
- Newborn factors
- Viral Factors

High viral load in pregnant mother could lead to high risk of transmission of the HIV to the child.

Maternal Factors

Sexual intercourse with multiple partners during pregnancy could lead to increased risk of transmission, Low CD4 counts in mother could lead to high risk of transmission to child as also the stage of the syndrome in the mother determines the risk of HIV transmission to child.

Prevention Strategies

Less frequent intercourse, sexual relationship with one partner and use of barrier contraception are important for prevention of HIV transmission.

Vitamin A supplementation to mother and anti-retro viral drug therapy to reduce the rival load in women.

Placental Factors

HIV can be isolated from the placenta. Any placental disruption could lead to higher risk of transmission and this can also happen with chorrioamionitis, cigarettesmoking or illicit drug use and sexually transmitted diseases in the mother.

Factors during delivery

Factors responsible for HIV transmission during delivery include amount of virus in the genital tract;.the infant's thin skin and mucus surface which can absorb the virus during the birth process; breaking of waters; any bleeding during labour; and prolonged labour after rupture.

Prevention Strategies

- Antiretroviral therapy to prevent infection of the placenta.
- Treatment of STDs, chorioamnionitis.
- Stop cigarette smoking and illicit drug use.

Foetal Factors

There are differences in the susceptibility of the foetal cells to infection by virus and this may be related to genetic factors. Swallowing of infected maternal fluids during the delivery and labour by the foetus may lead to increase the chance of infection.

Prevention Strategies

Adequate treatment of genital infections during pregnancy. Elective Caesarian section can reduce the risk of infection. Veridical cleaning of birth canal before vaginal delivery may also reduce transmission.Preventive therapeutic intervention. As mentioned previously the chance of the pregnant HIV positive mother producing an HIV infected baby is 25 to 30 per cent. By giving the mother an antiretroviral drug during the pregnancy the chance of transmission can be reduced by 70 per cent to about 80 per cent.

The drug most commonly used is called AZT or Azidothymidine or Zidoivudine. Sometimes two or three drug combinations can also be given. The baby should also receive AZT for six weeks after birth. Recently another drug is also found to be useful in reducing the transmission of HIV from mother to child. This drug is called Nevirapine. It can be given as a single dose to the mother at onset of labour, and to the newborn child as a single dose seventy-two hours after birth. Any treatment should be under the authentic prescription of a qualified physician. One should never opt for any type of self-medication.

HIV/AIDS AND BREAST-FEEDING

Transmission of HIV infection from a mother to her child can occur during breast-feeding also. However, fortunately a vast number of babies breast-fed by HIV positive mothers do not become infected through breast milk. Chances of transmission during breast-feeding are higher, if the woman becomes infected during the breastfeeding period and lower, among women already infected at the time of delivery.

Breast-feeding is extremely crucial for child survival in our country and especially among people of the poorer socio-economic status. Breast milk provides all the essential factors that makes a baby healthy and protects it from other infections. Without breast milk many infants can die from other infections or from malnutrition. A baby's risk of dying of AIDS through breastfeeding must be balanced against its risk of dying of other causes if not breast-fed.

The general recommendation is that in countries where the infant mortality rate is high, breast-feeding should be encouraged among pregnant women, including those who are HIV-infected. This is because the baby's risk of getting HIV infection through breast milk is likely to be lower than its risk of death from other causes, if the child is not breast-fed. Women, who know they are HIVinfected and for whom bottle-feeding is an affordable option, can resort to bottle-feeding rather than breastfeeding.

Sex Workers

In India, as in other countries, commercial sex workers (CSWs) are often singled out for special attention m the context of AIDS due to the multiplicity of their sexual contacts and high STD rates. Focusing on prostitution and its relationship to HIV infection has the detrimental effect of implying that women are responsible for the spread of HIV. They are viewed as transmitters for the HIV rather than as recipients.

Nevertheless, prostitution is on the list of behaviours, which can lead to HIV infection, because of the number of and the type of sexual contacts as well as the risk behaviours of the partners. Studies indicate that CSWs in India avoid using existing health structures because of the harsh and inhuman treatment they receive at the hands of the medical staff. They are also unaware of family planning services and how to protect themselves from STDs and HIV infection.

They may seek treatment from quacks to remain anonymous and to avoid facing ridicule from medical staff. From the public health point view it is very difficult to discover, educate and counsel the large number of women who are at risk of acquiring infection through heterosexual intercourse. It becomes the goal of HIV prevention programmes to educate all women about the risk of acquiring HIV/AIDS, and to encourage adoption of risk reducing sexual behaviours.

Another form of prostitution, which is practiced in parts of Maharashtra and Karnataka, is the Devadasi system, where young girls of poor family after attaining puberty are dedicated to Hindu goddess through a religious ritual, and later on channelised into prostitution. As this form of prostitution is linked to religion, it is very difficult to abolish. The reasons why women go into prostitution may be many. Some are forced into it because they are destitute or uneducated and have no other means of livelihood. Some others maybe even forced by their husbands or sexual partners, while, several are drug dependent and need money to meet their habit. Rarely they do it, because they want to.

Risk Reduction

Prostitution is found in all states of India. Many studies have revealed that a significant number of CSWs are HIV positive. Since the advent of AIDS it is important to empower these women to protect themselves from HIV infection by risk reducing behaviour. Whenever possible, CSWs have to be rehabilitated. CSWs must be provided with knowledge about STDs, and HIV and the means to protect themselves. CSW must be taught negotiating skills, so that they can negotiate with their clients for using condoms. CSWs must be provided with regular medical checkup so that STD can be promptly treated. As part of their rehabilitation, CSWs must be encouraged to undergo vocational trainings. Many women are at the mercy of middlemen or pimps who are the link between the CSWs and their clients. Often, there are powerful men at the helm of affairs and it may be very difficult for the women to leave their jobs even if they want to.

Many HIV/AIDS prevention programmes have been started by governmental and non-governmental organisations which target the CSWs. The Sonagachi project in West Bengal is cited as example of how CSWs can be empowered and educated to work towards HIV prevention.

Drug Addiction, HIV Disease and Women

There is an epidemiological relationship between drug abuse and HIV infection. Consumption of drugs and alcohol reduces the inhibitions of people and increases the chances of risk behaviours. In the Western countries intravenous drug usage is a major problem. In those countries a significant proportion of HIV infected women are IVDU. Thus, ensuring inclusion of HIV infected drug users and understanding drug use related issues become the key challenges to obtaining a comprehensive understanding of women affected by this epidemic.

Rape, Incest, Lesbianism, Teenage Pregnancies and Abortions When a male has sexual intercourse with a woman against her wish it constitutes rape. Incest is when there is sexual relationship between members of the family (father and daughter, mother and son etc.) Lesbianism means, women who have sex with woman. Homosexuality refers to sex relations between person of same sex, especially men. Teenage pregnancies occur among girls in their teens. An understanding of these specific issues become important in the context of HIV/ AIDS because these groups run the risk of acquiring HIV/ AIDS in addition to all the other social, physical and emotional problems that they are subjected to.

Another problem that exists in India is that of illegal abortions. These are still being practiced in the case of unwed mothers and those women who are unaware or embarrassed to seek proper medical facilities. It is possible that HIV positive expectant mothers may avail of these facilities to abort the foetus, but hide their own HIV status and therefore other complications may set in, as these centres do not take infection control into consideration. The counsellor must help and encourage women to avail of legal medical facilities.

Reproductive Health

It is important for women to know that their reproductive tract should be healthy and that very often women may have genital infections without even knowing that they have them. This in addition to all other factors previously mentioned, places them at increased risk of acquiring HIV infection.

WHY ARE WOMEN AT RISK

Women are at risk of acquiring sexually transmitted infections and HIV infection because their reproductive organs are structured in such a way. Also almost 60 per cent of all sexually transmitted infections have no symptoms. Therefore even if a woman has one, she would not know it. Women at the time of child birth may have several problems such as prolonged labour, caesarian section or forceps delivery. As a result of these procedures, injury to the genital tract, blood loss, risk of infection are common. Therefore it is important for women to take care of their reproductive health and have regular medical checks ups whether they have symptoms or not.

How are STDs Transmitted

Through sexual contact with an infected person. From a mother who is infected to her baby during the time of delivery. From blood and blood products given to women.

What are the Symptoms of STD in Women

Many of the Women are Asymptomatic

They may have discharge from the vagina, which could be large in quantity, white or yellow in colour and foul smelling. Women may have itching or pain, while passing urine. Ulcers or blisters may be seen on vagina/ vulva with or without pain. If these infections are not treated on time then women may not be able to conceive and have children. The infection can spread from the vagina to surrounding areas and the uterus. She is also easily prone to acquiring HIV infection from an infected partner and the infection can spread from her to her newborn child during her delivery.

The best way to prevent transmission of these sexually transmitted diseases is "safe sex" which means - abstinence (not having sexual relationship to all), fidelity or mutual faithfulness between partners. Also, proper condom usage can reduce the risk of HIV infection to some extent especially among CSWs and their clients. It needs to be highlighted that all programmes of women welfare now have reproductive health as a major component. Access to health care linked with women empowerment are the basic steps of successful HIV prevention programmes.

Empowerment of Women

In the Indian situation, a woman is usually completely dependent on her husband for food and shelter. The male partner controls the sexual interaction. The woman is at risk if her male partner has sexual relationship outside marriage. She does not have the capacity or the authority to demand that she has a right to protect herself from HIV/ AIDS and STIs, and therefore request her husband to be faithful or to use condom when indulging in sex outside marriage. Hence in a majority of cases the women become infected not through her behaviour but through that of her husband's, and once she is infected, she is at much greater risk of facing all the medical and social complications of HIV/AIDS.

She is the one who is then blamed, stigmatized and discriminated against. The issue of women is clearly a survival issue. In order to survive, women will need to know that they have a choice, a choice to say no to high-risk behaviours, a choice to protect themselves from infection, a choice to take care of their health if they don't want to get infected, a choice to make decisions regarding pregnancy, and a choice to have a significant role in the marital union lives. This act, to make women aware of their choices to strengthen them in all areas of their lives is referred to as empowerment of women.

Empowerment of women is one of the key issues in keeping women safe and healthy. In western countries, there is woman's advocacy and right groups, which empower women. Many of these groups are headed and run by HIV positive women themselves. The 1970's saw the rise of a wave of NGOs known as social action groups within which women's organisations from a distinctive band. They have taken the lead in the campaigns against sexual abuse, the dowry system and violence against women. They also provide health services for women, vocational training and income generating schemes.

Sonagachi Project

This is a unique project and was started in 1992 in the Sonagachi area of Kolkota, West Bengal, where around 5000 commercial sex workers reside in nearly 370 brothels, apart from 1500 street based sex workers.

The project has the following objectives:

- To enable modifications of sexual behaviour of sex workers and their clients so as to make their activities safe.
- To enable sustained sexual behaviour change.
- To develop an effective strategy and guidelines for an intervention programme, so that this can be replicated in other areas.

The basic approach of the project was based on service, respect and recognition.

Major Components of the Programme

Provision of Health Services

Basic health care services including diagnosis and treatment of STDs were started and these are continuing through established clinics. 30-40 per cent of those CSWs who attended the clinics were suffering from STDs. *Information, Education & Communication (IEC)* This programme was good example of empowerment. Sixty-five educators were selected from among the sexworkers themselves, and these highly motivated peer educators were trained for six weeks. They educated the CSWs by personal discussions, small group meetings, giving out informative handouts and flip charts.

Condom Programming

Condom promotion and distribution are important activities of the project. Others:

- Non-formal education
- Immunization programmes for children of the sexworkers
- Exposure to various social activities
- Formation of the multi-purpose cooperative society to encourage self-employment and impart vocational training.

Legal Training

Case Study

Rajini sat at outside her thatched house and buried her head in her hands and cried in loud, heart wrenching sobs. She cried for her life, which was now in ruins, she cried for her unborn child, she cried for the uncertain future that she now faced. Rajini was only 19 years old. She was the fifth of nine children. She had a sad childhood, living with her parents, her paternal grandparents and her eight brothers and sisters. Her parents earned their livelihood by breaking stones in quarries. She stopped attending school after the fourth standard, as she had to stay at home and look after the younger four boys and cook for them. When she was sixteen years old, she was married off to a 35-year-old man who had lost his wife 3 years ago.

Her married life was a living hell. Her husband was a truck driver and an alcoholic. When he was at home from his long journeys he would spend the days lying around in a drunken state and beating her up. He never gave her any money. She already had a girl child who was 2 years old. She realized that her husband was not a healthy man and he would frequently fall sick. She borrowed money from her family and from friends and went from hospital to hospital to cure his condition. Finally they were told that he had tuberculosis, but even with treatment he was not getting better. At one hospital, a doctor told them that he had AIDS. There was no cure, the doctor said. He would die anyway. They were asked to go away from the hospital.

She had taken one of her neighbours with her to the hospital. On hearing this neighbour ran away. On reaching her house with her husband, she found all neighbours staring at her and then turning away their faces. She spent a lot of her energy looking after him, caring for his needs, getting him the medicines etc. and finally three months later, he died. She was so tired. A week later, she went for a checkup for her pregnancy and the doctor told her that she too was infected with HIV. Her future was bleak. She got up and went into the house. She closed the door; she looked at the fire burning in the chullah (place in kitchen where food is prepared). She looked at the bottle of kerosene nearby. She found her way out of this miserable life by self-immolation.

HIV/AIDS AND CHILDREN

PROFILE OF THE CHILDREN SUFFERING FROM HIV/AIDS

It is estimated that about 4.5 million children below the age of 15 years have been infected with HIV since the beginning of AIDS epidemic to the end of 1998. On a global scale, children are becoming infected at about the rate of one child at every minute. Inl998, one in ten of all newly infected persons was a child and the majority of them acquired the virus from their infected mothers. Though Africa accounts for only 10 per cent of the world's population, it is home to 90 per cent of world's HIV- infected children, largely as a consequence of high fertility rates combined with very high levels of HIV infections among women. According to the UNAIDS report (2004) there were 2.1 million children living with HIV at the end of 2003. 6,30,000 new infections occurred and there were 4,30,000 deaths among children below the age of 15 years.

As far as India is concerned, an estimated 30,000 newly born babies are infected every year and the country has over 1,20,000 orphans who are infected with HIV. Most of HIV cases among children are reported from Maharashtra, Tamil Nadu and among intravenous drug users in the North-eastern State of Manipur. HIV affects children in many ways.

Some of the known sources or situations are given below:

- Mother to child transmission: This transmission could occur in the womb, during the time birth, and through breast-feeding.

- Children who may be sexually abused
- Children who are at risk of infection include street children, child prostitutes and devadasis. Institutionalized children like those who are kept at remand homes/juvenile homes and similar institutions, where child abuse takes place are also at risk of getting infected with HIV.
- Children with diseases like Hemophilia and Thalassemia are also at risk of getting infected with HIV.
- A child can also be infected due to cultural practices like circumcision, tattooing and genital mutilation.

MODES OF TRANSMISSION OF HIV AMONG CHILDREN

Let us try to discuss some of the routes of HIV transmission among children.

Mother-to-Child Transmission

Mother-to-child transmission is by far the largest source of HIV infection in children below the age of fifteen years. In countries where blood for transfusion and blood products are regularly screened and where clean syringes and needles are widely available in health centres and hospitals, mother to child transmission is virtually the only source of infection among young children. The extremely high rates of HIV infection among women of child bearing age in some parts of the world and increasing risk of infection among women everywhere is therefore a profound cause for worry.

A child whose mother is: HIV positive can be infected in three ways:

- In the womb before birth: HIV has been detected in very early foetus and in umbilical cord blood.
- A baby can also be infected during delivery by the mother's infected blood or vaginal secretions. This is because during the time of birth the child's skin is very soft and thin which paves the way for the virus to get into its body.
- The third means of transmission from the mother to child is from breast-feeding. Researchers now believe that the handful of documented cases where mothers did transmit HIV by breast-feeding was atypical. In each instance, the mother had received infected blood during blood transfusion immediately following birth and was therefore unusually infectious while she was breast-feeding because of high levels of virus ' in her blood. It is estimated that about 90 per cent pregnant rural women are anemic, requiring blood transfusions. Medical researchers estimate that the risk of transmission via breast milk is about 30 per cent for mothers who are post-natally infected. The risk is even higher for women who are infected, which is as much as 41 per cent.

It may be noted that human milk supplied to infants from milk banks operational in some of the hospitals in the country could also be a source for HIV infection, if the milk is not tested for HIV. Similarly infants should not be fed with breast milk of women whose HIV statusis unknown.

Prevention

There are various ways and means to prevent motherto- child transmission at various stages.

Some of these prevention methods are as follows:

- *The protection of girls and women from HIV infection*: HIV transmission can be minimized among women of childbearing age if they are provided adequate information on HIV/AIDS. This strategy is sometimes referred to as "primary prevention". It involves promoting abstinence before marriage, responsible sexual behaviour among couples, providing them with knowledge about HIV/AIDS and how to prevent infection and ensuring that they have the necessary personal skills and access to marital and sexual health counselling services so that they can act on their knowledge. It also means providing good quality, user-friendly prevention and treatment programmes for other sexually transmitted diseases (STDs), the presence of which increase the risk of HIV transmission to as much as from 6 to 10 fold. And, crucially, it means taking steps to deal with the cultural, legal and economic factors that make girls and women vulnerable to HIV infection by protecting them from such exposures.
- *The provision of safe/healthy and accessible family planning services*: Safe, healthy and accessible family planning services will enable women to avoid unwanted pregnancies. The aim is to ensure informed reproductive choice. If a woman is found to be HIV positive, counselling should enable her to give up the desire for conceiving which will further cause her health to deteriorate. Besides the chances of a child being born HIV positive is 25 to 30 per cent.
- *Provision of HIV counselling, testing and treatment*: An integrated package of measures consisting of voluntary HIV counselling and testing (VCT), the provision of antiretroviral drugs for HIVpositive pregnant women, counselling on infant feeding, and support for the feeding method(s) chosen by the mother can also minimize the chances of HIV transmission among children. This package is often referred to as the PPTC programme (Prevention of Parent To Child).
- *Caesarean section*: An HIV positive mother should opt for a caesarean section, which will reduce the chances of the child getting infected during delivery.

- *Breast-feeding*: The choice of breast-feeding or not breast-feeding should be made by the mother. The benefits as well as disadvantages must be conveyed to the mother and she should be allowed to make a choice. Her choice needs to be respected.

CHILDREN AT RISK OF INFECTION

Street Children

India has the dubious distinction of having the highest number of street children. Most of these children are found in the big cities of the country. They earn their living through rag picking, working in hotels, involvement in prostitution etc. This group is the most vulnerable because of the nature of work and resultant exposure. The most vulnerable are the girl street children. We will dwell at some length on the risks that they are exposed to. Puberty brings new stresses into young street girls' lives. These girls do not have mothers or female relatives to explain to them that menstrual periods are part of normal life, or help them cope with their anxieties. Most of them are sexually abused even before they are ten. The street girl may not also develop a positive attitude about menstruation or reproductive cycle. Their poor nutritional status can make their menstrual cycles irregular. They may not understand why months pass in between their periods and may incorrectly conclude that they are pregnant or sick.

Avoiding an unwanted pregnancy may be constant stress for an adolescent girl. This is especially true when viewed in the context of the high incidence of sexual abuse, rape and victimization suffered by the girls on the streets. They hardly have the emotional, physical and financial resources needed for a pregnancy or for motherhood. An unsafe abortion, often the only option for street girl, can cause severe health problems as well as emotional distress and in some cases death. Street girls needing abortion usually approach roadside "doctors" i.e. quacks. This further increases the risk to their reproductive health and also exposes them to other exploitative situations. The tenderness of the age of street girls does not appear to reduce their risk of sexual abuse. Very often girl children of all age groups are sexually abused or raped. In big cities, hooligans pressurize families to vacate the shanties they occupy and very often use rape as a weapon to terrorize them. Many of them land in brothels against their will. They have no marriage or family life. Under such circumstances, a girl child is exposed to risk factors causing HIV infection. Street girl children may also indulge in drug abuse. Most of them pick up the habit unknowingly.

Devadasies

The devadasi system is a practice in India since ancient times, when young girls of certain sections of society were trained as skilled courtesans and were initiated into the profession through a ritual in temple. This was propagated by the Hindu Goddess Yellamma. This practice is still prevalent in India, especially in the states of Karnataka and Maharashtra, particularly among some of the economically weaker sections of the society. Young girls are offered to the temple priests and others sexually exploit these girls before they have their first menstruation. Many of these girl children get infected with HIV and several of them also land up in brothels or the flesh market.

Children of Commercial Sex Workers

While other communities in India dread the birth of a girl child and celebrate the birth of a son, her mother, the brothel keeper, and pimps welcome the girl child of a prostitute as a potential source of income. The estimated six million children of prostitutes in the country have no other options than to follow the profession of their mothers. Given the present situation of HIV/ AIDS in the country, many of these children of prostitutes are likely to be HIV infected either from their infected mothers or through customers who engage them for sex at very tender ages.

Prevention

Some of the ways to prevent the spread of HIV among children at risk of infection are:

- Strict enforcement of available legislations to protect and safeguard children from exploitation.
- Rehabilitation of street children and children of commercial sex workers.
- Awareness programme and education for street children and child labourers.
- Sensitization of the general masses to enable them to see children as precious gift of God and not as commodities to be exploited and abused.
- Adopting measures

CHILDREN SUFFERING FROM THALASSEMIA, HEMOPHILIA AND DRUG ABUSE

Thalassemia

Thalassemia is a hereditary disease, widespread in the Mediterranean countries, Asia and Africa. In this disease there is an abnormality in the protein part of the hemoglobin molecule. The affected red cells cannot function normally leading to anemia. Other symptoms include enlargement of spleen and abnormalities of the bone marrow. The spleen is the scavenger of the body. It destroys the dead blood corpuscles but in case where spleen cannot get adequate blood, it also takes over the function of making it. This does great harm. The body does not get good quality blood and the spleen enlarges to be able to meet the demands of the new role. Hence it starts destroying more red blood cells. The exact number of thalassemic cases in the country is not known. Every year approximately 5000 thalassemic babies are born in India. Patients with this disease have to undergo repeated blood transfusions. Several patients are believed to have contracted the dreaded disease from infected blood transfusion. Twenty-one cases of HIV infection were reported from one of the hospitals in New Delhi in 1994. There are similar reports from hospitals situated across the country.

Hemophilia

Hemophilia is an inherited condition, which mainly affects men. The condition involves a reduced capacity for the blood to clot due to a deficiency of factor VIII. Consequently, an otherwise minor accident can in such patients be dangerous because the person continues to bleed. Most bleeding occurs internally. The patient suffering from hemophilia is prone to HIV infection because they also require transfusions of blood or use of blood products and these may be infected with HIV.

Intravenous Drug-Users

HIV is easily transmitted, when person share infected needles. Small volumes of contaminated blood remain inside previously used needles and syringes thereby providing opportunities to transmit virus via their infected contents. In India the entire Northeastern region and specifically the state of Manipur is threatened by the spread of HIV through intravenous drug abuse. Drug use is rampant among the millions of street children whom the Indian cities shelter.

Prevention

Some of the methods of prevention to reduce HIV transmission through blood and blood products are given below:

- Compulsory Testing of blood for HIV before blood transfusion.
- Testing of blood for HIV has been made mandatory in all developed nations and some of the developing countries. In these countries, every unit of blood is tested for HIV and the governments guarantee full safety of every unit of blood. But in India and many other developing nations, the testing facilities are not adequate. There is also a dearth of trained personnel in blood banks. Therefore one should make sure that every unit of blood is screened for HIV before transfusion through ELISA, western blot or PCR test depending upon the source and timegap between donation and transfusion.
- Professional blood donation should be avoided. In India a large number of professional blood donors have been found to be HIV

infected. Therefore, accepting blood from professional blood donors has to be discouraged. Instead, every institution and agency in the country should promote voluntary blood donation to meet the blood requirement in the country. Although the Supreme Court of India has banned professional blood donation, one should not take anything for granted. One should make sure that fresh needles are used each time to collect blood from a person through ELISA, western blot or PCR.

Compulsory Sterilization of Lab Instruments

Sterilization is defined as destruction of all the microbes, including bacterial spores. High level disinfection is defined as the destruction of all microbes. Therefore equipment used for procedures that draw blood e.g. dental and clinical equipment, or instruments piercing of the skin must be sterilized. Instruments, which involve piercing of the skin by needles as in the case of tattooing, piercing of the ear/nose, acupuncture etc. if not sterilized in a proper manner, present a degree of risk of transmission of the HIV virus. When outside the human body, the HIV virus has been known to be delicate and difficult to transmit. It is easily deactivated by heat (at 56°C). Chemicals such as bleach are effective sterilization agents. It is important to note that antiseptics such as 'dettoF are ineffective for sterilization.

PROGRAMME ELEMENTS FOR CHILDREN IN FAMILIES AFFECTED BY THE HIV EPIDEMIC

Many of the striking images of HIV epidemic are found in families: a grandparent surrounded by grandchildren; adolescent-headed families; siblings and cousins bonded together; dying adults being taken care of by their children and communities. It is important to focus on such families rather than, only on children, youth or adults. This allows for an interfamilial and longitudinal analysis of needs, skills and resources of families affected by HIV, which provides a different basis for determining and ranking the required responses. While specific programme components will vary according to the stage of disease progression, the situation, culture and resources of each country or community, five main some strategic programme elements, have been identified. These are not meant to be exhaustive nor are they operational in nature. The specific means of addressing each area may vary from one situation to another. Let us briefly examine each of these areas suggested by Elizabeth Reid (1993).

Components of this program element could include:

- Access to voluntary, confidential and affordable counselling and testing for adults and the motivation to use available services.
- Disclosure of a child's infection to both parents through counselling.
- Continued employment of the HIV infected people.
- Simple treatment of opportunistic infections.

- Passing on to children production-and-incomegenerating skills.
- Planning children's future care.
- Protection of children's inheritance and other legal rights. Prevention of infection while caring for the sick.

Assisting Children whose Parents have Died

Children whose parents have died of HIV-related illness have often also lived through the deaths of the others close to them; brothers and sisters, aunts and uncles, cousins, friends and, increasingly, grandparents. Their very will to live has often been undermined. If they are to grow and develop as human beings and as members of civil society, they need love and care and the opportunity to form and maintain emotional ties with adults. Their material and psychological needs will have to be met; their right to remain integral members of their communities and their legal rights may be at risk and need protection. Consideration can be given to the provision of services to all children within an area heavily affected by the epidemic rather than only to those whose parents have died of AIDS. The latter approach may lead to resentment and stigmatization of children who receive targeted assistance.

Components of this programme element could include:

- Minimizing children's psychological and emotional trauma.
- Keeping survivors as integral members of their communities.
- Providing basic material needs. Affected families often require direct assistance.
- Education, training and employment creation.
- Children's social and adolescent's development needs. To grow and develop into an adult capable of constructive social interaction, children need to be nurtured and stimulated.
- Adolescents sexual development needs.

Meeting the special needs of HIV-infected children

As with adults most symptomatic HIV-infected children do not know that they are infected. They continue to lead normal daily lives. Simple infection control procedures can protect all family members or institutional workers from transmission of the virus. Both mandatory and voluntary testing has been advocated to determine the HIV status of orphans. However, there are serious ethical issues involved in testing and disclosure to children. Issues, which need to be determined, include: Who wants to know and why? Will it benefit the child tested and how? Who should determine this and how? Can a child give informed consent to testing? Perspectives and policy needs to be drawn up in this area. Infants and children with HIV-related illness may have special care needs. Meeting them is more difficult where one or both of the parent's is/are also infected or has died. Components of this programme element could include:

- Support to families with a sick child.
- Promotion of non-discrimination policies and programmes.

Reaching children and adolescents who are vulnerable Among and within families affected by the HIV epidemic, there will be some children or families of children at particular risk of destitution and of HIV infection: urban families without the support of their extended families, families who for whatever reasons are on the streets, children suffering sexual abuse within families, etc. For many of these young people survival sex, sex in exchange for money, clothing, affection, shelter, food etc., is a basic coping strategy. Components of this programme element could include: Assistance to street children. Reducing the susceptibility of young women to infection.

Reducing the number of Affected children

This objective can be achieved by decreasing the number of adults becoming HIV-infected. Highest priority must be given to bringing about attitude and behavioural change and the change in the community norms and values required to bring this about. Because those with less control over their own lives are at greater risk, efforts to improve the socio-economic status of the most destitute and measure to empower women are critical to reduce the spread of the virus.

RIGHTS OF THE CHILD SUFFERING FROM HIV/ AIDS

The United Nations Convention on the rights of the child in the context of HIV/AIDS has spelt out principles for reducing the children's vulnerability to infection and for protecting children from discrimination because of their real or perceived HIV/AIDS status. Governments need to ensure that the best interests of the children with regards to HIV/ AIDS are promoted and addressed. They can use this human rights framework:

- States should include HIV/AIDS, as disability laws exist to strengthen: the protection of people living with HIV/AIDS against discrimination.
- State the profile of children suffering from HIV.
- Special measures to be taken by the governments to prevent and minimize the impact of HIV/AIDS caused by trafficking, forced prostitution, sexual exploitation, inability to negotiate safe sex, sexual abuse, use of injecting drugs and harmful traditional practices.
- Children's right to life, survival and development should be guaranteed.
- Children's right to confidentiality and privacy in regard to their HIV status should be recognized. This includes the recognition that HIV testing should be voluntary and done with the informed consent of theperson involved which should be obtained in the context of pretest counselling. If the children's legal guardians are involved, they should pay due regard to the child's view, if the child is of an age or maturity to have such views.

- Children should have access to social benefits, including social security and social insurance.
- Children should have access to HIV/AIDS prevention, education and information, and to the means of prevention. Measures should be taken to remove social, cultural, political and religious barriers that block children's access to these.
- Children should have access to HIV/AIDS prevention, education and information both in school and out of school, irrespective of their HIV/AIDS status.
- Children should have access to health care services and programmes and barriers to access encountered by especially vulnerable groups should be removed.
- Children should enjoy adequate standards of living.

HIV/AIDS AND SUBSTANCE ABUSE

SUBSTANCE ABUSE AND ITS EFFECTS

Before looking at the connection between HIV/AIDS and substance abuse it is good to know something about substance abuse. The very term substance abuse means using a substance or a chemical in an improper way or using a chemical in a wrong way. A substance as it is used in the term 'substance abuse' is a chemical or a drug that is used for the purpose of mood altering or intoxication. Some of these substances may have medicinal value when used under prescription by a physician. When they are used for the purpose of getting mood alteration, it is called substance abuse. Most of these substances are addictive by nature.

According to the definition of WHO a person becomes an addict when:

- He has the compulsive desire to continue to take the drug.
- He is willing to get it by any method.
- He increases the dose in such a way that'he becomes psychologically and physically dependent on its effect.
- If the physical or mental faculties or both are affected due to taking the drug, the person may be termed an addict.

It must be noted that all those who take drugs do not become addicts. But anyone who abuses drugs can be called a substance abuser.

Health Hazard

Addiction leads to many health hazards. It spoils the physical health and mental health of a person and some of the damages are irreversible. Many abused drugs can cause instantaneous death if they are consumed in excess. In the same way the withdrawal symptoms when some of the drugs are stopped are equally horrible and painful. Take for example, a heroin addict who stops taking the drug. He will have unbearable sweat, feel cold, and have painful twitches and muscular spasms. An overdose of cocaine may cause undue anxiety and panic resulting in an extreme state of agitation, which causes hallucination.

Addiction to cocaine will cause nervousness and insomnia (sleeplessness) and a mental state similar to paranoid psychosis. The use of stimulants like amphetamine produces delirium, panic and hallucinations and also experience panic and restlessness and can get respiratory diseases such as bronchitis, LSD may cause an unprecedented depression even giving rise to suicidal tendency. Alcohol consumption leads to accidents caused by double vision, lack of coordination of movements and reflexes and impaired judgment. It causes many physical and neuro-psychiatric disorders.

Economic and Family Ruin

It is also a known fact that a substance abuser pays heavily for his habit. Addiction drains one's finances and leads to untold miseries in families. It interferes with the tranquility of family life. Very often addiction is the major cause of domestic violence.

Crime

It also serves as the causes for crimes. An addict loses respect in society and is usually found to be dishonest in dealing with money. Street children involved in substance abuse often have an untimely death due too lack of care and treatment. Stealing, selling, borrowing and pawning are some of the ways in which an addict raises money to get the drugs. Addiction leads to loss of manpower and is also the cause behind many industrial and road accidents. Intravenous drug taking is one of the major causes for the spread of Human Immunodeficiency Virus and Hepatitis B/C Virus. AIDS was detected in heroin drug abusers in West Jersey, USA in 1982.

Vulnerability of Substance Abusers

How are substance abusers more vulnerable to getting infected by HIV? In basic course on HIV/AIDS we discussed different ways by which HIV spreads. Having multi-partner sex, transfusion of infected blood and use of unsterilised needles have close association with substance abuse. In order to understand this one should know something about the life of an addict, how a substance abuser makes money and the different ways of taking drugs. Have you ever come across one who takes hard-core drugs? Do you know the different kinds of substances abused by people?

Have you ever thought of how these substances abusers get money to sustain this habit? A knowledge of all these is necessary to understand the connection between substance abuse and the spread of HIV/AIDS. It is a known fact that the incidence of the HIV infection is higher among substance abusers. For example HIV infection is a great problem among those who inject drugs in some of the North- Eastern states as well as the metropolitan cities in the country.

In fact this is the case with substance abusers all over the world. The sections below will explain to you the link between substance abuse and HIV infection.

DIFFERENT KINDS OF DRUGS

Those who study substance abuse divide the substances into different categories:

- *Gateway drugs:* Gateway drugs are those initiate a person into the world, of drugs. Cigarette, cigar and various preparations of tobacco meant for chewing and the 'gutkas' now very popular with the students and youth are examples of this. A person who takes gateway drugs is more prone to slipping into the world of drugs.
- *Legal drugs:* Legal drugs are those that are allowed to be sold in the market. Very often it is the government, which serves as the seller, or distributor and it has control over the sale and distribution. As it is sold with the knowledge of the government, the government has various methods of regulating the distribution through licensing, imposing heavy taxes, restricting timings of sale and taking legal action on those who do not follow regulations. In India alcohol, and narcotics are controlled in this way.
- *Illegal or hardcore drugs:* Hardcore drugs or illegal drugs are those substances prohibited by the law. The Government machinery can take legal action like imprisonment, imposing fine etc. on those who possess, distribute or consume it. Substances like cannabis, opiuni, brown sugar and cocaine belong to this category.

There are many who abuse substancesor drugs that are available in the form of tablets, liquids and injections in medical shops.

Classification of Drugs Based on their Pharmacological Actions

Various types of drugs of addiction are available to our youth. Some are addicted to many drugs whereas some are addicted to one drug.

The commonly abused drags may be categorized as:

- *Depressants:* Depressants are those drags, which tend to depress the central nervous system. Though popular belief is that alcohol provokes a person, it in fact comes under this category: Barbiturates, methaqualone and benzodiazepines and tranquilizers like valium and calm pose are depressants.
- *Stimulants:* Stimulants are those drugs, which tend to stimulate the central nervous system. They temporarily enhance wakefulness, stimulate the 1 mood and even make one forget fatigue. Amphetamines, which some use to keep themselves awake belong to this category.
- *Hallucinogens:* Hallucinogens distort the perception and the users may feel confused and disoriented. The experience of one who takes hallucinogens may vary from visions of joy and splendor to unbearable waking nightmares. LSD is a popular hallucinogen. As

LSD interferes with perception there is a higher incidence of accidents due to wrong judgments. There is also high risk to life as a slight overdose can cause instantaneous death.

- *Narcotics:* Narcotics are used to suppress pain but they are abused to alter moods. Most of the abused drugs are derivatives from the narcotic substances in three plants, namely, poppy, coca and cannabis. Drugs derived from a poppy plant are known as opiates. Opium, which is the dried milk of poppy, contains morphine and codeine.

Various synthetic opiates are used as painkillers, pethidine; a synthetic opiate is commonly abused drug. Heroin, a white crystalline powder, bitter in taste is an opium derivative. Regular users have health problems as it affects food intake. Brown sugar, which is a crude form of heroin, is a very commonly misused illegal drug in India. It is a dangerous drug as it has highly addictive properties. Cocaine, which was not known to the Indian youth until the early 90's is now available in Indian cities. Various.derivatives of the plant cannabis are popular drugs among the Indian youth. Compared with the price of other illegal drugs the various forms of cannabis-hashish, bhang, ganja and marijuana are available at affordable price. You should be aware that due to various reasons, a youth who comes into contact with drugs and tries it once out of curiosity may continue to take it and become a confirmed addict in due course.

The Different Methods of Drug Intake

Table

Types of drugs and how they are taken

SI.NO 1	Cetegory 2	Drugs 3	Methods of Use 4
1.	Narcotics	Opium	Oral and smoked
		Morphine	Oral, smoked and injected
		Codeine	Oral, injected
		Heroin	Injected, smoked, snorted and oral
2.	Depressants	Barbiturates	Oral, injected
		Methaqualone	Oral, injected
		Benzodiazepines	Oral, injected
		Alcohol	Oral
3.	Stimulants	Cocaine	Snorted, orally taken, smoked injected
		Amphetamines	Oral injected
4.	Halluciogens	LSDS	Oral
		Mescaline	Oral
		Phencyclidine	Oral, smoked, injected
5.	Cannabis	Ganja/Hashish Marijuana	Smoked, Oral

There are many ways in which the drug abusers consume drugs or substances. The most common way is oral intake that is drinking or swallowing. Alcohol is usually drunk and opium is swallowed. Smoking is another way of taking drugs. For example cannabis or ganja is usually smoked. Drugs like heroin and cocaine are sniffed. This is called inhalation. Another method of intake is to inject the drug into the body especially into the veins (Intravenous). Drug injection is the method that has a close link with the spread of HIV/AIDS. This will be discussed in depth in the following sections. The table below gives information about the different types of drugs and how they are taken.

LIFE OF AN ADDICT

Now you have an idea about the type of substances, the different drugs of abuse and the different methods of intake. But to understand how a substance abuser is more prone to contracting HIV/AIDS we should know something about the life of an addict. Probably you have never seen a hard-core addict. In the Indian social context it may not be possible for many to see a hardcore drug abuser injecting a drug. Some of you may not even be aware of this method.

It is sad to note that many of our youth today are caught unawares in drug trap. Drugs have become easily accessible to the youth. An article published in 'India Today' January 31, 1994 says that 35 per cent of our young people in the cities occasionally indulge in smoking, 30 per cent in drinking beer, 12 per cent in consuming alcohol and 0.5 per cent in taking drugs. Various studies ten years later showed that the drug abuse especially of alcohol is increasing in the country. The statistical data available are frightening. Now people in their teens and 20's land themselves in psychiatric clinics with drugs-related problems. It is estimated that 20 per cent of the admissions in NIMHANS, Bangalore have alcohol-related problems.

In this section our main-aim is to understand the life and behaviour of an addict. It is good to know the names of the above addictive substances. Some of these are easily available. You should also know that some of these substances are very expensive. Some substances are so addictive that an addict finds it almost impossible to survive without it. The withdrawal symptoms are so severe that a drug-addict dreads it. As there is a compulsive desire and as an addict is physically and psychologically dependent on substances he usually tries to raise money to buy his drugs at any cost.

Have you ever thought how an addict manages to get money when all his attempts to raise money to buy drugs fail? An addict usually begs, borrows, steals; tell lies, cheats to get money to keep his habit going. Probably some of us might have had the experience of encountering an addict, trying to extract money from us under some pretext. It will be a worthwhile exercise to closely watch the life of an addict and observe his fund-raising enterprise. When all other doors are closed he embarks on a selling spree. He starts selling whatever he can lay hand on - vessels, watch, furniture, and jewellery and, if a student, even his textbooks. What more does he have to sell? Two easily available factors with an addict are his or her blood and body. This is how substance abuse is closely linked with professional blood donation and prostitution.

SUBTANCE ABUSE, BLOOD DONATION AND HIV/ AIDS

From what you have been reading till now you would have understood how addictive substance abuse is. Probably you never thought that an addict raises quick money by selling his own blood. It is established that many of the hardcore drug addicts are HIV positive. Don't you think there is a great risk of the recipient of blood getting HIV if it is from an unknown professional blood donor who happens to be a drug addict?

SUBSTANCE ABUSE AND SEXUAL ACTIVITIES

After going through the case study in the previous study in the previous section you would be asking a very pertinent question: How did the donor get HIV? You may have asked another question too: Do only addicts carry HIV? Some of you would have even said, "as if those who do not abuse substance never get HIV". If you have reacted in any of these ways, it shows you have started thinking about the substance abuse very deeply. We will try in this section to find out the connection between substance abuse and prostitution.

Addiction has close connection with lewd thinking and action. Though we may not be justified in making a sweeping statement, it is a known fact that alcohol provokes sexual desire. With all the problems that are likely to be created in an alcoholic's home and the bad company an alcoholic will have, it is natural that an alcoholic indulges in multipartner sex. It has already been mentioned in the previous sections that having multi-partner sex is responsible for the spread of HIV.

We have also established that with the compulsive desire, an addict makes money just to keep his habit going. Selling one's body is the easiest way for a drug addict to earn money for the procurement of drugs. Many of the women in prostitution are in the habit of taking drugs. Drug abusers, especially women, do not hesitate to take up prostitution, as they need a lot of money to keep their habit going. If they are in the habit of injecting drugs they are more vulnerable to contracting HIV. Even within a group of drug abusers, there is a possibility for having multi-partner sex and this also leads to the spread of HIV. So a substance abuser, whether male or female has more chances of contracting HIV/AIDS.

INJECTING DRUGS AND HIV/AIDS

We discussed the various ways in which drugs are usually taken. Do you remember them? Oral intake (drinking, chewing and swallowing) smoking, injecting and sniffing or snorting are the ways in which drugs are taken. Of these, injecting the drug has a very close link with the spread of HIV/ AIDS. Before establishing the link between injecting drugs and HIV/AIDS, we should know some basic facts about the habit of injecting drugs and the drugs usually injected. A question that you may raise is why do some people go for injecting drugs? It is the hard-core drugs that are used for injecting. There are three ways in which drugs are injected. Some inject it under the skin (skin popping) while some go for intramuscular injection (injecting deep into the muscles) Intravenous intake (mainlining) or injecting directly into the vein is the third method of injecting.

Morphine, codeine, heroin, methadone, methaqualonee, tranquilizers like benzodiazepines, cocaine, amphetamines etc. are the drugs that are usually injected. People indulge in injecting drags for different kinds of experiences with substances. But little do the drug abusers realize the risk involved in injecting drugs. As you are aware, usually substance abusers take drugs in company. When people sit in a group and take drugs, usually the same needle is used to prick different persons. In the previous sections we saw that drug addicts are more prone to contract HIV/AIDS either because of their multi-partner sexual behaviour or because of the close link between prostitution and substance abuse. Now in a group of substance abusers using the method of injecting the drug, if one person is HIV positive, the other members of the group who share the same needle are at a greater risk of getting HIV. Remember, even if the drug abusers are aware of the risk involved in sharing the needle, they won't have the patience to sterilize the needle every time or change it as substance abusers are usually, in a desperate hurry to inject the drug.

In states like Manipur, the HIV prevalence rate is very high among substance abusers who inject drags. A case study presented in the book "Broadening the Front and NGO Responses to HIV/AIDS in India" is worth presenting here as it shows the close link between substance injecting and HIV/AIDS.

LINK BETWEEN SUBSTANCE ABUSE AND HIV/ AIDS AND THE WAY OUT

We have seen in the previous sections that there is a close link between substance abuse and the spread of HIV/AIDS. This link is true not only of India but also worldwide. Now that this link has been established we should be in a position to suggest ways out of this predicament that are effective and practical. Though what we suggest here may not be exhaustive and may not be applicable to all parts of the world and all sections of the society, the suggestions may be useful.

Motivating the Youth

The youth should be motivated to keep off drugs. Conscientisation, awareness programmes, using the media, including lessons on the evils of substances abuse are some of the ways through which we can motivate the youth. The youth should be equipped in such a way that they will never experiment with drugs and they will boldly say "NO TO DRUGS".

Enacting and Implementing Laws

Strict laws and severe punishments may deter a person to some extent from becoming an addict. In India drug trading is a serious offence and strict vigil and implementation of the laws will prevent drug trade to a very great extent. Conscientisation programmes as suggested above, along with implementing the law will do good job in supply and demand reduction.

Health Care to Substance Abusers

Care should be given to substance abusers in such a way that neither do they get HIV/AIDS nor are they allowed to infect others. When supply and demand reduction tactics fail, in some parts of India and also in the Western world, methods like needle exchange are adopted.

STDS AND THEIR MANAGEMENT

DEFINITION AND MEANING

STD stands for Sexually Transmitted Diseases. Earlier, STDs were known as venereal disease or VD. STDs are diseases, which are communicable and are transmitted by an infected man or woman to his/her partner during sexual intercourse. For this reason they are called Sexually Transmitted Diseases.

A person becomes infected with STDs when he or she has:

- Vaginal sexual intercourse or
- Anal sexual intercourse or
- Oral sex with an infected person

The vagina, penis, rectum and mouth are the sources from which the STD germs can invade the body.

Statistics

India has a high incidence of STDs with annual incidence rate of 5 per cent. Thus on an average 40 million new cases are reported every year. An established 3-4 percent of the total population is suspected to be having STDs.

History of STDs

STDs have been in existence for centuries. Syphilis, one of the best known STDs before AIDS came into picture, took away lives of thousands of people. Later, Gonorrhea became known as another common STD. Fortunately with the discovery of penicillin, both these STDs could be treated. Since then more than twenty STDs have now been identified and they affect millions of men, women and even children every year.

Misconceptions

There are many misconceptions prevalent in India regarding sexually transmitted diseases. It is important to know about these misconceptions.

Regarding STD Transmission

Lack of genital hygiene, for example visiting dirty toilets, using unclean underclothing etc. causes STDs 'Excessive Heat' caused through eating spicy food or drinking alcohol or through constitutional or occupational reasons leads to STDs. Non-sexual contact with an infected person e.g. touch, sharing objects, sharing the same toilets etc. causes STDs.

Regarding STD Prevention

The only way to prevent STDs is to wash the genital area with one's own urine, water, soda or limejuice.

Regarding STD Treatment

Home remedies are believed to be adequate for STD treatment. Sexual intercourse with a child, a virgin or an animal is said to cure STDs. All these misconceptions lead to spread of STD infections in the community.

IMPORTANCE OF STDS

Why are STDs Important

STDs are important for many reasons, which include: Millions of men, women and children are infected with STDs each year India provides a vast playground for the rapid spread of STDs. The main cause for this spread is ignorance. Many STDs show early symptoms, which then disappear without treatment, but the germs continue to remain in the body. Anyone with an STD may look healthy but can still keep infecting others.

Very often, the infected people do not inform their sexual partners:

- STDs can occur again and again in the same individual because the human body cannot build immunity against them and there is no vaccination for them. These diseases can have serious consequences on those suffering from them. For e.g. they can cause blindness, sterility and even death.
- Some of the STDs produce ulcers on the genitalia. These STDs, which produce ulcers, are collectively called genital ulcer disease or GUDs. These GUDs are associated with an increased risk of HIV transmission.
- STDs can cause profound problems in women. STDs in women can occur without any symptoms. These STDs can then spread into the uterus and the fallopian tubes and cause pelvic inflammatory disease, which can be quite painful. As a result of this, the tubes can get blocked and the woman may not be able to produce children

(sterility). In other instances, a tubal pregnancy can occur and sometimes this can be fatal.

- Another important problem, which STDs can cause in women, is; cancer, especially of the cervix, which is the lower portion of the uterus. One of the STDs, namely, Human Papilloma Virus (HP V) can result in genital warts and also leads to! cancers.
- Untreated STDs can cause several complications in adults and these include liver problems, heart problems and brain problems.
- If women had untreated STD and she is pregnant, then it can cause problems in the newborn child such as conjunctivitis (inflammation in the eyes) blindness or pneumonia. Sometimes these children may be born with defects in their organs and therefore are permanently disabled.
- Health education and counselling to STD patients is an importantcomponent of prevention and control of STDs. Those who are in risk of acquiring STDs are also at risk acquiring HIV infection.
- It is important that a person with STD should complete the full courseof treatment, even if he feels better. Incomplete treatment may lead to chronic infection, with potential, serious, long-term consequences. It is important for the patients to return for further treatment also, if he is not feeling better with the first treatment.

Importance of STDs in Relation to HIV/AIDS

The relationship between STD and HIV infection is manifold:

- First of all STD and HIV infection are associated with the same risk behaviours, that is sexual intercourse with multiple partners. Thus the same measures that prevent STD also prevent sexual transmission of; HIV infection.
- The presence of STD has been found to facilitate the acquisition and transmission of HIV infection. It is believed that for those STDs associated with genital ulcer disease such as syphilis, cancroids and herpes, the risk of HIV transmission increases ten-fold.
- Ulcer diseases have a break in the mucosa. There is a rich collection of CD4 cells on the broken mucosa. The virus easily enters the broken mucosa and infects the CD4 cells. Presence of ulcerative disease increases the risk of acquiring HIV infection ten fold.
- For those STDs associated with discharge such as Gonorrhea, Chlamydia and Trichomoniasis the risk of HIV disease is four-fold. Thus early diagnosis and the treatment of STD can contribute significantly to a reduction in HIV transmission.
- Other routes of transmission of HIV and STDs are also similar. In addition to sexual transmission, HIV/ AIDS also be transmitted through blood, blood products, donated organs or tissue, and from mother to newborn infant.

- Many of the measures for preventing the sexual transmission of both HIV infection and STDs are the same. Therefore STD clinical services are important access points for persons at high risk for both HIV and STD, not only for diagnosis and treatment but also for education for prevention.

Increasing evidence suggests that there is increased severity of manifestations of STDs and reduced response to conventional therapeutic regencies in HIV infected persons. Trends in STD incidence can be used as indicators of changes in social behaviour. It is easier to monitor trends in STD reduction than the spread of HIV.

STDS AND TREATMENT OPTIONS

Let us now try to understand some of the common STDs, their signs and symptoms and treatment options.

Syphilis

Syphilis is the oldest of the STDs, and was discovered centuries ago. It is caused by a bacterium called Treponema Palladium.

The course of Syphilis can be divided into four stages:

- Primary stage
- Secondary stage
- Latent stage - Early and late latent stage.
- Tertiary stage

A person who is infected can pass on the disease to others during the first two stages and during early latent stage if he or she does not get treatment. These three stages usually last about one to two years. Late latent syphilis (late) and tertiary syphilis are not transmitted through sexual route. However, the tertiary stage, which can occur several years zafter the primary stage can cause problems of the brain, heart and blood vessels and can even cause death. Syphilis is one of the most dangerous STDs. It is transmitted almost always by sexual contact, but can be spread also by contact with broken skin. Transmission through kissing, blood transfusion and percutaneous injury has been reported.

Symptoms

The first symptom of primary syphilis is a sore called chancre. This may appear within one week to three months after exposure, but generally appears within two to six weeks. It is ordinarily painless. It usually occurs on the penis, the vulva, the vagina, the cervix, the tongue, lips or other parts of the body. It disappears within a few weeks with or without treatment. If it is not treated at this stage, it may progress on to the other three stages.

Secondary Stage

This occurs from 3 to 6 weeks after the chancre appears. It is marked by a reddish, skin rash, which may occur all over the body or only in a few areas such as the palms of the hands or soles of the feet. It usually heals within several weeks or months. Other symptoms include fever, tiredness, headache, sore throat, as well as patchy hair loss and swollen lymph glands throughout the body. The signs of secondary syphilis may come and go over the next one or two years.

Latent Stage

The latent stage may continue for many years after the secondary stage. The organisms dormant in the body and does not produce any symptoms, but the titers in the blood are positive. Latent stage is further categorized into early latent syphilis and late latent syphilis. Early latent syphilis is the period when the person is asymptomatic and it lasts for two years after the primary infection. Late latent syphilis is the stage when a person is asymptomatic and two years have lapsed after the primary infection. During this time person will not transmit the infection through sexual route but he can transmit through blood or a mother can transmit to the feotus. In about two-third of the cases, the latent stage continues for the rest of the patient's life without the development of any clinical lesion.

Tertiary Stage

If syphilis is not treated during the primary, secondary or the latent stage it can progress on tertiary syphilis, which causes chronic destructive changes in the brain, heart, bones, liver, stomach, eyes or other tissues. The skin mucous membranes and other organs may develop rubbery tumors called gummas.

Blood Test for Syphilis

These tests are referred to as non treponemal tests and the most common test is the VDRL test (Venereal Disease Research Laboratory test). They are not very specific. This test becomes positive within 7 to 14 days after appearance of the syphilitic chancre. It is almost always positive in the secondary and recurrent stages and in the early latent stage. It may be positive in a majority of cases in the late latent stage also, but in cases of late tertiary syphilis where heart and brain are involved, it may be negative in proportion of cases. The specific tests are called the Treponema tests. They are Treponema antigen-based enzyme immunoassay (EIA), Treponema hemoglobin assay (TPHA) or fluorescent treponemal antibody absorbed assay (FTS-ABS).

Treatment and Prevention

Syphilis is usually treated with the antibiotic, penicillin, administered by injection. Patients allergic to penicillin can be treated with other antibiotics. Within 24 hours of starting treatment, a person can no longer transmit syphilis. Normally, in all stages of syphilis, proper treatment will cure the disease. However, in tertiary syphilis, damage has already been done to the body organs and these cannot be reversed. If not treated, a pregnant woman with active syphilis may pass the infection to her unborn child. The only sure and safe method to prevent getting infected with syphilis is abstinence before marriage and fidelity within married life. Testing and treatment early in pregnancy is the best way to prevent syphilis in infants and should be a routine part of prenatal care.

Complication of Untreated Syphilis

Approximately 3 to 7 per cent of persons with untreated syphilis develop Neurosyphilis. Some persons with Neurosyphilis never develop any symptoms, while others may have headache, stiff neck and fever due to inflammation of the lining of the brain. Some people may have convulsions (fits). Some others may have the symptoms of the stroke with resulting numbness, weakness or visual complaints. The duration from time of infection up to development of neurosyphilis may take up to 20 years. Untreated syphilis can also affect the spine and cause what is called Tabes Dorsalis, which can give rise to excruciating pains. Untreated Syphilis can also affect the heart and cause syphilitic aortitis and involve the valves at the base of aorta. Aorta is the largest blood vessel in the body. Sometimes parts of this vessel can become thin walled and bloated like balloon. This is referred to as Aneurysm of the aorta and is a serious complication of untreated syphilis.

Chancroid

Chancroid is another fairly common STD. It is very common among men who have frequent contact with commercial sex workers. Its importance also lies in the fact, that it is one of the genital ulcer diseases that is associated with an increased risk of transmission of HIV disease.

Symptoms

The disease is caused by bacterium called H. ducreyi. It usually occurs within seven days of exposure. There are open and painful sores on the genitalia accompanied by swollen tender lymph nodes in the groin. in women there can be painful urination, painful defecation, painful intercourse, rectal bleeding and vaginal discharge.

Treatment and Prevention

Successful treatment for chancroid cures the infection, resolves the clinical symptoms and prevents transmission to others. In severe cases: scarring may result. Drugs usually advised include Azithromycin Ceftriaxore, and Ciprofloxacin. Sex partners of patients with chancroid should also be treated irrespective of whether they have symptoms. All patients with chancroid should be tested for HIV disease, since they require longer courses of therapy. The disease is generally more severe in HIV positive individuals and the healing is slower. Treatment failures can occur in certain cases.

Granuloma Inguinal

This is an STD, which occurs in Tropical areas such as India, Papua New Guinea, Central Australia and Southern Africa.

Symptoms

It is caused by a gram-negative bacterium called Klebisella granulomatis. It causes painless, one or more beefy red open sores that slowly enlarges. They bleed easily to touch. There is no associated lympadenopathy. They usually appear within seven days of exposure but may take long as 3 months also. A secondary bacterial infection may occur on top of this one or it may co-exist with other STDs.

Prevention and Treatment

Drugs usually given are Septran, Doxycycline, Ciprofloxacin or Erythromycin for a minimum period of three weeks for all four drugs. Recurrence can occur 6- 18 months later in spite of effective initial therapy. Patients should be followed regularly till all signs and symptoms have been resolved. Sex partners who report history of sexual -contact during 60 days preceding onset of infection should also be treated.

Genital Herpes

It is an STD. It is caused by a virus, contagious and affects millions of people each year. The virus called the Herpes Simplex Virus or HSV. HSV are two types-1 and 2. Both viruses cause diseases.

Symptoms

The early symptoms of the disease occur within 2 to 30 days of exposure and may last on a average 2 to 3 weeks. There is an itching burning sensation, pain in the legs, buttocks and genital area. Vaginal discharge may also occur. The sores appear around the vaginal area, penis, oral opening, buttocks as well as thighs. The sores appear as small red lumps, which may develop into blisters or painful open sores. There may also be fever, headache, muscle aches, painful urination, vaginal discharge and swollen glands in the vaginal area. The virus reactivates from time to time and remains in certain nerve cells of the body for life.

Treatment and Prevention

The most commonly used anti-viral drug is called Acyclovir. It should be taken within 24 hours of onset of the symptoms. However, Acyclovir is not a cure for Herpes, but if taken regularly, the drug interferes with the virus' ability to reproduce itself. The treatment is usually given for 7-10 days. It may be extended if healing is incomplete. Counselling is an important aspect of managing patients who have genital herpes. Many patients benefit learning about the chronic aspects of the disease after the acute illness subsides.

Counselling of these patients should include the following:

- That there is a potential for recurrent episodes, a symptomatic viral shedding and sexual transmission. Patients should abstain from sexual activity when lesions are present. Sexual Transmission of "HSV can occur even if the patients have no symptoms or no sores. This is more common for HSV-2 than HSV-1 infection and those who have infection for less than 12 months.
- Pregnant women with genital herpes who can spread the infection should be told that taking episodic antiviral therapy can shorten the duration of illness.

Continuous therapy can ameliorate or prevent recurrent outbreaks. Precautionary measures include:

- Keep the infected area dry and clean to prevent secondary infections.
- Avoid touching sores with the hands. Hands should be washed after contact with the sores.

Gonorrhea

Gonorrhea is caused by bacterium called Nesseira gonorrhea. It grows and multiplies quickly in moist, warm areas of the body such as the cervix, urethra, rectum etc. From the cervix, it can spread to the uterus and the fallopian tubes also, resulting in inflammation of all these pelvic organs and causing pelvic inflammatory disease. All cases of Gonorrhea may not necessarily develop symptoms, but when they do, usually appear within 2 to 20 days after exposure (sexual contact) with an infected partner. Men usually have severe burning on passing urine and white discharge from urethra. A smear may reveal the Gonococcus or it may be cultured from the discharge. In women, many may have no symptoms, some may have an abnormal vaginal discharge. The other symptoms include severe abdominal pain, bleeding between menstrual periods, vomiting or pain. Symptoms of rectal infection include discharge, anal itching and sometimes painful, bowel moments.

Treatment and prevention

Usually amoxicillin, quinolones, and tetracyclines may be given for the reatment of Gonorrhea. Gonorrhea may occur in combination with Chlamydia, so physicians prescribe a combination of antibiotics to treat both diseases. It is important to complete the full course of medication and return for the follow up. All sex partners of a person with gonorrhea should be treated even if they do not have symptoms of the infection. If Gonorrhea is not treated, the bacteria can spread to the blood stream and infect the joints, heart valves and the brain. Constant awareness and precautions are necessary, because a person who has once contracted the disease does not become immune. The infection can recur.

Chlamydia

Chlamydia is yet another common STD prevalent among both men and women. Very often it occurs in conjunction with gonorrhea. In many cases, the infection does not produce any symptoms at all. In women, complications of Chlamydia infection include pelvic inflammatory disease, ectopic pregnancy and infertility. It can affect newborn children at the time of the birth if the mother is infected. In these newborns it can cause infection in the eye, throat, urethra and rectum. It can also cause pneumonia in children from the age of 1 to 3 months.

Symptoms

Chlamydia is caused by a bacterium called Chlamydia trachomatis. The transmission occurs during the sexual contact either vaginal or oral or anal. Symptoms usually occur 1 to 3 weeks after exposure and include abnormal genital discharge and pain on passing urine. Half the patients may have no symptoms at all. In men there may be swelling and pain in the scrotal area, which is a sign of epididymitis. It can also cause inflamed rectum, conjunctivitis and throat infection.

Treatment and Prevention

The drug usually given for this infection includes Doxycycline, Azithromycin or erythromycin. They should be given for at least 7-10 days. Azithromycin may be given as a single dose. Of course, these drugs should be given only under the treatment of a physician. Pregnant women should not take tetracycline and should opt for erythromycin. Women should get themselves examined for Chlamydia before conceiving, as this infection can cause tubular pregnancy. All sex partners should also be treated. Since both Gonorrhea and Chlamydial infection co-exist, routine dual therapy without testing for Chlamydia is recommended. This has resulted in decrease in the prevalence of Chlamydial infection.

Bacterial Vaginosis

This is an STD that is caused by a variety of bacterial organisms that replace the Lactobacillus in the vagina. Although it occurs in women who have multiple sex partners, it can also occur in those who are sexually not active. The most important symptoms are the presence of an abnormal, white discharge from the vagina, which has a fishy odour. The treatment is with metronidazole or clindamycin cream for seven days. Bacterial" vaginosis during pregnancy has adverse outcomes, i.e. premature rupture of the waters, pre-term labour and pre-term birth.

Trichomoniasis

This is another STD that often develops without any symptoms. A protozoan called Trichomonas Vaginlis causes it. Symptoms occur usually within 4-20 days of exposure. In women there may be a yellow green or grayish, malodorous vaginal discharge and painful urination. Irritation and itching of the female genital area and the lower abdominal pain can also occur. Men may not have any symptoms, but can transmit the infection. It is therefore recommended that both partners be treated simultaneously for this infection. The drug of the choice is Metranidazole, either as a single dose for seven days. Patients taking this drug should avoid alcohol as it can cause nausea and vomiting. HIV positive people should receive the same regimen as HIV negative people.

Pubic Lice

Pubic lice are parasites, which often spread by sexual contacts. These tiny insects are visible to the naked eye. They are pinhead size, oval in shape and appear reddish brown when full with blood of the host. The eggs of the lice are called nits, which can be seen clinging to the pubic hair. The main symptoms are itching and by this the lice can spread to the other parts of the body. Creams and lotions and shampoos are available to kill the lice. The bedding and clothing should be decontaminated as re-infection can occur. All sex partners should also be treated. HIV positive people should receive the same treatment as HIV negative people.

Scabies

Scabies is usually transmitted through sexual contact. However, it is also transmitted through contacts with sheets, towels, furniture etc. The scabies mite is called Sarcoptes Scabeii, and causes intense itching. In addition to affecting the genital area, it can also affect the hands between the fingers, wrists, elbows and lower abdomen. After the exposure, it usually takes about a month or more to develop skin reaction. However during this period one can pass on the infection to another person. The entire family needs to be treated simultaneously to eradicate this infection. Bedding and clothing should be de-contaminated at the same time. Many solutions and ointments are available for treatment. HIV infected patients who develop scabies, are at risk for Norwegian scabies, a disseminated skin infection. Such patients should be managed under consultation with, an expert in the field.

Lymphogranuloma Venereum

It is caused by certain strains of C. Trachomatis. It causes painful inguinal lymphadenopathy that is usually onesided. Others may cause involvement of the rectum and can result in fistulas and strictures.

Prevention and Treatment

Doxycycline or erythromycin for a period of 3 weeks should be given. Sex partners should be treated within 30 days of onset o infection in the affected person. Again treatment might have to be prolonged in HIV positive individuals.

Cytomegalovirus Infection

Cytomegalovirus (CMV) is a member of the herpes virus family. It is found in various body fluids. It can spread by sexual contact as well as by other forms of physical touch. Once infected it remains in the body like the herpes virus. Infected mother can pass on the CMV to their babies before birth. Such a baby may suffer from mental retardation, blindness and deafness and even epilepsy. Such a baby can also infect others, as it will have CMV in its saliva and urine.

Human Papillomavirus Infection (HPV)

HPV is one of the STDs that can affect men and women. There are over 60 types of HPV, but only certain types can cause STD (6, 11, 16, 18, 31, 33 and 35). This disease is characterized by the presence of warts (Cauliflower like growths, which vary from a tiny size to very large ones) on the genitalia, as well as on the mouth or anus if one has indulged in anal or oral intercourse. The importance of these warts lies in the fact that these HPV types are associated with the development of cancer especially cervical and anal cancers. Removal of these warts does not remove the risk of cancer. Applications of certain resins, surgical cryotherapy etc. can remove the warts, but these treatment modalities are not curative. Examination of sex partners is not necessary. Patients with HIV disease may not respond to any treatment as well as those without any recurrences are more common.

Pelvic Inflammatory Disease or PID

This is an infection, which affects women. This happens when infection spreads from the lower reproductive tract i.e. vagina and cervix to the upper reproductive tract i.e. uterus, ovaries and fallopian tubes. Sexually transmitted organisms, especially N. gonorrhea and C.Trachomaatics are responsible in most cases, but others that generally reside in the vagina can also cause disease, if left untreated. It can lead to tubal pregnancy, primary infertility or acute emergency.

Symptoms

It has been found that sexually active teenagers are more likely to develop PID than older women. Those who have more sexual partners IUD insertion, induced abortions etc. are more at risk of developing PID. The symptoms can vary from asymptomatic to abnormal symptoms acute and severe. The patients may have irregular menstrual bleeding pain on intercourse, abnormal vaginal discharge, pain and tenderness in lower abdomen, high temperatures, severe abdomen pain etc. Hospitalization is required if the pain is acute and severe or if the patient is pregnant or has high fever with vomiting or has not responded to oral medication. In these cases intra-venous antibiotics have to be given.

Treatment and Prevention

Oral antibiotics such as Metranidozole and Doxycyline are given. In hospital, second or third generation cephalosporins, fluroquinolones etc. are given. Antibiotics may have to be continues for two weeks. Patients who have received treatment should have regular follow up. Sex partners of these women should be examined and treated as asymptomatic infection in them can cause recurrent infection in the women. The patient should receive drugs, which will cover both Gonorrhea and Chlamydia. Pregnant women with PID have high risk of death, foetal death or early delivery and they should be hospitalized and treated. HIV positive women with PID tend to have more severe symptoms than HIV negative women, but respond equally well to the standard drugs. Sometimes they require very aggressive treatment especially if the CD4 count is low.

Hepatitis

Hepatitis is basically an inflammation of the liver and manifests as jaundice. In many cases, hepatitis are caused by viruses and these virus is named from A to E. Vaccines are available for prevention of Hepatitis 1 A and Hepatitis B.

Hepatitis B

Hepatitis B is a common STD. In the United States, sexual transmission has accounted for 30-60 per cent of Hepatitis B infectious in the last 10 years.

These diseases can spread by:

- Having sexual intercourse with an infected person
- Through needles
- Mother to child transmission at birth
- Blood transfusions
- Personal contact with an infected person, blood, semen and saliva are the major sources of infection.

The importance of Hepatitis B infection lies in the fact that a percentage of this group can develop acute fulminant disease, chronic liver disease or cancer of the liver. This disease can also be transmitted from mother to child at birth or by personal contact during first five years of life. Supportive and symptomatic care is the mainstay of therapy Alpha-2 interferon has been 40 per cent successful in eliminating chronic HBV infection and so also the drug lamivudine.

Prevention

Hepatitis B vaccination is the most effective means of preventing infection.

Other measures of prevention include:

- Routine screening of all pregnant mothers
- Routine vaccination of all newborns

- Vaccination of older children
- Vaccination of persons who report a history of STDs

HBV infection in HIV infected persons is more likely to lead to chronic HBV infection. HIV infection can also impair the response to hepatitis B vaccine. Revaccination with three more doses should be considered for those who do not respond initially.

Vaccination

Both the immunoglobin for short-term protection (contacts) and the vaccine are available. All STD require proper and adequate dose of the drugs. It is essential that the patients are seen by a qualified doctor.

Syndromic Management

As the facilities for diagnosing many of these STDs are not available in the field, a new paradigm of diagnosis has been evolved. This is known as the syndromic management of STD. Under this scheme the.presentation of the symptoms is taken into consideration and a suitable treatment that covers the entire organism is given.

PREVENTION OF STDS

The prevention and control of STDs is based on five major concepts:

- Education of those at risk on ways to reduce risk of STDs.
- Detection of asymptomatically infected persons and persons unlikely to seek treatment.
- Effective diagnosis and treatment of infected persons.
- Evaluation, treatment and counselling of sex partners of those who are infected.
- Pre-exposure vaccination of persons at risk for vaccine preventable STDs.

Prevention Measures

It is important to take a good sexual history from the person and identify the risk factors for STDs. This then, provides an opportunity to deliver prevention measures. Counselling skills are important. The messages should be tailored to the patient. Other prevention measures include , getting both partners tested for STDs, using condoms etc. Those on drugs must enroll or continue in a drug treatment programme.

Government Response STD Control Programme in India

The importance of treatment and control of STD in relation tb HIV infection was recognized by NACO. After taking over the STD control programme, NACO made it an integral component of AIDS control policy. Suitable strategies were devised for the control and prevention of STD as a priority in the overall planning to control the spread of HIV infection.

Objectives of the STD Control Programme

The STD control component of the National AIDS control programme has two major objectives:

- Reduce STD cases and thereby control HIV transmission by minimizing the risk factor.
- Prevent the short-term as well as long-term morbidity and mortality due to STD. In order to accomplish these objectives, the following strategies have been incorporated in the strategic plan for the prevention and control of AIDS in India.

Strategies

The broad strategies for controlling STD, as outlined in the strategic plan for prevention and control of AIDS in India are the following:

- Adequate and effective programme management.
- Prevention of the transmission of STD/HIV infection through IEC and promotion of safer sexual behaviour by the use of condoms.
- Adequate and comprehensive case management including diagnosis, treatment, individual counselling, partner notification and screening for the other diseases.
- Increasing access to health care for STD by strengthening existing facilities and structures and creating new facilities where ever necessary.

Early diagnosis and treatment of mostly asymptomatic infections through case finding and screening.

The following major actions have been taken along the lines suggested in the strategies:

- Training of health care workers in both public and private sectors in comprehensive STD case management.
- Development of appropriate laboratory services for the diagnosis of STD.
- Conduct have microbiological, socio-behavioural and operation research.
- Surveillance to follow the epidemiological situation, monitor and evaluate the on-going STD control programme.

Organisation of Training Programmes

- 5 Regional STD referral centres upgraded to conduct training, research, supervision and monitoring.
- All the districts have been provided facilities for the management of STD control programme.
- 18,558 medical officers from various states trained in STD case management through syndromic case management.
- 1132, new STD clinics with the existing 372 clinics, upgraded to function as referral centres of primary health care facilities.

- More than 10,000 private health care providers trained in STD case management by Indian Medical Association (IMA) in collaboration withNACO.
- Guidelines for syndromic management and treatment of STD revised and updated.
- Training module on STD surveillance prepared and finalized for training AIDS/STD programme officers.

Laboratory Services

Laboratory services in the five regional STD referral centres and in the STD clinics in medical colleges and districts as well as taluk hospitals have been upgraded.

Surveillance

Guidelines on STD surveillance based on syndromic approach as well as ethological diagnosis have been developed for district down to health centres for implementation in a phased manner.

HIV/AIDS AND THE WORKPLACE

HIV AND WORKPLACE

In order for people to live they need to work and earn money. The work place creates an environment for the people to interact with many others. Most of the active period of one's life is spent at the workplace. Thus the work place plays an important role in the lives of people. Hence, there has been a growing concern about HIV/ AIDS at the workplace. The effect of HIV will reduce the productivity of the working population. More children and elderly people will have to be supported by a smaller active labour force.

This epidemic has started attacking skilled labourers and professional workers in many industries. This will result in labour shortage in the near future, which will lower production, which in turn will affect the economy. Thus our wealth and prosperity are under a gigantic threat. In the light of this concern, workers and organisations around the world have been trying to explore the opportunity to decide, what is the best approach to promote health in the workplace, ameliorate discrimination and maintain status and dignity.

Estimates of the International Labour Organisation (ILO) show that globally there are 20 million workers living with HIV/AIDS. Also the size of the labour force in high prevalence countries will be between 10 and 30 per cent smaller by 2020 than it would have been without AIDS; 14 million children would have lost one or both parents to AIDS and many of them would be forced out of school and compelled jobs for subsistence, hence aggravating the problem of child labour. Obviously HIV/AIDS has an enormous potential impact at the workplace''. A recent global report indicates that the majority of new infections are in young people between the age of 15 and 24, some times younger. In India, although surveillance is patchy, all indications are that there are four million people living with HIV. India is reported to be the second country with the largest number of HIV infected people in the world after South Africa. As the pandemic gathers momentum, its effects at the workplace are being felt more accurately, especially in the Developing Nations. The International Labour Organisation (ILO) projects that the labour force in 38 countries (all but four in Africa) will be between 5% and 35% smaller by 2020 because of AIDS

Vulnerability at the Workplace Migration

Migration is a major risk factor with regard to HIV infection. According to the Ministry of Labour, Government of India, in 1996, there were about 180 million migrant workers in India, most of who are either single or living apart from their wives and families. At any given time, they comprise 30-40 per cent of the population of the large cities, where they also account for much of the clientele of the red light areas. Rapid industrialisation coupled with unemployment, results in attracting thousands of young people to big cities in search of jobs. Most of the migrants to the cities and industrial areas are either unmarried or staying away from the family. They are also unskilled or semiskilled labourers. Life in cities gives them more freedom and privacy and many a time they indulge in multipartner sex and drug abuse. Studies have confirmed that migration does play a role in spread of HIV.

One study on the relationship between mobility, sexual behaviour and HIV infection in an urban population interviewed a representative sample of 1913 men and women in Yaounde, Cameroon. The study measured mobility over a one-year period. It found HIV prevalence of 7.6% among men who had been away from home for periods longer than 31 days. Prevalence among those who had been away for less than 31 days in the year was 3.4%, while prevalence among those who had not been away from home in the previous 12 months was 1.4%. The association between men 's mobility and HIV was apparently related to risky sexual behaviour and remained significant after controlling for other important variables. There was no association between women's mobility and HIV infection.

A study in South America confirmed that migration does play an important role in spreading HIV but revealed a more complex picture than had been expected, which challenged some basic assumptions. Looking at discordant couples (that is, couples in which just one partner is HIV-positive), the study found that, in nearly 30% of cases the infected person was the female partner who stayed home in the rural area, while her migrant partner was HIV-negative. In other words, migration may create vulnerability to HIV exposure at both ends of the trail, and the virus may spread in both directions.

HIV and Sexually Transmitted Disease in the Workplace

HIV/AIDS is predominantly a sexually transmitted disease (STD). It mainly afflicts people in the sexually active group. Being the productive members in the community, major corporations can expect to find at least a few HIV infected persons among their staff.

The reason as to only a very few problems related to HIV/AIDS have emerged till date in the workplace in India may be attributed to many of them being still asymptomatic, besides keeping their HIV status confidential. However, as the latency period advances, opportunistic infection would gradually develop and as the number of such persons increases, the impact at the workplace will naturally become more obvious. Therefore, pertinent issues need to be considered with regard to the HIV infected workers.

These include:

- The fitness to work during the so-called incubation period and adjustments in the duties of the workers who turn out to be HIV/AIDS patients.
- Implementation of adequate precautions in the workplace to reduce risk of transmission of HIV during accidental exposure such as deep penetrating injuries from hollow injection needles with an AIDS patient as the source.
- Mandatory HIV antibody testing of employees without their informed consent and counselling, which is an infringement of their civil rights. Besides, it is not the solution because it does not guarantee that they will not acquire the infection following a negative ELISA test.

Workplace and HIV/AIDS - Some Facts

The workplace varies in its nature based on various factors such as whether it is organised/unorganised, the attitude of the management towards the employees union etc. Vulnerability to HIV infection and the impact of HIV/AIDS will also vary based on the same factors.

For example the organised sector that usually gives permanent employment to its employees will have more difficulties in adjusting to the challenges of HIV/AIDS. Whereas in the unorganised sector, the workers may not get any benefit from their employers and their families will also be immediately affected with the HIV infection of any family member.

ISSUES THAT HIV/AIDS BRINGS TO THE WORKPLACE

Infection with the human immunodeficiency virus and the acquired immunodeficiency syndrome represent an urgent worldwide problem with broad social, cultural, economic, political, ethical and legal dimensions and impact. We will now analyze these issues in detail.

Cost of HIV/AIDS at the Workplace

As business issue, HIV/AIDS continues to make an impact, companies have felt the loss of tremendous talent since the epidemic began. AIDS has become the second leading killer of adults in their prime working years in Europe. Co-workers have grieved the loss of many colleagues, family members and friends. Unwarranted fear and ignorance of the disease have caused discrimination and disrupted work and employee productivity at a time when the competitive global market place demands nothing less than total efficiency and outstanding performance. There are various issues related to HIV and AIDS that can have a direct or indirect impact on the productivity of the workers in any workplace.

HIV Absenteeism

HIV affects the most productive age group 15-50 years. Due to physical, psychological and social reasons, a HIV positive person shows reluctance to report for work. This increases the level of absenteeism, thus reducing the productivity of the entire organisation. An employee, who has developed AIDS, has lot of physical problems and frequently becomes sick. He may not be fit enough to perform his duties and hence may abstain from work. This results in a long-term deficiency of manpower. Hence AIDS absenteeism can turn out to be a severe problem with respect to an industry.

Labour Turnover along with its Impact on Costs to the Company

AIDS is likely to reduce the labour force's growth rate. The epidemic also affects workforce quality, since AIDSaffected workers are replaced by younger, lessexperienced men and women. At the same time, the loss of teachers and trainers results in future generations with lower skill levels. Thus, the organisation will have to handle two issues; turnover of its experienced and skilled employees and the training of new recruits who may need some time to adjust to the new situation and to learn the work.

Productivity

HIV affects the most productive age group, AIDS reduces output by squeezing productivity, adding costs, diverting productive resources, depleting skills and distorting the labour market. For employers, employee health expenses and funeral costs are rising as productivity and profits decline. The epidemic increases absenteeism, organisational disruption, and the loss of skills.

Loss of Supervisory Workers

The loss of supervisory workers can have an especially harsh impact, since their acquired knowledge and skills are seldom replaced simply by hiring others. In hard-hit areas, the general shortage of skilled workers and management-level staff can mean positions stay vacant for months or even years at a significant cost to productivity. The effects can be even harsher for small businesses.

Employment Benefits

The liability on the part of the employer will increase when the employer has to give all benefits to the employee who is infected with HIV since, sooner or later the person is going to develop symptoms of AIDS. The monetary liability due to the death of an employee to his/her family will be very high. When there are more infections and number of deaths due to the AIDS, the employer will have to spend, a huge amount on the employment benefits like paying back the provident fund. The insurance companies will have to pay back huge amounts due to premature death of persons. Most of the companies will have to give employment to the next kin of the employee on the basis of provision of died-inharness.

Health Care

Despite the fact that the Indian Government evolved a Health Policy as far back as 1983, health care services have been deteriorating and do not meet people's expectation. Thus, they turn to private health care, which is not regulated by any statute, or laws unlike the public health care sector. According to the National Sample Survey' conducted by the National Council for Applied Economic Research, sixty to eighty per cent of health care is sought in the private sector for which households contribute four to six percent of the total income.

With the numbers of HIV infections on the rise daily, there will be a pressing and urgent need for the health care infrastructure to provide treatment for people living with HIV/AIDS. As of today, very few private hospitals are willing to admit and treat people living with HIV/AIDS. Most of the workforce is eligible for, health care services under the Employee State Insurance (ESI) Act. ESI is administered by the Government. The burden of HIV will increase the expenditure of the government. Industries that do not come under the ESI scheme have to make provision for providing health care. Some industries have evolved medical insurance schemes for their workforce.

For people living with HIV/AIDS, the health care setting is the most conspicuous environment for HIV/AIDSrelated discrimination. The denial of services vis-a-vis care and support represents one of the most immediate and pressing concerns of people living with HIV/AIDS. There are innumerable instances of discrimination against people living with HIV/AIDS viz. refusal of doctors to touch patients during routine medical examination, delays in treatment, breach of confidentiality, mandatory or routine testing without informed consent, wrapping dead bodies of HIV positive people in plastic sheets etc.

In case workers are detected as HIV positive, they cannot just be removed from the rolls. Medical care has to be given to them and the cost of reducing the effect of HIV/ AIDS on the health of the individual is very high. More than that AIDS related symptoms can cause several health problems for the individuals infected with HIV. For example in India, where 50-60 per cent of the population are already carriers of the Tuberculosis Bacillus (T.B), the HIV epidemic is likely to lead to a dramatic increase in active TB cases.

This will result in huge amount of expenses from the part of the emplpyer on taking care of health issues of the employees. Since most of the companies have a limited health care delivery system, and the public health system is inadequate to provide care to AIDS patients, a lot of work needs to be done to tackle the pandemic.

Social Issues Related to HIV and Workplace

Denial

A common misconception is that HIV is someone else's problem. It is a disease of selected groups commonly referred to as "high risk groups" i.e., promiscuous people, intravenous drug users, and foreigners. This ignores the evidence that the greatest single mode of transmission of HIV is heterosexual activities outside marriage. The virus does not put groups at risk. Statistics demonstrate that the virus already spread at an alarming rate in Asia. Continued beliefs that HIV only affects a selected population is dangerous allowing large sectors of the society to feel protected from the epidemic thus blocking the understanding of the necessity to develop effective intervention strategies.

Fear

Over twenty five years into the epidemic and still the most common response to the subject of AIDS is fear. Misinformation, misconceptions and dread of the unknown heighten the anxiety felt by those who have first encountered with a person with HIV/AIDS, or someone known to have HIV disease. Fear is best handled by allowing people to express their concerns openly. Acknowledgement of their feelings and discussion about them helps to dissipate the fear.

Discrimination

Fear often leads to discrimination against people who have HIV. Loss of jobs, friends, and homes are riot uncommon occurrences. Mistaken beliefs that casual contacts can spread the virus have led to the isolation and loss of dignity and respect to which people infected with the virus often become subject. Presenting medically incorrect facts and discussing the misconception that cause fear will reduce the discrimination that results from it.

Confidentiality

A person's medical history is confidential. Revelation of items such as a person's HIV status can lead to the consequences of his/her being stigmatized and subjected to discrimination. HIV is still associated with discrimination due to misconceptions of how the virus is transmitted. Cases of people losing their jobs, home and families have occurred after disclosure that they are infected with the HIV virus.

The medical facts regarding transmission of the virus clearly prove that ordinary workplace behaviour and interaction does not lead to the spread of infection. To reduce disruption in the workplace and protect the infected individual, privacy about his/her status is required. United Nations policy states, "Confidentiality regarding all medical information, including HIV/ AIDS status, must be maintained.

Applicants for Employment

The National AIDS Control policy does not allow for HIV testing as a pre condition for employment. Numerous Supreme Court rulings have upheld that people suffering from HIV have a right to employment. They can not be denied a job if they are capable of performing the job. Some companies screen blood for HIV as part of the assessment of fitness to work. Screening of this kind includes direct methods (HIV testing), indirect methods (Assessment of risk behaviour) and questions about HIV tests already taken. Pre-employment HIV/AIDS screening for insurance or other purposes raises serious concerns about discrimination and merits further close scrutiny.

There is no scientific reason to do a pre employment check up. First of all, there is no guarantee that the person will not have HIV even if he/ she is tested negative for once due to the fact that he/she may be in the window period or may acquire the infection after the test has been done. Secondly, it is known that HIV will not spread through casual contacts in the context of work, it is highly discriminatory to deny employment to a person infected with HIV. Thirdly it is highly unethical to screen the blood of a person without his consent. National and international bodies endorse this point of view.

Persons in Employment

Persons in employment usually undergo screening while applying for promotion or as part of routine by the organisation. A lot of issues related to testing while a person is in service are being debated such as:

Informed Consent

Most of the time, the testing is done without consent from the employee, which is against the national policy on HIV testing. Very often, blood samples are taken in the name of routine checkup.

Confidentiality

Confidentiality regarding all medical information including HIV status is supposed to be maintained by the employer even if the test is done with the consent of an individual, which often does not happen. Most of the time rumors spread and the employers as well as the co-workers often harass the infected person. Very often, the test is associated with loss of job for HIV positive person.

Informing the Employer

There is no obligation for the employee to inform the employer regarding his or her HIV/AIDS status.

Legal Issues Related to HIV/AIDS and Workplace

The Universal Declaration of Human Rights (Article 25) upholds the right to a standard of living adequate for the health and the well-being of individuals and their families Article 12.1 of the International Convention on Economic, Social and Cultural Rights recognises the right to the enjoyment of the highest attainable standard of physical and mental health. In terms of HIV, this means that people living with HIV or who are at risk of contracting HIV can safely seek information, voluntary testing, and counselling and medical care.

Human Rights and HIV

The reason why human rights are so important in the context of HIV arises from the fact that many of the people who have been or will be most affected by the epidemic are people who are already in a socially disadvantaged position. The people who remain vulnerable are those who are denied the means of protecting themselves against HIV because of economic need, for example, or powerlessness to control the basis upo n with their sexual relationship takes place.

Many factors come into play here. These are poverty, geographical isolation, inadequate health care and health education, and cultural values that compel certain practices that expose some members of the community to the risk of HIV infections are those who are already socially and economically vulnerable means that the need to incorporate human rights issues into HIV policy is essential.

The Law and HIV

The law has an important impact on how the HIV epidemic is experiencecd in any country. This became evident very early on in the epidemic because many of the people affected, such as sex workers, gay men and drug users, were already the target of punitive legal provisions. Creating a supportive legal environment can involve both positive and negative legal interventions. The laws that we do not need are the laws which discriminate against people with HIV, which distance them from their communities and which makes it less likely that these people will share in the common interest to reduce the effects of epidemics.

Ethics and Law

Ethics and laws have become common in the context of HIV policy. This is done for obvious reasons because the ethical dilemmas that arise are invariably played out in legal terms. Nonetheless, the blurring of the distinction between law and ethics can sometimes obscure the fact that tensions may exist between ethical imperatives and legal obligations. It is therefore worth considering the interaction between the law, ethics and HIV.

ADDRESSING ISSUES OF HIV/AIDS AT THE WORKPLACE

The disruption in the workplace caused by the fear of HIV can be minimized by providing an HIV education and support system to all employers and employees and by establishing HIV related personnel policies well in advance of any problems. However, only a comprehensive educational programme supported by top management will encourage employees to comply. Successful workplace education programmes have approached executives first to help them develop an understanding of the basic facts regarding HIV. This knowledge can be used to develop appropriate policy measures that will maintain a high level of worker productivity, ensure the rights and dignity of all, clarify legal issues and create an atmosphere conducive to caring for and promoting the health of all workers.

The ILO encourages a comprehensive approach to workplace polices and programmes based on protecting infected and affected workers' rights, and offering prevention and care services. Its Code o f Practice on HIV/AIDS and the world of work is a framework for action that establishes policy development principles, and provides practical programming guidance on prevention and behaviour change. In partnership with the Global Fund to fight AIDS, Tuberculosis and Malaria, and the Global Business Coalition on HIV/AIDS, the ILO works to extend care and treatment access through occupational health services, and supports community outreach. But many HIV-positive workers are reluctant to participate in such programmes because they fear losing their jobs or being ostracized.

Developing a climate that encourages workers' participation can be facilitated by involving trade unions or workers' representatives in planning and implementing workplace programmes. Trade unions, and confederations of trade unions, are playing an increasingly important role in strengthening national AIDS responses. For example, the South African Clothing and Textile Workers' Union provided HIV and AIDS training to 1100 shop stewards between 2002 and 2004. In India, Confederation of Indian Industry (CII) is starting programmes to improve the HIV/AIDS awareness among the workers. A workplace education programme meeting the needs of all workers must be developed. Each programme must be tailored to the particular audience and company. Union representatives or worker spokes persons can be involved in the design of the educational programme. Logistic decisions regarding whom, where how and when this programme should be undertaken must be determined both to meet the objectives of the programme and to create the minimum disruption in the workplace.

Planning HIV/AIDS Education Programme

The first step in addressing the issues is acknowledging the need for an HIV/AIDS education programme. This needs to be followed up by contacts with professional groups which can assist in the development of th'at programme. In some communities, local health departments or national AIDS committees may have material to assist in this process. The UN AIDS and WHO has several publications for this purpose. In other countries, local non-governmental agencies may be the strongest ally. Steps for Planning HIV/ AIDS Education programme: Approach management and then, take the steps necessary to get support from the chief executive officer and senior management.

- Compile information on HIV/AIDS and on what other organisations similar to yours have done.
- Identify a leader who can champion the cause for an HIV/AIDS education programme. If there is more than one person who is well suited for the opportunity, then develop a team.
- Encourage Teamwork.
- Educate yourself on this issue so that you can educate others.
- Gather information about resources and use them as needed. There are a number of excellent providers for HIV education programmes for workplaces.
- Plan for budget including the cost of material (brochures, videos, flyers, reprints etc.).
- Plan to train managers and supervisors so that they are knowledgeable, about HIV/AIDS.
- Develop a marketing communications plan with a message that you intend to send and communicate the basic information needed to avoid potential confusion around the issue.
- Plan to hold employee sessions to explain organisation's HIV/AIDS workplace policy, information on how HIV/AIDS is transmitted, prevention methods, company benefits available to employees afflicted with the disease, confidentiality requirements etc.

Advocacy

Though legal position is clear that public sector health care institution/ providers cannot refuse medical care for people living with HIV/AIDS, people living with HIV/ AIDS encounter much discrimination vis-a-vis their access to health care. There is an urgent need for advocacy with the health care sector in order to improve the quality of health care available to HIV positive people. Lawyers collective HIV/AIDS Unit, in a participatory process with health care workers, AIDS Unit and people living with HIV/AIDS have developed draft protocols on patient management relating to health care services of those affected by HIV/AIDS. The protocols have been developed with a view to improving the access and quality of health care services available to people living with HIV/AIDS while respecting the rights of health care workers.

WORKPLACE POLICY ON HIV/AIDS

Policy

Every company should have in place a policy that should address how communicable diseases should be handled in the workplace. The policy is an important first step. It sets the tone for communicating information about HIV as a workplace and productivity issue. Policy statements should be educational in tone and provide guidance for employees in terms of procedures and resources. However, companies do need a policy that deals with treatment of employees who are HIV positive.

The policy can be quite extensive or stated in a few simple paragraphs. The agency culture and management attitude will determine the length and extensiveness of the policy. Managers and supervisors should be involved in developing the policy. If this is not possible, they should be given the policy prior to other employees to become familiar with it so they may address employees concerns. When writing the policy many issues need to be considered. The workplace policy should spell out how the company will treat and protect employee's confidentiality regarding HIV. As a person dealing with HIV infected person, you are keenly aware of the importance of confidentiality for clients.

The same care and compassion should be extended to the workers with confidential issues. One way this point is illustrated in the manner in which healthcare claims are filed in the company. Many people (employees) in large companies file claims with their human resource department. This means that any claims for reimbursement identify the presenting problem in the claim form or the medical bill. When these claims are turned in, the company personnel handling them know the diagnosis of the employee. Many employees, might feel awkward and embarrassed in this situation but it certainly affects employees living with HIV. The workplace policy should address this problem. A solution would be a recommendation to management to contract out the claims process to an external business.

The policy will also need to address the company's nondiscrimination policy related to HIV infection. The policy will need to address employee education and where to go for help within the company. As with many work assignments, if time and energy are invested initially, the implementation and effectiveness phase will be much smoother. After the policy is written, it is important that it is not to be filed and forgotten. The policy should be posted in a common area so that it becomes a part of everyday work life.

Policy Development and Implementation

Policy development and implementation is a dynamic process not a static event.

Therefore, HIV/AIDS workplace policies should be:

- Communicated to all concerned
- Continually review the policy in the light of epidemiological and other scientific information
- Monitor for their successful implementation
- Evaluate for effectiveness
- Policy components

HIV/AIDS screening as a part of the assessment of fitness to work is unnecessary and should not be required.

Some of the suggested policy components are listed below:

- *Confidentiality*: Confidentiality regarding all medical information, including HIV/AIDS status, must be maintained.
- *Informing the employer*: There should be no obligation for the employee to inform the employer regarding his or her HIV/AIDS status.
- *Protection of employee*: Persons in the workplace affected by, or perceived to be affected by HIV/AIDS, must be protected from stigmatization and discrimination by co-workers, unions, employers or clients. Information and education are essential to maintain the climate of mutual understanding necessary to ensure this protection.
- *Access to services for employees*: Employees and their families should have access to information and educational programmes on HIV/AIDS as well as to relevant counselling and appropriate referral.
- *Benefits*: HIV infected employees should not be discriminated against, and should have access to and receive standard social security benefits and occupationally related benefits.
- *Reasonable changes in working arrangements*: HIV infection by itself is not associated with any limitation in fitness to work. If fitness to work is impaired by HIV related illness, reasonable alternative working arrangements should be made. This is similar to impairment caused by any medical condition.
- *Continuation of employment*: HIV infection is not a cause for termination of employment. As with many other illnesses, people with HIV related illness should be able to work as long as they are medically fit for available, appropriate work.

First Aid

In any situation requiring first aid in the workplace, standard precautions need to be taken. If the person has a wound or is bleeding, gloves have to be worn.

NGO AND CORPORATE SECTOR INITIATIVES IN INDIA FOR PREVENTION OF HIV/AIDS IN THE WORKPLACE

As the epidemic spreads at an increasing rate, many Non Government Organisations (NGOs) and corporate companies have realized the importance of developing preventive programs. Many have targeted the workplace as an appropriate setting for their efforts. Training modules, videos, peer training programs and written materials have been developed to assist in comprehensive workplace intervention programs. Business/NGO collaboration is important for workplace initiatives for HIV/AIDS prevention. In India, a number of Corporate Houses have initiated programmes for prevention of HIV/AIDS in the workplace. The Confederation of Indian Industries (CII) has developed certain modules on HIV/AIDS Prevention and Care. They also have training and communication materials and modules that are being extensively used by their member Industries.

An NGO, after providing basic education about the medical facts and socio-cultural implications of HIV can help management prepare workplace policies that will guide the company's response to questions and concerns about HIV. An NGO can also be asked to prepare management to deal with HIV related issues that are likely to arise in the workplace. Then, in conjunction with management it can draw up the most effective and efficient method of providing training to line workers. If necessary the NGO can offer ongoing support in the form of pre- and post-test counselling, individual sessions/ training of trainers; others can offer legal guidance, support for condom distribution, family counselling or education and an opportunity to allow people openly to discuss sexuality.

The need to Collaborate

India must address the crisis of AIDS. Each day the number of infected persons is growing. All efforts must be made to curb the rate of infection. AIDS cannot be stopped by any one sector of society. Only through alliances and partnerships, which maximize available human material resources, can we hope to control the epidemic. Non-governmental organisations have a front-line role to play in response to the HIV epidemic. In some developing countries, NGOs have already developed new community-based forms of care, counselling and support for people with HIV and their families. NGOs are also involved in educating communities about HIV/AIDS.

5

Social Institution of Marriage

MARRIAGE AND FAMILY: CHOOSING LIFE PARTNER

MEANING OF MARRIAGE

Marriage is a common term that we come across in our daily life. Have you ever thought of it seriously? What is the meaning of marriage? Is it a mere relationship between a man and woman to live together and have children? Is it a man-made institution? When did such an institution come into existence? It will be really interesting to ponder over the answers to the above questions – much more so about the meaning, scope, purpose and history of marriage. The term 'marriage' has different meanings and connotations for different people. To some, marriage is a relationship between men and women for the propagation of the human species. Some people take it as a license for sex. Yet another group considers marriage as a means for companionship. Marriage comprises all these views and much more. It is a very complex institution which can not be defined in a sentence or two. Many sociologists and philosophers have given differing views about the meaning and scope of marriage. Marriage is not an integral part of human nature, but it is a man-made custom or institution which was present even in prehistoric times. It is not a natural relationship but a conscious commitment between a man and a woman. With the advancement of civilization marriage became a social function with religious and legal sanction. As stated earlier, marriage has different meanings and connotations. Let us look at some of them.

Marriage as a Relationship

Marriage is one of the deepest and most fulfilling of human relationships. It has existed in varying forms throughout the history of man, responding to the fundamental needs and social aspirations of each generation.

Marriage as an Institution

Marriage is a union of man and woman their bodies, minds and souls, emotions and desires. The essence of this union is love. Marriage is considered to be a primary relationship, because it is a personal relationship between the partners. Lin Yutan gives a beautiful explanation of marriage. He says "woman is water and man is clay and the clay holds the water and gives it substance in which water moves and lives and has its full being".

The Biological Aspect of Marriage

The animal mates, but man marries. Looking from the biological point of view, we can say that mating is a biological matter, while marriage is a social affair. The sex instinct is one of the basic instincts for reproduction. In the case of man, however, from the beginning of society, this instinct has been subjected to distinct regulations and control. Marriage may be defined as the mechanism of regulation and control of biological reproduction. In the animal kingdom there are no definite rules for mating because they have no society and social norms. But in human society there are various kinds of social controls, religious limitations and even laws of marriage. For human beings, the sex relations are allowed within certain permitted limits. Marriage is a holy sanctifying, life long, comprehensive, loving union of a man and a woman, leading to the procreation of children.

The Social Aspects of Marriage

We have seen that there are certain biological aspects of human marriage, while there are more social aspects in it. These social aspects are most important in human society. The basic factor in marriage is love. True love between the man and woman in marriage is a complete giving of one to another. There should be a union of the souls and minds. There should be a union of emotions and wills. All these imply complete, exclusive and life long giving of ones self to the other.

The Psychological Aspect of Marriage

Marriage is an integral part of human existence. In marriage man's basic longing for communication and completeness finds its natural culmination. Human beings find their fulfillment as men and women. Marriage is the means by which two persons seeking a more perfect life give themselves totally to each other. In a marriage the male and female compliment each other. It fills the physical and psychological void which exists in human being, if they are alone. Marriage makes possible the satisfaction of the strong and natural tendency of male and female to be together in the union for which nature has designed them.

The Legal Aspect of Marriage

The union between man and woman must be legitimate. So marriage should get legal, social and civil acceptance. Legal sanction of marriage is based on prevailing social norms and customs. It varies from one society to another. The marriage can be legally contracted only by those who are able to perform the basic act of marriage. The legal minimum age for marriage in India is 18 years for girls and 21 years for boys.

THE FUNCTIONS AND PURPOSES OF MARRIAGE

Have you ever thought of the question why a person should get married? The first answer that comes to your mind may be for the propagation of the human species. Let us try to find the answer.

Marriage for Union and Procreation

What is the purpose of marriage? If it is only for procreation, marriage is not a must. Of course, one of the important purposes of marriage is union and procreation. The union in marriage is a medium of physical, psychological and spiritual communication of love and commitment of self.

Marriage for Sex

The natural end of sexual relationship is conception of children. Hence the procreation of children is an essential purpose of marriage. An equally important purpose is the union itself, the mutual love, pleasure and happiness of the husband and wife. Marriage, therefore, fosters mutual love and attachment. It provides for the legitimate expression of sexual satisfaction.

Marriage for Companionship and Friendship

The most important need of the human being is the intimacy in living with and making a commitment to another human being. What is friendship? According to Jennet Kid, "Friendship is having a privileged position in someone else's life and giving them a privileged position in our own. It is sharing ourselves with those we like". Friendship is the cornerstone of marriage which lasts even when the sexual desire is over. It remains even after the children are grown up and settled. It only deepens with years. This is what is meant by companionship or friendship. It enriches man and woman by increasing unselfishness and by deepening his/her capacity for love, and sacrifice. Hence marriage is love, it is sex, it is family, but ultimately and essentially it is companionship or friendship.

Marriage for Socialization

Marriage is a means through which the socialization and growth of a person reach its fulfillment. It provides numerous opportunities to bring about security, cooperation and love. Another purpose of marriage is to create a family to provide the natural environment in which a person can realize himself/herself and reach out to others in an attitude of dedication and service. It gives society a firm base, and children a stable environment to grow.

Marriage for Matured Relationship

Still another purpose of marriage is attainment of maturity through the establishment of relationships in marriage. Rearing and educating the children also is a purpose of marriage. The parent-child relationship is an intimate relationship.

Some Practical Purposes or Utilitarian Aspects of Marriage

- It ensures security to women who have to undergo long periods of pregnancy.
- It provides security to the offspring.
- It ensures the health life which gives stability to society.
- It makes society more cohesive through relationships.
- It simplifies blood relationships.

THE HISTORICAL DEVELOPMENT OF MARRIAGE

It is interesting to study the historical development of marriage. When did it commence? How did it attain its present structure and status? It is not easy to get the facts about marriage in the prehistoric era. We have to depend upon the studies of anthropologists and other available details of folklore and traditions. Even though the religious books mention marriage, we cannot conclude that marriage came into existence with the beginning of human life on earth. In the pre-historic ages people lived like animals and there were no social norms and rules to guide them. But gradually due to his superiority over the animals, man began to formulate some social patterns of behaviour.

In the early stages of human life, sexual life and procreation was a natural process. The earth was not owned by anybody. Nobody bothered to own the land. But gradually man began to cultivate the land and came to know about the productivity of the soil. This knowledge motivated him to own the land. This also led to many disputes and fights for the ownership of land. Finally they reached on agreement with regard to some type of control or laws about the ownership of land.

This is evident from social contract theory. The desire of man to own the land, which is productive, led him to the idea of owning any thing that is productive. Knowing that the woman can procreate children, men tried to own more women and thereby get more and more children. This also ended the conflicts and fights. Gradually restrictions and regulations came in procuring women. This finally culminated in the form of a social institution of marriage with all its laws and regulations and customs.

THE FAMILY

Just like marriage, family is also a very familiar term. We all come from families. We see families around us. Family is an integral part of our life. Can we answer these questions: What is a family? What is the need for a family? Who constitute the family? Is it a mere union of parents and children? What is the relationship between the members in a family? Is the family a human invention or a natural evolution? Is it found among animals also? What are the forms of family in different ages and different cultures?

The Need for a Family

The family was a necessary precondition for human evolution, for without it human existence would not have been possible. The human infant is born helpless. It has a potential for physical and mental development. But it requires years to achieve its maturity. In the case of animals, their young ones are able to take care of themselves shortly after birth. But for human beings the long period of pregnancy and the prolonged helplessness in infancy and childhood, needs a long association of parents. This has resulted in the formation of a family.

The Evolution of the Family

The family as a group of parents and offspring's existed even before the appearance of man upon this planet. Family like association is seen among birds and higher mammals. The chimpanzee is a highly social creature which lives in family groups. The family life of apes and human beings can be compared. There is a selection of a mate, interaction between male and female, levels of control among father, mother and children and a child is taken care of primarily by mother. There is a great deal of difference between the family life of apes, mammals and birds and that of man. In the former case, the nature of family life throughout the world is the same in any given species. But in the case of man, family behaviour varies greatly from one society to another. In the animal family, the behaviour of the members is motivated by instinct, whereas in the human family it is motivated by culture. The animal family is largely biological in nature, while in the human family its structure and functions are shaped by culture.

According to many sociologists, man in course of his evolution might have developed one or another family form as determined by situational and historical factors. In short we can say that geographic environment, economic conditions and culture rather than biological factors were the determinants of human family patterns. In man, the family is not only a biological group it is first and foremost a social institution.

The Definition of Family

We have seen that the structure and function of the family varies from place to place. So it is difficult to give a definition of the term 'family'. However, the definition of the family must include that which is common to the great variety of human groups to which the term 'family' has been applied. There are certain characteristics that are common to the human family in all times and in all places that differentiate the family from other social groups.

According to Ernest W Burgess and Harvey. J. Lock, these characteristics are:

- The family is composed of persons united by the ties of marriage, blood or adoption. The bond between husband and wife is that of marriage, and the relationship between parents and children is generally that of blood and sometimes that of adoption.

- The members of the family typically live together under one roof and constitute a single household. Sometimes, as in the past, the household is large consisting of three or four or even five generations. Today the household is small, consisting of the husband and wife with or without one or two children.
- The family is a unity of interacting and intercommunicating persons. They play the roles of husband and wife, father and mother, son and daughter, brother and sister. These roles are defined by the community.
- The family maintains a common culture derived mainly from the general culture. Usually this culture is the outcome of the merging of the two cultures of the husband and wife.

On the basis of the above characteristics the family may be defined "as a group of persons united by the ties of marriage, blood or adoption, constituting a single household; interacting and communicating with each other in their respective social roles as husband and wife, mother and father, son and daughter, brother and sister and creating and maintaining a common culture". A family is a community of people living together in an environment which is a centre of healing, a place where one can live, where one can admit one's frustrations, stupidities and anger to people who do not retaliate.

It is in the school of everyday family life, with all masks dropped and hypocrisies exposed, that man, woman and child acquire the potential to know what it is to be truly human, and fully human people have tried alternative arrangements for a family. But none of them are as efficient as a family. Children thrive best when they have a father and mother to love and protect them in a home. The parents also need the life long commitment in which love is proved.

The Indian Family

The family system all over the world are changing today and family relations are becoming weaker and weaker day by day. The influence of the family over the children is weakening due to the great social, political and economic changes. In the midst of these changes, India still has a time tested heritage of stable family structure. It is still the basic unit of our society and the medium of cultural transmission. The family still holds its solidarity and plays an important role in the formation of values in our society. In spite of the solidarity in the Indian families, a salient social transformation is taking place in the Indian families also.

With the empowerment of women and the women getting more and more educated, the traditional family patterns are gradually disappearing. Modernization has its roots in westernization and it has questioned the traditional family values and structures. Parental influence is also weakening day by day. The religious and moral values present in the family are giving way to secular and pragmatic values.

TYPES OF FAMILY PATTERN

The three chief historical stages in the evolution of the family are:

- The large patriarchal family characteristic of ancient society;
- The small patriarchal family which had its origin in the medieval period; and
- The modern democratic or nuclear family which is the product of the industrial revolution and the economic and social changes that followed.

The large patriarchal family was prevalent in China, India and Japan. Here the senior male member was the head of the family. He lived with his children and grand children which came up to four or five generations. The patriarch, the head of the family, had supreme authority over all other members of the family. This type of family was a result of the agricultural and pastoral mode of existence.

The small patriarchal family was the second stage in the evolution of the family structure. It consisted of husband and wife and children and one or two grandparents and one or two unmarried brothers and sisters of the husband and wife. This type of family was mostly seen in urban areas where the members used to work in industries. Here also the senior male member had the supreme authority over the whole family.

The democratic or nuclear family consists of only the husband and wife and the children. This type of family system is more prevalent in modern society. Here the husband and wife share more responsibility and are more free. They can take their own decisions. Children can also join in the decision making consistent with the advancement in age. In India we find three types of family structures which are almost identical with the historical family patterns.

They are:

- The large joint family;
- The nuclear family; and
- The stem or extended family

Joint Family

The large joint family is almost like the large patriarchal family where three or four generations of parents and off springs live together. This is mostly seen in rural areas. These families are mostly agricultural families.

Advantages of the Joint Family

The joint family assures shelter for the aged and sick, social security for the unemployed and support for the young couple. Children grow up in an atmosphere of security and affection. The newly married couple get training in family life and child care. The sons get the training from their father, uncle and grandfathers. The daughters get it from their mothers, aunts and grandmothers. In a joint family, the wisdom and experience of the elders are shared. The joint family has its own codes of behaviour and its own values which are transmitted from one generation to the other generation. On the whole, we can say that the joint family provides an umbrella of support which covers financial loss, social security and even provides informal counselling.

Disadvantages of the Joint Family

In the joint family the supreme authority is vested in the senior male member. So the whole life of the family goes according to his efficiency and attitudes. The junior members may not take up any responsibility and initiative. There is no freedom for the individuals, especially women. The head of the family may not be able to adjust to the social changes that are taking place outside the family. There will be a perpetuation of old customs and values.

Nuclear Family

In a nuclear family, the husband and wife live with their children. This is mostly seen in urban areas. Both the husband and wife may be earning members in such families.

Advantages

The husband and wife have the full freedom to act according to their own ideas. There is more financial security and individual freedom. This type of families can easily adapt to social changes. There is more responsibility and initiative for all the members.

Disadvantages

There is nobody to help and guide the members, especially when some conflict arises. The practical wisdom and emotional security offered by the joint family is lacking in a nuclear family. There is nobody to look after the children. Children miss the protection and affection of grand parents. Working mothers are forced to leave the children either with the servants or in a day care centre.

The Stem or Extended Family

This is midway between the joint family and the nuclear family. The husband, wife and children live with one of their grand parents.

Advantages

This type of family has all the advantages of the joint family and the nuclear family, provided the grandparents do not dominate. Children are looked after properly. Grandparents also may not feel the loneliness and will be happy with their children and grandchildren. Parents can give all the security and guidance to their son and daughter, who are newly married.

Disadvantages

If the parents who live with their son/daughter are too dominating, the young couple may loose their freedom and individuality. There are chances of problems with in-laws. For growth in marriage, it is desirable that the couple live on their own. Each system of family has its own advantages and disadvantages. But if the members are cooperative and have concern for each other, the disadvantages can be reduced to the minimum. The newly married couple who start their family life should have the freedom and initiative of a nuclear family and the emotional security and practical wisdom of a joint family. They should have the feeling of the 'home' where one has full relaxation and recreation and can live without masks.

Functions of the Family

The family is the basic unit of society. Today's family faces lot of problems due to the social changes. In spite of the problems in the family, it continues to exist because it meets the needs of children, adults and society at large.

The family:

- Provides for the reproduction of the race;
- Passes on the cultural heritage of the group;
- Provides physical security, protection and the material opportunities for living and growth;
- Meets the deep emotional needs of both children and adults and provides for their social, emotional, intellectual and spiritual development;
- Develops in its members socially desirable character traits and acceptable moral standards;
- Develops an orderly system of living among its members with provision for eating, sleeping, school, work, etc., and
- Develops sound relationships among members of the family and between them and their neighbours.

The family thus meets the basic physiological and psychological needs of its members.

The Social Role of the Family

Apart from the above functions the family has a social role also. The family, being the basic unit of society, has a vital and organic link with society. It is from the family that the citizens come and it is within the family that they find the first school of social virtues. The family is the bridge between the child and society. In the family, the child learns mutual respect, concern for others, generous service, deep solidarity, personal responsibility etc. These are the basic steps of social life. The family is thus the most effective means of humanizing and personalizing society. The family is the custodian and transmitter of values.

Society should also respect and foster the family. The family is the very first cell in the social structure and the very first social union, which is indispensable. The so-called developed countries have now realized the fact that their broken families are heading towards a great social disaster so they are exhorting the parents to strengthen the family ties. "Marriage and family are a union for which there is no substitute. Nothing can take their place. You can even say: as the families are, so will mankind be".

CHOOSING A PARTNER

Now that you have learned so much about marriage and family, you will be in a position to answer the question "How will you choose your partner for life" ? Marriage is a life-long commitment and relationship and hence the selection of a partner is very important. The choice of an ideal partner is one of the basic requirements for a successful marriage. Suppose you are going for a journey. You would like to have a companion who is agreeable to you in all respects. So what about your companion, who is to travel with you through your whole life, till death? Marriage is one of the three great events in life along with birth and death. Birth just happens and death is beyond our control. Marriage is however something which can be decided. We can decide whom to marry and when to marry.

There is a common saying among the Arabs " If you want to select a horse, select from among hundred horses. If it is a friend it should be one among thousand. But if it is a wife, it is should be from thousands". This implies the importance of choosing a partner in marriage. It should not be a casual or careless selection. It should be a long thought out process. Very few people are inclined to analyse the factors that are to be looked into in selecting a partner. There is a common belief that marriages are made in heaven or it is fate, luck or providence. But this issue of choice of spouse is not something to be completely left to fate or luck.

A scientific approach is necessary in the selection. There are certain determinants for mate selection. The patterns of arrangement for the selection of the mate differ from culture to culture. In certain cultures marriage is primarily a social and economic arrangement between two families. Here the choice of the mate is still the responsibility of the parents. Parents select the bride or bridegroom for their children. The young couple have little choice in this matter. They may not have the opportunity to become acquainted before the wedding. This type of marriage is known as arranged marriage.

Arranged marriages are now giving way to selection by the young people themselves. Both procedures have their advantages and disadvantages. Mate selection, when arranged by parents, stressed social and economic considerations. They minimized or even ignored the sentiments of love and interpersonal relations of the young people. The youngsters make the choice on the basis of compatibility and personal attraction. They may not conform to parental standards like caste, religion, economic security etc. The best pattern is to let the young people find out heir own mates with the guidance and consent of the parents.

This pattern is known as guided choice. Anyway, parents should guide their children without showing too much worry or haste. Allow the young people to decide on their partners as far as they can. But in every case, their elders should be the controlling factor. At the same time, parents should not give the impression that they have a readymade decision in their minds. Youngsters on their part should rely on their parents, recognizing their experience and their sincere desire for the good of their children.

As said earlier, marriage is a life-long relationship and commitment. There are certain qualities or social expectations that are commonly appreciated in a partner. There should be compatibility between the partners in maturity, health, behaviour patterns or character, caste and religion, economic status, education and intelligence, attitudes, and values or the basic orientation to life etc. Let us consider them one by one.

Maturity

Under 'maturity' come physical maturity, emotional maturity and social and intellectual maturity. Maturity is a term which comprises many things. When we say that the partner should have the maturity for a married life, it means the ability to take up the full responsibility of a family. Age is one important factor that comes under physical maturity. According to the Indian Marriage Act, the minimum age for marriage for woman is 18 and for man is 21. But from practical experience it is seem that the ideal age for woman is 21 to 24 and for man is 25 to 30. By that time they are physically mature and emotionally stable. If the man or woman lacks physical maturity he/she may find it difficult to make marital adjustments and to take up the responsibility as husband and wife and as parents.

What should be the age difference between the partners? Who should be older? The social expectation is that the man should be older and there should not be much difference of age between the partners. But for so many practical reasons, it may not be possible to strictly adhere to this. Still, it is always good to stick on to these expectations to avoid further complications later on. One of the reasons for marital breakdown is the great or wide disparity of age between husband and wife.

Emotional Maturity

It consists of the ability to control one's emotions and passions. Emotional maturity helps to develop selfrestraint and the attitude of self sacrifice. These are the essential requisites for a happy married life. Emotional maturity can be tested only at the times of crisis. He will adapt his course of action, overcome obstacles and accept the inevitable with grace and calmness. To an immature person, any frustration may bring about temper tantrums. An emotionally matured person is able to avoid frequent bad mood and has the ability to establish and maintain personal relationships. He is able to endure normal discomforts and disappointments and to overcome suspicion and jealousy. In short, he has the ability to give and receive that is ability to love.

Empathy is another characteristic of an emotionally matured persons. It is ability to perceive the feelings of others. It involves the willingness to recognize the needs of others and to assume the responsibility of meeting them. Getting married means taking up a responsibility for a life time. The partners have to meet each other's needs, bring up children, support the family financially and look after the members of the family. Life long commitment is one feature of the responsibility of marriage. It is related to the stability that comes with maturity.

A clear sign of emotional maturity is the ability to reflect before speaking and the readiness to talk with others. This is highly essential in husband/wife relationship. An emotionally mature person has, first of all, insight and foresight in his thinking. He can evaluate himself as well as the world around him in a realistic manner. He can also face the facts of life realistically and anticipate the results of his action. He develops a sense of independence. He is able to make his own judgments and decisions.

The maturity which marriage requires is not the achievement of one day. Emotional maturity can be achieved only by the satisfaction of the various needs of the child at each stage of development. Proper disciplining of emotions is necessary during the childhood for attaining emotional maturity, which results in self-confidence, self-control and affectional maturity. What is affectional maturity? It may be an unfamiliar term for you. It is the capacity to relate with people of different groups. The infant is at first interested in himself/herself or his/her mother.

This interest is then shifted to playmates of his own sex during school age and to the opposite sex during adolescence. When the person comes to maturity, the affectional maturity is towards his partner. One who is ready for marriage should have this affectional maturity so as to develop a good husband wife relationship. This is basic requirement for marital harmony.

Social Maturity

Social maturity is evident when one can relate oneself to others in a selfless and responsible way. One should not think only in terms of immediate wish fulfillments or satisfaction or personal desires. The main signs of social maturity are respect for others, honesty, frankness, courage and the ability to provide whatever a family needs. An emotionally mature person need not necessarily be socially mature if he has not experienced a social life. Social maturity comes from the fulfillment of one's quota of premarital living. Every boy and girl should have an experience of social life before marriage. Usually after completing this education, youngsters are employed and they have a 'free' time to assume the responsibilities of life and mingle with people. During this time they may come across persons of other sex, whom they may choose as their partners in life. This is a time of fantasy. Any way, this free time before marriage is essential for acquiring social maturity.

After exploring for a partner, they finally settle down, and are ready for marriage. One characteristic of social maturity is one's willingness to disregard unknown potential marriage partners in their fantasy. They will be ready to commit themselves to build up a relationship with a particular person. It is also important to be independent for a while. Having just become free from parents, it is too early to take one the bonds of matrimony. Spare time can be used as one may deem fit. Jobs can be changed. Travels can be made according to the availability of money and time.

Nobody else's wishes have to be consulted, nor moods catered to. Since they were more closely supervised than boys during childhood and adolescence, they have yet to achieve a full sense of personal identity. Usually many girls in India, especially in the rural areas, do not get this free time for socialization and acquiring social maturity. This is because they are married immediately after their schooling or graduation. Most of them are not permitted to work outside their homes. This is a real drawback as far as marriage is concerned.

Intellectual Maturity

Intellectual maturity lies in the ability to understand persons, events, situations and problems. It is the capacity to formulate one's ideas, opinions and judgments without depending on others. For developing intellectual maturity one must have a certain level of education according to his/her social status. One must be able to give a meaning and purpose to his/her life, if he/she is intellectually mature. As we grow up, we gradually learn to understand and evaluate ourselves better. We come to know of our own strengths and weaknesses, our abilities and disabilities. We gain insight into our feelings, thinking and behaviour. We also develop foresight. We learn to face realistically the facts of life and to anticipate the results of our action. We learn to foresee the possible consequences of our behaviour. We no longer permit our desires to dominate completely our thinking or action.

Mature thinking and feeling express themselves in mature action and behaviour. We show control and flexibility in our behaviour. We are neither rigid nor compulsive but adapt our actions according to the situation. We can accept authority and discipline as well as responsibility and power. We learn to co-operate with the people and make the necessary adjustments and adaptation in life. An individual should show these signs of intellectual maturity before he/she plans to marry. It is essential for promotion of desirable personality development and adjustments in marriage. Self realization is essential to understand the behaviour of others. "Know thyself" is an important principle in mental health. For good marital adjustments, knowledge of self is an essential factor. Only an intellectually matured person can know the limitations of others. A person who aims at an unattainable goal meets with frustrations. Intellectual maturity is essential for having 'frustration tolerance'. The married partners need high frustration tolerance to face problem situations wisely and to make wise decisions.

Now we have seen how important maturity in selecting a mate is. Only a person having all the above types of maturation will be a good partner in married life. Often it is not easy to evaluate correctly, the herself in the best high, hiding the negative aspects on his/her personality. Therefore in mate selection, it is necessary to go beyond the external appearance and behaviour. You will have to closely observe the behaviour of the person in different situation and circumstances. How a person acts in a crisis or a critical situation will show his/her real self and maturity.

Health and Physical Structure

A happy married life is very closely related to the health of the partners. So this is an important factor to be looked into in selecting a mate. The parents should be healthy to have children of good health. In some western countries, the partners have to produce a medical certificate before marriage. This is ideal, especially to eliminate people with hereditary diseases. It is advisable not to have marriage relations between person having a close blood relationship. The children born from such couples may have hereditary diseases of both the families. It is also necessary to look out for the RH factor of the blood. If the husband and wife have different RH groups i.e positive and negative, it may affect the children. So care should be taken to see that the partners has compatible blood groups. HIV testing also should be done before marriage, wherever scope for doubt exists, to avoid future problems and breakdowns. The presence of a health defect in a person may not prevent one from marrying, but it is necessary that both know about it and are ready to face its consequences together.

Physical structure is another factor in the selection of mate. There should not be much disparity in physical structure (height, weight etc. colour and general appearance). However, physical attraction or physical expectation in the Indian context is that the husband should have a bigger structure than the wife. Regarding general beauty, the usual practice is that woman's beauty is more looked into than a man's. In a man "manliness" is the usual criteria that is looked for. Physical appearance and beauty are relative terms and vary according to cultures. This is not a very important factor in selecting a mate. Anyway, beauty should not be the main criteria for selection. There is a Chinese proverb "Marrying a woman only on the basis of her beauty is like buying a building merely by looking at the outside painting". Young people give too much importance to this criteria which is not wise.

Behaviour Patterns or Character and Conduct

If you want to enroll for any course, you need a character or conduct certificate. In order to enter into a profession also, very often you need a conduct certificate, but to get married do you produce any conduct certificate? Unfortunately many persons do not give enough importance to this aspect, which is one of the most important criteria for mate selection. Even if your partner has all the other physical qualities, economic and social status and education, if his character is not satisfactory, married life will be a real hell.

At the same time even if there is disparity in age, caste, religion, education etc. and the partner has good character the marriage will still work. Character in married life means good will, sense of humor, the ability to love, honesty, responsibility, concern for others, give and take attitudes, cheerfulness, discipline, faith in God, fidelity openness, values in life, etc. The couple has a long life before them to spend together. Much of their happiness will depend upon their ability to share, to agree and to work together. All this presuppose in them the presence of strong similarities with regard to basic concepts of life. There is no doubt that a certain amount of differences can be useful to enrich the partners. But ultimately the person who shows more similarities should be considered as the best make.

According to the perspectives in psychology, a person's character is formed during his/her early years of life. So his/her family is mainly responsible for character formation. As in the case of maturity, it is very difficult to assess the character of a person with whom we do not have an intimate personal relationship. In choosing a partner this is not always possible. His/her family relationships and the life of the family can be taken as one of the important sources for assessing the character. Persons brought up in unhappy, insecure, and broken families may have many personality disorders and peculiar behaviour patterns. Some parents consider marriage as a solution for the behaviour problems of their children, especially sons. A drunkard, a drug addict or a criminal may marry a poor girl having low socio-economic status. The poor girl is supposed to 'change the prodigal son'. Usually this ends up with a marital breakdown and lot of misery for the girl. The innocent girl becomes a scapegoat.

Caste and Religion

When the selection of the bride or bridegroom is made by parents they insist on caste and religion. But when the selection comes to youngster, we come across many inter-caste and inter-religious marriages. Many of them are successful. These types of marriages are good for social and national integration – and harmony among different castes and religions. But there are many practical problems of adjustments in such marriages. In India marriages are between two families. The families may not accept such marriages and interfere with each one's customs and life-style. When two persons from two different castes or religions marry, they must be willing to accept and respect each other's faith and values. Usually the problem comes with the birth of a child. Both the parents will consciously or unconsciously try to practice his/her own customs and values which result in a conflict for the children. If both parents are strictly secular, such problems can be eliminated to some extent. It is safer to choose a mate from the same caste, religion and culture. Even in the developed countries, where mate selection is done mostly by couples, preferences are for mates from the same race, religion and culture.

Social and Economic Status

The partners should have as far as possible, the same economic and social status. The family should have a stable income to pull on. Today dowry has become a great social problem in India. Men are demanding huge amounts of money from the wife's home. Many bride burnings are due to the problems of dowry. Of course, the girl should have an equal share of her father's wealth. Usually this share is handed over to the boy at the time of marriage. In many cases, the wife has no say about the dowry money, and it is considered as the property of the husband and his family. In many marriages, dowry is the main criteria for selecting the wife. This is very unfortunate. The partners should have the financial stability to establish and run a family. But the whole financial assistance should not be expected from the wife's family. As far as possible the wife also should have an independent income. Marrying a person who is very much above or below the economic and social status may cause many adjustment problems for both the partners. In many love marriages, economic disparity may not be looked into which may result in marital problems later on. It is very difficult for love to flourish in a 'poor' circumstance.

Education and Intelligence

There should not be much disparity in these factors. In Indian villages, most women are still illiterate, men do not consider literacy as a pre-requisite for marriage. This is very sad state of affairs. Women should be educated to be intelligent wives and efficient home managers. An educated mother is the best insurance for the education of her children. As in the case of physical structure, men in India prefer partners with equal or a little lower level of education. If the wife is more educated, the husband may develop an inferiority complex. Regarding intelligence, both the partners should be intelligent enough to manage a home. Intellectual companionship between the partners is a very important factor which is not given adequate emphasis in Indian marriages. It is not advisable to marry persons who are mentally retarded. The intelligence of the parents will be inherited by children to a very large extent. So intelligence is an important factor in mate selection.

Attitudes and Values – Basic Orientation to Life

Areas where strong similarity is required are attitudes and values and the basic orientation to life. These include goals, values, religious convictions and general ideas about justice, honesty, truth etc. A simple tolerance of other's beliefs or conceptions is not enough to establish a life long partnership. The partners should fully agree with the idea of marriage, its meaning and purpose. It is very important for them to have the same concept about fidelity, reciprocal roles in the family, sex, children and inlaws. It is good to have a spontaneous agreement in fields such as entertainment, participation in cultural, social and political activity, religious practices and community life. Temperamental compatibility of the mates prevents problems in marriages. Temperament means the physiological activity level and response patterns of the individual. The behaviour controlling glands of one individual may be different from that of another individual. Such biological differences help to explain many of the conflicts in marriage. For example, why one spouse is always active and the other inactive. To avoid all these problems, temperamental compatibility should be given due importance in mate selection. Compatibility of needs is another factor which should be looked into the choice of the mate. There is evidence that persons seek a mate who will compliment their strengths and deficiencies. Person with complimentary needs tend to marry. Many boys and girls are attracted to each other because each satisfies the other's need. The need so satisfied may be the need for love, affection, sympathy, understanding etc.

Now we have seen some of the important qualities that are to be looked for in a mate. The selection of partner is not an easy process. It is an ongoing process which requires time and experience. It is better for the partners to have an opportunity to become well acquainted with each other. This called courtship. It provides the two persons the opportunity to test each other's feelings, ideas and orientations to life. This may help them to decide whether a life together will possible. It also provides them occasions to reveal to each other the different sides of their temperaments. Inspite of the above advantages of courtship, it is generally not followed or accepted in Indian marriages. But it is a must in western countries. Anyway, it is good to have some acquaintance with the partner before marriage. One may not get a partner who can satisfy all the above criteria of mate selection. Some compromises have to be made in some aspects. But once the selection is made, one should accept his/her partner totally. 'Accept toto' is a key word in marital success. Since it is not easy to change the behaviour of an adult the only way is to accept your partner with his/her merits and demerits and adjust accordingly.

There is no 'I' or 'You' in a marriage relationship, but only the 'We'. The husband and wife should become one and at the same time keep their own identities and individualities. The new Mathematics of marriage is 1+1 should be 'big one'; it should never be a -2- or a -11- where the partners proceed in two parallel lines which never meet.

MARRIAGE IN INDIA

CONCEPT OF MARRIAGE

Every individual has to play a number of roles in his or her life. Of the various roles one plays, two roles have a very great significance in life. One is the economic role and the other is the marital or family role. The former is prominent in life because one devotes quite a good part of one's carrier in performing it. Consider one starts earning one's livelihood at the age of 20 to 24 years and continues to do so, up to the age of 58 to 62 years. That is, the economic career is spread over to about four decades and that every day one devotes 8 to 10 hours to job/work. Thus one can well assume the period which one's economic role consumes in one's life. The marital role also involves about 40 to 50 years of one's life. But of these two roles, the marital role is more important than the economic role, because the latter involves secondary relations whereas, the former involves personal or primary relations. In order to understand this, more clearly, we have to see the difference between primary and secondary relations.

Primary relations are essentially unlimited, particularistic, emotionally involved, altruistic and spontaneous. But, secondary relations are typically limited, standardized, unemotional, utilitarian and contractual. Again, primary relationship in marriage is different from primary relationship in other primary groups like friendship, neighbourhood, village etc. It is in the sense that primary relationship in marriage is based on sexual relationship and this sexual relationship brings further intimacy and permanence in the relationship between a man and a woman. Primary relation in marriage has two important functions: one of need gratification and other of social control. It gratifies biological (sex satisfaction), psychological (affection and belongingness) and economic needs (food, clothing and shelter) of the individuals and also acts as a primary source of morality and ethics. When one finds one's partner performing certain tasks for him/her, he/she considers it his/her moral obligation to care for the other or to listen to the other. One is, thus, no longer free to be immoral and irresponsible.

Another sociological way of conceptualizing family is how marriage involves performing new and varied roles such as husband, wife, father, mother, son, daughter, brother, sister and so on. Whether the persons involved are capable of performing those new roles or not, and how the inadequacy of performing these roles lead to family disorganisation. What is important in marriage is how the role enactment of one partner corresponds to the role expectations of the other. According to Koos, a Sociologist, marriage is a dividing line between the family of orientation and family of procreation in terms of the nature of roles one performs in the two families. The roles in the family of orientation vary in infancy, childhood and adolescence and carry no responsibilities and obligations. But the roles one performs in the family of procreation after marriage as a husband/wife, a father/mother, a wage-earner, a grand-father/grand-mother, a retired person etc. have different expectations and obligations.

Thus marriage is a miniature social system which must be kept in equilibrium if it is not to fall apart. Equilibrium requires adjustments, which in turn require give and take or some sacrifice on the part of both husband and wife. To maintain equilibrium it requires certain tasks to be performed by someone, for example, of cooking, cleaning, wage earning, child-care and so on. Who performs which role is immaterial (though society has certain expectations from both husband and wife). What is significant is that somebody should perform these roles for the stability of marriage.

VIEWS OF MARRIAGE

Various views have been expressed on this institution by anthropologist, sociologists and in religious texts. Marriage is an institution in which men and women are admitted to family life, to live in the intimate personal relationship, primarily for a purpose of begetting and rearing children. From the social point of view, marriage is an institution that serves to ensure propagation and socialization of children of a particular society. From the individual point of view, it provides assistance in bearing and raising of children and controls for the receipt and extension of affection. Another view is that marriage is a socially legitimate sexual union, begun with a public announcement and undertaken with some idea of contract, which spells out reciprocal rights and obligations between spouses and their future children.

Indian Views on Marriage

The above views represent western thinking about marriage. Now we are going to look at how Indian experts talk about marriage. Marriage has been considered a ceremonial gift of the bride by her father, or other appropriate relative to the bride groom in order that both may together fulfill their duties which are necessary for human existence. These duties are "Dharma, Artha and Kama". Dharma is religious duty based on ethical values, that is to do good and attain Moskha or salvation. Artha is the economic aspect of life and Kama is the physical or sexual duties to the partner and to produce children to perpetuate race. Marriage is not for sense of enjoyment, but to perpetuate the race. This is the Indian conception of marriage. It is a social duty towards the family and community. Indian religious texts say that marriage is a religious sacrament which is considered primarily a complex of obligations, religious and moral on the one hand, and social and economic on the other hand.

The Hindu concept of marriage is that it is a sanskara (tradition) and a religious sacrament, not a contract. It is a holy union of the two souls and not simply of two bodies. It is an indissoluble bond which could be broken only by death. On the other hand Islam says that marriage is an institution ordained for the protection of the society and in order that human beings may guard themselves from foulness and unchastity. Marriage is not a sacrament but civil contract, the objectives of which are the promotion of normal family life and the legalization of children. Among the Christians marriage has been viewed as " a voluntary union for life of one man and one woman to the exclusion of others". This type of marriage is monogamous. Summarizing the above views, you might have learnt that marriage is a union of two persons of different sexes to lifelong reciprocal possession of their sexual qualities, which aims at the individual's biological, emotional, social and spiritual fulfillment and development and which cannot be achieved in isolation.

Hindu Marriage as Sacrament

The Hindu view of marriage is that it is for fulfilling dharma and the need for pleasure (Kama). It is considered as a sacrament.

There are several reasons for considering the Hindus marriage a sacrament:

- Dharma (fulfillment of religious duties) is the most important aim of marriage
- Performance of religious ceremonies including certain rites like kanyadan, panigrahana, saptapadi etc. which are based on certain sacred formulae.
- The rites are performed before Agni (the most sacred god) by reciting mantras (passage) from Vedas (the most sacred scriptures) by a Brahmin.
- The union is considered indissolvable and irrevocable and husband and wife are bound to each other not only until death, but even after death.
- Though a man can perform several sacraments during the course of his life, a woman can perform only one sacrament in her life i.e. marriage, hence it has great importance for her.
- Emphasis is on chastity of a woman and the faithfulness of a man.
- Marriage is considered a "social duty" towards the family and community and there are no ideas of individual interest and aspiration.

FORMS OF MARRIAGE

Till now you have read about the concept, meaning and different views on marriage. Now you are going to learn about different forms of marriage. There have been different opinions regarding the original form of marriage. Some theorists say that primitive man lived in a state of group marriage. The group marriage in which men in a group or tribe had indiscriminate access to all women of the group and children born out of this union were considered children of the general community. There are some other social scientists who believed that monogamy was its original form. Whatever may have been the original form of marriage, at present the most prevalent form is monogamy. But polygamy, polyandry levirate and sorrorate forms are also found.

Monogamy

Monogamy is the only form of marriage found in most societies; a man marries one woman, raises children within the wedlock and performs all rites with his mate. Monogamy has a long history of its own. Ancient Hindus regarded monogamy as the most ideal form of marriage.

Polygamy

Polygamy is marriage of one male with more than one female, or what may be called the "plurality of wives". A polygamous marriage may be unrestricted or restricted or conditional. In early Hindu society conditional polygamous marriage was practiced. According to the Dharmashastra, a man could marry again after ten years of his first marriage, if his wife is barren, or he could marry after thirteen or fourteen years if he had only daughters from his wife and wanted a son. Manu said that, a man can marry another woman after eight years of his first marriage, if his wife is barren, after ten years if children produced by his wife do not remain alive; after eleven years if his wife produces only daughters, and immediately after first marriage if his wife is quarrelsome, rebellious, or harsh. The Mahabharata says that a man who marries twice without any rational cause commits a sin for which there is no penance.

Today polygamy has been legally prohibited. Besides the legal restrictions, people do not practice polygamy because:

- Maintaining higher living standards is not possible with more than one wife in the house,
- Plurality of wives increase tension in the family, and
- Women having economically independent status refuse to accept men's dominance over them.

Polyandry

Polyandry is a marriage in which one woman marries more than one man. This was found among the Todas and Kotas of Nilgiris in South India. There are two types of polyandry which are prevalent in India. They are fraternal and non-fraternal. In the fraternal, the husbands are all brothers or possibly from cousins from the father's side. In the non-fraternal, they are not related, as among the Nairs of Kerala. In the 19th century the Nairs among the Hindus in Kerala practiced polyandry. But Westernmarck, a sociologist referring to these marriages, has said that polyandrous marriage unions of Nairs can hardly be called marriages because the male partners never lived with the woman and that the duties of fatherhood entirely were ignored. In 1896, the Malabar Marriage Act was passed which stabilized marriage norms among Nairs.

In the ancient literature the only example of Draupadi's marriage with five Pandavas in Mahabharata period was justified by Yudhishtra on the basis that similar marriages were performed by some of his ancestors and described it as "mother's command". Obeying the mother's command was a son's dharma. In the Mahabharata, referring to polyandry, it is said, "to have many wives is no dharma on the part of men, but to violate the duty owned to the first husband would be a great adharma in the case of woman".

Levirate

Levirate is a form of marriage under which a woman is taken as the wife of the late husband's younger brother or even during the life time of the elder brother and the younger brother exercises sexual rights over the wife of the elder brother. The form prevails among the Ahirs of Haryana, some Jats and Gujars and some other castes of U.P.

Sorrorate

In sorrorate wives of a man are invariably the sisters. The origin of the word sorrorate lies in the Latin word 'Sorror' which stands for sister. In this form of marriage several sisters are simultaneously or potentially the spouses of the same man. It is usually observed among the Nagas, Gonds and Baigas of India who pay a high bride price. It has been observed that the death of the wife or her being barren is compensated by supplying a new spouse who is generally the younger sister of the deceased women.

MARRIAGE AMONG HINDUS, MUSLIMS, CHRISTIANS AND TRIBALS

In the Mahabharata four distinct forms of marriages are mentioned. They are: Brahma, Gandharava, Asura and Rakshasa. Gautama and Asvalayana, two of the ancient law-giver of the Hindus, refer to eight different forms of marriage. They are Brahma, Daiva, Arsha, Prajapatya, Asura, Gandharva, Rakshasa and Paisacha. Among them four were considered proper and desirable (dharmya) which had the approval of the father/family. The other four were regarded as undesirable (adharmya) which did not have the approval of the father. The proper marriages recognized by the "Smritis" were Brahma, Daiva, Arsha and Prajapatya while the four undesirable marriages were Asura, Gandharva, Rakshasa and Paisacha.

Brahma was the form of marriage in which a fully dressed girl – with proper decorations and ornaments – was given to a man of the same class by performance of the ceremony mentioned in the holy texts. The bridegroom used to be learned person of pure character and selected/approved by the bride's father. Daiva form of marriage was one in which the father of the girl gave her to a sacrificial priest as a part of his fee for officiating at the ceremony. The bride was properly dressed, decorated with jewellery which formed part of his fees.

In the Arsha form of marriages, instead of the dowry, the marriage was based on a system of barter in which the father of the bride was given a pair of cattle or two cows by the young man in exchange for his daughter. The Prajapatya form of marriage is one in which the bridegroom is duly worshipped and married to the bride with due honors and blessing with these words, "go both of you and fulfill the duties of a householder". In the Asura form of Marriage, bride-price is given by bridegroom to the bride's father. This is sort of economic contract. There is no limit of the amount given.

The Gandharva form of marriage was the union of a willing girl with a man in solitude when both of them were in love. In this form of marriage, neither the consent of the parents nor the rites of dowry was essential. Only the will of the marrying parties was given importance. This marriage is believed to spring from desire and had sex satisfaction as its chief purpose.

The Rakshasa form of marriage was marriage by capture in which the girl was forcibly abducted by the man. If she cried for help and if her kinsmen came to her rescue, they were killed. The Paisacha form of marriage was marriage by seduction, stealing or fraud, where the girl was sexually violated while she was asleep, intoxicated or unconscious or when incapable of protecting herself.

Of these eight forms of marriage Brahma is considered to be the best marriage, where a girl is married to a boy of merit in the same caste or in a caste of equal status. In the Mahabharata age, the two most prevalent forms of marriage were Brahma and Gandharva. Gandharva marriage was declared to be proper for a Kshatriya. Many of the heroes of Mahabharata contracted this form of marriage; for instance, Arjun married Ulupi and Chitrangada, and Dushyanta married Shakuntala. Swayamvara: A variant of the Rakshasa form marriage was considered to be the norm for princely houses; for instance, Arjun won Draupadi and Nala won Damayanti.

Marriage within the caste was the prevalent order of things during the period of the Smritis and the Puranas. Marriage was rigidly regulated by the caste system and caste laws. As a matter of fact, a man of higher caste could marry a woman of lower caste which is called anuloma marriage. But a woman of high caste marrying a man of lower caste which is called pratiloma marriage was not allowed. Another custom relating to marriage was the law of consanguinity – close relationship by blood over generations. There are sapinda, gotra and pravara degrees of relationship. They are intended to prevent marriage among certain kins and gotras.

The present custom of Hindus is that marriage within the same gotra is to be avoided:

Endogamy

Endogamy is a social custom that requires a person to select a spouse from within certain groups. These endogamous groups specifically refer to Varna, caste and sub-caste. Thus, a boy from a particular caste marries a girl from the same caste.

Caste endogamy was functional in early society because:

- It made marital adjustments easier,
- It preserved the occupational secrets of the caste,
- It maintained the solidarity of the caste, and
- It checked the decrease in the membership or strength of the castes.

The most typical endogramous rules are enforced by tribe race, religion and social class. Hindu couples planning to marry are obligated to belong to the same caste and sub- caste. Sub-caste refers to a further subdivision of castes into endogamous categories which, for all practical purposes, are themselves independent castes.

The negative effects of caste endogamy are that, it creates:

- Inter-caste tensions which adversely affect the political unit of the country,
- The problem of marital adjustment, because the field of selection remains limited, and
- Problems of child marriage and dowry system.

Exogamy

The term 'exogamy is essentially covered by the incest taboo which is prohibited universally. Similarly, universally banned is the marriage between brother and sister. An interesting exception to the latter prohibition occurred in the royal families of ancient Egypt, Hawaii and the Incas of Peru. The explanation for this is the determination to maintain intact a royal line of descent in societies which had not developed a system of inter marriages with foreign royalty. Close blood relationship is typically a bar on marriage for all people in all times and places. Frequently first cousins may not marry. Alliance of affinity, as well as blood relationship, has been included within exogamous rules. Among some people, marriage between persons belonging to the same village or other territorial group is banned, or at least discouraged. Exogamy is a social custom which forbids selection of a spouse from certain groups. There are two types of exogamy practiced by Hindus. They are Gotra exogamy and Sapinda exogamy. They are intended to prevent marriage among certain kins and gotras.

Gotra Exogamy

Gotra is a group whose members are believed to have descended from a common mythical ancestor. Initially there were only eight Gotras, but gradually their number increased to thousands. The Gotra exogamy prohibits marriage between members of the same gotra.

Sapinda Exogamy

Sapinda means one who carries the particles of the same body. Sapinda relationships arise from being connected by having particles of the same ancestor. Marriage between such persons is prohibited. Since there is no limit to persons related by blood, some limit is prescribed for avoiding persons for marriage related to each other within certain generations on the father's and mother's side. In practice and according to law, five generations from father's side and three generations from mother's side are avoided. However, breach of sapinda exogamy was never penalized, though breach of gotra exogamy was considered a heinous practice.

Cousin Marriage

There are four types of cousins:

- Chachera (father's brother's son/daughter),
- Mamera (mother's brother's son/daughter),
- Phuphera (father's sister's son/daughter) and,
- Mausera (mother's sister's son/ daughter).

Of these, chachera and mausera cousin (where the two sibling parents of the child belong to the same sex) are called parallel cousins and mamera and phuphera cousins (where the two sibling parents of the child are of opposite sex) are called cross cousins. Of these two forms of cousins, cross cousin marriage was practiced in ancient Hindu society. Even now crosscousin marriages are practiced among Hindus and Muslims.

The main arguments for and against cousin marriages are biological, social, psychological and cultural.

The arguments against cousin marriages are:

- It will lead to biological degeneration of family because parental defects will be transmitted to their children,
- It will create secret relations between primary relations in the family and thereby lead to immorality; and
- It will be against our religious norms.

Arguments in favour of cousin marriage are:

- One's property will remain in one's own family;
- It will create stronger bonds of love between brother and sister, and
- With the breakdown of joint family cousins no longer live together in the same house.

Hypergamy and Hypogamy

As a matter of fact, a man of higher caste could marry a woman of lower caste which is called anuloma marriage (hypogamy). But a woman of high caste marrying a man of lower caste which is called pratiloma (hypogamy) marriage was not allowed.

Inter-caste Marriage

It is a marriage between man and woman belonging to different castes. Inter-caste marriage in India is generally understood to mean not only marriage between sub-castes of a major caste group (as between Brahmin sub-castes), but also marriage between two major castes (as for eg. Brahmins and Vaishyas). Inter-caste marriages which are increasingly common in India, especially in urban and industrial areas, are not between high and low caste people but between the members of various sub-castes within a large caste group (as between Brahmin sub-caste).

At present, many of the modern minded and liberal people in India believe that inter-caste marriages should be accepted (legally such marriages are permitted) by the people/ society. Also they believe that inter-caste marriages would help breakdown the traditional caste system. It will also help wipe out caste distinction and untouchability.

Formerly marriage outside one's caste was not to be even thought of. Today many men and women are prepared to break through the bonds of caste if mutual love or attraction demand it. However, studies conducted on inter-caste marriages show three features.

- When a person outside the caste is wealthy and had a social prestige, there has been a general approval.
- Persons with higher education and who are older marry outside the caste.
- Even today, the large number of marriages are within the caste and these are marriages arranged by parents. The only significant change is with respect to the restriction against sub-castes which has now been practically eliminated at least in the urban areas among the educated persons.

Arranged marriages are the marriages arranged by the parents of the bride and the bridegroom, considering all the norms and customs of the society and religion.

Inter-religious Marriage

Inter-religious marriage in India is basically understood to mean marriage between persons belonging to different religions.

Influence of Legislations on Hindu Marriage

Over a period of time many beliefs, values and ideals related to Hindu marriage have lost their original meaning and purpose. People started questioning certain evil practices like child marriage, sati system, restrictions of widow remarriage etc. consequently during the British rule and even after independence various legislations were enacted.

Some of them were; The prevention of Sati Act, 1829, The Hindu Widow Remarriage Act, 1856, The Civil Marriage Act, 1872, The Child Marriage Restraint Act, 1929 and its amendment in 1978, The Hindu Marriage Act, 1955 and The Dowry Prohibition Act, 1961 and its amendment in 1986. The above mentioned legislations have led to significant changes in the Hindu marriage system.

Some of the important impacts of legislations on the institution of Hindu marriage are:

- Divorce is now socially and legally permissible. Thus marital relation has ceased to remain unbreakable.
- Provision for widow remarriage and divorce has affected the ideal of 'pativrata'.
- Marriage is no more a religious duty rather it is performed for lifelong companionship.

Marriage among Muslims

Marriage among Muslim is universal and obligatory. Since the Muslim community discourages celibacy, marriage has to be performed. It is true that marriage among Muslim is a civil contract as it is meant for procreation of children and legalizing sexual intercourse; it is a religious duty also. It is considered an 'ibadat'. Characteristic features of Muslim marriage are; acceptance of the proposal of marriage by the bride; capability of the bridegroom to enter into a marriage contract; preference system i.e. parallel cousins (father's brother's daughters) and cross cousins (mother's brother's daughters) are given preference; and marriage is valid only if it is free from legal complications.

It may be noted that man and women did not enjoy equal rights with regard to the provision of divorce. Women have always been at the receiving end. However, industrialization, urbanization, modernization and spread of modern education have drastically changed the perspective. Spread of small family norm and lesser incidence of divorce are some of the impacts of social change on the institution of Muslim marriage.

Marriage among Christians

The Christian community has two major denominations: Catholics and Protestants. The Catholic owe allegiance to the Pope. The Pope is the supreme authority in the Catholic Church. All the teachings of the Catholic Church has the approval of the Pope. The Protestants have several denominations or groups. Hierarchical approach is limited within each denomination. As per the teaching of the Catholic Church marriage is a sacrament. There is no provision for divorce. However a marriage can be declared null and void if one of the spouses is already married and the partner from the first marriage is still alive. A marriage can also be declared null and void in case if the spouse is of unsound mind, impotent etc. at the time of marriage. But the procedure to get a marriage declared null and void from Church is very tedious as the clearance has to come from the Vatican.

Among the Catholics mixed marriages are permitted (with a person from any other religion). However the Catholic spouse has to make an undertaking that the offsprings would be brought up in the Catholic faith. Among the

Protestants divorce is permitted. Marriages are usually performed within the church in the presence of relatives and friends. Married couples are free to register their marriage for legal purpose. Protestant couples usually seek divorce from a court of law. Among the Protestants, remarriage is also permitted after divorce. According to the teaching of the Church free consent from both the parties is must. Consent must be an act of the will of each of the contracting parties, free of coercion or grave external fear.

Tribal Marriage

Family comes into being only through the establishment of culturally controlled and sanctioned marital relations. Marriage, therefore, is universal. We find various forms of prescriptions and proscriptions regarding marriage among tribes, also. However, uniqueness of tribal marriage lies in the ways by which mates are acquired.

There are: probationary marriage among Kuki; marriage by capture among Nagas, Ho, Kharia and Birhor; marriage by trial which is recognition of personal courage and bravery among Bhil; marriage by what has been called purchase or bride price prevalent all over tribal India: marriage by service—a solution to the problem of high bride price among Gonds and Baigas; marriage by exchanging women of two households for avoiding the payment of high bride price prevalent all over India except Khasi Tribe; marriage by mutual consent and elopment among those tribes who have youth dormitories, and marriage by intrusion among Birhor and Ho.

SOCIETY, CULTURE, RELIGION AND FAMILY VALUES

FAMILY LIFE: CHANGING PATTERNS

Definition of Family

A family is a community of persons related to one another, living together in an environment of understanding and acceptance. A family is a place where one can freely express one's feelings, emotions and needs without being threatened or ashamed of them. Family is a place where one can feel security, wholeness and a sense of being wanted. Family can also be defined as "Those related persons who live together within a household, usually with common eating habits or one kitchen." It is experienced and proved that children grow best in an atmosphere of security and affection and that material attributes can never be substituted for true love.

Types of Family

Development in society in the recent years have focused their attention on man's self-fulfillment through individualism, materialism and consumerist values isolating man from his need to belong to one another as persons.

Authentic fulfillment and happiness is experienced not in the acquisition of the external, material wealth and possessions, isolated from one's relations to the rest of humanity, but in his intimate and significant experiences of other people starting with the family. In fact every human being is bound together in family and in the earliest experience of interacting with the father, mother and other significant people, one learns to find meaning and identity for the rest of one's life. The traditional pattern of family living in India was that of joint family, in which members were bound together by ties of common ancestry and common property.

Now in India we find three types of family structures:

- The large Joint Family
- The Nuclear Family
- The Extended Family

A joint family is one that has a greater generation depth than the nuclear family, in which members are related to one another by property, income, mutual rights and obligations. The care and maintenance of dependents is a moral obligation. Members of the family are closely knit together and share the problems and joys of social living, having strong feelings of mutual obligations during crises and regard self-interest as being identical with family welfare. The joint family provides an "umbrella" of support, which covers financial loss, decease of a spouse and social security.

Children brought up in a joint family are more secure, affectionate and have a well-developed personality. Joint family can be found more frequently among Hindus than amongst any other community; among agriculturists rather than traders, clerical and professional workers. Joint families can be found in the lowest income groups too. Men grow up with the knowledge of people around, confidence and skill in family business matters. Children grow up with the experience of life cycles: birth, maturation, marriage and death. There is no difficulty of boy-girl relationship, no problem of single woman, no problem of single or neglected child and marriage are arranged by parents.

The positive aspects of joint family system are based on the advantages of the members such as:

- Family survival
- Care in old age
- Increase in family income
- More share in the property
- To follow the pattern in the community
- To make the home happier

Nuclear Family

Nuclear family is one in which the parents and their unmarried sons and daughters live together.

Extended Family

The extended family is a later development of the joint family system with a transformed image. It mediates the nuclear family and the large joint family. In this type the nuclear family is extended with sons marrying, bringing up children and remaining within the original family of the parents.

Traditional in Family Patterns

We live in a fast changing world. We have reached a time in history when sitting at home, we are able to know what is happening around the world. We are able to move around the world in a shorter time than before. We are living with all the modern technologies that dictate easy life, pleasure, comfort and provide automatic answers for most of our problems. Many are doing their own business sitting at home. The science and technologies have progressed to such an extent that man only has to sit in homes press a button in order to send a written message across the world and receive the reply. Any information one needs on any topic can be obtained through our family computer.

Over the years, the Indian Family has gone through many transitions. The larger families of six and eight children have been replaced by families of one or two children who learn constantly to compete with each other over toys and personal possessions from their infancy. In place of joint families where adults, children and the elderly interacted with one another in a secure atmosphere, now we have strangers and lonely individuals living in separate worlds. The elderly are conveniently put into old-age homes and children are kept waiting at the school gates or in front of family T.V. till their parents return from the offices.

Children who spend long hours in closed houses or in the company of servants or other school children develop a sense of rejection, depression and isolation. All that they are able to interact with for long hours after school are toys, story books, T.V. computer games and cartoons that contribute to the formation of a mechanical, dehumanizing, individualistic, and narrow-minded attitudes in children.

Significance of Transitions in Families

The joint family cannot be dismissed as outdated. Many Hindus as well as Muslim still families follow that life-style. Rank and wealth are not the conditions for this system but blood relations and social value are. They are mostly found in non-urban, non-industrialized settings. It is interesting to note that even when the members of an extended family do not live in the same household, they still share a common budget and follow the same family leader. Besides, even among the members, who live separately, we observe that all belong to a joint family system and believe in this value.

There are problems connected with all extended families, as the joint family is based on the relations among the adult males rather than on the conjugal bonds between spouses. The spouses do not feel the allegiance toward the large units as the husbands feel and there are quarrels, competitions and dissatisfaction among women and children. In recent years majority of Indians prefer to live in nuclear families. The role of religion is to give a perspective to human life, hence, to family life and through it to society.

ASPECTS OF VALUE FORMATION IN FAMILY

Definition of Values

Values are those ideas which direct our thinking and living and give meaning to our existence. The values we hold dear are expressed in our actions by which our lives receive a certain amount of identity. It is the value one possesses which gives him/her an image by which others judge or measure him/her. In order to make values meaningful, they have to be practical and directive.

Classification of Values

Values can be classified into three groups—personal, social and neutral. This classification is based on the traditionally held on customs and beliefs inherited by the person which make a society proud and protective of the culture which is inherited. Values can also be classified as material values and higher values. Material things have their own values: food, physical health, and clothes are such visible values by which one exhibits one's identity and are essential for survival in a society. Higher values are seen only by way of behaviour. Since food is a necessity for human life, working for daily food is a value, but to share what one has with other needy people is a higher value. Even though joy is a value, all things which give joy need not be values, though there can be a desire to possess all things. Higher values are eternal values: they can be understood as human or divine.

Whenever, there is a doubt; a need for the expression of values becomes apparent. Life is made up of small and big decisions. Where families are authentic in loving one another and caring for each other, obeying God and working for Him as the source and centre of the universe, progress, peace, harmony and human development will be the outcome.

Socialization and Value Formation

Social, religious, and cultural values affect family life to a great extent. In fact no family can exist independently of these factors. One of the most significant stages of one's life is socialization. Socialization is a process through which the child absorbs, assimilates and internalizes socio-cultural and religious practices from the significant persons in his/her life e.g. parents, teachers, siblings. Thus, a child acquires attitudes and values, some of which pertain to moral standards and others relating to people love and hate, superior and inferior, etc. These attitudes and values exist in children in different ways, at different levels according to the atmosphere, psychological stages and physical conditions.

Socialization is seen by sociologist as a process toward cultural conditioning. For an individual infant to survive, it must be socialized. There is a structural relationship socialization. As result of being socialized by parents, one becomes an agent of socialization for one's children and grand children. These obligations become fixed and specified for generations. It is easy to understand that such a conditioning attached to a joint family system can be so strong in the Indian society as it has existed for over 2000 years with its culture, beliefs and socialization process give a meaningful values to family life that are inseparable from society.

Thus we see that the individuals and the families are motivated to serve the society's interests and keep up the system. In this sense the socialization process is more or less a natural process to make the individual conform to the social norms and cultural pattern of a society. There is a tendency in many individuals, to deviate from this type of forced pattern, since all human beings have an inmate longing for freedom and selfexpression, for spontaneity and personal identity. This explains the reason for teenagers and young adults growing up with antagonism and rebelling against parents and those in authority.

Value Formation in Parent Child Interaction

The mother-child ties is emotionally intimate which facilitates the process of socialization. The span of human life is long and hence socialization continues. The pattern of dominance by father or mother gives further authority to what is learned and fixes attitudes and values in the minds of children. Already learned experience of children through families are made forceful and commanding by the way the society lives and interacts. At this stage, the experience of the father and mother and the strength of the parentchild relationship will determine the values of selfhood (identity, security and self image of the child), which form the core of a child's personality.

Children of pre-school age are already exposed to a competitive world. Parents, out of enthusiasm for proving their identity and getting approval for their status, pressurize their children to achieve excellence in studies, sports, music and other fields and push them beyond their capacity and speed up their performance. But gradually this creates stressful feelings and inferiority complexes in children and they become victims to physical and verbal humiliation in school and at home.

Women's Role Affecting Family Values

We cannot satisfactorily talk about the formation of family values, by passing the nature and role of women in both society and family. The house is the pivot of society and the woman is its centre. The home – the family – is the first institution which imparts self identity to an individual and where he/she formulates a self image. The respect and esteem the mother is given in the family greatly determines the values with which the family looks at others in society. "A women's position in the family is lowered if she gives birth to female children, and she is looked down upon by others. On the other hand producing sons is considered to be a great achievement". Such families cannot give a positive self-concept to female children who in turn look at women negatively and pass on negative values to the coming generations. "The cultural conditioning has gone so deep into the psychology of people of India that even among the educated and so called enlightened and well-to do urban-dwelling people, the birth of son is much more desired".

Though some change is evident in cities, most of the village women still live under the subjugation of men and traditional social customs. It is clear from what has been said that one of the important aspects of family values depends on the position that women occupy in home and in society. The women's self-image, the opportunities and congenial environment for utilizing the rights and privileges due to her has a great deal to do with the type of families and the quality of values imparted to the family members. Hence women's empowerment is necessary for the formation of new values in Indian families.

FAMILY VALUES AND INFLUENCE OF SOCIO-CULTURAL AND RELIGIOUS DIMENSIONS

Values in Family and Society

The family is made up of individuals but it is also a part of the larger social network. Thus, individuals are initiators and promoters of culture. Individuals and society are mediated by families. It is in and through families that people learn and pass on values. But all members of a society are under the constant supervision of parents in childhood, of friends in teenage, and of the public in adulthood. Family is where children are trained; the adults feel free to praise, criticize, suggest and order so that the children learn family preferences. They are taught what is right and wrong, what to tell others and not, how to behave inside and outside the home, who must be their friends etc. All these influence and communicate to the children directly and indirectly the attitudes, values and conduct which remain with them for the rest of their life. What they learn is part of that culture and customs of the society which are valued by the adults.

Family as a social institution is the basic structure of the society. Hence the flow of values between the family and society is very lucid and they interact very closely, intrinsically and inter-dependently before the effect is apparent. It is not wrong to say that it is through the family that the values and attitudes are absorbed by the child in his/her early age, cultural transmission of particular society is kept up and the major agent for all these is the woman. The significance of the family is the mediating function of family in the larger society, as it links the individual to the larger social structure. As part of the society, families like to keep their identity linked to it, hence the family values remain mostly undifferentiated from the values of the society. Socially, man's relationship with other human beings is diminishing. His engagements are more with the machine and technically produced means of communication. Communication, which is the medium of relationship and social connection, is no more concerned with human relationships, but media and media-related learning and knowledge. Media also has helped to replace human interactions with group interactions.

Studies have shown that in societies where human life and peaceful living are valued, there is little competition and there seems to be hardly any exploitation of one another. Work is done essentially in co-operation and there is no economic rivalry. Women are respected and included in the decision making processes. We can also see that the opposite is true in societies where wealth and success are valued over human life. When money, position and power are valued, individuals grow up with aggression, violence, competition and manipulation. Families become unable to foster human values that can sustain and uphold members, as they are subjected to the negative influences of peers, employees, neighbours and organisations in the society. According to Mahatma Gandhi, truth and love are the most admirable and cherished values of youth.

Values in Family and Culture

The Indian family is no more unicultural following customs, practices and beliefs of definite pattern but a plurality of practices and patterns. The elders used to be the central persons whom the youngsters looked up to, learned from and were agents of imparting the traditions and values of family, life, parent-child relationship and discipline. The uniqueness of the Indian culture is being engulfed by the global culture. However, the villages still hold on to the traditional values of hospitality, simplicity, submissiveness, and belief in God. They have been excluded from the modernism by deprivation of economic and technological development.

Man's uniqueness consists in developing language and preserving meaningful, creative behaviour and in communicating the internal conditions and feelings through external expressions. The cultural implications of values are tied up with practices, symbols, religious rituals and the customs of a society. Also, traditions and languages of the different regions or nationalities are expressions of values of the ethnic group to which one belongs. Though India is known for its unique culture, the different religions have specific cultures. Culture expresses itself in one's life-style, food habits, dress and symbolic expressions. Indian culture is unique in comparison to the West, but each culture has its won richness and inherent in it are specific messages, interpretations and expressions of values the people of that society hold dear. The diversity of perception, experience expressed through different and creative ways become integrated in the life of individuals through learning, understanding and accepting in the given cultural contexts. The family is the place where the atmosphere of unity, integration, harmony and respect of different beliefs and expressions become a necessarily parts of unified consciousness.

India is a land of many striking contrasts, and a great cultural complexity, social diversity and regional variation can be found among the people. And in the diversity of the Indian scene it is very difficult to make any generalized judgments concerning the values in family life. But it is the unity running through diversity which reveals the positive dimensions of social and cultural values in family life. Older attitudes and prejudices still persist and social opinion is taking its time in changing itself. As values are integrated with culture, religion as well as socially determined attitudes, behaviour and customs, an evaluative and critically questioning methodology is required for the promotion of family values. In course of social change people adopt new ways of living. Old customs and practices fail to make meaning to younger generations. Hence, the need for introducing meaningful values become a necessity. For example, the role of women was considered to be within the family, taking care of the husband and children, but now as women are working on equal terms with men, outside home the attitude toward women cannot remain the same. This perception affects family values.

Values in Family and Religion

The world is not the ultimate reality. This is the teaching of all Religions. The Bible, Gita, Koran and other scriptures affirm and acknowledge the one and only powerful and omnipotent God who is invisible to the external eyes and to the physical world in which we live. All religions emphasize the need for forming a mature conscience in people. Religion provides a code of norms which will guide and enable persons to have an objective understanding of God. Religion must help people to grow in a balanced, harmonious, altruistic attitude which will result in accepting all people as one's relations, regardless of their caste, creed, religion, or customs/ language.

It is difficult to differentiate the socio-cultural and religious values as they affect family life. Religion in its purest form deals with one's faith in God and shows how he/she must live in this world. Hence religion frames 'law' or teaches one's duty to God and towards others, which we call Dharma. All religious founders taught how to live our lives in worship to God and our duty towards our neighbour. Hence Buddha taught compassion and less desire for worldly pleasure. Jesus taught of love for neighboure to the extent of giving up one's life for the other in service. Hinduism talks of Nishkamakarma; doing one's duty toward others and not expecting the results of the actions. However, the truth is that it is the religious beliefs of a society that sweeps under all other values in family and society.

Family Values and Attitude toward Sex

According to the study and analysis of number of psychologists and educationists, the attitudes and values (either positive or negative) which the parents have, become the most powerful instrument in the hands of the children for later years. The self-image, as well as the ability to interact with other in children from childhood to later years are affected by the early experience of sex-related values taught in the family. According to a classic concept a little boy at the age of five or six chooses his mother as the first object of his sexual desires. The same thing is true about girls concerning their father. The upbringing of children with a positive, balanced, relationship with family members and outsiders at this age is essential for the growth of proper values regarding sexuality in children. The understanding of sex as part of the body for a special purpose in the plan of God for the world has to be taught to children gradually as they mature in life.

Respect for all persons, regardless of sex difference is a higher value which very few people possess. At the same time a family that does not respect persons and considers sex as an object of pleasure and a means of play can cause negative understanding of sex in children who may grow up to be exploiters of women in society.

Values in Family and Role of Media

As we have already seen earlier, with the breakdown of the joint family and the advent of industrialization, the family atmosphere has changed drastically. The family has become small in size, the elderly and children are left alone at home and the parents are burdened with over time jobs. The rise of materialism and consumerism has created unnecessary anxieties of isolation and loneliness in families and among families. The advertisements set the norms for values concerning food, dress and friends. The concepts of values are created in children by what they see and hear in the media. T.V., internet, computer and other technological devices have become source of entertainment for both children and adults. In place of listening to the stories of parents and grand parents while going to sleep, children seek music, serials and cartoons before going to bed. Role models for the present generation are film stars who constantly appear on televisions. Balance in the media against the values of families has gone beyond the control of parents.

On the positive side, children are becoming aware of the wider dimension of human life and interactions. Young children are growing rapidly in their intellectual curiosity and general knowledge of the world around them.

Teenagers, youth and adults themselves are becoming more aware of their rights. Environmental Preservation, Animal Protection and Human Rights are becoming issues of priority for the young people of today. The demands of children and adults in families to upkeep with the media-world has become an obsession affecting the dignity and self-worth of family members.

FAMILY AS THE AGENT OF A NEW SOCIETY

Family in Process of Value Formation

The truth that family is the foundation for a stable and strong society is becoming more and widespread throughout the developing countries. The topic is complicated one, as family, society, culture and religion are inseparable factors and each one has something to do with the shaping of values in the individual and families. The family is a 'mini school' and it is there the children learn to relate with others. According to physiologists the child perceives and experiences its parents in the first year of life. The child's personality and attitude to a great extent are shaped by the age of four. The significant persons of the child's life in this stage are the mother, father, brothers, uncles and aunties. This is the period in which parents can play a great foundational role in families.

The future of humanity passes by way of family. Philosophers and social analysts have noted that society is a structure made up of families, and that peculiarities of given society can be described by outlining its family relations. The earliest moral and ethical writing concentrated much on family due to its importance as the base of the society. True happiness and progress of a society depends on the positive attitudes and behaviour of the members of the family. When these attitudes and relatedness extends from family to society, the society mirrors the family. When the influence is vice-versa, the family becomes the mirror of the society. In either situation, both family and society influence each other and one of them will always be dominant.

Family must become the Basic Unit of Change

Families as the basic and most important unit of social institution must be given special attention by any educational field that deal with society and progress. Being the fundamental constituting unit of the society, the family concerns itself with the well being and growth of persons. A happy family is where the parents and children together experience the joy of belonging, and the feeling of being cared for the deepest needs. Food, clothing and shelter are the basic needs of all human beings, but the happiness of a family depends on higher needs such as being loved, trusted, understood, for given, recognized for one's talents, gifts and the ability to reach out to those less fortunate.

The fulfillment of family life is in bringing forth persons strong in body, mind and spirit, with emotional maturity and altruistic outlooks as citizens of the nation. Persons must be socialized and educated for bringing about a social change. Hence, schools have a vital role in the attitudinal change and inculcation of values in children. This has to be done in co-operation with families. Parent-Teacher Associations and Management Committees are such means through which schools and families can take co-operative responsibility for education of children in the true spirit of formation.

Personality Traits and Basic Life Orientations

- Basic trust vs. basic mistrust;
- Autonomy vs. shame and doubt;
- Initiative vs. guilt;
- Industry vs. inferiority;
- Identity vs. role confusion,
- Intimacy vs. isolation;
- Generativity vs. stagnation; and
- Ego integrity vs. despair.

Men and woman are made in the image of God so that they can think, question and differentiate between good and bad, design their own destiny and reach the ultimate goal.

Parents' Focus on Value Clarification

In order to function as moral human beings in society, children need to grow in an atmosphere of clearly defined values which are practiced by adults. Children need to see/hear parents doing and talking what they believe in. Mostly, children learn from adults through imitation when they are young, and through reasoning when they grow up. They look for impartiality in behaviour and preaching in practice. Hence there is a need for clarification of values in the day-to-day life of the families. Initiated by parents, children seek guidance and answers to question in order to understand and accept values in the light of their purpose in life. Therefore, every family's first priority in training and educating children must begin with the question of personal identity.

Who am I? Where have I come from? Where am I going? This basic foundational principles of life must become a stepping stone for the positive socialization of children. Religious and moral values of God as the Creator-Father and the Universe as His Creation – Home should occupy important place in their value domain. A relationship with self, with God and with others will pave the way through to the child's mind. Children then will learn to relate to others as extension of themselves and develop social consciousness. The understanding of personal, social and spiritual relationships will grow in children through their experience in the family with the interaction with one another, day in and day out.

Family Values and Positive Strokes

Psychologists have come to the conclusion that positive thinking is the secret of happiness. In order to grow up in positive thinking, one must be exposed to positive strokes. The families where parents accept one another and encourage what they are and their contributions, health and happiness abound. From childhood on, children need to feel secure in themselves from the recognition and understanding they get from their significant people. Positive strokes can be effective in families for the proper self-image and upbringing of children. Case studies show that the most unhappy and violent people have been those whose childhood was spent with adults who were strict, constantly nagging, criticizing, and condemning.

Allowing children to grow up with clearly defined freedom, respect, love, encouragement and appreciation will result in making new generations of good citizens for the nation. The quality of change thus brought about in persons through families will prepare the groundwork for causing a gradual change in the society. Therefore, the parents must concentrate on giving positive strokes to the children in order to direct them toward a new value system making families agents of social change. Marriage is a point of departure in which boys and girls, brothers, and sisters realize themselves as persons with responsibilities in life, from individual ties with other persons and appear mature and able to make decisions for life.

Recommendations

In order to form families with lasting value that can influence society and change it for the better, the following values must be inculcated and transmitted to children both by parents and social institutions.

- Family life must be based on truth, faith and justice.
- A culture of peace, brotherhood and tolerance must be taught in families.
- Respect for life and respect for different views regardless of religions, ethnicity and regions must be fostered in families.
- A sense of responsibility for the welfare of others; family must be recognized by society and educational systems as a primary unit of society.
- Adults must become examples of inter-faith dialogue, critical analysts of social issues and promoters of Nation Building.
- True patriotism must be affected in children through parent's efforts and social institutions.
- Education at home and in an institutional set up must direct the yearning of human communion and self-realization.
- Young people must be recognized for their energy, enthusiasm and new knowledge and the elderly must be respected for their wisdom and practical knowledge.
- Correct judgment and common sense must be cultivated in children right from childhood.
- Opportunities for making personal decisions and evaluating the choices be made and carried out.

- Children must be brought up with consideration for their aesthetic, moral, intellectual and emotional development.
- Boys and girls must be brought up at home with equal participation in the household duties, given equal treatment and respect.
- A sense of compassion for the elderly and those less fortunate due to cosmic, social or economic situations must be part of children's curriculum.
- Sacredness of sex, beauty of growing up and happiness of family life must become experiences for children in families.
- Lastly, there must be the conviction that every parents in this world has a privileged duty of being an agent of re-creating the society and transforming the world.

MARITAL LIFE AND ROLE EXPECTATIONS

ROLE EXEPTATIONS IN MARITAL LIFE

Shakespeare wrote that the world is a stage upon which men and women are acting out the drama of life. The same thing can be said of marriages. There are many cultural and social expectations about appropriate behaviour for males and females. The goals, purposes and functions in marriage can be achieved only when each family member plays his or her particular role.

Marital Roles

What is meant by marital roles? Marital roles are the behavioural expectations of husbands and wives in a particular society at any given time. Roles are cultural creations, rather than biological imperatives. Roles provide the facility for the smooth running of society by a division of labour for men and women.

Changes in Gender Roles

Are there any hard and fast rules for assigning sex type roles? Can we change the gender roles? Of course there are no definite rules to assign roles to men and women. Cultural variations and the purposes of spouses may bring about changes in marital roles. But they cannot violate nature's goals for marriage. So we can find that some marital roles are unchangeable.

Disparity in Role Conceptions

In the past there were clearly defined roles for man and woman. Today we all are living in a rapidly changing society. In the modern society, there are no definite patterns of behaviour or roles for men and women. There is wide disparity in role conceptions. This changing nature of gender roles creates problems for all types of couples as they settle down to live together.

Factors Affecting Changes in Roles

The industrial revolution, emancipation of women, urbanization, employment of women, preoccupation of men with career etc. are some factors which have left their imprint upon family roles.

Role of Man

Role patterns for each sex are based on masculinity and feminity. Men and women are born with certain basic characteristics. Each culture has its own expectations of the roles of males and females.

Unique Male Roles

What is the key role of man? On what basis do we assign this role to the male? In most cultures strength and courage are still considered to be the qualities of men. They are also independent, tough and can control their emotions in better ways than women. Physical strength and social dominance are more functional for the male roles. So man is generally expected to be the provider and protector of the family. He is the master of the family. According to the traditional role expectations, he is the bread earner and the head of the family. He is expected to acquire a job to support his wife and children. He has to show determination in the achievement of difficult goals.

Leadership Role

The man is also entrusted with the role of leader and supervisor of all family endeavours. For the child, his/her first heroes will be his/her own parents, particularly the father who holds the position of authority in the family.

Role as a Husband

As a husband he has the role of sex partner, companion, confidant, decision maker and accountant. He must train himself to be a better observer so that he can be of great help to his wife. He must notice his wife and praise her performance and ability. He should also give emotional support to her.

Role as a Father

The father holds a dominant position in the family. In our culture, he is the chief authority in the home. Children need him for their all round development. They learn many good qualities from him. Some of the qualities are sense of justice and fairplay, steadfastness, inspiration to be useful etc. Hence he should be firm without being despotic, decisive without being dictatorial and gentle but not weak.

Role of Woman

Females, in most cultures, have been conditioned to carry out the reproductive function.

Traditional Roles

The woman is biologically, psychologically and emotionally prepared for motherhood. She is trained to carry out the roles of birth, nurture, protection, gratification and giving comfort to children and men. In the life of woman, these functions are given priority over all other engagements. According to the traditional role expectations, she is oriented towards rearing capable children, helping her husband to achieve the goals of the family and being useful to the community in which she lives. But are all women satisfied with this role concept? Talented and ambitious women, in addition to these functions, want to develop their special aptitudes.

Role as Wife

As a wife, she is expected to be an affectionate companion, a good sex partner, confidant and social secretary of her husband. She has to take charge of the social life of the couple. She should develop interest in her husband's work. She should be able to understand his world of activities. Moreover she should be able to give intellectual companionship to her husband.

As a Home Maker

It is the duty of the woman to make her house a beautiful place to live in. She has to take care of the basic needs of the family such as nutrition, clothing, recreation etc.

Role as a Mother

-She represents to her children the ideas and ideals of perfect womanhood working in harmony with her husband. The child's first attachment is to his/her mother. She is his/her source of nourishment, warmth and comfort.

Changing Roles of Man and Woman Today

You may be wondering whether the couples are following the traditional roles of man and woman today. What are the changes that have occurred in their roles? Why? Let us look at the changed role concepts and the reasons for these changes.

Reasons for Role Changes

Today family roles are changing largely because they have become less appropriate for the social and economic realities of the modern world. Most of the families are small in size and more women are employed. We can see changes in the styles of femininity as well as masculinity. The man is not maintaining the image of the brave, strong, tough, aggressive male of the past. The gentle, passive, submissive female is a character of yesterday. Opportunities are open for both sexes in education, work and family life. So greater flexibility is required in the role expectations of husbands and wives.

You may be interested to know what exactly are the changes in role concepts. Is there confusion in male's roles? We shall discuss these changes one by one.

Sharing Roles

Originally the husband was the head of the home and the chief authority in the family. But now the domination of the man seems to be giving way to equalitarian roles between husband and wife. More women have moved into employment outside the home. So the husband has to share the provider role with his wife. He also has to give up his position as the custodian of family wealth as the wife has come to share spending. He has to accept her equality in community affairs also. They share household chores including the care of children.

Economic Equality

A working wife plays an important role in decision making. When the women are employed, there is a tendency for the couple to share power equally. Wives are less dependent upon their husbands. The husbands in turn are freed from the burden of total support to their wives. Husbands provide more emotional support to working wives.

Changes in the Leadership Role of Man

The vocational demands may take the man away from home for long periods of time. In his race for achievement and success, he may forget his major duty towards his family. Naturally we can find a decline in the respect given to husbands and fathers. The leadership role of man also tends to be reduced proportionately. At times, they stay away from home to avoid responsibility in difficult situations. Then, the handling of the situation falls on the shoulders of the mother. What happens when fathers are reluctant to take up their responsibilities? In such cases, children may develop certain behaviour problems such as anxiety, aggressiveness and antagonism. You can observe the shrinking of father's role and an enlargement of the mother's role within the family. The masculine role has been greatly modified by the new role demands of the female.

Role Expectations in different Classes of Society

Do you think that role concepts are the same among people of different social strata? There are differences. In the case of lower class males and females, the traditional definitions of masculinity and femininity persist. For them, roles are strictly segregated. But for the middle and upper classes, the spouses have sharing roles. They share responsibility in providing family finances, in bringing up children, and in giving them good education. Even in the middle and upper classes, is this type of relationship accepted by everybody? The answer is no. In actual practice in India, the husbands have more say in the family.

Woman's Expectations of Man's Role

Do you feel men are becoming more effeminate in today's culture? What do women expect from men? Men are taking more interest in domestic tasks, and in the care of children. But they are still less gentle, less family oriented and less domestically oriented than women. There is no doubt that men are still trained to be more materialistic, and more success-minded than women. They have more efficiency, competence and material success. A women still expects many of these traits in a man. Many women still want the male to be strong and at times they want to depend upon males. They still admire and feel safe with a strong male. The man has to exhibit some courage and strength to meet the role expectations of his wife.

What do Husbands expect from the Wife

The wife should become the companions of the husband. She is expected to give love and affection to him. He expects an equal sharing of responsibilities. He expects cooperation, support and recognition for his efforts.

Factors Influencing Choice of Marital Roles

Marriage roles differ from many other roles in everyday life. There are no definite general role patterns. Each couple has to work out a role pattern for themselves. There are many factors influencing the choice of marital roles. Some of them are the followingL

Family

Customary roles are learnt largely from the family. It is through the attitudes, expectations and habits formed in the family that a boy or girl gets basic training in role expectations for him or her as well as for the opposite sex. In some families the parents consciously instill what they feel is the appropriate sex role behaviour in their children. Children also learn sex roles and authority patterns by imitating the behaviour of their parents.

The Peer Group

The peer group is oriented towards new attitudes and expectations for both sexes. They create new role expectations. These are usually in direct contrast to customary roles.

Culture

In our culture, men have more freedom of action. The women are expected to behave according to the norms dictated by society. Education has given her social and economic equality. But still she is restrained to traditional roles by our culture. This ties here down to house keeping and child care in addition to outside employment.

Employment of Women

This is a role assigned by culture, not by nature. Today, women are bearing a double load of work. Employment gives economic independence to the woman and she shares the financial burden of the family. She is fatigued after a day's work. There are more emotional and physical strains for the working woman. She may neglect her duties at home and may even refuse sexual rights to her husband. In some cases the husband may feel inadequate in his roles as provider. Children also suffer from lack of care and supervision. She may not be able to satisfy her role expectations.

She may face the following problems:

- Good health
- Willingness of the husband to share household duties
- Adequate pay
- A mother substitute if there are young children in the family and
- Co-operation from all family members A couple has to face many adjustmental problems, if both of them are committed to their jobs.

ROLE CONFLICTS

You have already learnt that couples should have a clear concept of their roles when they marry. This concept forms the basis of marital adjustment. The goals in marriage can be achieved when these roles are played properly. Do you expect that the couple can adhere to role expectations always? If not, why? When do role conflicts arise? Role conflicts occur when there are discrepancies in role expectations and the actual behaviour of the couple. It also occurs when partners relate to each other in some new or different ways because of emotional changes.

Reasons for Role Conflicts

No two persons are exactly alike. There are differences in attitudes, behaviour and beliefs. Husbands and wives gather different role concepts from their families. For success in marriage, each one has to produce in his/ her personality some resemblance of the partner's image of a man/woman. They have to change their values, attitudes and behaviour to fit in with the new role concepts. In the case of the woman living along with her husband and other family members, the mother-in-law may criticize her. She may be forced to change her behaviour in order to fit in with her mother-in-law's concept of an ideal wife.

Role conflicts are brought about by the strain put upon the wife in meeting the role expectations of her husband and his family and in adapting to the demands of his work. The husband also faces problems when his wife is having an established role in her life. Money management is another area creating role conflicts. Money management is the handling and spending of the family income. Usually conflicts arise over the issues of who should handle money and how it should be spent. You may think it is a simple question touching only the surface. But the decision has far reaching effects on family life. It affects the attitudes and relationships of the couple. Problems of domination, submission, insecurity, inferiority feelings etc. are created by the decision regarding the spending of family income. This in turn leads to conflicts between husband and wife.

The other areas bringing about conflicts in marriage are unrealistic expectations from marriage, sexual incompatibilities, the discipline of children, struggle for domination etc. However, the most difficult problem is difficult in communication. The failure in communication occurs at a deeper level of sharing feelings, expectations, intentions and personal needs.

How can we Resolve Role Conflicts

In marriage, spouses are involved in the lives of each other. Hence disagreement in some areas is inevitable. How couple manage conflicts is more important.

Conflict Management

There are many ways in which conflicts can be managed by the couple. In the first method, compatibility can be achieved when one partner is dominant and he/she attempts to get the other person comply with his/her desires and the partner agrees and accepts the complementary role. But when the disagreement is very strong and both partners are not willing to give in, tension is intensified. They may emotionally withdraw from each other's relationships without finding out an actual solution for the problem. An uneasy peace is achieved. There may not be any quarrels, but both of them are not happy or satisfied. How can one manage conflicts without hurting the personalities of both the spouse? The best method to solve the problem in a reasonable way is by negotiating with each other. Changes are to be made in the roles of both partners. This helps them to learn and understand more about themselves and about each other. This will deepen their relationship.

Personal Factors to be Remembered

In quarrels, be very careful in the use of words. Pay attention to the good things your partner does. Do not pay too much attention to his/her faults. Don't fall asleep without making up a quarrel. Control you temper. Don't compare your spouse with your parents. Learn to compromise to forget and to forgive. The partner's should have flexible personalities. They should understand each other. Avoid scathing criticism and curb the impulse to make cutting retorts. Settle a problem through mutual discussion. If things cannot be resolved mutually, you will need to seek help from a family counselor or spiritual counselor. Although seeking help from a counselor is not common in India, we need to adapt ourselves to changing situations.

ROLE CHANGES IN DIFFERENT PHASES OF MARRIAGE

As you have gone through the changes in marital roles you may have noticed that the relationship in marriage is not a static one. It is an ongoing process. In marriage you will find a variety of separate stages. Each stage requires new adjustments and re-valuation of the old ones. The couple has to re-organise their ideas, values and goals for the smooth running of their married life.

Early Years of Marriage

Marriage takes the new couple to new and unfamiliar ways of life. Every day they have to take some decisions, solve some problems and make plans for the future. The first year of marriage is one in which the husband and wife belong predominantly to each other, expenses are low, health is usually good and needs are simple. Their unique plan of life is in the making. Each one is becoming established in the routine of his/her job. During the first year or two of marriage the couple faces a multitude of adjustments. The following are some of the areas of adjustments in marriage which will be affecting their behaviour or role in early marital life.

Relationship between Husband and Wife

When you get married you say "I take you". It is not just the company, thoughts or the body of the partner that you take. You take the whole of the other person.

Accepting each Other

The husband and the wife have to accept each other with all their shortcomings. At the same time, they should maintain their individually, personal worth and self-respect.

Communication

The spouses should show the ability and willingness to communicate with each other. Communication is the breath of married life. It is not enough to love, to care or to respect. The lover must express affection.

Give and Take

The couple should possess the ability to give and take. To give oneself to the other means to share one's most intimate feelings. They should be co-operative and should be capable of emotional interdependence.

Personality Factors in Relation to Role Expectation

You know man and woman differ in their physical structure. Do they show differences in their emotional and psychological structure too? As every cell of the body is different, so also every feeling, every reaction, and every attitude of man and woman have particular characteristics according to one's sex. The respective nature of man and woman determines their roles in marriage. Success in marriage can be attained when the couple respects the characteristic qualities which nature has given to each of them and when they adhere to their respective roles. Do not expect one's own characteristics in the other partner and do not try to change him/her.

Personal Habits

Most of the problems faced by the couples arise from their basic personality patterns. Each person learns particular habits and attitudes from early childhood. So regardless of their similarities, each partner, always brings to marriage enough differences in their attitudes, punctuality, formality and informality in housekeeping and management of home, observing social conventions etc. may bring about role conflicts in marriage. Only if both partners are willing to compromise from the beginning of marriage, can they get along smoothly.

Sexual Relations

Why do you consider sex as an important factor for the success of marriage? It is because; sexual relationships directly and indirectly influence the adjustment in other areas of life. It is the physical foundation of marital relationships. If there is any frustration in sexual relationship it will affect the emotional, mental and social adjustment of the concerned person.

Sexual Adjustment in Marriage

You know that biological factors are important in determining the sexual satisfaction of the individual. Cultural factors are also equally important. What are the other factors? From where does an individual gain his sexual attitudes? The sexual attitudes and expectations are learnt by an individual from his/ her early childhood from his/her family and his peer group. The cultural norms of the society in which he/she grows up and matures and his/her biological structure modify the acquired attitudes of the person. Knowledge of sexual anatomy and appropriate sexual activities are also necessary for good adjustment. The other factors conducive for good sexual relationship are complete emotional acceptance of each other and an understanding of each other's behaviour.

Sexual Maladjustments in Marriage

Unfavourable attitudes towards sex, ignorance about sex and sexuality lack of proper sex education, unfavourable sexual experiences of early years of life, unrealistic expectations about sex in marriage and the unwillingness to be open with one's partner etc. are some of the reasons for sexual maladjustment. Psycho sexual development influences an individual's sex life.

Fixation or regression at any stage of development will adversely affect the sexual adjustment. According to Freud at one stage of development, the male and female children are attracted to the parent of the opposite sex – the boy to the image of his mother, the girls to the image of her father. For the boy this phenomenon is known as Oedipus complex, for the girl it is Electra complex. Normally the boy and girl will pass through this stage and begin to identify with the parent of one's own sex. If they are fixated to this stage, in their later marital life it will cause problems in sexual relationship with the partner.

Confusion about Sex and False Attitudes Towards Sex

In Indian society discussion on sex continue to be a taboo since long. This conservative attitude of elders prevents the imparting of healthy facts about sex to the teenagers. So they may turn to some other source to get information. They may be knocking at the wrong doors and getting wrong and dangerous information. Inaccurate and distorted information creates unhealthy attitudes towards sex. Later on in married life it will create a number of problems. The role of man and woman in sexual adjustment depends upon the attitudes and expectations each person brings into marriage. Both the spouses should have balanced and positive attitudes towards sex.

Relations with In-Laws

Marriage joins not only the man and woman together, but their families also. Hence, in-laws are the new relatives acquired through marriage. You may wonder whether in-laws are bringing problems to every marriage. The relationship with in-laws may bring about problems in some marriages. The circumstance in which each person lives is different. If the son-in-law or daughterin- law fits in with the expectations of the respective family he/she will be accepted easily. Otherwise problems may arise.

Interference of Mothers

Usually it is the mother-in-law who is more involved in in-law problems. Mother's lives are tied up with the lives of their children. They are very close to children. Some mothers are reluctant to give up their roles and try to maintain their responsibilities and expect privileges from their married children. The boy or the husband should understand this phenomenon and manage the situation accordingly.

Husband's Mother Interferes more Often

The mother is the first woman in the life of her son. After the son's marriage some mothers cannot accept another woman loving and caring him, even though it is his wife. The wife feels the mother-in-law to be a threat to her marital happiness. Only an intelligent and understanding husband can solve this problem. He should give due importance to both of them. Don't make them rivals. The wife should not be in competition with the mother. Give mothers time to find out new interests.

Other In-Laws

Sister-in-law also creates problems in the life of married couple. Brothers-in-law and fathers-in-law also share a small part in the in-law problems. Care of elderly relatives also creates troubles.

Why do the Parents Interfere

Parents are concerned with the growth and achievements of their children from the time of their birth. Hence, when children get married it is difficult for the parents to ignore or to be indifferent about their lives. At the same time the young couple is eager to be independent. They do not like the interference of parents. In many cases, the parents are not economically independent. They are forced to live with their married children. This also creates problems.

Positive Contribution of In-Laws

The in-law relationships are not always a problem. If the young wife appreciates her husband's mother and loves her as a second mother, she will find her very helpful.

Cultural Factors Affecting Role Changes

The role expectations vary with different cultures. Culture conditions the personality of an individual. Marital roles are determined by the culture in which one grows up. The couple coming from two different cultures will behave differently in a given situation. They will be having different expectations and their goals in marriages will be different. There may be few common interests. Each brings from his/her culture quite often different values, attitudes, customs and styles of living.

Cultural differences make mutual understanding and communication difficult. What should the couple do to adjust to each other? The couple requires more adjustment than others in a homogenous marriage. Before marriage, they should think carefully whether they are capable of making all the adjustments in such a marriage. To achieve marital satisfaction they should work with more maturity, understanding and determination than a couple marrying from similar backgrounds. If the couple can accept one another without trying to recast the mate into one's own particular mould, they may get along well.

Religion

Society may accept inter-racial marriages. But it seldom approves inter-religious marriages. The chances for success of an interfaith marriage depend upon the ability of the couple to face the situation maturely and realistically. Before marriage, they should have a clear evaluation of the difficulties they have to encounter and overcome.

Areas of Conflict

One's desire to make the other person adopt his/her religion causes major marital problems. Whether the parents and friends will accept the match is another difficulty. This affects the relationship of the parents. The religion to which children shall belong their education, choice of child training methods, the use of birth control measures etc. are some of the major areas of conflict.

Adjustments

If they are of an understanding nature and tolerant of each other's religion and have no desire to impose their own religion on the mate, they will get along well. If they have a clear idea of the many obstacles they have to encounter and if they are flexible enough to make their adjustments, their marriage may became successful.

Importance of Early Years

During the early years the couple has to make all the above adjustments for the success of their marriage. Each partner must learn how far he/she can take the mate in different areas and which are the things he/she must avoid. A couple may be able to make adjustments successfully in the early years. But marital life is a continuous process. Aging and maturity bring about changes in the lives of the couple. The new and changing situations in life makes further adjustments in the roles of husbands and wives necessary and inevitable.

Role Changes with the Arrival of Children

The next phase in marriage starts with the arrival of children in the family. It signals the beginning of a new stage in the relationship of husband and wife.

Life Along with Offspring

There are radical role changes to be made with the birth of children. Parenthood brings fulfillment and completion to marriage. It fundamentally changes the whole character of marital relationships.

Problems Related to Transition to Parenthood

The coming of the child is early anticipated, loved and cherished by the parents. But transition to parenthood brings about a number of readjustments in the lives of parents. The arrival of the child upsets the balance maintained in the family.

Parental Role

Parental role brings personal, social and economic privations.

Economic Problems

The father is worried about his responsibility and additional expenses. The wife may have to give up her career and take up the role of a full time housewife. This affects the income and expenditure of the family.

Personal Difficulties

The wife may be embarrassed about the conditions of pregnancy and its effects on her social life and marital relations. Men also have to make role changes. When the wife is overburdened with child care and other household chores, he may have to share her duties.

Social Participation

The social life and recreation of the parents are severely affected. The young couple is tied down with the care of children. When they can entrust some one else for child care, they can have joint participation in social activities. Otherwise they attend social functions separately. However, joint participation gives more satisfaction to the couple. You have already learnt that, in the early phase of marriage, the couple had a child-centered relationship. They had very few outside interests. Their lives were built around their children.

Feelings of Uselessness

Some women feel that their lives are empty and futile. When parental responsibilities diminish, they may be having a feeling of uselessness. For such women, ending of parental role is a traumatic experience. It may cause neurotic difficulties. They can try to learn new skills and become engaged in some activities. Husbands are occupied with their work. In this way, they can adjust to the changes in the family.

Adjustment with In-Laws

Children may get married and the parents have to adjust to the children's spouses. Another adjustment is the care of aging parents. Caring for the elderly may help to fill the gap created when children leave home. But in many cases the care of aging parents deprives the couple of the opportunities for social participation and development of new interests.

Role as Grandparents

You may be well aware that many men and women become grandparent before grand parent middle age ends. This is a new role in the life of the couple.

Formal Roles

Some grandparents play a formal role following a hands off policy as far as care and discipline of grandchildren are concerned.

Surrogate Parent Role

In some other cases they assume the responsibility for the care of children. Grandmothers are more active in this role.

Fun Seeker Role

Another role is that they impart special knowledge to their grand children and teach them certain skills. The role of grand parents gives couple more satisfaction than their earlier role of parents.

Role Changes in Old Age

You must have observed the role changes in early adulthood and middle ages of the couple. What are the changes during old age? How does the couple adjust to these changes? You also know that the couple had a close, intimate relationship in the early phase of their marriage. Later on, it changed into a child-centered relationship. In old age, the relationship between a husband and wife again takes the form of a pair centered relationship.

Effects of Retirement

The pattern of family life undergoes further changes with the retirement of the husband. Perhaps the greatest adjustment of all occurs during this period. The husband retires and suddenly faces the insults of old age. He feels unwanted and has no motivation to compete with other men. He feels lost and does not know what to do with his free time. He tends to be depressed and unhappy. He is irritable in his treatment of his wife. He always criticizes and finds fault with the spouse. He does not want to help the wife in her household duties thinking it is woman's work.

Common Interests

Retirement forces the couple to be together most of the time. They can develop a pattern of togetherness in recreational activities. The same pattern can be applied to other areas of life. With the change of time mutual interests can be developed. When children leave home the parents are drawn towards each other more closely.

6

Family Planning: Programmes and Policies

Family planning is the planning of when to have children, and the use of birth control and other techniques to implement such plans. Other techniques commonly used include sexuality education, prevention and management of sexually transmitted infections, pre-conception counseling and management, and infertility management.

Family planning is sometimes used as a synonym for the use of birth control, however, it often includes a wide variety of methods, and practices that are not birth control. It is most usually applied to a female-male couple who wish to limit the number of children they have and/or to control the timing of pregnancy (also known as *spacing children*). Family planning may encompass sterilization, as well as abortion.

Family planning services are defined as "educational, comprehensive medical or social activities which enable individuals, including minors, to determine freely the number and spacing of their children and to select the means by which this may be achieved".

PURPOSES

Raising a child requires significant amounts of resources: time, social, financial, and environmental. Planning can help assure that resources are available. The purpose of family planning is to make sure that any couple, man, or woman who has the desire to have a child has the resources that are needed in order to complete this goal. With these resources a couple, man or women can explore the options of natural birth, surrogacy, artificial insemination, or adoption. In the other case, if the person does not wish to have a child at the specific time, they can investigate the resources that are needed to prevent pregnancy, such as birth control, contraceptives, or physical protection and prevention.

HEALTH

Waiting until the mother is at least 18 years old before trying to have children improves maternal and child health. Also, if additional children are desired after a child is born, it is healthier for the mother and the child to wait at least 2 years after the previous birth before attempting to conceive (but not more than 5 years). After a miscarriage or abortion, it is healthier to wait at least 6 months.

When planning a family women who are over at least 30 years of age should be aware of the risks of having a child at that age. Like older men, older women are at higher risk of having a child with autism and Down syndrome, the chances of having multiple births increases, which cause further late-pregnancy risks, they have an increased chance of developing gestational diabetes, the need for a Caesarian section is greater, older women's bodies are not as well-suited for delivering a baby. The risk of prolonged labor is higher. Older mothers have a higher risk of a long labor, putting the baby in distress.

"Family planning benefits the health and well-being of women and families throughout the world. Using contraception can help to avoid unwanted pregnancies and space births; protect against STDs, including HIV/AIDS; and provide other health benefits."

MODERN METHODS

Modern methods of family planning include birth control, assisted reproductive technology and family planning programs. In cases where couples may not want to have children just yet and plan with time family planning programs help a lot. Federal family planning programs reduced childbearing among poor women by as much as 29 percent, according to a University of Michigan study.

Adoption sometimes used to build a family. There are seven steps that one must make towards adoption. You must decide to pursue an adoption, apply to adopt, complete an adoption home study, get approved to adopt, be matched with a child, receive an adoptive placement, and then legalize the adoption.

BIRTH CONTROL

Birth control are techniques used to prevent unwanted pregnancy. There are a range of contraceptive methods, each with unique advantages and disadvantages. Any of the widely recognized methods of birth control is much more effective than no method. Behavioral methods that include intercourse, such as withdrawal and calendar-based methods have little up front cost and are readily available, but are much less effective in typical use than most other methods. Long-acting reversible contraceptive methods, such as intrauterine device (IUD) and implant are highly effective and convenient, requiring little user action. When cost of failure is included, IUDs and vasectomy are much less costly than other methods. In addition to providing birth control, male or female condoms protect against sexually transmitted diseases (STD). Condoms may be used alone, or in addition to other methods, as backup or to prevent STD. Surgical methods (tubal ligation, vasectomy) provide long-term contraception for those who have completed their families.

ASSISTED REPRODUCTIVE TECHNOLOGY

Some families use modern medical advances in family planning. For example in surrogacy treatments a woman agrees to become pregnant and deliver a child for another couple or person. There are two types of surrogacy: traditional and gestational. In traditional surrogacy, the surrogate uses her own eggs *and* carries the child for her intended parents. This procedure is done in a doctor's office through IUI. This type of surrogacy obviously includes a genetic connection between the surrogate and the child. Legally, the surrogate will have to disclaim any interest in the child to complete the transfer to the intended parents. A gestational surrogacy occurs when the intended mother's or a donor egg is fertilized outside the body and then the embryos are transferred into the uterus. The woman who carries the child is often referred to as a gestational carrier. The legal steps to confirm parentage with the intended parents are generally easier than in a traditional because there is no genetic connection between child and carrier.

In sperm donations, pregnancies are usually achieved using donated sperm by artificial insemination (either by intracervical insemination or intrauterine insemination) and less commonly by invitro fertilization (IVF), usually known in this context as assisted reproductive technology (ART), but insemination may also be achieved by a donor having sexual intercourse with a woman for the sole purpose of initiating conception. This method is known as natural insemination (NI). Mapping of a woman's ovarian reserve, follicular dynamics and associated biomarkers can give an individual prognosis about future chances of pregnancy, facilitating an informed choice of when to have children.

FINANCES

Family planning is among the most cost-effective of all health interventions. "The cost savings stem from a reduction in unintended pregnancy, as well as a reduction in transmission of sexually transmitted infections, including HIV". Childbirth and prenatal health care cost averaged $7,090 for normal delivery in the United States in 1996. U.S. Department of Agriculture estimates that for a child born in 2007, a U.S. family will spend an average of $11,000 to $23,000 per year for the first 17 years of child's life. (Total inflation-adjusted estimated expenditure: $196,000 to $393,000, depending on household income.)

INTERNATIONAL OVERSIGHT

The world's largest international source of funding for population and reproductive health programs is the United Nations Population Fund (UNFPA).

The main goals of the International Conference on Population and Development Program of Action are:

- Universal access to reproductive health services by 2015

- Universal primary education and closing the gender gap in education by 2015
- Reducing maternal mortality by 75% by 2015
- Reducing infant mortality
- Increasing life expectancy
- Reducing HIV infection rates in persons aged 15–24 years by 25% in the most-affected countries by 2005, and by 25% globally by 2010

The World Health Organization (WHO) and World Bank estimate that $3 per person per year would provide basic family planning, maternal and neonatal health care to women in developing countries. This would include contraception, prenatal, delivery, and post-natal care in addition to postpartum family planning and the promotion of condoms to prevent sexually transmitted infections.

REGIONAL VARIATIONS

CHINA

China's *one-child policy* forces couples to have no more than one child. Beginning in 1979, the policy was instated to control the rapid population growth that was occurring in the nation at that time. With the rapid change in population, China was facing many impacts of the rapid population growth including poverty and homelessness. As a developing nation, the Chinese government was concerned that a continuation of the rapid population growth that had been occurring would hinder their development as a nation. The process of family planning varied throughout China, as many different people differed in their responsiveness to the one-child policy, based on location and socioeconomic status. For example, many families in the cities accepted this policy more readily based on the lack of space, money, and resources that are often offered in the cities.

However, the people in rural areas of China were more hesitant in accepting this policy. Since the policy was put into place in 1979, over 400 million births have been prevented in China. China's population policy has been credited with a very significant slowing of China's population growth which had been higher before the policy was implemented. However, it has come under criticism that the policy has resulted in the abuse of women in China. Often implementation of the policy has involved forced abortions and forced sterilization. However, while the punishment of "unplanned" pregnancy is a large fine, both forced abortion and forced sterilization can be charged with intentional assault, which is punished with up to ten years' imprisonment.

Another aspect of family planning in China due to the one-child policy is the differentiation between the desire for male and female children in both urban and rural locations. In the Chinese culture, the desire for a male child is much harder, making the abandonment or abortion of female infants or fetuses common in the rural areas of the nation. Another issue that is raised in the one-child policy in China is the information in regards to naturally giving birth to twins or triplets. If this situation arises, the family is allowed to keep the children because of the natural causes of this impregnation.

HONG KONG

In Hong Kong, the Eugenics League was found in 1936, which became The Family Planning Association of Hong Kong in 1950. The organisation provides family planning advice, sex education, birth control services to the general public of Hong Kong. In the 1970s, due to the rapidly rising population, it launched the "Two Is Enough" campaign, which reduced the general birth rate through educational means. The Family Planning Association of Hong Kong, Hong Kong's national family planning association, founded the International Planned Parenthood Federation with its counterparts in seven other countries.

INDIA

Family planning in India is based on efforts largely sponsored by the Indian government. In the 1965-2009 period, contraceptive usage has more than tripled (from 13% of married women in 1970 to 48% in 2009) and the fertility rate has more than halved (from 5.7 in 1966 to 2.6 in 2009), but the national fertility rate is still high enough to cause long-term population growth. India adds up to 1,000,000 people to its population every 15 days.

IRAN

While Iran's population grew at a rate of more than 3% per year between 1956 and 1986, the growth rate began to decline in the late 1980s and early 1990s after the government initiated a major population control program. By 2007 the growth rate had declined to 0.7 percent per year, with a birth rate of 17 per 1,000 persons and a death rate of 6 per 1,000. Reports by the UN show birth control policies in Iran to be effective with the country topping the list of greatest fertility decreases. UN's Population Division of the Department of Economic and Social Affairs says that between 1975 and 1980, the total fertility number was 6.5. The projected level for Iran's 2005 to 2010 birth rate is fewer than two.

In late July 2012, Supreme Leader Ali Khamenei described Iran's contraceptive services as "wrong," and Iranian authorities are slashing birth-control programs in what one Western newspaper (USA Today) describes as a "major reversal" of its long standing policy. Whether program cuts and high-level appeals for bigger families will be successful is still unclear.

IRELAND

The sale of contraceptives was illegal in Ireland from 1935 until 1980, when it was legalized with strong restrictions, later loosened. It has been argued that the resulting demographic dividend played a role in the economic boom in Ireland that began in the 1990s and ended abruptly in 2008 (the Celtic tiger) was in part due to the legalisation of contraception in 1979 and subsequent decline in the fertility rate. In Ireland the ratio of workers to dependents increased due to lower fertility — the reality of which has been questioned — but was raised further by increased female labor market participation.

PAKISTAN

In agreement with the 1994 International Conference on Population and Development in Cairo, Pakistan pledged that by 2010 it would provide universal access to family planning. Additionally, Pakistan's Poverty Reduction Strategy Paper has set specific national goals for increases in family planning and contraceptive use. In 2011 just one in five Pakistani women ages 15 to 49 uses modern birth control. Contraception is shunned under traditional social mores that are fiercely defended as fundamentalist Islam gains strength.

RUSSIA

According to a 2004 study, current pregnancies were termed "desired and timely" by 58% of respondents, while 23% described them as "desired, but untimely", and 19% said they were "undesired". As of 2004, the share of women of reproductive age using hormonal or intrauterine birth control methods was about 46% (29% intrauterine, 17% hormonal). During the soviet era high quality contraceptives were difficult to obtain, and abortion became the most common way of preventing unwanted births. Since the dissolution of the Soviet Union abortion rates have fallen considerably, but they are still higher than rates in many developed countries.

PHILIPPINES

In the Philippines, the Responsible Parenthood and Reproductive Health Act of 2012 guarantees universal access to methods on contraception, fertility control, sexual education, and maternal care. While there is general agreement about its provisions on maternal and child health, there is great debate on its mandate that the Philippine government and the private sector will fund and undertake widespread distribution of family planning devices such as condoms, birth control pills, and IUDs, as the government continues to disseminate information on their use through all health care centers.

SINGAPORE

Population control in Singapore spans two distinct phases: first to slow and reverse the boom in births that started after World War II; and then, from the 1980s onwards, to encourage parents to have more children because birth numbers had fallen below replacement levels.

UNITED KINGDOM

Contraception has been available for free under the National Health Service since 1974, and 74% of reproductive-age women use some form of contraception. The levonorgestrel intrauterine system has been massively popular. Sterilization is popular in older age groups, among those 45–49, 29% of men and 21% of women have been sterilized. Female sterilization has been declining since 1996, when the intrauterine system was introduced. Emergency contraception has been available since the 1970s, a product was specifically licensed for emergency contraception in 1984, and emergency contraceptives became available over the counter in 2001. Since becoming available over the counter it has not reduced the use of other forms of contraception, as some moralists feared it might. In any year only 5% of women of childbearing age use emergency hormonal contraception. Despite widespread availability of contraceptives, almost half of pregnancies were unintended in 2005. Abortion was legalized in 1967.

UNITED STATES

Despite the availability of highly effective contraceptives, about half of U.S. pregnancies are unintended. Highly effective contraceptives, such as IUD are underused in the United States. Increasing use of highly effective contraceptives could help meet the goal set forward in Healthy People 2020 to decrease unintended pregnancy by 10%. Cost to the user is one factor preventing many American women from using more effective contraceptives. Making contraceptives available without a copay increases use of highly effective methods, reduces unintended pregnancies, and may be instrumental in achieving the Healthy People 2020 goal.

In the United States, contraceptive use saves about $19 billion in direct medical costs each year. Title X of the Public Health Service Act, is a U.S. government program dedicated to providing family planning services for those in need. But funding for Title X as a percentage of total public funding to family planning client services has steadily declined from 44% of total expenditures in 1980 to 12% in 2006. Medicaid has increased from 20% to 71% in the same time. In 2006, Medicaid contributed $1.3 billion to public family planning. The 1.9 billion spent on publicly funded family planning in 2008 saved an estimated $7 billion in short-term Medicaid costs. Such services helped women prevent an estimated 1.94 million unintended pregnancies and 810,000 abortions. More than 1 out of 3 women in the United States have an abortion by the time they are 45 years old.

WORLD CONTRACEPTION DAY

September 26 is designated as World Contraception Day, devoted to raising awareness of contraception and improving education about sexual and reproductive health, with a vision of "a world where every pregnancy is wanted". It is supported by a group of international NGOs, including Asian Pacific Council on Contraception, Centro Latinamericano Salud y Mujer, European Society of Contraception and Reproductive Health, German Foundation for World Population, International Federation of Pediatric and Adolescent Gynecology, International Planned Parenthood Federation, Marie Stopes International, Population Services International, The Population Council, The United States Agency for International Development (USAID), Women Deliver.

POLICIES AND PROGRAMMES FOR FAMILY WELFARE

FAMILY STRUCTURE, FUNCTIONS, AND RELATIONSHIPS

Family may be defined as a group of persons united through the ties of marriage, blood or adoption or consensual unions, usually constituting a single household, interacting and communicating with each other and creating and maintaining a common culture.

Family Functions

There are three major areas of functions which have been particularly accentuated. Thus a functional analysis of the family emphasizes the relationship flanked by the family and the superior society, the internal relationship flanked by the sub-systems of the family, and the relationship flanked by family and the personality of individual members. The former may be termed macro functionalism and the latter two micro-functionalisms.

Family Patterns

Family patterns are conceptualized in terms of family composition. A household is one of the dimensions of the family pattern. It is a residential and domestic unit composed of one or more persons living under the same roof and eating food cooked in a single kitchen. The normative family patterns in India are extended or joint family and elementary or nuclear family. The term joint family is used more commonly in India than extended family. The joint family comprises movable or immovable property, and all the members of the family may or may not be staying together. The elementary or nuclear family comprises couples and their unmarried children and is usually financially self-governing of other families.

Family Structure

Family structure is conceptualized as the configuration of role, power and status and relationships in the family. It depends upon the family's socio-economic background, family pattern, and extent of urbanization. Family structure has implications for family unity and stability and development of individuals. The functions that the family as an institution performs are divided in the middle of family members in the form of roles. Roles are culturally defined and are passed on to succeeding generations as correct behaviour. Role expectations are thus learnt from family orientation. Norms of family relationships may comprise norms and dyadic relationships, families and kinship orientation.

The dyadic relationships cover the following dyads in the family:

- *Filial Relation*: Parent-child relation
- *Fraternal Relation*: Relation in the middle of siblings
- *Conjugal Relations*: Relation flanked by husband and wife
- *In-law Relation*: Relation flanked by family members related through marriage and not through blood.

Family Practices

Family practices depend upon the family's ethnic background, extent of urbanization, family structure, and family laws. Marriage practices cover marriage patterns, selection of marriage partner, and age at marriage, age at consummation of marriage, marriage rituals, financial swap, and divorce. Other family practices relate to lineage, residence, child bearing, child birth, adoption, guardianship, and custody of children, maintenance, death and inheritance and succession. Families are classified into patrilineal and matrilineal families according to the lineage or descent through the father or through the mother. Patrilineal families are usually patrilocal and matrilineal families are usually matrilocal through residence. Neolocal families establish a new residence after marriage.

Role of the Family in the Socialization of the Child

Socialization is the procedure through which persons learn the ways of a given society. Children are taught the ways and values of their society through get in touch with already socialized individuals. The family is significant because it maintains get in touch with children in excess of a longer period of time than any other group, and through close emotional association is able to exert maximum power in their lives. Both adult and other sibling members (brother and sisters) act as role models in providing examples for children in the development of their personality, attitudes, and behaviour.

FAMILY DYNAMICS

Family dynamics broadly comprise family interactions and family development as influenced through socialization of family norms of individual members.

Family Interactions

Family interactions refer to the distinctive character of interpersonal relationships which occur flanked by members of the family. An interpersonal relationship is a relation based on personal interaction rather than on any legal or structural foundation. The main features of family interactions may comprise cohesion, communication, role performance, decision-making, and adaptability. Each subsystem of the family has dissimilar interactional patterns.

Family Cohesion

Family cohesion is defined as the emotional bonding that family members have towards one another. There are four stages of cohesion, ranging from disengaged (very low) to separated (low to moderate), to connect (moderate to high), to enmeshed (very high). It is hypothesized that the central stages of cohesion (separated and linked) make for optimal family functioning. The extreme stages (disengaged and enmeshed) are usually seen as problematic.

Family Communication

Family communication is defined as all the verbal and non-verbal behaviour that occurs within the family, and flanked by the family and its social environment.

Role Performance

The following are the dissimilar characteristics of role performance:

- Role enactment, role performance and role behaviour
- The behaviour dimension of roles either validates the cultural expectations or emerges to create new roles.

Role Commitment

Role competence is the evaluation of one's own and another's performance.

Role Disagreement

Inter-role disagreement takes place when the norms or behaviour patterns of one role are inconsistent with those of another role of the same individual. Intra-role disagreement takes place when two or more categories of people hold conflicting expectations concerning the behaviour appropriate to a single role.

Decision-making

Decision making involves recognition of need for decision, identification, and weighing of acceptable alternatives, selection of an alternative and facilitating its action.

Family Adaptability

Family adaptability is defined as the ability of a family system to change its power structure, role relationships, and relationship rules in response to situational and developmental stress. It is hypothesized that the central stages of adaptability (structured and flexible) are more conducive to marital and family functioning with the extremes (rigid and chaotic) being the mainly problematic.

Family Development

The concept of family development gives a longitudinal view to compare family interactions in dissimilar stages of family life span. These stages may be determined through the age and developmental needs of the adults and the children in the family. The Family Life Cycle is a way of taking look at the family life. It is based upon the recognition of the successive patterns within the stability of family living in excess of the years.

Evelyn Duvall depicts the family life cycle as consisting of 8 stages:

- Stage I Beginning families (married couple without children)
- Stage II Childbearing Families (oldest child, birth to 30 months)
- Stage III Families with Preschool Children (oldest child 2½ to 6 years
- Stage IV Families with School Children (oldest child 6 to 13 years)
- Stage V Families with teenagers (oldest child 13 to 20 years)
- Stage VI Families as launching centers (1st child gone to last child's leaving home)
- Stage VII Families in the middle years (empty nest to retirement)
- Stage VIII Aging Families (retirement to death of one or both spouses)

Development Tasks

A family's development task is a growth responsibility that arises at a sure stage in the life of a family, successful attainment of which leads to satisfaction and success with later tasks, while failure leads to unhappiness in the family, disapproval through society, and difficulty with later developmental tasks. Family development tasks are vital family tasks specified for a given stage to development in the family life cycle. Family life development programmes aim at development of knowledge, attitudes, and skills towards democratic family functioning and strong family ecology.

These goals may be achieved through the following tasks:

- Attitude development in favor of family rights and responsibilities.
- Social training for enrichment of family dynamics and development at each stage of family life span for strengthening family's interactions with its social ecology.
- Information dissemination in relation to the family possessions such as laws, policies and implementation systems and services.

SOCIAL CHANGES AFFECTING INDIAN FAMILY

The family has been and continues to be one of the mainly significant elements in the fabric of Indian society. The bond that ties the individual to his family, the range of the power and power that the family exercises make the family in India not merely an institutional structure of our society, but accord provide it a deep value. The family has indeed contributed to the stability to Indian society and culture.

Today, the Indian family is subjected to the effects of changes that have been taking place in the economic, political, social, and cultural spheres of the society. In the economic sphere, the patterns of production, sharing, and consumption have changed greatly. The procedure of industrialization and the consequent urbanization and commercialization have had drastic impacts on the family. Migration to urban areas, growth of slums, change from caste oriented and hereditary occupations to new patterns of employment offered through a technological revolution, the cut-throat competition for economic survival and several other economic changes have left their impact on the family.

Briefly speaking, these changes in the socio-economic political- cultural milieu of our society have led to changes in the structures, functions, roles, relationships and values of the family. In the context of the changes in the economic system, more and more members of the family are moving absent from the superior family circle and living as individuals or members of a nuclear unit in urban areas. The patterns or loyalties, obligations and expectations have changed. The case of the child and the aged in scrupulous have become a problem for several due to structural changes in the family.

Change in Traditional Functions

Several functions performed through the traditional family are being taken in excess of through other agencies such as schools, day care centers, commercial and entertainment centers, etc. For instance, a significant function of cultural transmission performed through the family has been affected because the nuclear families are scattered cultures. The function of setting moral standards for the rising children and adolescents has been taken in excess of to a large extent through the peer group culture, mass media or through commercial entertainment. A major area of the family that has been affected through the social and economic changes in the society is that of the role performed or expected of the dissimilar members of the family. The traditional role allocation based on sex, age, or kinship has changed. With more and more women taking up jobs outside the home, the traditional role of the wife has changed. Likewise the role of the father, the mother, the husband, the child, and the elders in the family has all undergone several changes. The degree of role-overlap depends on the version of the scrupulous family to the changed situations.

The changes in roles have inevitable affected the relationships, in the middle of the members of the family. The concept of freedom, individuality, and rights of the individual has had their impact on the relationships too. The attitudes of implicit obedience to elders, concern for others, self-denial for the sake of others in the family, acceptances of the power of parents and superior status of the male are being displaced through attitudes of self-centeredness, assertion of individual rights, clamor for equality and right for self-determination etc. In the realm of values, today's family is moving towards materialism, individualism, and liberalism. The cherished values such as respect for age, concern for the weak, devotion to one's duty, co-operation are being replaced through competition and "getting ahead". It is not surprising that the family in India is also succumbing to the pressures of the time.

The consequences of these changes are several. Troubles such as child neglect, behaviour troubles in children, indiscipline in the middle of the youth, alcoholism, drug addiction, neglect of the elderly, material disharmony etc. are on the augment today and are indications that the family is not able to handle the change in a desirable manner. There is need so, to help the families to cope with the pressures and challenges of their life situation which are affected through the interacting forces to change in the economic, political, and cultural spheres.

Alternative Family Patterns

One of the mainly striking characteristics of contemporary societies is the attendance of a range of family variations, from the mainly traditional, extended families with strict, gender based sex roles to the modern dual career families based on liberal, equal sex roles and to adults cohabiting without marriage. The term "alternative family patterns" suggests family patterns that result from personal circumstances outside one's control (death of a partner, infertility) or from socio-economic circumstances (male migration, work participation of women). In the Indian context, mainly family variations are a result of personal or socio-economic circumstances. Experimental or chosen lifestyles like living without marrying, and being childless voluntarily are restricted to a very small group of people.

The following are the mainly commonly observed family variations in India:

- Single parent families
- Female headed households
- Dual earner/career families
- Childless families
- Adoptive families

TROUBLES ENCOUNTERED IN THE FAMILY AND INTERVENTION PROGRAMMES

Programmes

The following is a list of major family problem situations which may be entry points for family intervention. The causal factors of the situations may be multiple, situated in the family ecology, socialization of authoritarian family norms, dysfunctional family interaction patterns, or troubles with individual member's developmental tasks.

These areas are, so, not mutually exclusive. Some of these problem situations are:

- Families with individuals having troubles:
- Families of the disabled
- Families of the chronically/terminally ill
- Families of substance abuse addicts

Troubles with child bearing:

- Infertility
- Unwed motherhood

Marital troubles:

- Marital disharmony
- Marital breakdown

Abuse and violence in families:

- Child abuse in family
- Family violence against women
- Elderly abuse in family
- Family abuse of the disabled

Families in disagreement with other systems:

- Families with unemployment/indebtedness
- Families with inadequate or no land/housing

Families affected through dis-equilibrium in other systems:

- Families facing political violence
- Families facing environmental disasters
- Uprooted/refuge/migrant families

Family deprivation:

- Destitute children
- Destitute adults
- Destitute aged

These family situations, in turn, may affect the family functions, interactions, and individual members. The family may become incapable of carrying out some individual members. The family interaction patterns may change as a coping mechanism. Harm may be caused to physical and mental development and health of individual members, particularly children, women, and the aged. In the extreme situation family may disintegrate and individual members may become destitute.

Family Intervention

A family practitioner's role comprises planning and implementing a combination of interventions ranging from development to remedial, by individual, group, as well as community methods to strengthen these families, coping mechanisms and then rehabilitate them. Family counseling, marital counseling, family, and marital therapy crisis intervention, encouraging self help groups and legal aid are specific methods that may be used. The groups needing family intervention may be children, adolescent, youth, women, couples, or the aged; but the family as a whole may be measured the unit for intervention. Besides, planning and implementing the services, the practitioner needs to monitor and evaluate them and raise public awareness in relation to these services.

GOVERNMENT POLICIES AND PROGRAMMES FOR FAMILIES

Family policy means everything that the government does for the family explicitly or implicitly. The Constitution of India does not make an explicit reference to the family. Though, it lays down the fundamental rights of individual citizens in terms of equality, nondiscrimination, and protection. Its Directive Principles of State Policy state that, "The state shall strive to promote the welfare of the people through securing and protecting as effectively as it may a social order in which justice, social, economic, and political shall inform all the institutions of the national life". Article 41 specifically lays down that, "the state shall, within the limits of its economic capability and development, make effective provision for securing the right to work to education and to public assistance in cases of unemployment, old age, sickness, and disablement".

Social Policies and the Family

Reviewing the social policies of India that affect the family, one can conclude that India has explicit family policy with explicit goal for the family only in the form of the Family Welfare Programme of the Ministry of Health and Family Welfare. This programme pursues family planning as an integral part of a comprehensive policy, covering the total health care delivery system. Though, the policy has the limited goal of promoting Planned Parenthood with a two children/one child norm, through the self-governing choice of family welfare methods. We have a National Policy for Children that aim at full physical, mental, and social development of children.

As far as the family is concerned, it states that, "In organizing services for children efforts would be directed to strengthen family ties so that full potentialities of growth of children are realized within the normal family, neighborhood, and community environment". In 1992, India adopted a "National Plan of Action" for children, based on the recommendations of the World Summit of Children contained in the plan of Action for Survival, Protection, and Development of Children. The extensive-term goals of the National Housing Policy are eradication of home—lessens improvement of the housing circumstances of the inadequately housed, and provision of minimum stage of vital services and amenities to all.

The National Policy for Child Labour, the National Youth Policy, the National Policy Education, and the National Health Policy aim at specific services for select groups of individuals and implications for the family are implicit. India has a forest policy which aims at protection, conservation, and development of forests. Thus, we have several policies for the family and its members. A draft of the national policy for the aging is being discussed. A National Policy for Women is yet at the stage of recommendations of the National Perspective Plan for Women. Our social security legislation is applicable only to work force in the organized sector. A large number of families at risk remain uncovered through any social security against poverty, old age, disability, illness, and environmental disasters.

Family Laws in India

India has dissimilar personal laws for families belonging to dissimilar religions, and so, do not have any agreed upon goals in relation to the significant aspect of civic life. Hindus, Muslims, Christians, Jews and Parsis, have their own personal laws, which cover matters of personal relations and family practices such as marriage, divorce, adoption, maintenance, guardianship and custody of children, and inheritance and succession. As these laws draw from the respective religious norms, they often perpetuate traditional patriarchal norms and slow down the procedure of reforms.

Although Article 44 of the Constitution maintains that, "The State shall endeavour to secure for the citizens a uniform civil code throughout the territory of India", very few attempts have succeeded in enacting secular family laws that apply to family practices of all Indians. These secular family laws are, the Child Marriage Restraint Act, 1929. The Medical Termination of Pregnancy Act, 1972, Special Marriage Act, 1974, Dowry Prohibition Act, 1961 and provisions made in the Criminal Procedure Code and Indian Penal Code.

Government Schemes and the Family

In the absence of an overall family policy, the government schemes that affect/benefit families and their members are divided in the middle of dissimilar ministries.

Provisions Under Ministry of Welfare

The Ministry of Welfare has five bureaus for the following purposes. The Bureau of Social Defense controls the troubles of family and social disorganization which are manifest in the shapes of delinquency, juvenile vagrancy, drug addiction, alcoholism, and other such troubles of personal and social deviance, within the framework of specific laws and allied events.

This Bureau implements the following schemes:

- For the welfare of children in need of care and protection;
- For the prevention and control of juvenile special maladjustment;
- For spreading awareness in relation to the ill effects of drug abuse and providing counseling, de-addiction, after-care and rehabilitation services;
- For refugees from other South Asian countries (Relief and Rehabilitation schemes);

- For grant-in-aid to welfare programmes of the aged; and
- A scheme for the development of street children.

Provisions Under Ministry of Human Possessions Development

The Ministry of Human Resource Development runs the Department of Women and Child Development which has two bureaus: Bureau of Nutrition and Child Development and Bureau of Women's Welfare and Development.

The Department runs the following schemes for children:

- Integrated Child Development Services for Children;
- The Adolescent Girls Scheme;
- A Scheme of Crèches/Day Care Centers for Children of Poor, working and ailing women and;
- Early Childhood Education Programme.

The Department runs the following schemes for women:

- Hostels for Working Women Belonging to Low Income Group;
- The Scheme for Employment cum Income Generating Production Units for Women;
- The Scheme for Training Centers for Rehabilitation of Women in Distress;
- The Scheme for Short Stay Homes for Women and Girls;
- Public education for the Prevention of Atrocities against Women; and
- The Support to Training cum Employment Programme (STEP)

The Central Social Welfare Board, which is an autonomous organization working under the Department of Women and Child Development, offers the following schemes:

- The scheme of Opportunities for Education For Adult Women;
- The Socio-Economic Programme provides opportunities for work and wages to needy women that contain the economically backward, the destitute, the widowed, the deserted, the physically handicapped, and so on;
- The Awareness Generation Project for Rural and Poor Women Programme;
- Mahila Mandals;
- Family Counseling Centers;
- Voluntary Action Bureaus;
- Welfare Extension Project; and
- Scheme of Balika Mandals for Adolescent Girls.

Provisions Under the Ministry of Urban Development

The following Social Housing Schemes are implemented through the Ministry of Urban Development:

- Housing Scheme for economically weaker sections;
- Housing Scheme for low income groups;

- Housing Scheme for middle income groups; and
- Rural housing sites cum construction assistance scheme for landless workers;

The Ministry is also implementing the following programmes related to urban poverty alleviation:

- The Nehru Rozgar Yojana;
- The urban vital services for the poor; and
- Environmental improvement of urban slums aims at ameliorating the living condition of urban slum dwellers.

Provisions Under the Ministry of Rural Development

The Ministry of Rural Development implements several schemes. Though, with the formation of every new Ministry and Government at the centre, each of the programmes gets a new name or is put into dissimilar categories.

Some of the well recognized programmes contain:

- Integrated Rural Development Programme (IRDP)
- National Scheme for Training of Rural Youth for Self-Employment (TRYSEM); and
- Development of Women and Children in Rural Areas (DWCRA).

HUMAN RIGHTS IN THE FAMILY

The goal of the International Year for the Family (IYF), 1994 is "Building the smallest democracy at the heart of the society". The plans for the IYF seek to promote the vital human rights and fundamental freedoms accorded to all individuals through the set of internationally agreed instruments formulated under the aegis of the United Nations, whatever the status of each individual within the family, and whatever the form and condition of the family.

According to the United Nations, "Human rights could be usually defined as those rights which are inherent to our nature and without which we cannot live as human beings. Human rights and fundamental freedoms allow us to fully develop and use our human qualities, our intelligence, our talents and our spiritual and other needs", their being met is, so, not a matter of choice, but an imperative of vital justice. The human rights need to be applied to the family for enriching family life. Denial of them creates circumstances of use, deprivation, and destitution of families and their individual members. Family responsibilities are as significant as family rights to ensure family happiness.

The following human rights instruments are applicable to the family:

- The U.N. Declaration of Human Rights;
- The U.N. Convention on the Elimination of All Shapes of Discrimination against Women; and
- The U.N. Convention of the Rights of the Child.

Desai has applied these human rights instruments to family and added family responsibilities at three stages:

- The individual's right to have a family;

- The individual's rights and responsibilities within the family, and
- The family's rights and responsibilities with reference to its environment. These family rights and responsibilities can form the goals for family well-being that cut crossways the diverse shapes of families.

The Individual's Right to Have a Family:

- Every child has the right to be reached through his or her natural family. Parents have the primary responsibility to rear their children.
- Every adult has the right to marry and form a family
- Every elderly person has the right to be cared through his or her children.

The Individual's Rights and Responsibilities within the Family

There are natural humane and caring qualities in family relationships. These may be used and strengthened through promoting and protecting every individual's rights for status, worth and dignity; equality and nondiscrimination; freedom and choices in family life; social security from family members; and protection from family abuse and violence. It is the responsibility of every individual, family, community and the state to promote and protect these rights. Every individual has responsibility to enrich family interactions.

These rights and responsibilities are further elaborated below:

- Every family member is equal in dignity and worth, irrespective of age and gender. Every family member, so, has the right to equal allocation of family possessions, and equal responsibility towards household work.
- Both the married partners have the right to gender equality in marriage with respect to monogamy, role, power and status; parenting, guardianship and custody of children; title to matrimonial home and property; and dissolution of marriage and division of matrimonial property.
- Every family member has the right to freedom and choice in family life.
- Every family member has the right to care and support from other family members in crisis events such as disability, illness and in old age.
- Every family member has the right to life and security of persons.
- Individuals need legal protection of the state for their rights within the family.
- It is the responsibility of every family to register birth, marriage, and death of every family member.
- It is the responsibility of every family member to promote sensitivity and responsiveness, positive communication patterns, democratic decision making and peaceful and nonviolent approaches for resolving conflicts in their family interactions.

PLANNING FOR FAMILY AND FOR RESPONSIBLE PARENTHOOD

A marriage undergoes a transformation when husband and wife suddenly become parents. The word "suddenly" is appropriate because the transition to the status of parent is quit unlike the transitions to other major statuses in life, such as marriage or an occupation. People have relatively greater preparation and experience for entering marriage or an occupation, and they also have a grace period throughout which they slowly assume the responsibilities of the new status. The transition to parenthood is quite dissimilar and often dramatic. It may constitute a crisis in the life of married couple, as it forces them to take on a significant and demanding responsibility. The task of parenting allows the wife and husband much less time to devote to each other. And as the child becomes an interacting individual in the family, intricate relationship pattern emerge.

Once the motivation for the good life is created, couples will be able to come to mutual decision concerning each pregnancy so that every child in the family will be a 'wanted child' and not a "product of chance". Every pregnancy will place husband and wife in a new human setting and far from experiencing pregnancy as a pathological condition. It will place them in a revived experience at the very centre of human destiny. The decision to marry and to bring a child into the world is the couple's decision. They necessity responsibly prepare for parenthood so as to give for themselves and their children in an environment in which they can grow personally and as a family. Marriage and conjugal love are through their nature ordained towards the begetting and educating of children. Children are really the supreme gift of marriage and contribute very substantially to the welfare of their parents. Hence conjugal love requires in husband and wife an awareness of their mission of "responsible parenthood".

Characteristics of Responsible Parenthood

- Responsible parenthood means the knowledge and respect of their functions.
- The deliberate and generous decision to raise a family, or through the decision, made for some motives and with due respect for the moral law, to avoid for the time being or even for an indeterminate period, a new birth.
- The responsible exercise of parenthood implies that husband and wife recognize fully their own duties towards God, towards themselves, towards the family and towards the society, in a correct hierarchy of values.

Future Trends

The future of parenthood will contain a greater awareness of what the role involves, increased sharing through both spouses of the birth of their child or children, new techniques of delivery, and more emphasis on fatherhood. There is need for preparation for parenthood classes accessible to potential parents as Lamaze classes (the Lamaze method emphasizes active involvement of the father in the delivery procedure).

FAMILY PLANNING POLICIES

OBJECTIVES AND SCOPE OF FAMILY PLANNING

An Expert Committee of the WHO defined Family Planning as: a way of thinking and living that is adopted voluntarily, upon the foundation of knowledge, attitudes, and responsible decision through individuals and couples, in order to promote the health and welfare of the family group and thus contribute effectively to the social development of a country".

Objectives of Family Planning

Family planning refers to practices that help individuals or couples to attain sure objectives:

- To avoid unwanted births
- To bring in relation to the wanted births
- To regulate the intervals flanked by pregnancies
- To control the time at which births occur in relation to the ages of the parent and
- To determine the number of children in the family

Now you have learnt the definition and objectives of family planning. Let us see the scope of family planning services.

Scope of Family Planning Services (lh2)

It is not synonymous with birth control, but is in fact more than mere birth control. A WHO Expert Committee has stated that, family planning comprises in its purview.

- The proper spacing and limitation of births
- Advice on sterility,
- Education for parenthood
- Sex education,
- Screening for pathological circumstances related to reproductive system,
- Genetic counseling
- Premarital consultation and examination
- Marriage counseling,
- Carrying out pregnancy tests,
- Preparation of couples for the arrival of their first child,
- Providing services for unmarried mothers.
- Teaching home economics and nutrition and,
- Providing adoption services.

These activities vary from country to country according to national objectives and policies with family planning. This is the modern concept of family planning. Rapid population growth in less urbanized countries is a key factor in limiting the ability of these countries to raise standards of living. Significant obstacles to their socio-economic development contain limited possessions, food sharing troubles high rate of diseases and infant mortality, lack of proper sanitation, scarcity of funds and shortage of educational facilities and work opportunities. In this context, the Planning Commission clearly, recognized the need for population control right at the beginning of the planning exercise.

To quote the First Five Year Plan:

- "The recent augment in the population of India and the pressure exercised on the limited possessions of the country have brought to the forefront the urgency of the problem of family planning and population control. It is, so, apparent that, population control can be achieved only through the reduction of the birth-rate to the extent necessary to 'stabilize the population' at a stage constant with the requirements of national economy. This can be secured only through the realization of the need for family limitation on wider scale through the people".

NATIONAL POPULATION POLICY 2000

A social policy signifies consensual social purpose, and aims at progressive and structural changes. It pays appropriate attention to economic-cultural, political, and social factors as also to short-term and extensive term perspectives. A population policy can be nothing less than a social policy. Population programme necessity works itself in the whole fabric of social environment and necessity power and be influenced through all other events of social changes. When a policy is translated into programmes and activities, it causes social development, with due involvement of integrated diverse range of sectoral programmes and activities.

National Population Policy 2000

- Address the unmet needs for vital reproductive and child health services, supplies and infrastructure.
- Make school education up to age 14 free and compulsory, and reduce drop outs at primary and secondary school stages to below 20 percent for both boys and girls.
- Reduce infant mortality rate to below 30 per 1000 live births.
- Reduce maternal mortality ratio to below 100 per 100,000 live births.
- Achieve universal immunization of children against all vaccine preventable diseases.
- Promote delayed marriage for girls, not earlier than age 18 and preferably after 20 years of age.

- Achieve 80 percent institutional deliveries and 100 percent deliveries through trained persons.
- Achieve universal access to information/ counseling, and services for fertility regulation and contraception with a wide basket of choices.
- Achieve 100 per cent registration of births, deaths, marriage, and pregnancy.
- Contain the spread of Acquired Immunodeficiency Syndrome (AillS), and promote greater integration flanked by the management of reproductive tract infections (RTI) and sexually transmitted infections (STI) and the National AIDS Control Organisation.
- Prevent and control communicable diseases.
- Integrate Indian Systems of Medicine (ISM) in the provision of reproductive and child health services, and in reaching out to households.
- Promote vigorously the small family norm to achieve replacement stages of TFR.
- Bring in relation to the convergence in implementation of related social sector programs so that family welfare becomes a people centered programme.

Strategic Themes

- Decentralized Planning and Programme Implementation
- Convergence of Service Delivery at Village Stages
- Empowering Women for Improved Health and Nutrition
- Child Health and Survival
- Special efforts for Under-Served Population Groups who are people living in Urban Slums, Tribal Communities, Hill Area Populations, Displaced and Migrant Populations, Adolescents. Efforts to augment participation of men in Planned Parenthood
- Diverse Health Care Providers including private parishioners, private hospitals, NGOs, etc.
- Collaboration With and Commitments from Non- Government Organisations and the Private Sector
- Mainstreaming Indian Systems of Medicine and Homeopathy
- Contraceptive Technology and Research on Reproductive and Child Health (xi) Providing for the Older Population
- Information, Education, and Communication

Legislation

It is recommended that the 42nd Constitutional Amendment that freezes till 2001, the number of seats to the Lok Sabha and the Rajya Sabha-based on the 1971 Census be extended up to 2026.

Public Support

Demonstration of strong support to the small family norm, as well as personal instance, through political, community, business, professional, and religious leaders, media and film stars, sports personalities, and opinion makers, will enhance its acceptance throughout society. The government will actively enlist their support in concrete ways.

New Structures

- *National Commission on Population*: A National Commission on Population, presided in excess of through the Prime Minister, will have the Chief Ministers of all states and UTs, and the Central Minister in charge of the Department of Family Welfare and other concerned Central Ministries and Departments, for instance Department of Woman and Child Development, Department of Education, Department of Social Justice and Empowerment in the Ministry ofHRD, Ministry of Rural Development, Ministry of Environment and Forest, and others as necessary, and reputed demographers, public health professionals, and NGOs as members. This Commission will oversee and review implementation of policy. The Commission Secretariat will be provided through the Department of Family Welfare.
- State / UT Commissions on Population
- Coordination Cell in the Planning Commission
- Technology Mission in the Department of Family Welfare

Funding

Funding to obtained form a variety of sources including international sources, national governments, state governments, NGOs etc. Promotional and motivational events for adoption of the small family norm, the following promotional and motivational events will be undertaken:

- Panchayats and Zila Parishads will be rewarded and honored for exemplary performance in universalizing the small family norm, achieving reductions in infant mortality and birth rates, and promoting literacy with completion of primary schooling.
- The Balika Samridhi Yojana run through the Department of Women and Child Development, to promote survival and care of the girl child, will continue. A cash incentive of ₹ 500 is awarded at the birth of the girl child of birth order 1 or 2.
- Maternity Benefit Scheme run through the Department of Rural Development will continue. A cash incentive of ₹ 500 is awarded to mothers who have their first child after 19 years of age, for birth of the first or second child only. Disbursement of the cash award will in future be connected to compliance with ante-natal check up, institutional delivery through trained birth attendant, registration of birth and BCG immunization.

- A Family Welfare-connected Health Insurance Plan will be recognized. Couples below the poverty row, who undergo sterilization with not more than two living children, would become eligible (beside with children) for health insurance (for hospitalization) not exceeding ₹ 5000, and a personal accident insurance cover for the spouse undergoing sterilization.
- Couples below the poverty row, who marry after the legal age of marriage, register the marriage, have their first child after the mother reaches the age of 21, accept the small family norm, and adopt a terminal method after the birth of the second child, will be rewarded.
- A revolving fund will be set up for income-generating activities through village-stage self help groups, who give community-stage health care services.
- Creches and child care centers will be opened in rural areas and urban slums. This will facilitate and promote participation of women in paid employment.
- A wider, affordable choice of contraceptives will be made accessible at diverse delivery points, with counseling services to enable acceptors to exercise voluntary and informed consent.
- Facilities for safe abortion will be strengthened and expanded.
- Products and services will be made affordable through innovative social marketing schemes.
- Local entrepreneurs at village stages will be provided soft loans and encouraged to run ambulance services to supplement the existing arrangements for referral transportation.
- Increased vocational training schemes for girls, leading to self-employment will be encouraged.
- Strict enforcement of Child Marriage Restraint Act, 1976.
- Strict enforcement of the Pre-Natal Diagnostic Techniques Act, 1994.
- Soft loans to ensure mobility of the ANMs will be increased.
- The 42nd Constitutional Amendment has frozen the number of representatives in the Lok Sabha (on the foundation of population) at 1971 Census stages. The freeze is currently valid until 2001, and has served as an incentive for State Governments to fearlessly pursue the agenda for population stabilization. This freeze needs to be extended until 2026.

Socio-Demographic Goals in 2010

- Implementation in totality of the Minimum Needs Programme in scrupulous, universalisation of primary education and reduction in the drop-out rates of primary and secondary school students, both boys and girls, abolition of child labour and priority to primary health.

- Reduction in the incidence of marriage of girls below the age of 18 years to zero.
- Augment in the percentage of deliveries mannered through trained personnel to 100 percent.
- Reduction in maternal mortality rate to less than 100 per 100,000 live births.

FAMILY WELFARE PROGRAMMES THROUGH FIVE YEAR PLANS

You have read in relation to the Family Planning Policies urbanized through the Government of India throughout the Plan periods. Now let us look at the Family Welfare Programme urbanized through the Five Year Plans. The country is committed to attaining the goals of "Health for All" and a "Net Reproduction Rate of Unity" through the year 2000 A.D. through the universal provision of comprehensive primary health care services to all and an easy access to family welfare planning and maternal and child health facilities. The National Family Planning Programme is the expression of the communal concern for the population problem. After 10 years of its introduction, the Department of Family Planning was organized at the Centre. Now it is described the Department of Family Welfare. At the State or Union Territory stage, there are directorates of Family Welfare Planning. In excess of the years, the programme has evolved a nationwide physical infrastructure and vast reservoir of skills.

Family Planning Programmes Under the First Five Year Plan (1951-56)

While formulating the First Plan, it was assumed that the population would continue to grow at the rate of 1.25 percent per annum. So, under the Medical and Public Health Plan, a component entitled Family Planning and Population Control was incorporated for the first time with an allocation of ₹ 6.5 million for this action. The main appeal for family planning was based on thoughts of health and welfare of family. It was understood that family limitation or spacing of children was necessary and desirable in order to secure better care and upbringing of the children. It was then firmly believed that all progress in this field depended on creating a sufficiently strong motivation in favor of family planning in the minds of people. After that it would only remain to give the necessary advice and service, based on acceptable, efficient, harmless, and economic methods. For carrying out the programme of family planning two committees were constituted one to deal with population policy and the second for research and for framing programmes relating to family limitation. Thus, India was the first country in the world to have an official policy on population and to a lunch a National Programme of Family Planning in 1952.

The Family Planning programmes in this plan were expected to obtain:

- An accurate picture of the factors contributing to the rapid population increase,

- To discover appropriate techniques of family planning,
- To devise methods through which knowledge of these techniques could be widely disseminated,
- To make advice on family planning an integral part of the services of government hospitals and public health agencies.

Family Planning Programmes under the Second Five Year Plan (1956-61)

Throughout the Second Plan the strategy was the same as in the First Five Year Plan that is expansion of family planning services facilities through clinics. The budgetary provision for family planning increased from Rs.6.5 million in the First Plan to ₹ 50 million in second Plans. The sharing of contraceptives was extended through Primary Health Centers, Government Hospitals and Dispensaries, and Maternity Homes run through the State Governments.

In both the rural and urban areas, contraceptives were issued free to those with a monthly income below ₹ 100, and at half price to those in the Rupees 100-200 income group. The Central Family Planning Board recommended the inclusion of sterilization operations in the family planning programme in hospitals and institutions where facilities lived. An incentive scheme paying Rs.10/- to a sterilization acceptor as compensation for he loss of wages was first introduced in Tamil Nadu followed through other States.

Research and Training Activities

Research activities were extended to the fields of reproductive physiology, demography, and communication action. Considerable progress was achieved at the contraceptive testing units in Bombay under the guidance of the Indian Council of Medical Research and the All India Institute of Hygiene and Public Health in Calcutta. Demographic research centers were set up in Bombay, Calcutta, Delhi, and Trivandrum. The United Nations Regional Demographic Training and Research Centre at Bombay, recognized in 1956, became a reputed centre for training students in Demography and population studies from dissimilar countries of Asia and the Pacific region.

Many valuable field investigations were accepted out throughout 1951-61 such as the India-Harvard Ludhiana Population Study, the Mysore Population study, and the Lodhi Colony Study in Delhi and the Singur Study in Calcutta. A broad-based training programme was urbanized which incorporated establishment of centers for family planning. Family Planning was incorporated in the normal training programme of a number of training institutions for doctors and medical auxiliaries.

In this plan, a Central Board for Family Planning and Population Troubles was set up at the national stage. Its responsibilities were to take care of extension of programme, training of personnel, and organizing biomedical and demographic researches. It was also responsible for carrying out inspection/supervision of governmental and non-governmental agencies getting grants, monitoring, and evaluation etc.

Family Planning Programmes Under the Third Five Year Plan Period (1961-66)

The Third Five Year Plan document sounded a note of concern that the Family Planning programme was a mainly hard one to carry out and it raised troubles of great complexity. It was realized that, sustained and rigorous efforts were described for in excess of a fairly extensive period before family planning could become a popular movement and part of the accepted attitudes of the people usually. Throughout the Third Plan period, the programme was strengthened further and an expenditure of in relation to the Rs.250 million was incurred.

The basically clinic oriented approach throughout the first two plans was replaced through an extension education through the network of primary health centers and sub centers in the urban areas. The change in strategy involved utilization of interest and influential local leader in villages for promoting a small-family norm and carrying the message of family planning to the couples. The objectives of this extension approach, which continues to be a pervasive methodology in the Indian Family planning programme to date, are:

- Creation of a group norm of a small family size in every community through educating and involving opinion leaders,
- Providing information to every eligible couple on accessible contraceptive methods, and
- Making provision for contraceptive service facilities in a socially and psychologically acceptable manner. In the clinic approach, the family planning personnel wait for eligible couples to come to their seeking advice and supplies. In the extension approach the crucial task of identifying, informing and motivating the eligible couples for family planning was given to the peripheral health workers, particularly to the auxiliary nurse midwives (anms) and family planning health assistants (fphas). In respect of advocates on methods of family planning, the 'cafeteria approach' was adopted, leaving the choice of the method to an acceptor. The responsibility of sharing of simple contraceptives and giving general advice on family planning was given on a much superior scale to voluntary organizations, paramedical personnel and to extension educators, trained in family planning.

The family planning programme was viewed mainly as a positive policy instrument for achieving the demographic goal. It was not measured as a social welfare measure for improving the status of women in the country or helping couples to space and limit the number of children according to their desire. The programme gained momentum in 1966 when a Department of Family Planning was constituted in the Ministry of Health and Family Planning at the Centre. It was to provide technical and administrative direction and guidance to the programme and to bring in relation to the effective co-ordination of its several facets. The emphasis was placed on time-bound and target oriented programmes. The Third Five Year Plan stated that "the objective of stabilizing the growth of population in excess of a reasonable period necessity is at the very centre of planned development".

Plan-Holiday (1966-69)

The period 1966-69 was termed as a "plan-holiday" when the earlier rogrammes were sustained with annual budgeting and target setting. The programme was integrated with the health programme in the country such as integrated with public health programme as maternal and child health (MCH) services operated through the primary health centers (PHCs) in rural areas and urban family welfare planning centers (UFWPCs) in town and cities. The expenditure throughout this period increased to ₹ 704.6 million. Two characteristics that characterized the programme at this stage were:

- The pattern of personnel to be deployed in the programme was decided at the national stage, purely on the foundation of the population size of a phc, district or state
- The choice of the methods accessible to couples was limited with emphasis on IUD and sterilization, although as a matter of policy, all methods were to be made accessible to the couples leaving the choice entirely to them.

Family Planning Programmes in the Fourth Five Year Plan (1969-74)

In the fourth five year plan, family planning was incorporated in the middle of the programmes of the highest priority. A numerical target was set for reducing the crude birth rate from 39 through the end of the Plan period and to 25 through 1979. These demographic goals were translated into targets of family planning acceptors to be recruited under the programme. To achieve these targets, a concrete programme was drawn up for expanding the facilities. It was through providing services and expansion of motivational and educational characteristics through the mass media. An outlay of Rs.3, 300 million was made in this Plan for the programme and the actual expenditure was ₹ 2884.3 million.

It is estimated that as a result of the programme 28 million couples were protected through 1973-74 and the births turned absent throughout this plan period were estimated at 12 million. Throughout this plan period, the programme for popularization of oral pills was also expanded. Surgical equipments were provided in rural and urban family welfare centers for vasectomy operations and a system for free sharing of condoms was introduced. Through the beginning of this Plan (1969), sterilization became the major task in the government strategy to be met. Increased emphasis was placed on the adoption of the 'camp approach'. In this approach sterilization operations were accepted out in villages at appropriate locations for conducting surgery and the infrastructure facilities were strengthened in the rural areas.

The incentive money was also raised. At the end of this Plan period the mass-camp approach was replaced through the "mini-lap approach" under which in any one camp not more than 25 persons could be operated. This change in excess of was felt necessary since a large number of complaints were received from persons operated upon in large camps. As a consequence, the programme suffered a set back in 1973-74, when the number of sterilization done declined to 0.9 million from 3.1 million in the previous year. In 1971, Parliament passed a law liberalizing induced abortions under an Act entitled "Medical Termination of Pregnancies Act" which became effective from 1st April 1972, making it possible for pregnant women to have legal abortion under sure specified circumstances.

Family Planning Programme under Fifth Five Year Plan (1974-79)

This plan witnessed a dramatic rise and fall in family planning acceptance in the country. The Fifth Plan document refixed the demographic goals so as to achieve a birth rate of 30 through 1979 and 25 through 1984. Throughout 1974- 78 a sum of Rs.4, 089.8 million was spent on the programme and it received an enormous boost from the government in 1976 with the announcement of the National Population Policy, a comprehensive policy formulated for the first time. The performance in the family planning programme throughout the year 1976-77 was the best to be realized ever, with a total of 8.26 million sterilizations, and all-time record. The programme suffered a serious set back after 1976- 77 and a revised policy on family welfare was announced in April 1977 (1.4.2). The term family planning was changed to "family welfare" to contain maternal and child health programmes as an integral part of the programme.

Family Welfare Programmes Under the Sixth Five Year Plan (1980-85) (lh3)

The sixth Five Year Plan in its objectives stated that one of the major areas of effort which was incorporated pertains to promoting policies for controlling the growth of population through voluntary acceptance of small family norm. The Plan envisaged the extensive term goal of reducing the Net Reproduction Rate to unity through 1995. for the country as a whole and through 2001 in all the states, This was expected to be made possible through reducing the birth rate to 21 and death rate to 9 and raising the proportion of couples protected through family planning to in relation to the60 percent. It is understood that the prime was required to be reactivated through education and persuasion of people, avoiding any form of coercion. The small family norm was to be built into the social and cultural ethos of the people. A multi-pronged but integrated approach was advocated.

It comprised of:

- Education and employment, particularly of women,
- Eradication of poverty,
- Provision of maternal and child care services including immunization, prophylaxis against anemia and nutrition,
- Building up of health care facilities in rural areas with due attention to control of communicable diseases,
- Promotion of preventive health,
- Water supply and sanitation.

Family Welfare services and supplies were sought to be made accessible on an extended scale through the health infrastructure in the country. All existing channels of communication including governmental extension machinery, voluntary organizations, youth organizations, women's organizations, village opinion leaders etc; were to be fully mobilized for promoting the widespread acceptance of family planning methods. While formulating the targets for family planning methods, adequate attention was given to raising the stage of acceptance of non-terminal/spacing methods in the contraceptive mix. Throughout the sixth plan, an allocation of ₹ 101.00 million was made for family welfare sector. At the end of the Plan, it was envisages that the couple protection rate due to contraception would go up to 36.6 percent. Throughout 1983, the government of India adopted a National Health Policy under which it was sought to be achieved through universalisation of primary health care and reaching Net Reproduction Rate of Unity through 2000 A.D.

Family Welfare Programme under the Seventh Five Year Plan (1985-90)

The Seventh Five-Year Plan document has declared the approval of the extensive-term demographic policy of reaching a net reproduction rate of 1 through the year 2000.A.D. In terms of specific family planning goals for the Plan period, the following targets have been stipulated.

- Effective couple protection rate (CPR) of 42 percent to be realized through 1990.
- Crude Birth Rate (CPR) 29.01 to be realized through 1990.
- Crud Death Rate (CDR) 10.4 to be realized through 1990.
- Infant Mortality Rate (IMR) 90 per 100 live births through 1990
- Immunization of children-universal coverage; and
- Ante-natal care -75 percent of all pregnant women.

In order to reach the above targets, particularly 42 percent couple protection, the Seventh Plan stipulated 31 million sterilizations, 21.25 million IUD (Intra Uterine Devices) insertions, and 14.5 million users of conventional contraceptive through the end of the Plan year 1989-90. Inter-sect oral co-ordination and cooperation and involvement of voluntary agencies in the programme are contemplated to be implemented in a better measure in the field of health and family welfare. Community participation is being achieved through the utilization of non-government organizations, informal leaders in the community, political leaders, and other social workers.

Special programmes to reduce the infant mortality rate to the stage of 90 per thousand per year through 1990 have been implemented. Special schemes for the reduction of diseases in the middle of children, such as diarrhea, dysentery and respiratory diseases are being implemented. A Universal Immunization Programme (UIP) providing immunization for children and oral dehydration therapy for treatment of diarrhea diseases was implemented.

The UIP sheltered all districts of the country through 1990. The Seventh Plan has provided an outlay of Rs.32560 million for the family welfare sector. Throughout the Seventh Plan, the oral pill sharing programme had been intensified. Besides, a subsidized marketing programme for promoting the oral pill with brand name MALA-D has been launched utilizing the sharing network and services of selected pharmaceutical companies.

Eighth Five Year Plan (1992-97)

- The vital premises of the Family Welfare Programme till now have been) Acceptance of the family welfare is voluntary.
- The Government's role is to create an environment for the people to adopt small family norm. This is done through spreading awareness, information, and education through ensuring easy and convenient availability of family planning aids and services and through giving incentives for adopting family planning.
- The programme, which is a 100% Centrally Sponsored Scheme has integrated family planning and Mother and Child Health (MCH) services and is being implemented through countrywide network of primary health centers and supporting institutions. Inspite of these efforts the results have been far for encouraging.

The following strategies will be adopted for achieving the goals of family welfare throughout the Eighth Plan:

- Convergence of services provided through several social services sectors.
- Decentralized planning and implementation will be another strategy.
- Panchayati Raj institutions like Gram Panchayat and Zila Parishads, etc., will have to play important role in planning, implementing and administering the programme. The role of the Centre will be limited to general policy planning and coordination, providing technological inputs of local self-government.

- The younger couples, who are reproductively mainly active will be the focus of attention, with necessarily a greater emphasis on spacing methods, although the terminal methods would continue to remain the significant means of birth control.
- The targeted reduction in the birth rate will be the foundation of designing, implementing and monitoring the programme against the current method of couple protection rate.
- The outreach and excellence of family welfare services will be improved through ensuring adequate drugs and other essential supplies at the Sub-centre and PHC through suitably raising the funds for this purpose.
- The whole chain of CHC, PHC and Sub-centers will be equipped to deliver general health and MCH services in an integrated manner with a strong referral support and linkage at the District stage.
- Child survival and safe motherhood initiatives will be vigorously pursued.

  These initiatives will contain:
  - Atrengthening of Universal Immunization Programme,
  - Greater emphasis on Diarrhoea Control Programme and effective implementation of art programme,
  - Acute Respiratory Infections Control Programme,
  - Anaemia Management Programme and not presently Anaemia prophylaxis,
  - Safe Motherhood Programme with high risk pregnancy approach and
  - Intensified effort for training of birth attendants.
- Training will not only aim at providing requisite knowledge and social, but also ensure development of such behavioral attributes that will him conducive to a closer interaction with the community. The methodology, the logistics and the content of training programme will be continuously reviewed. Special programmes would be chalked out for imparting pro-service and in-service training in programme management and IEC activities. To meet the training needs, several training institutions will be strengthened or new ones recognized, through providing adequate funds, staff, equipments and mobility.
- The whole package of incentives and awards will be restructured to make it more purposeful.
- There is an urgent need to secure involvement and commitment of practitioners of all systems of medicine in the Population Control Programme.
- The role of voluntary organisation in a mass movement such as population control is critical for generation of momentum and accelerating the pace of progress.

- As an extrapolation of the concept of voluntary organisations, is the role and place of organized corporate sector which covers almost 20 million workers and their families. Effective methods will he evolved to get the organized sector involved in the implementation of family welfare programme.
- Special efforts will he made to involve the community in the Family Planning Programme. The strategy will he to prepare the community to accept the responsibility, the ownership and the control of
- The village/neighborhood tea shops, pan shops, public sharing system shops, pharmacies, cooperatives, etc., will he utilized for community based contraceptive sale and sharing.
- The social marketing of oral pills as well as for market research and educational activities will be done with help for the Corporate Sector possesses special social and sensitivity.
- Information, Education and Communication, which are critical inputs will be further strengthened and expanded.
- A new thrust in the research and development of methods aimed at regulation of fertility in the male, and of vaccines for fertility regulation, both in the male and female, will be given. Fertility regulation practices such as the use of special herbs through the community particularly in the tribal areas, will also be subjected to research. While intensification of bio-medical research is necessary, research in social and behavioral sciences to explore the human dimensions is vital. Health systems research to optimize operational framework, to improve the efficiency and effectiveness of the service provided and to evolve cost-effective interventions in several areas of family planning operation, will be given high priority.
- A continuous monitoring, review and evaluation is an essential component for the successful implementation of the programme.

The Ninth Five Year Plan (1997-2002)

The reduction in the population growth rate has been recognized as one of the priority objectives throughout the Ninth Plan period.]

The current high population growth rate is due to:

- The large size of the population in the reproductive age-group (estimated contribution 60%);
- Higher fertility due to unmet need for contraception (estimated contribution 20%); and
- High wanted fertility due to prevailing high IMR (estimated contribution in relation to the20%).

The enabling objectives throughout the Ninth Plan period, so, will be to reduce the population growth rate through The objectives throughout the Ninth Plan will be:

- To meet all the felt-needs for contraception

- To reduce the infant and maternal morbidity and mortality so that there is a reduction in the desired stage of fertility

The strategies throughout the Ninth Plan will be:

- To assess the needs for reproductive and child health at PHC stage and undertake area- specific micro planning
- To give need-based, demand-driven high excellence, integrated reproductive and child health care. a) meeting all the felt-needs for contraception; and b) reducing the infant and maternal morbidity and mortality so that there is a reduction in the desired stage of fertility

The strategies throughout the Ninth Plan will be:

- To assess the needs for reproductive and child health at PHC stage and undertake area- specific micro planning; and
- To give need-based, demand-driven high excellence, integrated reproductive and child health care.

The programmes will be directed towards:

- Bridging the gaps in essential infrastructure and manpower through a flexible approach and improving operational efficiency through investment in social, behavioral and operational research
- Providing additional assistance to poorly performing districts recognized on the foundation of the 1991 census to fill existing gaps in infrastructure and manpower.
- Ensuring uninterrupted supply of essential drugs, vaccines and contraceptives, adequate in quantity and appropriate in excellence.
- Promoting male participation in the Planned Parenthood movement and raising the stage of acceptance of vasectomy.

Efforts will be intensified to enhance the excellence and coverage of family welfare services through:

- Rising participation of general medical practitioners working in voluntary, private, joint sectors and the active cooperation of practitioners of ISM&H;
- Involvement of the Panchayati Raj Institutions for ensuring inter-sectoral coordination and community participation in planning, monitoring and management;
- Involvement of the industries, organized and unorganized sectors, agriculture workers and labour representatives.

The NDC Committee on Population has recommended that there should be:

- Decentralized area specific planning based on the need assessment
- Emphasis on improved access and excellence of services to women and children
- Providing special assistance to poorly performing states/districts to minimize the inter and intrastate differences in performance

Creation of district stage databases on excellence and coverage and impact indicators for monitoring the programme IICPD has advocated similar approach. Concordance flanked by National (NDC Committee) and International (ICPD) efforts has improved funding and accelerated the pace of implementation of the family welfare programme.

- Decentralized area specific planning based on the need assessment
- Emphasis on improved access and excellence of services to women and children
- Providing special assistance to poorly performing states/districts to minimize the inter and intrastate differences in performance
- Creation of district stage databases on excellence and coverage and impact indicators for monitoring the programme.

Tenth Five Year Plan (2002-2007)

The NDC Sub-Committee on Population recommended that there should be a paradigm shift in the Family Welfare Programme and the focus should be on:

- Decentralized area-specific planning based on need assessment.
- Emphasis on improved access and excellence of services to women and children.
- Providing special assistance to poorly performing states/districts to minimize the differences in performance.
- Creation of district-stage databases on excellence, coverage and impact indicators for monitoring the programme.

Department has drawn up the National Population Policy 2000 (NPP 2000), which aims at achieving replacement stage of fertility through 2010. A National Commission on Population was constituted in May 2000, in row with the recommendations of the NPP 2000.

Currently some of the major areas of concern contain:

- The huge inter-state differences in fertility and mortality; fertility and mortality rates are high in the mainly populous states, where almost half the country's population lives;
- Gaps in infrastructure, manpower and equipment and mismatch flanked by infrastructure and manpower in primary health centers (phcs)/ community health centers (chcs); lack of referral services;
- Slow decline in mortality throughout the 1990s; the goals set for mortality and fertility in the ninth plan will not be achieved;
- There has been no decline in the maternal mortality ratios in excess of the last three decades, while neonatal and infant mortality rates have plateau throughout the 1990s;
- The routine service coverage has declined, perhaps because of the emphasis on campaign mode operations for individual components of the programme;
- In spite of the emphasis on training to improve skills for the delivery of integrated reproductive and child health (rch) services, the progress in in-service training has been very slow and the anticipated improvement in the content and excellence of care has not taken place;

- Evaluation studies have shown that the coverage under immunization is not universal even in the best performing states while coverage rates are very low in states like bihar; elimination of polio is yet to be achieved;
- The logistics of drug supply has improved in some states but remnants poor in populous states;
- Decentralized district-based planning, monitoring and mid-course correction utilizing the locally generated service data and Civil Registration has not yet been operationalised.

Approach throughout the Ten]th Plan

Throughout the Tenth Plan, the paradigm shift, which began in the Ninth Plan, will be fully operationalised.

The shift was from:

- Demographic targets to focusing on enabling couples to achieve their reproductive goals,'
- Method specific contraceptive targets to meeting all the unmet needs for contraception to reduce unwanted pregnancies;
- Numerous vertical programmes for family planning and maternal and child health to integrated health care for women and children;
- Centrally defined targets to community need assessment and decentralized area specific micro planning and implementation of program for health care for women and children, to reduce infant mortality and reduce high desired fertility;
- Quantitative coverage to emphasis on excellence and content of care;
- Predominantly women centered programmes to meeting the health care needs of the family with emphasis on involvement of men in planned parenthood;
- Supply driven service delivery to need and demand driven service; improved logistics for ensuring adequate and timely supplies to meet the needs;
- service provision based on providers' perception to addressing choices and conveniences of the couples.

Three of the 11 monitorable targets for the Tenth Plan and beyond are:

- Reduction in IMR to 45 per 1,000 live births through 2007 and 28 per 1,000 live births through 2012;
- Reduction in maternal mortality ratio to 2 per 1,000 live births through 2007 and 1 per 1,000 live births through 2012; and
- Reduction in decadal growth rate of the population flanked by 2001-2011 to 16.2.

Path Ahead and Goals Set

Reduction in fertility, mortality and population growth rate is major objectives of the Tenth Plan. These will be achieved through meeting all the felt needs for health care of women and children. The focus will be on improving access to services to meet the health care needs of women and children through:

- A decentralized area-specific approach to planning, implementation and monitoring of the performance and effective mid-course corrections;
- Differential strategy to achieve incremental improvement in performance in all states/districts;
- Special efforts to improve access to and utilization of the services in states/districts with high mortality and/or fertility rates;
- Filling the critical gaps, especially in chcs, in existing infrastructure through appropriate reorganization and restructuring of the primary health care infrastructure;
- Ensuring, that post of specialists in chcs do not remain vacant; upgrading skills and redeploying existing manpower to fill other critical gaps;
- Streamlining the functioning of the primary health care system in urban and rural areas; providing good excellence integrated rch services at the primary, secondary and tertiary care stages and improving referral services;
- Providing adequate supply of essential drugs, diagnostics and vaccines; improving the logistics of supply;
- Well coordinated activities for delivery of services through public, private and voluntary sectors to improve coverage;
- Involvement of pris in planning, monitoring and mid-course correction of the programme at the local stage;
- Involvement of industry in the organized and unorganized sectors, agriculture workers and labour representatives in improving access to rch services;
- Effective use of social marketing to improve access to simple in excess of the counter (otc) products such as ort and condoms;
- Effective IEC and motivation programmes; and effective inter-sectoral coordination.

EVALUATION OF FAMILY WELFARE PROGRAMMES

The National Family Planning Programmes (1951) is the expression of the communal concern for the population problem. After a decade, the Department of Family Planning was organized at the Centre. Now there is a close to universal awareness of family welfare planning, its concepts and techniques.

In excess of the years, the programme has evolved a nationwide physical infrastructure and a vast reservoir of skills. At the centre, there is a Department of Family Welfare and at the State and Union Territory stage, there is Directorate of Family Welfare Planning.

Although the National Family Planning Programme started in 1951, it has not made an important impact on reduction of fertility. Reduction in birth rate in excess of the years has fallen much short of the planned targets in excess of the successive Five Year Plans. Throughout 1970, the birth rate did not come down from in relation to the39 to 34, but from 1977 onwards it has been stagnating approximately 33 with a slight fall witnessed after 1984. it has been estimated that, the programme has been able to avert in excess of 106 million births, in the country at a total investment of ₹ 4683 crores (almost) upto the end of 1988-89.

Thus ₹ 442 has been spent per birth averted in the programme including the cost of infrastructure. Throughout the last 40 years Indian Health and Family Welfare Programme has grown manifold. At present in relation to the16,000 Primary Health Centers (PHCs) and 113,000 sub-centers are functioning in rural areas for providing Health and Family Welfare Services. Through several studies mannered on the Health and Family Welfare Programme, it is found that although it has attained remarkable organizational accomplishment, the programme as a whole has yet to succeed in either curbing population growth or reducing infant mortality to the desired stages

Accessible statistics also show that, performance of the programme is not uniformly poor all in excess of the country. For instance while States like Kerala, Mahrashtra, and Tamil Nadu have performed quite well in terms of both health and FP programme, the States in the Hindibelt, particularly UP, Bihar, Rajasthan and Madhya Pradesh have failed in their effort to implement the programme effectively and augment contraception to the desired stage. If India has to achieve its target of Health for All through 2000 A.D" and Net Reproduction Rate (NRR) equal to one through 2006, through lowering the infant mortality to less than 60 and birth rate to 21, a serious effort should be made to understand the reasons for the ineffective implementation of the programme, so that corrective events could be taken.

FAMILY PLANNING METHODS AND SPACING BETWEEN LIVE BIRTHS

FAMILY PLANNING METHODS

Family Planning Methods or contraceptive methods through definition are preventive methods to help couples to avoid unwanted pregnancies. There are a number of methods which are commonly used through the people. Let us talk about details on those methods one through one.

Condom

Condom is the mainly widely used barrier device through the males approximately the world. In India, it is recognized through its trade name NIRODH, a Sanskrit word meaning prevention. Condom is getting new attention today as an effective simple "spacing" method of contraception, without side effects. In addition to preventing pregnancies, condom protects both men and women form sexually transmitted diseases. There are two kinds of condoms latex and skin. Latex condoms are through far the mainly widely used. The condom is fitted on the erect penis before intercourse. The air necessity is expelled from teat end to make room for the ejaculation. The condom necessity is held cautiously when withdrawing it from the vagina to avoid spilling seminal fluid into the vagina after intercourse. A new condom should be used for each sexual act. Condom prevents the semen from being deposited in the vagina.

The advantages of condom are:

- Are easily accessible,
- Safe and inexpensive,
- Easy to use, do not require medical supervision.
- No side effects,
- Light, compact and disposable, and
- They give protection not only against pregnancy, but also against sexually transmitted diseases (STD).

The disadvantages are:

- It may slip off or tear throughout intercourse due to incorrect use and
- Interferes with sex sensation locally in relation to the some complain while others get used to it, through repeated use.

Although there is much publicity in relation to the use of condoms to avoid pregnancy and getting infected with STDs and HIV/AIDS you necessity keep in mind that the condom does not guarantee hundred per cent safety. There is certainly a risk involved. There are many reported and confirmed cases of condom failure as a preventive method for pregnancy as well as HIV/AIDS infection.

Diaphragm

The diaphragm is a vaginal barrier. It was invented through a German Physician in 1882. It is a shallow cap made of synthetic rubber or plastic material. It has a flexible rim made of spring or metal. It is significant that a woman be fitted with a diaphragm of the proper size. The diaphragm is inserted before sexual intercourse and necessity remain in place for not less than 6 hours after sexual intercourse. A spermidical jelly is always used beside with the diaphragm.

Advantages

The primary advantage of the diaphragm is the approximately total absence of risks and medical contraindications.

Disadvantages

Initially a physician or some other trained person will be needed to demonstrate the technique of inserting the diaphragm into the vagina to ensure a proper fit. After delivery, it can be used only after involution of the uterus is completed. Hence it is not very useful in Indian families especially in rural area where medical assistance and privacy hardly exist. Further repeated or frequent pregnancy is a barrier to regular use of diaphragm.

Intra-Uterine Devices (IUDs)

The IUD is devices used for the control of conception through introducing a foreign body into the uterus. There are two vital kinds of IUD: 'non-medicated' and 'medicated'. Both are usually made of polyethylene or other polymoss. In addition the medicated or bioactive IUDs release either metal ions (copper) or hormones (progestogens).

The IUDs are of dissimilar generations such as:

- The non-medicated or insert IUDs _ First generation IUDs
- The copper IUDs _ Second generation IUDs
- The hormone releasing IUDs _ Third generation IUDs
- The medicated IUDs or the second and third generation IUDs were urbanized to reduce the incidence of side effects and to augment the contraceptive effectiveness.

Though, they are more expensive and necessity be changed after a sure time to uphold their effectiveness.

The First Generation IUDs

The first generation IUDs comprise the inert or non-medicated devices. They appear in dissimilar shapes and sizes loops, spirals, coils, rings and bows. Lippes Loop, double-S-shaped device, is a very commonly used IUD in India.

The Second Generation IUDs

A new approach was devised in 1970s through adding copper to the IUD. It was found that, metallic copper had a strong anti-fertility effect. The addition of copper made it possible to develop smaller devices which are easier to fit. There are dissimilar kinds of copper IUDs – Copper- 7, Copper-T and Nova-T. The Indian Council of Medical Research in 1979 recommended to the Department of Family Planning the use of Copper-T. According to the recent reports copper devices have become very popular in India.

Advantages:

- Low expulsion rate,
- Lower incidence of side effects,
- Easier to fit even in nulliparous women,
- Better tolerated through nullipara,
- Increased contraceptive effectiveness, and
- Effective as post-coital contraceptives, if inserted within 3 to 5 days of unprotected sexual intercourse.

The Third Generation IUDs

A third generation IUDs is based on another principle that is release of a hormone. The mainly widely used hormonal device is progestseart, which is a T-shaped device filled with progesterone, the natural hormone. The hormone is released slowly in the uterus. Long-term clinical experience with hormone releasing IUD has shown it to be associated with lower menstrual blood loss and fewer days of bleeding than other copper devices. The hormonal devices would be valuable for women in developing countries in who excess blood loss caused through inert devices have shown to result in important anemia. But these devices are too expensive, to be introduced on a wider scale.

Advantages:

- Simplicity, that is no intricate procedures are involved in insertion; no hospitalization is required.
- Insertion takes only a few minutes.
- Once inserted IUD stays in place as extensive as required.
- Inexpensive
- Contraceptive effect is reversible through removal of IUD.
- Virtually free of systematic metabolic side-effects associated with hormonal pills.
- Highest continuation rate.
- There is no need for the continual motivation required to take a pill daily or to use a barrier method uniformly; only a single act of motivation is required.

Hormonal Contraceptives

Hormonal contraceptives when properly used are the mainly effective spacing methods of contraception. They give the best means of ensuring spacing flanked by one child birth and another.

Hormonal Contraceptives currently in use may be classified as follows:

- *Oral pills*: Combined pill; Progestogen – only pill; Post-coital pill; Once-a-month (extensive acting) pill; and Male pill
- *Depot (slow release) formulations*: Injections; Subcutaneous implants; and Vaginal rings

Oral Pill

The Pill is given orally for 21 consecutive days, beginning on the 5th day of the menstrual cycle, followed through a break of 7 days throughout which period menstruation occurs. When the bleeding occurs this is measured as the first day of the after that cycle. The bleeding which occurs is not like normal menstruation, but is an episode of uterine bleeding which from an incompletely shaped endometrial caused through the withdrawal of exogenous hormones. So it is described "withdrawal bleeding", rather than menstruation. If bleeding does not occur, the woman is instructed to start the second cycle one week after the proceeding one. Ordinarily the woman menstruates after the second course of pill intake. The pill should be taken every day at a fixed time, preferably before going to bed at night. The first course should be started strictly on the 5th day of the menstrual period, as any deviation in this respect may not prevent pregnancy. If the user forgets to take a pill, she should take it as soon as she remembers, and that she should take the after that day's pill at the usual time. If taken according to prescription combined pills are 100 percent effective in preventing pregnancy. There is the benefit of pregnancy prevention and risk of abnormal cycle bleeding. The other kinds of pills are to be taken according to the prescription of a medical practitioner.

Adverse Effects

- *Cardio vascular effects:* Based on some of the studies mannered in dissimilar parts of the world, it is reported that, women who had taken the pill had a 40 percent higher death rate than women who had never taken the pill. Virtually, all the excess mortality was due to cardio vascular causes, that is myocardial infraction.
- *Carcinogenesis:* Even though there is no clear proof , the WHO multi-centre Case Control Study on the possible association flanked by the use of hormonal contraceptives and neoplasia, indicated a trend towards increased risk of cervical cancer with rising duration of oral contraceptives.
- *Metabolic effect:* The metabolic effects incorporated the elevation of blood pressure, the alteration in serum lipids with a scrupulous effect on decreasing high density lipoproteins, blood clotting and the ability to vary carbohydrate metabolism with the resultant elevation of blood glucose and plasma insulin. These effects are positively related to the dose of the progestogen component.
- Other adverse effects:
  - Liver disorders
  - Effect on lactation
  - Effect on subsequent fertility
  - Ectopic pregnancies and
  - Effect on foetal development.
- Common unwanted effects:
  - Breast tenderness, fullness and discomfort
  - Weight gain
  - Headache and migraine
  - Bleeding disturbances.

Beneficial Effects

The single mainly important benefit of the pill is its approximately 100 percent effectiveness in preventing pregnancy. Women taking oral contraceptives should be advised annual medical checkup.

Depot Formulations

The depot formulations are effective, extensive acting oestrogen free for spacing pregnancies, in which a single administration suffices for many month or years. The injectible contraceptives, sub dermal implants, and vaginal rings come in this category.

- *Injectable contraceptives:* They offer more reliable protection against unwanted pregnancies than the other barrier techniques.
- *Subdermal (subcutaneous) implants:* The Population Council, New York has urbanized a subdermal implant recognized as 'Norplant' for long-term contraception. The Norplant ® -2, the Silastic capsules or rods are implanted beneath the skin of the forearm or upper arm. Effective contraception is provided for 5 years. The contraceptive effect of Norplant is reversible on removal of capsules. The main disadvantages, though, appear to be irregularities of menstrual bleeding and surgical procedures necessary to insert and remove implants.
- *Vaginal Rings:* Vaginal rings containing levonorgestrel have been found to be effective. The hormone is slowly absorbed through the vaginal mucosa, permitting mainly of it to bypass the digestive system and liver and allowing a potentially lower dose. The ring is worn in the vagina for 3 weeks of the cycle and removed for the fourth.

Post Conceptional Methods

- *Menstrual Regulation:* It consists of aspiration of the uterine contents 6-14 days of missed period, but before mainly pregnancy tests can accurately determine whether or not a woman is pregnant. Some regard menstrual regulation as a very early abortion; others view it as a treatment for delayed periods.
- *Abortion:* Abortion is theoretically defined as termination of pregnancy before the fetus becomes viable (capable of living independently). This has been fixed administratively at 28 weeks. Abortions are usually categorized as spontaneous and induced. Spontaneous abortions occur once in every 15 pregnancies. They may be measured "Nature's method of birth control". Induced abortions, on the other hand, are deliberately induced. They may be legal or illegal. Illegal abortions are hazardous. They are usually the last resort of women determined to end their pregnancies at the risk of their own lives.

Abortion Hazards

Abortions, whether spontaneous or induced, whether in the hands of skilled or unskilled persons are approximately always filled with hazards;

resulting in maternal morbidity and mortality. The early complications of abortion contain shock, septic condition, uterine perforation, cervical injury, thromboembolism, anesthetic and psychiatric complications. The late complications contain infertility, ectopic gestation, and increased risk of spontaneous abortion and reduced birth weight.

Other Methods of Family Planning

Abstinence

The only method of birth control which is totally effective is complete sexual abstinence. It is sound in theory, in practice it amounts to repression of a natural force and is liable to manifest itself in other directions such as temperamental changes and even nervous breakdown. So, it can hardly be measured a method of contraception to be advocated to the masses.

Coitus Interruptus

This is the oldest method of voluntary fertility control. It involves no cost or appliances. In this method, the male withdraws before ejaculation, and thereby tries to prevent authentication of semen into the vagina. Some couples are able to practice this method successfully, while others find it hard to manage. The chief drawback of this method is that, the precoital secretion of the male may contain sperm, and even a drop of semen is sufficient to cause pregnancy. Further, the slightest mistake in timing the withdrawal may lead to the authentication of a sure amount of semen. The alleged side-effects (e.g. Pelvic congestion, vaginismus, anxiety neurosis) were highly magnified. It is better than by no family planning methods at all. It is admitted to be true that coitus interrupts beside with abstinence and abortion played a major role in reducing birth rates in the urbanized world throughout the 18th and 19th centuries.

Safe Period (Rhythm Method)

This is also recognized as the "Calendar method", first described through Ogino in 1930. The method is based on the fact that ovulation occurs from 12 to 16 days before the onset of menstruation. The days on which conception is likely to occur are calculated as follows:

Regulation of the period and Safe Period Method

If you have irregular period, with a little treatment you can regulate your period. Then you divide your cycle in 3 equal parts. The infertile days are the 1st and the last parts of cycle. The shortest cycle minus 18 days gives the first day of the fertile period. The longest cycle minus 10 days gives the last day of fertile period. For e.g. if a woman's menstrual cycle varies from 26 to 31 days, the fertile period throughout which she should no have intercourse would be from the 8th day to 12th day of the menstrual cycle, counting day one as the first day of the menstrual cycle.

The drawbacks of calendar method are:

- Women's menstrual cycles are not always regular. If the cycles are irregular, it is hard to predict the safe period.
- It is only possible for this method to be used through educated and responsible couples with a high degree of motivation and co-operation.
- Compulsory abstinence of sexual intercourse for almost one half of every month may be described "programmed sex".
- This method is not applicable throughout the postnatal period.
- A high failure rate.

Natural Family Planning Methods

- Basal body temperature (BBT) method,
- Cervical mucus method, and
- Symptothermic method.

Here the woman employs self-recognition of sure physiological signs and symptoms associated with ovulation as an aid to ascertain when the fertile period begins. For avoiding pregnancy, couples abstain from sexual intercourse throughout the fertile stage of the menstrual cycle. They totally desist from by drugs and contraceptive devices. This is the essence of natural family planning.

Basal Body Temperature Method

The BBT method depends upon the identification of a specific physiological event —— the rise of BBT at the time of ovulation, as a result of an augment in the production of progesterone. The rise of temperature is very small, 0.3 to 0.5 degree C. When no ovulation occurs (e.g. as after menarche, throughout lactation) the body temperature does not rise. The temperature is measured preferably before getting out of bed in the morning. The BBT method is reliable if intercourse is restricted to the postovulatory infertile period, commencing 3 days after ovulatory temperature rise and continuing up to the beginning of menstruation. The major drawback of this method is that, abstinence is necessary for the whole preovulatory period.

Cervical Mucus Method

This is recognized as ovulation method. This method is based on the observation of changes in the features of cervical mucus. At the time of ovulation, cervical mucus becomes watery clear becoming raw egg white, smooth, slippery and profuse. After ovulation, under the power of progesterone, the mucus thickens and lessens in quantity. It is recommended that, the woman use a tissue paper to wipe the inside of vagina to assess the quantity and features of mucus. This method requires a higher degree of motivation than mainly other methods. The appropriateness of this method in countries like India, especially in the middle of the rural and poor is doubtful.

Symptothermic Method

This method combines the temperature, cervical mucus and calendar techniques for identifying the fertile period. If the women cannot clearly interpret one sign, she can 'double check' her interpretation with another. To sum up, natural family planning demands discipline, and understanding of sexuality. It is not meant for everybody. The educational component is more significant with this approach than with other methods.

Breast-feeding

Field and laboratory investigations have confirmed the traditional belief that, lactation prolongs post partum amenorrhea and provides some degree of protection against pregnancy. No more than 5-10 percent of women conceive throughout lactational amenorrhea, and even this risk exists only throughout the month preceding the resumption of menstruation. Though, one menstruation returns, sustained lactation no extensive offers any protection against pregnancy.

Birth Control Vaccine

Many immunological approaches for men and women are being investigated. The mainly advanced research involves immunization with a vaccine prepared from beta sub-unit of human chronic gonad tropic (HCG) a hormone produced in early pregnancy. Immunization with HCG would block continuation of the pregnancy. Antibodies appeared in relation to the4-6 weeks and reached maximum after in relation to the 5 months and slowly declined reaching zero stages after a period ranging from 6-11 months. The immunity can be boosted through a second injection. Research on birth control vaccines continues and uncertainties are great.

Terminal Methods (Sterilization)

Voluntary sterilization is a well-recognized contraceptive procedure for couples desiring no more children. Sterilization offers several advantages in excess of other contraceptive methods. It is a one-time method. It does not require sustained motivation of the user for its effectiveness. It provides the mainly effective protection against pregnancy. The risk of complications is small if the procedure is performed according to accepted medical standards. It is cost-effective.

Male Sterilization

Male sterilization or vasectomy being a comparatively simple operation can be performed even in primary health centers through trained doctors under local anesthesia. In vasectomy, it is customary to remove a piece of vas at least 1 cm after clamping. The ends are ligated and then folded back on themselves and sutured into position so that, the cut ends, face absent from each other. This will reduce the risk of decimalization at a later date. It is significant to stress the person is not immediately sterile after the operation, usually until intermediate period, another method of contraception necessity be used. If properly used vasectomies are 100 percent effective. Vasectomy is a simpler faster and less expensive operation than tubectomy.

Female Sterilization

Female sterilization can be done as an interval procedure; post partum or at the time of abortion. There are two such commonly used methods.

Laparoscopy

This is a technique of female sterilization through abdominal approach with a specialized instrument described "laparoscope". The abdomen is inflated with gas (carbon dioxide, nitrous oxide or air) and the instrument is introduced into the abdominal cavity to visualize the tubes. Once the tubes are accessible, the Falope rings (or clips) are applied to obstruct the tubes. This operation should be undertaken only in those centers where specialist obstetrician gynecologists are accessible. The short operating time, shorter stay in hospital and a small scar are some of the attractive characteristics of this operation.

Minilap operation

Minilaparotomy is a modification of abdominal tubectomy. It is a modification of abdominal tubectomy. It is a much simpler procedure requiring a smaller abdominal incision of only 2.5 to 3 cm mannered under local anaesthesia. It is found to be an appropriate procedure at the primary health centre. It has the advantage in excess of other methods with regard to safety, efficiency, and ease in dealing with complications. Minilap is appropriate for postpartum tubal sterilization.

SPACING FLANKED BY LIVE BIRTHS

Till now you have learnt the dissimilar methods of family planning. Now let us see what is spacing and how does it affect the health of mother and child. Spacing is the interval flanked by two lives births. There are a number of social and cultural factors which have tended to augment the spacing flanked by two births. The segregation of women after delivery, the taboo of sex relations when the child is young and abstinence on sure religious days are some of them. Prolonged lactation which has been observed may also be a significant factor.

The Hindu joint family has also helped in minimizing the frequency of sexual relationship. The prevalence of 'purdah' system did not allow the couples to meet very regularly. The so described rigid rules of social behaviour prevalent in traditional families did not allow undue sexual freedom to the couples. Social customs of the wife making frequent visits to her parental home, having the first child in her mother's home and such other customs have helped to augment spacing flanked by two births. The above mentioned factors which helped to augment spacing are slowly changing. With increased education, urbanization and economic prosperity, social atmosphere is changing. Widow remarriage is becoming more common; moral restraint is not much observed; and the joint family system is giving way to nuclear families. All these factors affect spacing. The birth of children is a voluntary decision of the couples rather than a culturally oriented phenomenon.

RELIGIOUS VIEWS AND SPIRITUAL GUIDANCE

Our lives are profoundly influenced through advancement in the field of science and technology. As a result of these advancements some people tend to consider religion and belief in God outdated and irrelevant. For them the teachings and heritage of the great religions make little or no sense. It is true to say that, the teachings and traditions of the significant religions have been the conscience keepers of the world. The ethical views of dissimilar religions have always condemned the violation of natural law. All religious accept regulating family size through way of self-control and regulating sexual union flanked by couples. The same way all religions condemn abortion and consider it as murder.

According to Hindu Vedas, abortion is measured to be a more serious sin than the killing of a Brahman. The 'Charka Samhita; a classical work on Hindu Medicine states that conception takes place in the womb through the union of semen and ovum, when the soul, beside with the mind, enters the zygote. The embryo is of unique constitution, because it is a composite of the vital information it receives from both parents. The humanization of the individual takes place at the moment of conception and all future growth is only the actualization of conceptual potency. Based of 'Shastras' and on the principle that the genetic components are complete at conception, the modern Hindu belief is that life begins with conception. Though Hindu ethics condemn abortions usually, it accepts abortion on the grounds of rape, incest and when the mother is at the risk of grave injury or death. This is because, Hindu ethics place greater weight on the maternal rights rather than on the unborn child's right.

The vital teaching of Islam is that, life is a gift of god. Hence the Koran warns men not to interfere with the work of God. It is on this faith that, Muslims usually oppose abortion. The laws of Islam prohibit abortion since the foetus is measured a living being. But as per the doctors, foetus is only a human being after the fourth month. Hence abortion is allowed in general throughout the first ninety days of pregnancy and it is prohibited immediately afterwards. Though, like Hindu ethics, Islamic ethics also permits abortion on the foundation of pregnancy which endangers the mother's life, and where it is the result of a rape that does not result in marriage. The Christian religion also condemns abortion. Christianity encourages couples to have self-control and promote natural family planning methods. Christianity considers abortion a grave sin and calls it murder. At the time of conception a new life has started and abortion is the killing of that new life. The Holy Bible warns emphatically against abortion at any stage of conception.

There are sure myths concerning religious faith, population, growth and family planning. Hindu religion promulgates monogamy and there is no law prohibiting family planning. But Muslim religion allows polygamy and prohibits family planning and hence there is rate of augmentin population in the middle of them. These myths are to be examined in the light of studies mannered in India. When these above mentioned myths are examined based on scientific study, it is understood that they remain as myths even now. In the middle of Muslims it was 23% in 1980 and increased to 34% (+11%) in 1989. Likewise, in the middle of scheduled castes it was 28% (1980) increased to 39% in 1989. In the middle of Scheduled Tribes it was 33 % in 1980 and sustained the same pattern in 1989 also. Muslims are politically and culturally against the attitude of western concept of sexuality and abortion, rather than on family planning. Christians are very conservative in relation to the artificial family planning methods. But it is deadly against abortion.

Even though, all these religious are not positively promoting family planning, in the State of Kerala where literacy rate is very high, education of women is high and a high index of social development exist, the small family norms has been accepted and has become a way of life in the middle of people of dissimilar walks of life, no matter to what religion they belong.

PREFERENCE FOR MALE CHILD

In India sons are significant from a religious point of view. According to Hindu religion, a man, attains salvation only when a son performs sure rites at his funeral. Preference for a son is not only a religious point of view, sons are measured as providers of security in old age and throughout prolonged illness. There are several other reasons as well. Once married, the girls are measured to belong to their husband's family, and so, they cannot be relied on for support in old age. In fact, there are strong taboos on taking any kind of help from a married daughter.

According to Blaikie the reasons for the importance of sons in Indian culture are:

- Sons are required to perform the last funeral rites (sraddha) for their parents. It is motivating to note that in Sanskrit 'put' means hell and 'putra' means literally 'one that saves from hell'.
- Sons, upon marriage, draw dowries for the parents.
- Sons, give economic and emotional security in old age. It is the son, not the daughter who remnants at the parent's home after marriage.
- Sons give income and help in the home and in the fields from an early age.

- Sons bring prestige and local political power (and even protection against the threat of physical force in confrontational situations) to the household, the kindship group and caste.

The question of son survivorship is so, so vital that people do not feel satisfied with presently one son. They seek safety in numbers. Women too have compelling reasons for desiring children, preferably sons. The mainly intense hope of a young woman is that she proves her worth to her husband's family through producing a healthy male child. The birth of a son entitles a woman to respect and status. She and her baby have been conditioned to see their success and destiny in terms of procreation especially of a son. In actual practice it is found that, the above arguments for male child are myth. Now as a result of the disintegration of joint family system and augmentin the number of nuclear families, the expectation on the son to give security at old age is coming down. With regard to the amount of work done through males and females, it is approximately equal. Hence preference for male child is a myth.

MEDICAL TERMINATION OF PREGNANCY AND ISSUES ASSOCIATED WITH IT

ABORTION – DEFINITION AND KINDS

Abortion is made up of two Latin words —*ab*- meaning off or absent *oriri* meaning to be born; abortion means taking absent a human life which would in the normal course of events be born. Abortion has two meanings—medically it can describe a case of miscarriage, without any outside intervention, occurring within the first three months of pregnancy. Abortions legalized through the Act on the other hand, are those deliberately procured with the intention of terminating the pregnancy, killing the unborn child. The terms abortion and miscarriage are sometimes used a synonyms. They are also used to describe the same happening at an earlier and at later stage of pregnancy. Abortion is restricted so as to describe the case occurring in the first three months of pregnancy and miscarriage to describe one throughout pregnancy from the beginning of the fourth month, until the foetus becomes viable.

Kinds of Abortion

- Spontaneous Abortion (Miscarriage) occurring naturally without any deliberate effort on the part of pregnant women or other persons.
- Indirect Abortion: This is an abortion which occurs as a side effect of treatment given to the mother for some diseases or haemorrhage which is endangering her life. The purpose is not to take absent the child's life. It occurs as the result of the therapeutic events taken to save the mother.
- Artificial or Induced Abortion is taking absent of life for the main purpose of removing the foetus or child. Induced abortion is the

result of deliberate effort on the part of the pregnant women or others with the intention of terminating pregnancy.

METHODS OF PROCURING AN ABORTION

There are several ways of aborting an unwanted foetus. The method chosen depends mainly on the duration of pregnancy to be interrupted as in the first or second trimester (3 months).

First Trimester

In the first trimester (upto 12 weeks) of pregnancy, two broad methods are used.

Medical

One single dose of Misetristone pills administered within 40 days of menstrual period, (within 10 days after missed period).

Surgical

- Menstrual Regulation by MR Syringe (upto six weeks of pregnancy)
- Suction: The mainly regularly used method of abortion is suction, also described Vacuum aspiration. It is used when the women is less than 3 months pregnant. This technique involves sucking out the contents of the uterus through a tube inserted into the uterus through the cervix. This operation can be performed while the women are awake, in five to ten minutes, with little blood loss and a low risk of complications.
- Tent Evacuation with Laminaria Tent (slow dilatation is achieved and evacuation is done later).
- Dilatation and Curettage (D&C): This procedure involves rising the size of the cervical canal through inserting a series of slowly – widening metal dilators. When the opening is wide enough the physician uses a curette (small metal surgical instrument) to scrape the embryo and placenta from the walls of the uterus. Since the D and C operation takes longer and is more complicated than the suction method, the women is put to sleep.

Second Trimester

In the second trimester of pregnancy, only very few methods are usually adopted:

- *Intra Uterine Saline Instillation*: After twelve weeks, the foetus is large enough to be removed safely through the suction or D&C methods. Pregnancies after this period are removed through inserting extensive needle abdominal and uterine walls into the cavity of the uterus. A concentrated salt solution is inserted into the amniotic sac destroyed, the uterus will contract until the foetus is pushed out into the vagina. Because saline abortion is a major surgical procedure, earlier termination of pregnancy through the suction method or D&C is being recommended through the physicians.

- *Hysterectomy*: This is used in the later stages of pregnancy when the foetus is too large. The mother is given a general anaesthetic and the uterus is cut open and the foetus is removed. This is usually performed in cases where foetal abnormalities are detected and when all the other methods have failed.

Two other methods of abortion are intra cervical prostaglandin E2, administration and oxytocin induction.

LIBERALIZATION OF ABORTION LEADING TO LEGALIZATION

Prior to 1950s in several countries, laws governing abortions were very restrictive; i.e. abortions were totally prohibited or permitted strictly on medical grounds. But laws could not prevent illegal abortions which were done mostly through non-medical persons and in unhygienic circumstances.

Consequences of Illegal Abortion

Illegal abortions regularly led to complications such as perforations of the uterus, hemorrhage and infection requiring gynecological care and hospitalization. In countries such as Venezuela, Nigeria, Chile and a few other countries sepsis due to illegal abortion was the leading cause of maternal deaths. Illegal and partial abortion was a major strain on medical possessions. It is also reported that in countries with restrictive abortion laws, the poor were made to suffer more than the affluent, the better educated and the urban elite.

The poor, with no possessions to obtain safe but expensive abortions and with little contacts or knowledge in relation to the places where such services were accessible, were often driven into the hands of unqualified abortionists which resulted in severe complications and deaths. Such loss of lives, impairment to mother's health and wastage of medical infrastructure as well as compassion for the poor led to the demand in many countries for liberal abortion laws.

Attempts to Legalize Abortion

The Soviet Union was the first country to legalize abortion. In 1920, Lenin's government enabled women in first trimester pregnancy (less than 12 weeks of pregnancy) to obtain abortion on request. Thereafter several countries introduced liberal clauses in their abortion laws from 1930 onwards. Presently, the laws on abortion vary from abortion on request at one extreme to total prohibition on the other. The four main countries which have liberalized abortion laws for medical termination of pregnancy are China, India, USA and Soviet Union.

Medical Termination of Pregnancy Act, 1971 (MTP)

In India, prior to 1972, abortion was illegal except to save the life of regnant women. In 1964, a committee under the Chairmanship of Shantilal Shah was constituted to study the question of liberalizing abortion laws. Based on the report submitted through this committee in 1966, the Medical Termination of Pregnancy (MTP) Act was passed through the Parliament in 1971 and came in to force all in excess of the country in April 1, 1972 (except in Jammu & Kashmir where it came into effect from November 1, 1976). This act is one of the mainly liberal in the world and has replaced one of the mainly rigid laws sections 312 of Penal Code, 1860 and the Code of Criminal Procedure 1898. The Medical Termination of Pregnancy Act 1971 lays down three norms for terminating a pregnancy.

THE CIRCUMSTANCES UNDER WHICH A PREGNANCY CAN BE TERMINATED UNDER THE MTP ACT 1971

There are 5 circumstances that have been recognized in the Act:

- Medical: Where continuation of the pregnancy might endanger the mother's life or cause grave injury to her physical or mental health.
- Eugenic: Where there is substantial risk of the child being born with serious handicaps due to physical or mental abnormalities.
- *Humanitarian*: Where pregnancy is the result of rape.
- *Socio-economic*: Where actual or reasonably foreseeable environments (whether social or economic) could lead to risk of injury to the health of the mother.
- *Failure of contraceptive devices*: The anguish caused through an unwanted pregnancy resulting from a failure of any contraceptive device or method can be presumed to constitute a grave mental injury to the mental health of the mother. This condition is a unique characteristic of the Indian Law virtually allows abortion on request, in view of the difficulty of providing that a pregnancy was not caused through failure of contraception.

The written consent of the guardian is necessary before performing abortion in women under 18 years of age, and in lunatics even if they are older than 18 years.

The person or persons who can perform abortion

The Act provides safeguards to the mother through authorizing only a registered medical practitioner having experience in gynecology and obstetrics to perform an abortion where the length of pregnancy does not exceed 12 weeks. Though, where the pregnancy exceeds 12 weeks and is not more than 20 weeks the opinion of two registered medical practitioners is necessary to terminate the pregnancy.

Where Abortion can be Done

The Act stipulates that no termination of pregnancy shall be made at any place other than a hospital recognized or maintained through the Government or a place approved for the purpose of this Act through Government. Abortion services are provided in hospitals in strict confidence. The name of the abortion seeker is kept confidential, since abortion has been treated as a statutory personal matter.

MTP Rules (1975)

Rules and Regulations framed initially were altered in October 1975 to eliminate time-consuming procedures involved in MTP and to make services more readily accessible. These changes have occurred in three administrative areas.

Approval through Board

Under the new rules, the Chief Medical Officer of the District is empowered to certify that a doctor has the necessary training in gynecology and obstetrics to do abortions. The procedure of doctors applying to Certification Boards was removed.

Qualification required doing Abortion

The new rules allow for registered medical practitioners to qualify through on the spot training. The doctor may also qualify to do MTPs under the new rules if he/she has one or more of the following qualifications which are similar to the old rules:

- 6 months housemanship in obstetrics and gynecology.
- a post-graduate qualification in OBG
- 3 years of practice in OBG for those doctors registered before the 1971 MTP Act was passed.
- 1 year of practice in OBG for those doctors registered on or after the date of commencement of the Act.

The Place where Abortion is Performed

Under the new rules, non-governmental institutions may also take up abortions provided they obtain a license from the Chief Medical Officer of the district, thus eliminating the requirement of private clinics obtaining a Board License.

Limitations of the Act

- The provisions for abortion under the Act such as pregnancy caused through rape, failure of a contraceptive etc. need not necessarily constitute grave injury to her mental health.
- Extending the period of pregnancy from 12 weeks to 20 weeks of pregnancy in sure situations gives more scope for abortion takers.

- The value of human life is challenged
- No consideration is given to the right of the foetus.

The New Act is indeed a liberal piece of legislation compared to the Old Act of 1860. The Act has been mainly adopted to eradicate a large number of criminal and clandestine abortions, which caused considerably mortality and morbidity in the middle of pregnant women. Though, the utility of the new act will depend to large extent on the number of localities that are provided with clinical facilities for abortion especially in rural areas, knowledge in relation to the facilities in the middle of the people and also on the attitude of the physicians. Due to inadequate data on the socio-economic status of women who had legal abortions, it is not clear whether liberalization has really helped the poor sections of the society.

ISSUES AND CONTROVERSIES ASSOCIATED WITH LEGAL ABORTIONS

Abortion has been a hotly debated issue. Both pro (for) and anti-abortion (against) groups have lobbied intensively on the local, state, national, and international stages. Abortion raises some hard questions to which there are no simple answers. Abortion issues may be divided into 1) Physical and Medical, 2) Psychological, 3) Social, and 4) Moral and Religious

Physical and Medical Issue

A woman is made physically and psychologically for motherhood. This is the vital fact of her life. If this procedure of becoming a mother is suddenly stopped, the shock will have its effect. This effect may be physical or mental immediate or extensive-term. If a pregnancy is to be terminated, it should be terminated as soon as possible. This is of special necessity from a biological and medical point of view. Medical complications arise due to patients spending so little time under observation after their initial operation and so troubles of infection tend to set in.

A woman who has undergone an abortion is also more likely to have subsequent children both physically and mentally handicapped. Damage to the wall of the uterus can affect the normal development of the placenta through which the baby takes its nourishment. There is an extensive-term medical effect of aborting first pregnancy. Repeated abortions may be associated with a later inability to conceive or to carry a child to full term and with several birth complications. Abortion should only be a backup measure not the primary method of birth control and they urge fuller usage of contraceptives in the middle of all sexually active person so that repeated abortions are not necessary.

Emotional Issue

There is emotional and physical unrest experienced throughout the first few weeks of pregnancy. Mainly women even experience feelings of rejection of the pregnancy at this time. It is at this time that the expectant mother may be subjected to maximum pressure to agree to an abortion. Each individual is dissimilar. For some, abortion provides great relief with little or not disturbance. For the others, the experience is upsetting. The key factor seems to be whether the woman wants an abortion or whether she is hesitant. Being refused an abortion and forced to bear an unwanted child can lead to psychiatric symptoms. But the woman who has health troubles and has to have an abortion or who is persuaded to have an abortion against her better judgment is also more likely to show negative psychological reactions following the operation. The common psychological reactions can be minimized if the decision is solely that of the women. So, Abortion Counseling can assist her in making the best decision she can live with and working her feelings ahead of time.

Social and Realistic Issues

Legalized abortion saves lives through reducing the number of illegal attempts. Antiabortionists emphasize their fears that without any restriction, except the individual woman and her conscience, an 'Abortion Mentality' develops so that abortion becomes too common and are performed too easily or for reasons that are not serious: For instance teenage pregnancy has become a common occurrence in the middle of college students in cities with a free access to abortion facilities. Even unplanned pregnancies in normal families, for want of spacing flanked by children, especially in the middle of the career women, are also some of the common groups taking up abortions. Thus, the majority of abortions today are not for medical cause, but for personal, social and economic reasons that have to do with woman's life situations and not with her health.

Moral Issues (Rights of the Unborn Child)

Much of the controversy in relation to the abortion has centered approximately the moral issues involved. In ordinary justice, the child has as much claim as the mother to life and should have even more claim to legal protection of its right, since it is incapable of defending itself.

Rights of the Unborn Child

The UN declaration on the Rights of the child maintains that "the Child through cause of his physical and mental immaturity, needs special safeguards and care including appropriate legal protection before as well as after birth". They emphasize the right to life of the foetus and that no individual or state should deprive the foetus of its constitutional and moral rights to live. The Anti abortionists claim that science has proven beyond any reasonable doubt that human life begins at fertilization. The foetus from the beginning has its own life, is a totally new human being, a new person, with a genetic code quite separate from the genetic code of its parents. The only life generated through human beings is human life. That new life is totally there at fertilization, lacking only development and growth. Abortion always takes absent an innocent's already existing life. Human life is the highest form of life on earth. The after that generation depends on the existing society for its survival.

On the other hand, the pro-abortion lobby emphasizes that the moral and legal rights of other parties necessity also be measured, not presently those of the foetus. What in relation to the rights of the mother, father, other family members? Should these lives be sacrificed for the sake of the child? Is it right to let the foetus live but to let the mother die so that her husband and other children are deprived of her love? The constitution guarantees equal protection under the law. Is it moral to force a woman to bear a baby she doesn't want, can't care for, or that might be deformed? Is it moral to insist that an unwanted child be born into the world and then to suffer all of its life because it was never wanted. Who has the right to decide? It is obvious to you know that the moral dilemmas raised through the abortion issue are not easy to solve.

RELIGIOUS VIEWS

The whole gamut of laws related to life is of several kinds—divine law, natural law, secular or civil law, religious law and the like. The mainly significant law related to life is the Divine Law or the Law of God. God is the giver and the author of life. No human being on earth has the power to destroy life. Abortion is equal to murder of the human being, a person created in the image and likeness of God and so a grave sin against God. The ethical views of dissimilar religions have always condemned the violation of natural law, the laws of the creator. Keeping this in view, let us look at the teachings of at least three major religions on human life and related issues, specifically on abortion which has posed the mainly serious ethical troubles to the modern world.

The Hindu View

According to Hindu religion, a woman who undergoes an abortion in this, life becomes barren in her subsequent lives. Hindu scriptures condemn abortion and consider it as murder. According to Hindu Vedas, abortion is measured to be a more serious sin that killing of a Brahmin. According to Shastras, life begins after the fourth month in the womb, when a ceremony is performed, blessing the foetus which is already living. Though Hindu ethics condemn abortion usually, it accepts abortion on the grounds of rape, incest, and when the mother runs the risk of grave injury or death. But still some of the Hindu religious leaders oppose such abortion on the ground that it is an act of interference with the Karmic development of the child.

The Islamic View

The Holy Quran warns men not to interfere with the work of God. It is one of the vital teachings of Islam that life is a gift of God and as such, no man has any right to commit any kind of act that is detrimental to, and extinguishing life. It is on this faith that Muslims usually oppose abortion, as it is felt that it amounts to extinguishing of life. The laws of Islam under sure circumstances prohibit abortion when the foetus is animated and measured a living being. As per the doctors of the law, the foetus is only a human being after the fourth month.

Abortion is allowed in general throughout the first ninety days of pregnancy, and it is prohibited immediately afterwards. Though, like Hindu ethics, Islamic ethics also permit abortion on the foundation of pregnancy which endangers the mother's life and where it is the result of a rape that does not result in marriage.

Christian Proposition

The Christian church in the first centuries after Christ, forbade abortion under all circumstances from the moment of conception and abortion at any time is measured a grave sin. Direct abortion of a foetus before viability is never lawful because this is to kill an innocent human being, who has a right to live. Every human being, even a child in its mother's womb has a right to life directly from God, and not from Parents or from any human society or power.

Hence there is no human power, no medical eugenic, social, economic or moral indication that can offer or produce a judicial title to the deliberate disposal of an innocent human life. There is an argument that the soul does not exist until the foetus really resembles a human being 'in form'. But from the time when the male sperm unites with the ovum fertilizing it, (conception) the minute embryo contains all the features which will make it a unique person. Hence the Christians believe that the soul enters at the moment of conception so that at whatever stage of growth, the new life is human.

View in Favor of and against Abortion

We have so far discussed the issues associated with the legal termination of pregnancy. The views of the two groups: Pro abortionists and anti abortionists are strong in their own ways and the debate seems to be unresolvable. It is likely to persist for sometime generating high sentiments on both sides. We will furnish here very briefly the views favoring legal abortion.

- Women should have the right to control their own bodies.
- No child should be brought into the world unwanted.
- Legal abortion should be mannered in authorized medical settings in which considerable care is taken to avoid harming the mother physically or psychologically.
- Women necessity has the option of a safe, legal abortion if they desire.

View against Legal Abortion

- Foetus is a living being and so its right to life necessity is respected – no one has the moral right to take that life.
- Persons other than the mother have rights as far as the unborn child is concerned – child itself and the father.
- Because the foetus is unable to defend itself, opponents of abortion believe that others are obligated to defend the foetus against the efforts of those who want to "kill it".

The mainly significant opposition to abortion is from organized religious groups who address abortion issue as that of questioning the ultimate power of God the Almighty.

Viable Alternatives to Unplanned Pregnancies

- Family Life Education should help the couples for a planned parenthood.
- Make people realize the value of human life to protect it through instilling in them the love of God.
- Girls in moral danger should be protected.
- Effective use of contraceptives should be promoted.
- Teenagers should be helped to imbibe the spiritual values in them and be aware of the consequences of ending countless innocent human lives through premarital sexual experiences.

7

Social Change: Population and Urbanization

POPULATION

We have commented that population growth is an important source of other changes in society. A generation ago, population growth was a major issue in the United States and some other nations. *Zero population growth*, or ZPG, was a slogan often heard. There was much concern over the rapidly growing population in the United States and, especially, around the world, and there was fear that our "small planet" could not support massive increases in the number of people. Some of the most dire predictions of the time warned of serious food shortages by the end of the century. Those predictions did not come to pass, and concern over population growth has faded as the world's resources seem to be standing up to population growth.

Widespread hunger in Africa and other regions does exist, with hundreds of millions of people suffering from hunger and malnutrition, but many experts attribute this problem not to overpopulation and lack of food but rather to problems in distributing the sufficient amount of food that actually does exist to people in poor nations. Concern over population growth also decreased because of criticism by people of color that ZPG was directed largely at their ranks and smacked of racism. The call for population control, they said, was a disguised call for controlling the growth of their own populations and thus reducing their influence. Still another reason for the reduced concern over population growth is that birth rates in many industrial nations have slowed considerably. Some nations are even experiencing population declines, while several more are projected to have population declines by 2050.

For a country to maintain its population, the average woman needs to have 2.1 children, the *replacement level* for population stability. But several industrial nations, not including the United States, are far below this level. Increased birth control is one reason for their lower fertility rates, but so are the decisions by women to stay in school longer and then to go to work right after their schooling ends and not having their first child until somewhat later. Ironically, these nations' population declines have begun to concern demographers and policy makers. Because people in many industrial nations are living longer while the birth rate drops, these nations are increasingly having a greater proportion of older people and a smaller proportion of younger people. In several European nations, there are more people 61 or older than 19 or younger.

As this trend continues, it will become increasingly difficult to take care of the health and income needs of so many older persons, and there may be too few younger people to fill the many jobs and provide the many services that an industrial society demands. The smaller labor force may also mean that governments will have fewer income tax dollars to provide these services. To deal with these problems, several governments have initiated *pronatalist* policies aimed at encouraging women to have more children. In particular, they provide generous child-care subsidies, tax incentives, and flexible work schedules designed to make it easier to bear and raise children, and some even provide couples outright cash payments when they have an additional child. Russia in some cases provides the equivalent of about $9,000 for each child beyond the first, while Spain provides 2,500 euros.

DEMOGRAPHY AND DEMOGRAPHIC CONCEPTS

As all of these issues indicate, changes in the size and composition of population have important implications for other social changes. The study of population is so significant that it occupies a special subfield within sociology called demographydemographyThe study of population growth and changes in population composition.. To be more precise, demography is the study of changes in the size and composition of population. It encompasses several concepts: fertility and birth rates, mortality and death rates, and migration.

Fertility and Birth Rates

FertilityfertilityThe number of live births. refers to the number of live births. Demographers use several measures of fertility. One measure is the crude birth ratecrude birth rateThe number of live births for every 1,000 people in a population in a given year., or the number of live births for every 1,000 people in a population in a given year. To determine the crude birth rate, the number of live births in a year is divided by the population size, and this result is then multiplied by 1,000. For example, in 2008 the United States had a population of about 304 million and 4,251,095 births. Dividing the latter figure by the former figure gives us 0.0140 rounded off. We then multiply this quotient by 1,000 to yield a crude birth rate of 14.0 births per 1,000 population. We call this a "crude" birth rate because the denominator, population size, consists of the total population, not just the number of women or even the number of women of childbearing age.

A second measure is the general fertility rategeneral fertility rateThe number of live births per 1,000 women aged 15–44. or the number of live births per 1,000 women aged 15–44. This is calculated in a manner similar to that for the crude fertility rate, but in this case the number of births is divided by the number of women aged 15–44 before multiplying by 1,000. The U.S. general fertility rate for 2007 was about 69.5. A third measure is the total fertility ratetotal fertility rateThe number of children an average woman is expected to have in her lifetime, sometimes expressed as the number of children an average 1,000 women are expected to have in their lifetimes., or the number of children an average woman is expected to have in her lifetime.

This measure often appears in the news media and is more easily understood by the public than either of the first two measures. In 2007, the U.S. total fertility rate was 2.1. Sometimes the total fertility rate is expressed as the average number of births that an average group of 1,000 women would be expected to have. In this case, the average number of children that one woman is expected to have is simply multiplied by 1,000. Using this latter calculation, the U.S. total fertility rate in 2007 was 2,100. The U.S. general fertility rate has changed a lot since 1920, dropping from 101 in 1920 to 70 in 1935, during the Great Depression, before rising afterward until 1955. The fertility rate then fell steadily after 1960 until the 1970s but has remained rather steady since then, fluctuating only slightly between 65 and 70 per 1,000 women aged 15–44.

The fertility rate varies by race and ethnicity. It is lowest for non-Latina white women and the highest for Latina women. Along with immigration, the high fertility rate of Latina women has fueled the large growth of the Latino population. Latinos now account for about 16% of the U.S. population, and their proportion is expected to reach more than 30% by 2050.

The fertility rate of teenagers is a special concern because of their age. Although it is still a rate that most people wish were lower, it dropped steadily through the 1990s, before leveling off after 2002 and rising slightly by 2007. Although most experts attribute this drop to public education campaigns and increased contraception, the United States still has the highest rate of teenage pregnancy and fertility of any industrial nation. Teenage fertility again varies by race and ethnicity, with Latina teenagers having the highest fertility rates and Asian American teenagers the lowest.

Fertility rates also differ around the world and are especially high in poor nations. Demographers identify several reasons for these high rates. First, poor nations are usually agricultural ones. In agricultural societies, children are an important economic resource, as a family will be more productive if it has more children. This means that families will ordinarily try to have as many children as possible. Second, infant and child mortality rates are high in these nations. Because parents realize that one or more of their children may die before adulthood, they have more children to "make up" for the anticipated deaths. A third reason is that many parents in low-income nations prefer sons to daughters, and, if a daughter is born, they "try again" for a son. Fourth, traditional gender roles are often very strong in poor nations, and these roles include the belief that women should be wives and mothers above all. With this ideology in place, it is not surprising that women will have several children. Finally, contraception is uncommon in poor nations. Without contraception, many more pregnancies and births obviously occur. For all of these reasons, then, fertility is much higher in poor nations than in rich nations.

Mortality and Death Rates

MortalitymortalityThe number of deaths. is the flip side of fertility and refers to the number of deaths. Demographers measure it with the crude death ratecrude death rateThe number of deaths for every 1,000 people in a population in a given year., the number of deaths for every 1,000 people in a population in a given year. To determine the crude death rate, the number of deaths is divided by the population size, and this result is then multiplied by 1,000. In 2006 the United States had slightly more than 2.4 million deaths for a crude death rate of 8.1 deaths for every 1,000 persons. We call this a "crude" death rate because the denominator, population size, consists of the total population and does not take its age distribution into account. All things equal, a society with a higher proportion of older people should have a higher crude death rate. Demographers often calculate *age-adjusted* death rates that adjust for a population's age distribution.

Migration

Another demographic concept is migrationmigrationThe movement of people into or out of specific regions., the movement of people into and out of specific regions. Since the dawn of human history, people have migrated in search of a better life, and many have been forced to migrate by ethnic conflict or the slave trade. Several classifications of migration exist. When people move into a region, we call it *in-migration,* or *immigration;* when they move out of a region, we call it *out-migration,* or *emigration*. The *in-migration rate* is the number of people moving into a region for every 1,000 people in the region, while the *out-migration rate* is the number of people moving from the region for every 1,000 people. The difference between the two is the *net migration rate.*

Migration can also be either domestic or international in scope. *Domestic migration* happens within a country's national borders, as when retired people from the northeastern United States move to Florida or the Southwest. *International migration* happens across national borders. When international immigration is heavy, as it has been into the United States and Western Europe in the last few decades, the effect on population growth and other aspects of national life can be significant. Domestic migration can also have a large impact. The great migration of African Americans from the South into northern cities during the first half of the 20th century changed many aspects of those cities' lives. Meanwhile, the movement during the past few decades of northerners into the South and Southwest also had quite an impact: the housing market initially exploded, for example, and traffic increased.

POPULATION GROWTH

Now that you are familiar with some basic demographic concepts, we can discuss population growth in more detail. Three of the factors just discussed determine population growth: fertility, mortality, and net migration. The *natural growth rate* is simply the difference between the crude birth rate and the crude death rate. The U.S. natural growth rate is about 0.6% per year. When immigration is also taken into account, the total population growth rate has been almost 1.0% per year. The annual population growth rate of all the nations in the world.

Note that many African nations are growing by at least 3% per year or more, while most European nations are growing by much less than 1% or are even losing population, as discussed earlier. Overall, the world population is growing by about 80 million people annually. To determine how long it takes for a nation to double its population size, divide the number 70 by its population growth rate. For example, if a nation has an annual growth rate of 3%, it takes about 23.3 years for that nation's population size to double. As you can see from the map in several nations will see their population size double in this time span if their annual growth continues at its present rate. For these nations, population growth will be a serious problem if food and other resources are not adequately distributed.

Demographers use their knowledge of fertility, mortality, and migration trends to make *projections* about population growth and decline several decades into the future. Coupled with our knowledge of past population sizes, these projections allow us to understand population trends over many generations. One clear pattern emerges from the study of population growth. When a society is small, population growth is slow because there are relatively few adults to procreate. But as the number of people grows over time, so does the number of adults.

More and more procreation thus occurs every single generation, and population growth then soars in a virtual explosion. We saw evidence of this pattern when we looked at world population growth. When agricultural societies developed some 12,000 years ago, only about 8 million people occupied the planet. This number had reached about 300 million about 2,100 years ago, and by the 15th century it was still only about 500 million. It finally reached 1 billion by about 1850 and by 1950, only a century later, had doubled to 2 billion. Just 50 years later it tripled to more than 6.8 billion, and it is projected to reach more than 9 billion by 2050.

Eventually, however, population growth begins to level off after exploding, as explained by *demographic transition theory*, discussed later. We see this in the bottom half of which shows the average annual growth rate for the world's population. This rate has declined over the last few decades and is projected to further decline over the next four decades. This means that while the world's population will continue to grow during the foreseeable future, it will grow by a smaller rate as time goes by. The growth that does occur will be concentrated in the poor nations in Africa and some other parts of the world. Still, even there the average number of children a woman has in her lifetime dropped from six a generation ago to about three today.

VIEWS OF POPULATION GROWTH

Earlier we talked about the zero population growth movement and concern about overpopulation that received so much attention a generation ago. Social observers have actually worried about overpopulation since the 18th century. One of the first to warn about population growth was Thomas Malthus, an English economist, who said that population increases *geometrically*. If you expand this list of numbers, you will see that they soon become overwhelmingly large in just a few more "generations." Malthus said that food production increases only *arithmetically* and thus could not hope to keep up with the population increase, and he predicted that mass starvation would be the dire result.

Fortunately, Malthus was wrong to some degree. Although population levels have certainly soared, the projections show that the rate of increase is slowing. Among other factors, the development of more effective contraception, especially the birth control pill, has limited population growth in the industrial world and, increasingly, in poorer nations. Food production has also increased by a much greater amount than Malthus predicted, although, as noted earlier, hunger remains a serious problem in poor nations because of inequalities in food distribution.

Demographic Transition Theory

Other factors also explain why population growth has not risen at the geometric rate that Malthus predicted and is even slowing. The view explaining the interaction of these factors is called demographic transition theorydemographic transition theoryA theory that links population growth to the level of technological development across three stages of social evolution., mentioned earlier. This theory links population growth to the level of technological development across three stages of social evolution.

In the first stage, coinciding with preindustrial societies, the birth rate and death rate are both high. The birth rate is high because of the lack of contraception and the several other reasons cited earlier for high fertility rates, and the death rate is high because of disease, poor nutrition, lack of modern medicine, and other problems. These two high rates cancel each other out, and little population growth occurs. In the second stage, coinciding with the development of industrial societies, the birth rate remains fairly high, owing to the lack of contraception and a continuing belief in the value of large families, but the death rate drops because of several factors, including increased food production, better sanitation, and improved medicine.

Because the birth rate remains high but the death rate drops, population growth takes off dramatically. In the third stage, the death rate remains low, but the birth rate finally drops as families begin to realize that large numbers of children in an industrial economy are more of a burden than an asset. Another reason for the drop is the availability of effective contraception. As a result, population growth slows, and, as we saw earlier, it has become quite low or even gone into a decline in several industrial nations. Demographic transition theory gives us reason to be cautiously optimistic regarding the threat of overpopulation. As poor nations continue to modernize—much as industrial nations did 200 years ago—their population growth rates should start to decline.

Still, population growth rates in poor nations continue to be high, and, as the "Sociology Making a Difference" box discussed, inequalities in food distribution allow rampant hunger to persist. Hundreds of thousands of women die in poor nations each year during pregnancy and childbirth. Reduced fertility would save their lives, in part because their bodies would be healthier if their pregnancies were spaced farther apart. Although world population growth is slowing, then, it is still growing too rapidly in much of the developing and least developed worlds. To reduce it further, more extensive family-planning programs are needed, as is economic development in general.

URBANIZATION

An important aspect of social change and population growth over the centuries has been urbanizationurbanizationThe rise and growth of cities., or the rise and growth of cities. Urbanization has had important consequences for many aspects of social, political, and economic life. The earliest cities developed in ancient times after the rise of horticultural and pastoral societies made it possible for people to stay in one place instead of having to move around to find food. Because ancient cities had no sanitation facilities, people typically left their garbage and human waste in the city streets or just outside the city wall; this poor sanitation led to rampant disease and high death rates.

Some cities eventually developed better sanitation procedures, including, in Rome, a sewer system. Cities became more numerous and much larger during industrialization, as people moved to be near factories and other sites of industrial production. First in Europe and then in the United States, people crowded together as never before into living conditions that were often decrepit. Lack of sanitation continued to cause rampant disease, and death rates from cholera, typhoid, and other illnesses were high. In addition, crime rates soared, and mob violence became quite common.

VIEWS OF THE CITY

Are cities good or bad? We asked a similar question—is modernization good or bad?, and the answer here is similar as well: cities are both good and bad. They are sites of innovation, high culture, population diversity, and excitement, but they are also sites of high crime, impersonality, and other problems. In the early 20th century, a group of social scientists at the University of Chicago established a research agenda on cities that is still influential today. Most notably, they began to study the effects of urbanization on various aspects of city residents' lives in what came to be called the human ecology schoolhuman ecology schoolThe study by early University of Chicago sociologists of the effects of urbanization on various aspects of city residents' lives..

One of their innovations was to divide Chicago into geographical regions, or zones, and to analyze crime rates and other behavioral differences among the zones. They found that crime rates were higher in the inner zone, or central part of the city, where housing was crowded and poverty was common, and were lower in the outer zones, or the outer edges of the city, where houses were spread farther apart and poverty was much lower. Because they found these crime rate differences over time even as the ethnic backgrounds of people in these zones changed, they assumed that the social and physical features of the neighborhoods were affecting their crime rates. Their work is still useful today, as it helps us realize that the social environment, broadly defined, can affect our attitudes and behavior. This theme, of course, lies at the heart of the sociological perspective.

Urbanism and Tolerance

One of the most notable Chicago sociologists was Louis Wirth, who, in a well-known essay entitled "Urbanism as a Way of Life", discussed several differences between urban and rural life. In one such difference, he said that urban residents are more tolerant than rural residents of nontraditional attitudes, behaviors, and lifestyles, in part because they are much more exposed than rural residents to these nontraditional ways. Supporting Wirth's hypothesis, contemporary research finds that urban residents indeed hold more tolerant views on several kinds of issues.

LIFE IN CITIES

Life in U.S. cities today reflects the dual view just outlined. On the one hand, many U.S. cities are vibrant places, filled with museums and other cultural attractions, nightclubs, theaters, and restaurants and populated by people from many walks of life and from varied racial and ethnic and national backgrounds. Many college graduates flock to cities, not only for their employment opportunities but also for their many activities and the sheer excitement of living in a metropolis. On the other hand, many U.S. cities are also filled with abject poverty, filth and dilapidated housing, high crime rates, traffic gridlock, and dirty air. Many Americans would live nowhere but a city, and many would live anywhere but a city. Cities arouse strong opinions pro and con, and for good reason, because there are many things both to like and to dislike about cities.

Types of Urban Residents

The quality of city life depends on many factors, but one of the most important factors is a person's social background: social class, race and ethnicity, gender, age, and sexual orientation. These dimensions of our social backgrounds often yield many kinds of social inequalities, and the quality of life that city residents enjoy depends heavily on these dimensions. For example, residents who are white and wealthy have the money and access to enjoy the best that cities have to offer, while those who are poor and of color typically experience the worst aspects of city life. Because of fear of rape and sexual assault, women often feel more constrained than men from traveling freely throughout a city and being out late at night; older people also often feel more constrained because of physical limitations and fear of muggings; and gays and lesbians are still subject to physical assaults stemming from homophobia. The type of resident we are, then, in terms of our sociodemographic profile affects what we experience in the city and whether that experience is positive or negative. This brief profile of city residents obscures other kinds of differences among residents regarding their lifestyles and experiences. A classic typology of urban dwellers by sociologist Herbert Gans is still useful today in helping to understand the variety of lives found in cities.

Gans identified five types of city residents. The first type is *cosmopolites*. These are people who live in a city because of its cultural attractions, restaurants, and other features of the best that a city has to offer. Cosmopolites include students, writers, musicians, intellectuals, and writers. *Unmarried and childless* individuals and couples are the second type; they live in a city to be near their jobs and to enjoy the various kinds of entertainment found in most cities. If and when they marry or have children, respectively, many migrate to the suburbs to raise their families. The third type is *ethnic villagers*, who are recent immigrants and members of various ethnic groups who live among each other in certain neighborhoods.

These neighborhoods tend to have strong social bonds and more generally a strong sense of community. Gans wrote that all of these three types generally find the city inviting rather than alienating and have positive experiences far more often than negative ones. In contrast, two final types of residents find the city alienating and experience a low quality of life. The first of these two types, and the fourth overall, is the *deprived*. These are people with low levels of formal education who live in poverty or near-poverty and are unemployed, are underemployed, or work at low wages. They live in neighborhoods filled with trash, broken windows, and other signs of disorder. They commit high rates of crime and also have high rates of victimization by crime. The final type is the *trapped*. These are residents who, as their name implies, might wish to leave their neighborhoods but are unable to do so for several reasons: they may be alcoholics or drug addicts, they may be elderly and disabled, or they may be jobless and cannot afford to move to a better area.

Problems of City Life

By definition, cities consist of very large numbers of people living in a relatively small amount of space. Some of these people have a good deal of money, but many people, and in some cities most people, have very little money. Cities must provide many kinds of services for all their residents, and certain additional services for their poorer residents. These basic facts of city life make for common sets of problems affecting cities throughout the nation, albeit to varying degrees, with some cities less able than others to address these problems. One evident problem is *fiscal*: cities typically have serious difficulties in paying for basic services such as policing, public education, trash removal, street maintenance, and, in cold climates, snow removal, and in providing certain services for their residents who are poor or disabled or who have other conditions.

The fiscal difficulties that cities routinely face became even more serious with the onset of the nation's deep recession in 2009, as the term *fiscal crisis* became a more accurate description of the harsh financial realities that cities were now facing. Another problem is *crowding*. Cities are crowded in at least two ways. The first involves *residential crowding*: large numbers of people living in a small amount of space. City streets are filled with apartment buildings, condominiums, row houses, and other types of housing, and many people live on any one city block. The second type of crowding is *household crowding*: dwelling units in cities are typically small because of lack of space, and much smaller than houses in suburbs or rural areas.

This forces many people to live in close quarters within a particular dwelling unit. Either type of crowding is associated with higher levels of stress, depression, and aggression. A third problem involves *housing*. Here there are two related issues. Much urban housing is *substandard* and characterized by such problems as broken windows, malfunctioning heating systems, peeling paint, and insect infestation. At the same time, adequate housing is *not affordable* for many city residents, as housing prices in cities can be very high, and the residents' incomes are typically very low. Cities thus have a great need for adequate, affordable housing. A fourth problem is *traffic*.

Gridlock occurs in urban areas, not rural ones, because of the sheer volume of traffic and the sheer number of intersections controlled by traffic lights or stop signs. Some cities have better public transportation than others, but traffic and commuting are problems that urban residents experience every day. A related problem is *pollution*. Traffic creates pollution from motor vehicles' exhaust systems, and some cities have factories and other enterprises that also pollute. As a result, air quality in cities is substandard, and the poor quality of air in cities has been linked to respiratory and heart disease and higher mortality rates. Yet another issue for cities is the state of their *public education*. Many city schools are housed in old buildings that, like much city housing, are falling apart.

City schools are notoriously underfunded and lack current textbooks, adequate science equipment, and other instructional materials. Although cities have many additional problems, *crime* is an appropriate one with which to end this section because of its importance. Simply put, cities have much higher rates of violent and property crime than do small towns or rural areas. For example, the violent crime rate in 2008 was 489 for the nation's largest cities, compared to only 205 for rural counties. The property crime rate in the largest cities was 3,352 crimes per 100,000, compared to only 1,681 in rural counties. Crime rates in large cities are thus two to three times higher than those in rural counties.

GLOBAL URBANIZATION

Urbanization varies around the world. In general, wealthy nations are more urban than poor nations thanks in large part to the latter's rural economies. This variation, however, obscures the fact that the world is becoming increasingly urban overall. In 1950, less than one-third of the world's population lived in cities or towns; in 2008, more than half the population lived in cities or towns, representing the first time in history that a majority of people were *not* living in rural areas. By 2030, almost two-thirds of the world's population is projected to live in urban areas.

The number of urban residents will increase rapidly in the years ahead, especially in Africa and Asia as people in these continents' nations move to urban areas and as their populations continue to grow through natural fertility. Fertility is a special problem in this regard for two reasons. First, and as we saw earlier, women in poor nations have higher fertility rates for several reasons. Second, poorer nations have very high proportions of young people, and these high rates mean that many births occur because of the large number of women in their childbearing years. This trend poses both opportunities and challenges for poorer nations.

The opportunities are many. Jobs are more plentiful in cities than in rural areas and incomes are higher, and services such as health care and schooling are easier to deliver because people are living more closely together. In another advantage, women in poorer nations generally fare better in cities than in rural areas in terms of education and employment possibilities. But there are also many challenges. In the major cities of poor nations, homeless children live in the streets as beggars, and many people lack necessities and conveniences that urban dwellers in industrial nations take for granted. As the United Nations Population Fund warns, "One billion people live in urban slums, which are typically overcrowded, polluted and dangerous, and lack basic services such as clean water and sanitation."

The rapid urbanization of poor nations will compound the many problems these nations already have, just as the rapid urbanization in the industrial world more than a century ago led to the disease and other problems discussed earlier. As cities grow rapidly in poor nations, moreover, these nations' poverty makes them ill equipped to meet the challenges of urbanization. Helping these nations meet the needs of their cities remains a major challenge for the world community in the years ahead. In this regard, the United Nations Population Fund urges particular attention to housing:

- Addressing the housing needs of the poor will be critical. A roof and an address in a habitable area are the first step to a better life. Improving access to basic social and health services, including reproductive health care, for poor people in urban slums is also critical to breaking the cycle of poverty.

RURAL LIFE AND RURAL PROBLEMS

Before we leave the topic of cities and urbanization, it is important to note that one-fourth of the U.S. population and more than 40% of the world population continue to live in rural areas. The dual view of cities presented in this section also applies to rural areas but does so in a sort of mirror image: the advantages of cities are often disadvantages for rural areas, and the disadvantages of cities are often advantages of rural areas. On the positive side, and focusing on the United States, rural areas obviously feature much more open space and less crowding. Their violent and property crime rates are much lower than those in large cities, as we have seen. The air is cleaner because there is less traffic and fewer factories and other facilities that emit pollution.

On the negative side, rural areas are often poor and lack the services, employment opportunities, and leisure activities that cities have. Teens often complain of boredom, and drug and alcohol use can be high. Rural schools are often small and poorly equipped. Health and Medicine noted, rural areas often lack sufficient numbers of health-care professionals and high-quality hospitals and medical clinics. The long distances that people must travel make it even more difficult for individuals with health problems to receive adequate medical care. In a problem that only recently has been recognized, rural women who experience domestic violence find it especially difficult to get help and/or to leave their abusers.

Rural police may be unenlightened about domestic violence and may even know the abuser; for either reason, they may not consider his violence a crime. Battered women's shelters are also much less common in rural areas than in cities, and battered women in rural areas often lack neighbors and friends to whom they can turn for support. For all of these reasons, rural women who experience domestic violence face a problem that has been called "dangerous exits".

SOCIAL MOVEMENTS

Social movements in the United States and other nations have been great forces for social change. At the same time, governments and other opponents have often tried to thwart the movements' efforts. To understand how and why social change happens, we have to understand why movements begin, how they succeed and fail, and what impact they may have.

UNDERSTANDING SOCIAL MOVEMENTS

To begin this understanding, we first need to understand what social movements are. A social movementsocial movementAn organized effort by a large number of people to bring about or impede social change. may be defined as an organized effort by a large number of people to bring about or impede social change. Defined in this way, social movements might sound similar to special-interest groups, and they do have some things in common. But a major difference between social movements and special-interest groups lies in the nature of their actions.

Special-interest groups normally work *within the system* via conventional political activities such as lobbying and election campaigning. In contrast, social movements often work *outside the system* by engaging in various kinds of protest, including demonstrations, picket lines, sit-ins, and sometimes outright violence. Conceived in this way, the efforts of social movements amount to "politics by other means," with these "other means" made necessary because movements lack the resources and access to the political system that interest groups typically enjoy.

TYPES OF SOCIAL MOVEMENTS

Sociologists identify several types of social movements according to the nature and extent of the change they seek. This typology helps us understand the differences among the many kinds of social movements that existed in the past and continue to exist today. One of the most common and important types of social movements is the *reform* movement, which seeks limited, though still significant, changes in some aspect of a nation's political, economic, or social systems. It does not try to overthrow the existing government but rather works to improve conditions within the existing regime. Some of the most important social movements in U.S. history have been reform movements. These include the abolitionist movement preceding the Civil War, the woman suffrage movement that followed the Civil War, the labor movement, the Southern civil rights movement, the Vietnam antiwar movement, the contemporary women's movement, the gay rights movement, and the environmental movement.

A *revolutionary* movement goes one large step further than a reform movement in seeking to overthrow the existing government and to bring about a new one and even a new way of life. Revolutionary movements were common in the past and were responsible for the world's great revolutions in Russia, China, and several other nations. Reform and revolutionary movements are often referred to as *political* movements because the changes they seek are political in nature. Another type of political movement is the *reactionary* movement, so named because it tries to block social change or to reverse social changes that have already been achieved.

The antiabortion movement is a contemporary example of a reactionary movement, as it arose after the U.S. Supreme Court legalized most abortions in *Roe v. Wade* and seeks to limit or eliminate the legality of abortion. Two other types of movements are *self-help* movements and *religious* movements. As their name implies, self-help movements involve people trying to improve aspects of their personal lives; examples of self-help groups include Alcoholics Anonymous and Weight Watchers. Religious movements aim to reinforce religious beliefs among their members and to convert other people to these beliefs.

THE ORIGINS OF SOCIAL MOVEMENTS

To understand how and why social movements begin, we need answers to two related questions. First, what are the social, economic, and political conditions that give rise to social movements? They do not arise in a vacuum, and certain macro problems in society must exist for movements to begin. Second, once social movements do begin, why are some individuals more likely than others to take part in them? Answers to this question usually focus on personality and other micro factors. We will start with these micro factors and then turn to the macro conditions that make movements possible in the first place.

Micro Factors: Emphasis on the Individual

Over the years social scientists have tried to explain why some individuals are more likely than others to join social movements. Their explanations center on several factors.

The Question of Irrationality

One issue is whether social movement involvement is *rational* or *irrational*. Early thinkers such as Gustavo LeBon, a French intellectual, thought that social movement involvement and, more generally, crowd behavior were the product of *irrational impulses*. Writing in the wake of the French Revolution of 1789, these thinkers worried that social order was breaking down. LeBon in particular blamed crowds for turning normally rational individuals into irrational and emotional actors who are virtually hypnotized by the crowd's mind-set.

American sociologists early in the 20th century adopted LeBon's view. In so doing, they viewed social movement participation as more *expressive*, or emotional, than *instrumental*, or directed at achieving specific goals. Just after the mid-20th century, Ralph H. Turner and Lewis M. Killian presented their *emergent norm* view of collective behavior, which downplayed the irrationality emphasized in earlier formulations. According to Turner and Killian, when people start interacting in collective behavior, they are not sure initially how they are supposed to behave. As they discuss their potential behavior and other related matters, norms governing their behavior emerge, and social order and rationality then guide behavior. Adopting this view, most sociologists today feel that people taking part in social movements are indeed acting rationally and instrumentally, not just expressively. Although they have emotions, that does not mean their behavior is any less rational or political.

Relative Deprivation

Another important line of thought has centered on relative deprivationrelative deprivationThe feeling by individuals that they are deprived relative to some other group or to some ideal state they have not reached., or the feeling by individuals that they are deprived relative to some other group or to some ideal state they have not reached. This view was popularized by James C. Davies and Ted Robert Gurr, both of whom built upon the earlier work of social psychologists who had studied frustration and aggression. When a deprived group perceives that social conditions are improving, wrote Davies, they become hopeful that their lives are getting better.

But if these conditions stop improving, they become frustrated and more apt to turn to protest, collective violence, and other social movement activity. Both Davies and Gurr emphasized that people's *feelings* of being relatively deprived were more important for the involvement in collective behavior than their level of actual deprivation. Relative deprivation theory was initially very popular, but scholars later pointed out that frustration often does not lead to protest, as people can instead blame themselves for the deprivation they feel and thus not protest. Scholars who favor the theory point out that people will ordinarily not take part in social movements unless they feel deprived, even if many who do feel deprived do not take part.

Social Isolation Versus Social Attachments

A final micro issue has been whether the individuals participating in social movements are isolated from society or very much a part of it. Are they loners, or are they involved in social networks of friends, coworkers, and others? In his influential book *The Politics of Mass Society*, William Kornhauser wrote that because modern societies are impersonal with weak social ties, individuals who are loners become involved in social movements to provide them the friendships and social bonding they otherwise lack. Kornhauser's mass society theorymass society theoryWilliam Kornhauser's view that social isolation prompts involvement in collective behavior and social movements. was popular for a time, but much research finds that the people who join social movements are in fact very much a part of society instead of loners. They have many friends and belong to several organizations, and these friendship and organizational ties help "pull" them into social movements.

Macro Factors: Emphasis on Social Structure

Structural explanations of social movements try to understand why social movements are more likely to arise in some historical periods and locations than in others. In effect, they try to show how certain social, economic, and political conditions give rise to social movements. We discuss some of these explanations here.

Smelser's Structural-Strain Theory

One of the most popular and influential structural explanations is Neil Smelser's structural-strain theorystructural-strain theoryNeil Smelser's view that social movements and other collective behavior occur and persist when six conditions are present: structural conduciveness, structural strain, generalized beliefs, precipitating factors, mobilization for action, and weak social control.. Smelser wrote that social movements and other collective behavior occur when several conditions are present. One of these conditions is *structural strain,* which refers to problems in society that cause people to be angry and frustrated.

Without such structural strain, people would not have any reason to protest, and social movements do not arise. Another condition is *generalized beliefs,* which are people's reasons for why conditions are so bad and their solutions to improve them. If people decide that the conditions they dislike are their own fault, they will decide not to protest. Similarly, if they decide that protest will not improve these conditions, they again will not protest. A third condition is the existence of *precipitating factors,* or sudden events that ignite collective behavior. In the 1960s, for example, several urban riots started when police were rumored to have unjustly arrested or beaten someone.

Although conditions in inner cities were widely perceived as unfair and even oppressive, it took this type of police behavior to ignite people to riot. Smelser's theory became very popular because it pointed to several factors that must hold true before social movements and other forms of collective behavior occur. At the same time, collective behavior does not always occur when his factors do hold true. The theory has also been criticized for being a bit vague; for example, it does not say how much strain a society must have for collective behavior to take place.

Resource Mobilization Theory

Resource mobilization theoryresource mobilization theoryThe view that social movements are a rational response to perceived grievances and that they arise from efforts by social movement leaders to mobilize the resources, especially the time, money, and energy, of aggrieved peoples and to direct them into effective political action. is a general name given to several related views of social movements that arose in the 1970s. This theory assumes that social movement activity is a rational response to unsatisfactory conditions in society.

Because these conditions always exist, so does discontent with them. Despite such constant discontent, people protest only rarely. If this is so, these conditions and associated discontent cannot easily explain why people turn to social movements.

What is crucial instead are efforts by social movement leaders to mobilize the resources—most notably, time, money, and energy—of the population and to direct them into effective political action. Also important are *political opportunities* for action that arise when, say, a government weakens because of an economic or foreign crisis. Resource mobilization theory has been very influential since its inception in the 1970s.

However, critics say it underestimates the importance of harsh social conditions and discontent for the rise of social movement activity. Conditions can and do worsen, and when they do so, they prompt people to engage in collective behavior. As just one example, cuts in higher education spending and steep increases in tuition prompted students to protest on campuses in California and several other states in late 2009 and early 2010.

Critics also say that resource mobilization theory neglects the importance of emotions in social movement activity by depicting social movement actors as cold, calculated, and unemotional. This picture is simply not true, critics say, and they further argue that social movement actors can be both emotional and rational at the same time, just as people are in many other kinds of pursuits.

THE LIFE CYCLE OF SOCIAL MOVEMENTS

Although the many past and present social movements around the world differ from each other in many ways, they all generally go through a life cycle marked by several stages that have long been recognized.

- Stage 1 is *emergence*. This stage is obviously when social movements begin for one or more of the reasons indicated in the previous section.
- Stage 2 is *coalescence*. At this stage a movement and its leaders must decide how they will recruit new members and they must determine the strategies they will use to achieve their goals. They also may use the news media to win favorable publicity and to convince the public of the justness of their cause.
- Stage 3 is *institutionalization* or *bureaucratization*. As a movement grows, it often tends to become bureaucratized, as paid leaders and a paid staff replace the volunteers that began the movement. It also means that clear lines of authority develop, as they do in any bureaucracy. More attention is also devoted to fund-raising. As movement organizations bureaucratize, they may well reduce their effectiveness by turning from the disruptive activities that succeeded in the movement's earlier stages to more conventional activity by

working within the system instead of outside it. At the same time, if movements do not bureaucratize to at least some degree, they may lose their focus and not have enough money to keep on going.

- Stage 4 is the *decline* of a social movement. Social movements eventually decline for one or more of many reasons. Sometimes they achieve their goals and naturally cease because there is no more reason to continue. More often, however, they decline because they fail. Both the lack of money and loss of enthusiasm among a movement's members may lead to a movement's decline, and so might *factionalism*, or strong divisions of opinion within a movement. The government may also "co-opt" a movement by granting it small, mostly symbolic concessions that reduce people's discontent but leave the conditions that originally motivated their activism largely intact. As noted earlier, movements also may decline because of government repression.

HOW SOCIAL MOVEMENTS MAKE A DIFFERENCE

By definition, social movements often operate outside of the political system by engaging in protest. Their rallies, demonstrations, sit-ins, and silent vigils are often difficult to ignore. With the aid of news media coverage, these events often throw much attention on the problem or grievance at the center of the protest and bring pressure to bear on the government agencies, corporations, or other targets of the protest. As noted earlier, there are many examples of profound changes brought about by social movements throughout U.S. history.

The abolitionist movement called attention to the evils of slavery and increased public abhorrence for that "peculiar institution." The woman suffrage movement after the Civil War eventually won women the right to vote with the ratification of the 19th Amendment in 1920. The labor movement of the late 19th and early 20th centuries established the minimum wage, the 40-hour workweek, and the right to strike. The civil rights movement of the 1950s and 1960s ended legal segregation in the South, while the Vietnam antiwar movement of the 1960s and 1970s helped increase public opposition to that war and bring it to a close.

The contemporary women's movement has won many rights in social institutions throughout American society, while the gay rights movement has done the same for gays and lesbians. Another contemporary movement is the environmental movement, which has helped win legislation and other policies that have reduced air, water, and ground pollution. Although it seems obvious that social movements have made a considerable difference, social movement scholars until recently have paid much more attention to the origins of social movements than to their consequences. Recent work has begun to fill in this gap and has focused on the consequences of social movements for the political system, for various aspects of the society's culture, and for the lives of the people who take part in movements. Regarding political consequences, scholars have considered such matters as whether movements are more successful when they use more protest or less protest, and when they focus on a single issue versus multiple issues. The use of a greater amount of protest seems to be more effective in this regard, as does a focus on a single issue. Research has also found that movements are more likely to succeed when the government against which they protest is weakened by economic or other problems. In another line of inquiry, movement scholars disagree over whether movements are more successful if their organizations are bureaucratic and centralized or if they remain decentralized and thus more likely to engage in protest.

Regarding cultural consequences, movements often influence certain aspects of a society's culture whether or not they intend to do so and, as one scholar has said, "it is perhaps precisely in being able to alter their broader cultural environment that movements can have their deepest and lasting impact". Social movements can affect values and beliefs, and they can affect cultural practices such as music, literature, and even fashion. Movements may also have biographical consequences. Several studies find that people who take part in social movements during their formative years are often transformed by their participation. Their political views change or are at least reinforced, and they are more likely to continue to be involved in political activity and to enter social change occupations. In this manner, writes one scholar, "people who have been involved in social movement activities, even at a lower level of commitment, carry the consequences of that involvement throughout their life".

IMPORTANT POINTS

- Social change involves the transformation of cultural norms and values, behavior, social institutions, and social structure. As societies become more modern, they become larger, more heterogeneous, and more impersonal, and their sense of community declines. Traditions decline as well, while individual freedom of thought and behavior increases. Some sociologists view modernization positively, while others view it negatively. Tönnies in particular lamented the shift from the Gemeinschaft of premodern societies to the Gesellschaft of modern societies. Durkheim also recognized the negative aspects of modernization but at the same time valued the freedom of modern societies and thought they retain a good amount of social solidarity from their division of labor.
- A functionalist understanding of social change emphasizes that it's both natural and inevitable. Talcott Parsons's equilibrium model recognized that gradual change is desirable and ordinarily stems from such things as population growth and technological advances,

but that any sudden social change disrupts society's equilibrium. Taking a very different view, conflict theory stresses that sudden social change is often both necessary and desirable to reduce inequality and to address other problems in society. Such social change often stems from intentional efforts by social movements to correct perceived deficiencies in the social, economic, and political systems.

- Several sources of social change exist. These include population growth and changes in population composition, changes in culture and technology, changes in the natural environment, and social and ethnic conflict.
- Demography is the study of population. It encompasses three central concepts: fertility, morality, and migration, which together determine population growth. Fertility and mortality vary by race and ethnicity, and they also vary around the world, with low-income nations having both higher fertility and higher mortality than high-income nations.
- The world's population is growing by about 80 million people annually. Population growth is greatest in the low-income nations of Africa and other regions, while in several industrial nations it's actually on the decline because birth rates have become so low. The world's population reached 6.8 billion by the beginning of the 21st century and is projected to grow to more than 9 billion by 2050, with most of this occurring in low-income nations. The annual rate of population growth will decline in the years ahead.
- Thomas Malthus predicted that the earth's population would greatly exceed the world's food supply. Although his prediction did not come true, hunger remains a serious problem around the world. Although food supply is generally ample thanks to improved technology, the distribution of food is inadequate in low-income nations. Fresh water in these regions is also lacking. Demographic transition theory helps explain why population growth did not continue to rise as much as Malthus predicted. As societies become more technologically advanced, first death rates and then birth rates decline, leading eventually to little population growth.
- Urbanization is a consequence of population growth. Cities first developed in ancient times after the rise of horticultural and pastoral societies and "took off" during the Industrial Revolution as people moved to be near factories. Urbanization led to many social changes then and continues today to affect society.
- Sociologists have long been interested in the city and have both positive and negative views of urbanization and city life. Contemporary research supports Wirth's hypothesis that tolerance for nontraditional beliefs and behaviors will be higher in urban areas than in rural areas.

- Social movements have been important agents for social change. Common types of social movements include reform movements, revolutionary movements, reactionary movements, and self-help and religious movements.
- Explanations of social movements address both micro and macro factors. Important issues at the micro level include the question of irrationality, the importance of relative deprivation, and the impact of social isolation. Macro theories address the social, economic, and political conditions underlying collective behavior. Two of the most important such theories are Smelser's structural-strain theory and resource mobilization theory.
- Most social movements go through a life cycle of four stages: emergence, coalescence, bureaucratization, and decline. Decline stems from several reasons, including internal divisions and repressive efforts by the state.
- Social movements have political, cultural, and biographical consequences. Research finds that movements are more successful in the political arena when they use more rather than less protest and when they focus on a single issue rather than multiple issues.

8

Population Geography

INTRODUCTION

Human beings evolved under conditions of high mortality due to famines, accidents, illnesses, infections and war and therefore the relatively high fertility rates were essential for species survival. In spite of the relatively high fertility rates it took all the time from evolution of mankind to the middle of the 19th century for the global population to reach one billion. The twentieth century witnessed an unprecedented rapid improvement in health care technologies and access to health care all over the world; as a result there was a steep fall in the mortality and steep increase in longevity. The population realized these changes and took steps to reduce their fertility but the decline in fertility was not so steep. As a result the global population has undergone a fourfold increase in a hundred years and has reached 6 billion.

DEMOGRAPHIC TRANSITION

Demographers refer to these changes from stable population with high fertility and mortality to a new stability in population due to low fertility and mortality patterns as demographic transition. Demographic transition occurs in four phases; of these the first three phases are characterized by population growth. In the first phase there is a fall in death rate and improvement in longevity; this leads to population growth. In the second phase there is a fall in birth rate but fall is less steep than fall in death rates and consequently there is population growth. In the third phase death rates plateau and replacement level of fertility is attained but the population growth continues because of the large size of population in reproductive age group. The fourth phase is characterized by fall in birth rate to below replacement level and reduction in the proportion of the population in reproductive age group; as a result of these changes population growth ceases and population stabilizes.

Experience in some of the developed countries suggest that in some societies even after attainment of stable population there may be a further decline in fertility so that there is a further reduction in the population- so called negative population growth phase of the demographic transition.

Different countries in the world have entered the demographic transition at different periods of time; there are also substantial differences in the rate of demographic transition and time taken to achieve population stabilization.

GLOBAL POPULATION SCENARIO

In 1901 the world population was 1.6 billion. By 1960, it became 3 billion, and by 1987, 5 billion and in 1999, 6 billion. Currently, one billion people are added every 12 - 13 years. During the last decade there has been substantial decline in birth rate. The reasons for decline vary from society to society; urbanization, rising educational attainment, increasing employment among women, lower infant mortality are some major factors responsible for growing desire for smaller families; increasing awareness and improved access to contraception have made it possible for the majority of the couple to achieve the desired family size. In some countries slowing of the population growth has been due to an increase in mortality.

As a result of all these the decline in the global population growth during the nineties is steeper than the earlier predictions. Currently, the annual increment is about 80 million. It is expected to decrease to about 64 million by 2020 -25 and to 33 million by 2045 -50; 95 % of the growth of population occurs in developing countries. Most demographers believe that the current accelerated decline in population growth will continue for the next few decades and the medium projections of Population Division of United Nations, that the global population will grow to 8.9 billion by 2050 is likely to be achieved.

CHANGING AGE STRUCTURE OF THE POPULATION

During demographic transition along with the growth in number there are changes in the population age structure. While the importance of the population growth as a determinant of quality of life is universally understood, the profoundly serious consequences of changing age structure especially if it occurs too rapidly is not understood by many. Population pyramids graphically represent complex changes in age structure of the population so that it can be readily understood and interpreted. The population pyramids for the global population, developed and developing countries. Currently nearly half of the global population is below 25 years of age and one sixth are in the age group 15-24. Their choices, efforts and lifestyles will determine not only the population growth but also future improvement in the quality of life in harmony with global ecology.

In developed countries the reproductive age group population is relatively small; their fertility is low and the longevity at birth is high. Population profiles of these countries resemble a cylinder and not a pyramid.These countries have the advantages of having achieved a stable population but have to face the problems of having a relatively small productive workforce to support the large aged population with substantial non-communicable disease burden. Some of the developing countries have undergone a very rapid decline in the birth rates within a short period. This enabled them to quickly achieve population stabilization but they do face the problems of rapid changes in the age structure and workforce which may be inadequate to meet their manpower requirements.

In contrast the population in most of the developing countries consist of a very large proportion of children and persons in reproductive age. Because of the large reproductive age group the population will continue to grow even when replacement level of fertility is reached. It is imperative that these countries should generate enough employment opportunities for this work force and utilise the human resources and accelerate their economic growth. Planners and policy makers in developing countries like India have to take into account the ongoing demographic changes so that available human resources are optimally utilised as agents of change and development to achieve improvement in quality of life.

DEMOGRAPHIC TRANSITION IN INDIA

Over the last four decades there has been rapid fall in Crude Death Rate from 25.1 in 1951 to 9.8 in 1991 and less steep decline in the Crude Birth Rate from 40.8 in 1951 to 29.5 in 1991. The annual exponential population growth rate has been over 2% in the period 1961-90. During the nineties the decline in CBR has been steeper than that in the and consequently, the annual population growth rate has fallen below 2%. The rate of decline in population growth is likely to be further accelerated during the next decade. The changes in the population growth rates have been relatively slow, steady and sustained. As a result the country was able to achieve a relatively gradual change in the population numbers and age structure. The short and long term adverse consequences of too rapid decline in birth rates and change in age structure on the social and economic development were avoided and the country was able to adapt to these changes without massive disruptions of developmental efforts.

In spite of the uniform national norms set under the 100% Centrally Funded and Centrally Sponsored Scheme of Family Welfare , there are substantial differences in the performance between States as assessed by IMR and CBR. Though the decline in CBR and IMR has occurred in all States, the rate of decline is slower in some States. At one end of the spectrum is Kerala with mortality and fertility rates nearly similar to those in some of the developed countries. At the other end, there are four large northern States with high Infant Mortality Rate and Fertility Rates. Though the decline in CBR, IMR and CDR has occurred in all States, the rate of decline was slower in some States like U.P. and Bihar.

There are substantial differences in CBR and IMR not only between States but also between the districts in the same state. In view of these findings, the

NDC Committee on Population recommended that efforts should be made to provide reproductive and child health services at district level and undertake decentralized area-specific micro planning and implementation of appropriate interventions. In response to this recommendation Dept of Family Welfare has abolished the practice of fixing targets for individual contraceptives by the Central Government from April 1996 and had initiated decentralized district based, planning, implementation, monitoring and midcourse corrections of FW programme. The experience of states with district based planning, implementation and the impact are being closely monitored.

CONSEQUENCES OF POPULATION GROWTH

ENVIRONMENTAL AND ECOLOGICAL CONSEQUENCES

The already densely populated developing countries contribute to over 95% of the population growth and rapid population growth could lead to environmental deterioration. Developed countries are less densely populated and contribute very little to population growth; however, they cause massive ecological damage by the wasteful, unnecessary and unbalanced consumption the consequences of which could adversely affect both the developed and the developing countries. The review on "Promotion of sustainable development: challenges for environmental policies" in the Economic Survey 1998-99 had covered in detail the major environmental problems, and policy options for improvement; the present review will only briefly touch upon some of the important ecological consequences of demographic transition.

In many developing countries continued population growth has resulted in pressure on land, fragmentation of land holding, collapsing fisheries, shrinking forests, rising temperatures, loss of plant and animal species. Global warming due to increasing use of fossil fuels could have serious effects on the populous coastal regions in developing countries, their food production and essential water supplies. The Intergovernmental Panel on Climate Change has projected that, if current greenhouse gas emission trends continue, the mean global surface temperature will rise from 1 to 3.5 degrees Celsius in the next century. The panel's best estimate scenario projects a sea-level rise of 15 to 95 centimeters by 2100.

The ecological impact of rising oceans would include increased flooding, coastal erosion, salination of aquifers and coastal crop land and displacement of millions of people living near the coast. Patterns of precipitation are also likely to change, which combined with increased average temperatures, could substantially alter the relative agricultural productivity of different regions. Greenhouse gas emissions are closely linked to both population growth and development. Slower population growth in developing countries and ecologically sustainable lifestyles in developed countries would make reduction in green house gas emission easier to achieve and provide more time and options for adaptation to climate change. Rapid population growth, developmental activities either to meet the growing population or the growing needs of the population as well as changing lifestyles and consumption patterns pose major challenge to preservation and promotion of ecological balance in India.

Some of the major ecological adverse effects reported in India include:

- Severe pressure on the forests due to both the rate of resource use and the nature of use. The per capita forest biomass in the country is only about 6 tons as against the global average of 82 tons.
- Adverse effect on species diversity:
- Conversion of habitat to some other land use such as agriculture, urban development, forestry operation. Some 70-80 % of fresh water marshes and lakes in the Gangetic flood plains has been lost in the last 50 years.
- Tropical deforestation and destruction of mangroves for commercial needs and fuel wood. The country's mangrove areas have reduced from 700,000 ha to 453,000 ha in the last 50 years.
- Intense grazing by domestic livestock Poaching and illegal harvesting of wildlife.
- Increase in agricultural area, high use of chemical fertilizers pesticides and weedicides; water stagnation, soil erosion, soil salinity and low productivity.
- High level of biomass burning causing large-scale indoor pollution.
- Encroachment on habitat for rail and road construction thereby fragmenting the habitat. increase in commercial activities such as mining and unsustainable resource extraction.
- Degradation of coastal and other aquatic ecosystems from domestic sewage, pesticides, fertilizers and industrial effluents.
- Over fishing in water bodies and introduction of weeds and exotic species.
- Diversion of water for domestic, industrial and agricultural uses leading to increased river pollution and decrease in self-cleaning properties of rivers.
- Increasing water requirement leading to tapping deeper aquifers which have high content of arsenic or fluoride resulting health problems.
- Disturbance from increased recreational activity and tourism causing pollution of natural ecosystems with wastes left behind by people.

The United Nations Conference on Environment and Development acknowledged population growth, rising income levels, changing technologies, increasing consumption pattern will all have adverse impact on environment. Ensuring that there is no further deterioration depends on choices made by the population about family size, life styles, environmental protection and equity. Availability of appropriate technology and commitment towards ensuring sustainable development is increasing throughout the world. Because of these, it might be possible to initiate steps to see that the natural carrying capacity of the environment is not damaged beyond recovery and ecological balance is to a large extent maintained. It is imperative that the environmental sustainability of all developmental projects is taken care of by appropriate inputs at the planning, implementation, monitoring and evaluation stages.

URBANIZATION

The proportion of people in developing countries who live in cities has almost doubled since 1960, while in more developed regions the urban share has grown from 61 per cent to 76 per cent. Urbanization is projected to continue well into the next century. By 2030, it is expected that nearly 5 billion of the world's 8.1 billion people will live in cities. India shares this global trend toward urbanisation. Globally, the number of cities with 10 million or more inhabitants is increasing rapidly, and most of these new "megacities" are in developing regions. In 1960, only New York and Tokyo had more than 10 million people. By 1999, the number of megacities had grown to 17.

It is projected that there will be 26 megacities by 2015; more than 10 per cent of the world's population will live in these cities. India's urban population has doubled from 109 million to 218 million during the last two decades and is estimated to reach 300 million by 2000 AD. As a consequence cities are facing the problem of expanding urban slums. Like many other demographic changes, urbanization has both positive and negative effects. Cities and towns have become the engines of social change and rapid economic development.

Urbanisation is associated with improved access to education, employment, health care; these result in increase in age at marriage, reduction in family size and improvement in health indices. As people have moved towards and into cities, information has flowed outward. Better communication and transportation now link urban and rural areas both economically and socially creating an urban-rural continuum of communities with improvement in some aspects of lifestyle of both. The ever increasing reach of mass media communicate new ideas, points of reference, and available options are becoming more widely recognized, appreciated and sought. This phenomenon has affected health care, including reproductive health, in many ways.

For instance, radio and television programmes that discuss gender equity, family size preference and family planning options are now reaching formerly isolated rural populations. This can create demand for services for mothers and children, higher contraceptive use, and fewer unwanted pregnancies, smaller healthier families and lead to more rapid population stabilisation. But the rapid growth of urban population also poses some serious challenges. Urban population growth has outpaced the development of basic minimum services; housing, water supply, sewerage and solid waste disposal are far from adequate; increasing waste generation at home, offices and industries, coupled with poor waste disposal facilities result in rapid environmental deterioration. Increasing automobiles add to air pollution. All these have adverse effect on ecology and health. Poverty persists in urban and peri-urban areas; awareness about the glaring inequities in close urban setting may lead to social unrest.

RURAL POPULATION AND THEIR DEVELOPMENT

Over seventy per cent of India's population still lives in rural areas. There are substantial differences between the states in the proportion of rural and urban population. Agriculture is the largest and one of the most important sector of the rural economy and contributes both to economic growth and employment. Its contribution to the Gross Domestic Product has declined over the last five decades but agriculture still remains the source of livelihood for over 70 per cent of the country's population.

A large proportion of the rural work force is small and consists of marginal farmers and landless agricultural labourers. There is substantial under employment among these people; both wages and productivity are low. These in turn result in poverty; it is estimated that 320 million people are still living below the poverty line in rural India. Though poverty has declined over the last three decades, the number of rural poor has in fact increased due to the population growth. Poor tend to have larger families which puts enormous burden on their meagre resources, and prevent them from breaking out of the shackles of poverty.

In States like Tamil Nadu where replacement level of fertility has been attained, population growth rates are much lower than in many other States; but the population density is high and so there is a pressure on land. In States like Rajasthan, Uttar Pradesh, Bihar and Madhya Pradesh population is growing rapidly, resulting in increasing pressure on land and resulting land fragmentation. Low productivity of small land holders leads to poverty, low energy intake and under nutrition, and this, in turn, prevents the development thus creating a vicious circle. In most of the states non-farm employment in rural areas has not grown very much and cannot absorb the growing labour force.

Those who are getting educated specially beyond the primary level, may not wish to do manual agricultural work. They would like better opportunities and more remunerative employment. In this context, it is imperative that programmes for skill development, vocational training and technical education are taken up on a large scale in order to generate productive employment in rural areas. The entire gamut of existing poverty alleviation and employment generation programmes may have to be restructured to meet the newly emerging types of demand for employment.

Rural poor have inadequate access to basic minimum services, because of poor connectivity, lack of awareness, inadequate and poorly functional infrastructure. There are ongoing efforts to improve these, but with the growing aspirations of the younger, educated population these efforts may prove to be inadequate to meet the increasing needs both in terms of type and quality of services.

Greater education, awareness and better standard of living among the growing younger age group population would create the required consciousness among them that smaller families are desirable; if all the felt needs for health and family welfare services are fully met, it will be possible to enable them to attain their reproductive goals, achieve substantial decline in the family size and improve quality of life.

WATER SUPPLY

In many parts of developed and developing world, water demand substantially exceeds sustainable water supply. It is estimated that currently 430 millions are living in countries affected by water stress; by 2020 about one fourth of the global population may be facing chronic and recurring shortage of fresh water. In India, water withdrawal is estimated to be twice the rate of aquifer recharge; as a result water tables are falling by one to three meters every year; tapping deeper aquifers have resulted in larger population groups being exposed to newer health hazards such as high fluoride or arsenic content in drinking water.

At the other end of the spectrum, excessive use of water has led to water logging and increasing salinity in some parts of the country. Eventually, both lack of water and water logging could have adverse impact on India's food production. There is very little arable agricultural land which remains unexploited and in many areas, agricultural technology improvement may not be able to ensure further increase in yield per hectare. It is, therefore, imperative that research in biotechnology for improving development of foodgrains strains that would tolerate salinity and those which would require less water gets high priority. Simultaneously, a movement towards making water harvesting, storage and its need based use part of every citizens life should be taken up.

FOOD SECURITY

Technological innovations in agriculture and increase in area under cultivation have ensured that so far, food production has kept pace with the population growth. Evolution of global and national food security systems have improved access to food. It is estimated that the global population will grow to 9 billion by 2050 and the food production will double; improvement in purchasing power and changing dietary habits may further add to the requirement of food grains. Thus, in the next five decades, the food and nutrition security could become critical in many parts of the world especially in the developing countries and pockets of poverty in the developed countries. In India one of the major achievements in the last fifty years has been the green revolution and selfsufficiency in food production.

Food grain production has increased from 50.82 in 1950-51 to 200.88 million tons in 1998-99. It is a matter of concern that while the cereal production has been growing steadily at a rate higher than the population growth rates, the coarse grain and pulse production has not shown a similar increase. Consequently there has been a reduction in the per capita availability of pulses and coarse grains. Over the last five decades there has been a decline in the per capita availability of pulses. During the last few years the country has imported pulses to meet the requirement.

There has been a sharp and sustained increase in cost of pulses, so there is substantial decline in per capita pulses consumption among poorer segment of population. This in turn could have an adverse impact on their protein intake. The pulse component of the "Pulses and Oil Seeds Mission" need to receive a major thrust in terms of R&D and other inputs, so that essential pulse requirement of growing population is fully met. Rising cost of pulses had a beneficial effect also. Till eighties in central India wages of landless labourers were given in the form Kesari Dal which was cheaper than cereals or coarse grains.

Consumption of staple diet of Kesari Dal led to crippling disease of neuro lathyrism. Over the last three decades the rising cost of pulses has made Kesari Dal more expensive than wheat or rice and hence it is no longer given to labourers as wages for work done; as a result the disease has virtually disappeared from Central India. Over years the coarse grain production has remained stagnant and per capita availability of coarse grain has under gone substantial reduction; there has been a shift away from coarse grains to rice and wheat consumption even among poorer segment of population.

One of the benefits of this change is virtual elimination of pellagra which was widely prevalent among low income group population in Deccan Plateau whose staple food was sorghum. Coarse grains are less expensive than rice and wheat; they can thus provide higher calories for the same cost as compared to rice and wheat. Coarse grains which are locally produced and procured if made available through TPDS at subsidised rate, may not only substantially bring down the subsidy cost without any reduction in calories provided but also improve "targetting" - as only the most needy are likely to access these coarse grains.

Another area of concern is the lack of sufficient focus and thrust in horticulture; because of this, availability of vegetables especially green leafy vegetables and yellow/red vegetables throughout the year at affordable cost both in urban and rural areas has remained an unfulfilled dream. Health and nutrition education emphasizing the importance of consuming these inexpensive rich sources of micronutrients will not result in any change in food habits unless there is harnessing and effective management of horticultural resources in the country to meet the growing needs of the people at affordable cost. States like Tamil Nadu and Himachal Pradesh have initiated some efforts in this direction; similar efforts need be taken up in other states also.

NUTRITION

At the time of independence the country faced two major nutritional problems; one was the threat of famine and acute starvation due to low agricultural production and lack of appropriate food distribution system. The other was chronic energy deficiency due to poverty, low-literacy, poor access to safe-drinking water, sanitation and health care; these factors led to wide spread prevalence of infections and ill health in children and adults. Kwashiorkor, marasmus, goitre, beri beri, blindness due to Vitamin-A deficiency and anaemia were major public health problems.

The country adopted multi-sectoral, multi-pronged strategy to combat the major nutritional problems and to improve nutritional status of the population. During the last 50 years considerable progress has been achieved. Famines no longer stalk the country.

There has been substantial reduction in moderate and severe undernutrition in children and some improvement in nutritional status of all segments of population. Kwashiorkor, marasmus, pellagra, lathyrism, beri beri and blindness due to severe Vitamin-A deficiency have become rare.

However, it is a matter of concern that milder forms of Chronic Energy Deficiency and micronutrient deficiencies continue to be widely prevalent in adults and children. In view of the fact that population growth in India will continue for the next few decades, it is essential that appropriate strategies are devised to improve food and nutrition security of families, identify individuals/families with severe forms of CED and provide them assistance to over come these problem.

Operational strategy to improve the dietary intake of the family and improve nutritional status of the rapidly growing adult population would include:

- Ensuring adequate agricultural production of cereals, pulses, vegetables and other foodstuffs needed to fully meet the requirement of growing population.
- Improving in purchasing power through employment generation and employment assurance schemes;
- Providing subsidised food grains through TPDS to the families below poverty line.
- Exploring feasibility of providing subsidized coarse grains to families Below Poverty Line

Operational strategies to improve health and nutritional status of the growing numbers of women and children include:

- Pregnant and lactating women - screening to identify women with weight below 40 Kgs and ensuring that they/ their preschool children receive food supplements through Integrated Child Development Services Scheme; adequate antenatal intrapartum and neonatal care.
- 0-6 months infants - Nutrition education for early initiation of lactation protection and promotion of universal breast feeding exclusive breast feeding for the first six months; unless there is specific reason supplementation should not be introduced before 6 months immunisation, growth monitoring and health care.
- Well planned nutrition education to ensure that the infants and children do a) continue to get breasted; b) get appropriate cereal pulse - vegetable based supplement fed to them at least 3 - 4 times a day – appropriate help in ensuring this through family/community/ work place support; c) immunisation and health care.
- Children in the 0 - 5 age group; a) screen by weighment to identify children with moderate and severe undernutrition b) provide double quantity supplements through ICDS; c) screening for nutrition and health problems and appropriate intervention.
- Primary school children: a) weigh and identify those with moderate and severe chronic energy deficiency; b) improve dietary intake to these children through the mid-day meal.
- Monitor for improvement in the identified undernourished infants, children and mothers; if no improvement after 2 months refer to physician for identification and treatment of factors that might be responsible for lack of improvement;
- Nutrition education on varying dietary needs of different members of the family and how they can be met by minor modifications from the family meals. Intensive health education for improving the life style of the population coupled with active screening and management of the health problems associated with obesity.

POPULATION PROJECTIONS FOR INDIA AND THEIR IMPLICATIONS

Right from 1958 the Planning Commission has been constituting an Expert Group on Population Projections prior to the preparation of each of the Five Year Plans so that the information on the population status at the time of initiation of the Plan and population projections for future are available during the preparation of the Plan. Population projections have been utilised not only for planning to ensure provision of essentials necessities such as food, shelter and clothing but also prerequisites for human development such as education, employment and health care.

Over the years there has been considerable refinement in the methodology used for population projections and substantial improvement in the accuracy of predictions. The projections made by the Standing Committee on Population Projection in 1988 for the year 1991 was 843.6 million; this figure was within 0.3% of the 846.3 million reported in the Census 1991. In 1996, Technical Group on Population Projections, had work out the population projections for the country and the states for the period 1996 to 2016 on the basis of census 1991 and other available demographic data. Population pyramids for the period 1971 to 2016.

Economic Implications

Population growth and its relation to economic growth has been a matter of debate for over a century. The early Malthusian view was that population growth is likely to impede economic growth because it will put pressure on the available resources, result in reduction in per capita income and resources; this, in turn, will result in deterioration in quality of life. Contrary to the Malthusian predictions, several of the East Asian countries have been able to achieve economic prosperity and improvement in quality of life inspite of population growth.

This has been attributed to the increase in productivity due to development and utilisation of innovative technologies by the young educated population who formed the majority of the growing population. These countries have been able to exploit the dynamics of demographic transition to achieve economic growth by using the human resources as the engine driving the economic development; improved employment with adequate emoluments has promoted saving and investment which in turn stimulated .economic growth. However, not all countries, which have undergone demographic transition, have been able to transform their economies.

Sri Lanka in South Asia underwent demographic transition at the same time as South East Asian countries but has not achieved the economic transition. It is now realized that population growth or demographic transition can have favourable impact on economic growth only when there are optimal interventions aimed at human resource development and appropriate utilisation of available human resources. For India the current phase of demographic transition with low dependency ratio and high working age group population, represents both a challenge and an opportunity.

The challenge is to develop these human resources through appropriate education and skill development and utilise them fully by giving them appropriate jobs with adequate emoluments; if this challenge is met through well planned schemes for HRD and employment generation which are implemented effectively, there will be improved national productivity and personal savings rates; appropriate investment of these savings will help the country to achieve the economic transition from low economic growth - low per capita income to high economic growth - high per capita income. It is imperative to make the best use of this opportunity so as to enable the country and its citizens to vault to the high income- high economic growth status and stabilize at that level.

INTERSTATE DIFFERENCES

The projected values for the total population in different regions. There are marked differences between States in size of the population and population growth rates, the time by which replacement level of fertility is to be achieved and age structure of the population. If the present trend continues, most of the Southern and the Western States are likely to achieve TFR of 2.1 by 2010. Urgent energetic steps to assess and fully meet the unmet needs for maternal and child health care and contraception through improvement in availability and access to family welfare services are needed in the States of UP, MP, Rajasthan and Bihar in order to achieve a faster decline in their mortality and fertility rates.

The five states of Bihar, Uttar Pradesh, Madhya Pradesh, Rajasthan and Orissa, which constitute 44% of the total population of India in 1996, will constitute 48% of the total population of India in 2016. These states will contribute 55% of the total increase in population of the country during the period 1996-2016. In all the states performance in the social and economic sector has been poor. The poor performance is the outcome of poverty, illiteracy and poor development which co-exist and reinforce each other. The quality and coverage under health services is poor and the unmet need for FW services is about 30%.

Urgent energetic steps are required to be initiated to assess and fully meet the unmet needs for maternal and child health care and contraception through improvement in availability and access to family welfare services in the states of UP, MP, Rajasthan and Bihar in order to achieve a faster decline in their mortality and fertility rates. The performance of these states would determine the year and size of the population at which the country achieves population stabilisation. There are also marked differences between States in socio-economic development. Increasing investments and rapid economic development are likely to occur in the States where literacy rates are high; there is ready availability of skilled work force and adequate infrastructure.

In these States, population growth rates are low. If equitable distribution of the income and benefits generated by development is ensured, substantial increase in per capita income and improvement in quality of life could occur in these States in a relatively short time. In majority of States with high population growth rates, the performance in the social and economic sector has been poor. The poor performance could be the outcome of a variety of factors including paucity of natural, financial or human resources. Poverty, illiteracy and poor development co-exist and aggravate each other. In order to promote equity and reduce disparity between States, special assistance has been provided to the poorly performing States.

The benefits accrued from such assistance has to a large extent depended upon:

- The States' ability to utilise the available funds; improve quality & coverage of services and facilities, increase efficiency and improve performance
- Community awareness and ability to utilise the available services.

In spite of the additional assistance provided, improvement in infrastructure, agriculture and industry have been sub-optimal and the per capita income continues to be low in most of the poorly performing States. These States also have high birth rates and relatively low literacy rates. It is imperative that special efforts are made during the next two decades to break this vicious self perpetuating cycle of poor performance, poor per capita income, poverty, low literacy and high birth rate so that the further widening of disparities between States in terms of per capita income and quality of life is prevented. The higher population growth rates and low per capita income in poorly performing States are likely to have a major impact on several social sector programmes.

The health status of the population in these States is poor; the health sector programme will require inputs not only for improving infrastructure and manpower, but also increasing efficiency and improving performance. The Family Welfare Programme has to address the massive task of meeting all the unmet needs for MCH and contraception so that there is a rapid decline in mortality and fertility rates.

Due to high birth rate, the number of children requiring schooling will be large. The emphasis in the education sector on primary education is essential to ensure that the resource constraints do not result in an increase in either proportion or number of illiterates. Emphasis on prevocational and vocational training in schools will enable these children to acquire skills through which they will find gainful employment later.

Migration

The available data from census shows that until 1991 both internal and international migration has been negligible. The Technical Group while computing the population projection upto 2016, has assumed that the component of migration between major States and from India will be negligible. This assumption may not be valid if there is further widening of the disparity between States in terms of economic growth and employment opportunity. Given the combination of high population growth, low literacy and lack of employment opportunities in the poorly performing States, there may be increasing rural to urban migration as well as interstate migration especially of unskilled workers.

Such migration may in the short run assist the migrants in overcoming economic problems associated with unemployment. However, the migrant workers and their families may face problems in securing shelter, education and health care. It is essential to build up a mechanism for monitoring these changes. Steps will have to be taken to provide for the minimum essential needs of the vulnerable migrant population.

Labour, employment and manpower

Population, which is engaged in any economic activity and population seeking work constitute Labour Force. India has the second largest labour force in the world. Projection of labour force is pre-requisite ensuring optimal utilisation of available human resources. Manpower development is then taken up to provide adequate labour force, of appropriate skills and quality to different sectors so that there is rapid socioeconomic development and there is no mismatch between skills required and skills available. Planning also attempts to provide enabling environment for employment generation in public, private and voluntary sectors in urban and rural areas. Labour force in India will be increasing by more than 10 million per annum during 1997-2012.

It will be imperative to plan for and achieve adequate agricultural and industrial growth to absorb this work force. Most of the persons entering the labour force will be educated and have some skills. Increasing literacy and decreasing birth rates may result in more women seeking economically productive work outside home. It will be important to generate appropriate and renumerative employment at places where labour force are available so as to reduce interstate and urban migration in search of employment. Attempts should be made to eliminate bonded labour, employment of children and women in hazardous industries and minimising occupational health hazards. Planners face the challenge to have sustained high economic growth rate in sectors that are labour-intensive to ensure adequate employment generation for productively utilising this massive work force. If the massive work force of literate, skilled, aware men and women in age-group 20-60 years get fully employed and adequately paid they could trigger off a period of rapid economic development. As they have very few dependant children and elders there will be increased savings and investments at household level; this in turn will improve the availability of resources for accelerating economic growth. The current stage of demographic transition thus provides the country with the opportunity window for using human resources as the engine to power economic development and improving the quality of life of all the citizens.

Sex Ratio

The reported decline in the sex ratio during the current century has been a cause for concern. The factors responsible for this continued decline are as yet not clearly identified. However, it is well recognised that the adverse sex ratio is a reflection of the gender disparity. Higher childhood mortality in girl children is yet another facet of the existing gender disparities and consequent adverse effect on survival.

In the reproductive age group the mortality rates among women are higher than those among men. The continued high maternal mortality is one of the major factors responsible for this. Effective implementation of the Reproductive and Child Health Programme is expected to result in a substantial reduction in maternal mortality. At the moment, the longevity at birth among women is only marginally higher than that among men. However over the next decade life expectancy among women will progressively increase.

Once the reproductive age group is crossed, the mortality rates among women are lower as women outlive and outnumber men in the age group 65 and above. The needs especially of the widowed women have to be met so that quality of life does not deteriorate. The census 2001 will collect and report vital data on sex disaggregated basis; this will be of help in identifying and taking up appropriate interventions in correcting gender disparity; continued collection, collation, analysis and reporting of sex disaggregated data from all social sectors will also provide a mechanism to monitor whether girls and women have equal access to services. There are substantial differences in sex ratio at birth and in different age groups between states.

The SRS based estimates of average sex ratio at birth for the period 1981-90 for the major States and India. The observed sex ratio of 110 is higher than the internationally accepted sex ratio at birth of 106. There are substantial differences among states in the reported sex ratio at birth. There had been speculations whether female infanticide, sex determination and selective female foeticide are at least in part responsible for this. The Government of India has enacted a legislation banning the prenatal sex determination and selective abortion. Intensive community education efforts are under way to combat these practices, especially in pockets from where female infanticide and foeticide have been reported.

INCREASING LONGEVITY

The projected populations of India in the three major age groups. Over the coming decades the country will be facing a progressive increase both in the proportion and number of persons beyond 60 years of age. Over the next 20 years the population of more than 60 years will grow form 62.3 million to 112.9 million; the subsequent decades will witness massive increase in this age group. Increasing longevity will inevitably bring in its wake increase in the prevalence of non-communicable diseases. The growing number of senior citizens in the country poses a major challenge and the cost of providing socio-economic security and health care to this population has to be met. Currently several region and culture specific innovative interventions to provide needed care to this population are underway; among these are efforts to reverse the trend of break up of joint families. If these efforts succeed, it will be possible to provide necessary care for rapidly increasing population of senior citizens in the subsequent two decades within the resources of the family and the country.

Majority of the people in their sixties will be physically and psychologically fit and would like to participate both in economic and social activities. They should be encouraged and supported to lead a productive life and contribute to the national development. Senior citizens in their seventies and beyond and those with health problems would require assistance. So far, the families have borne major share in caring for the elderly. This will remain the ideal method; however, there are growing number of elderly without family support; for them, alternate modes for caring may have to be evolved and implemented. Improved health care has "added years to life". The social sectors have to make the necessary provisions for improving the quality of life of these senior citizens so that they truly " add life to years."

HEALTH IMPLICATION OF THE DEMOGRAPHIC TRANSITION

It was earlier assumed that population growth during demographic transition will lead to overcrowding, poverty, undernutrition, environmental deterioration, poor quality of life and increase in disease burden. Experience in the last few decades have shown that this may not always be correct. India is currently in the phase of demographic transition when the increase in population is mainly among younger, better educated and healthy population with low morbidity and mortality rate. The challenge for the health sector is to promote healthy life styles, improve access to and utilisation of health care so that the country can achieve substantial reduction in mortality and morbidity.

Occupational health and environmental health programme need be augmented to ensure that working population remain healthy and productive. If these challenges are fully met, it is possible to accelerate reduction in morbidity and mortality rate in this age group and improve health indices of the country. With growing number of senior citizens there may be substantial increase in health care needs especially for management of non-communicable diseases.

Increasing availability and awareness about technological advances for management of these problems, rising expectations of the population and the ever escalating cost of health care are some of the problems that the health care system has to cope with. Health care delivery systems will have to gear up to taking up necessary preventive, promotive, curative and rehabilitative care for growing population of senior citizens.

POPULATION PROJECTIONS AND THEIR IMPLICATIONS FOR THE FW PROGRAMME

There will be a marginal decline in the population less than 15 years of age. The health care infrastructure will therefore be not grappling with ever increasing number of children for providing care and they will be able to concentrate on.

- Improving quality of care;
- Focus on antenatal, intranatal and neonatal care aimed at reducing neonatal morbidity and mortality;
- Improve coverage and quality of health care to vulnerable and underserved adolescents;
- Promote intersectoral coordination especially with ICDS programme so that there is improvement in health and nutritional status;
- Improve coverage for immunization against vaccine preventable diseases.

The economic challenge is to provide needed funds so that these children have access to nutrition, education and skill development. The challenge faced by the health sector is to achieve reduction in morbidity and mortality rate in infancy and childhood, to improve nutritional status and eliminate ill-effects of gender bias. There will be a massive increase of population in the 15-59 age group. The persons in this age group will be more literate and have greater access to information; they will therefore have greater awareness and expectation regarding both the access to a wide spectrum of health care related services and the quality of these services.

Under the Reproductive and child health care programme efforts are underway to provide:

- Needed services for this rapid growing population
- To broaden the spectrum of services available and
- To improve quality and coverage of health care to women, children and adolescents, so that their felt needs for health care are fully met.
- To improve the participation of men in the planned parenthood movement.

The components of the comprehensive RCH services are given in the text box. While providing the package of services, efforts will have to be made to improve the quality of services, make services more responsive to users' needs, ensure that health workers and health care providers have the necessary skills and supplies they need and there is a strong and effective referral system to manage all the risk cases. Family welfare Programme is attempting to improve the logistics of supply of drugs and vaccine to make sure good quality drugs are available at appropriate time.

Simultaneously the IEC efforts are being directed to:

- Ensure responsible reproductive /sexual behavior;
- Improve awareness about reproductive health needs;
- Promote community participation and optimal utilisation of available services

ESSENTIAL REPRODUCTIVE AND CHILD HEALTH SERVICES

Though it is desirable that the entire package of services indicated under comprehensive RCH care is made available to all those who need it, it will not be possible to immediately implement such a comprehensive package at primary health care level on a nationwide basis. After consultation with experts a package of essential reproductive health services for nationwide implementation at primary health care settings has been identified.

Essential components recommended for nationwide implementation include:

- Prevention and management of unwanted pregnancy,
- Services to provide antenatal, intra-natal and post-natal, and neo-natal care
- Services to promote child health and survival,
- Prevention and treatment of RTI/STD.

Most of these services are already being delivered under the Family Welfare Programme. However, there are wide variations in the quality and coverage of services not only between states but also between districts in the same state. The focus under RCH Programme is therefore on the improvement in the quality and coverage of the services over and above the existing level in all districts/states in an incremental manner so that there is over all improvement maternal and child health indices.

Index

I

M

O

P

R

S

T

U

V

Z